Motif Programming
in the X Window
System Environment

Other McGraw-Hill Titles of Interest

*To order or to receive additional information on these or
any other McGraw-Hill titles, in the United States please
call 1-800-822-8158. In other countries, contact your local
McGraw-Hill office.*

MH92

Motif Programming in the X Window System Environment

William A. Parrette

Vice President of Education Services, ITDC Cincinnati, Ohio

McGraw-Hill, Inc.

New York   San Francisco   Washington, D.C.   Auckland   Bogotá
Caracas   Lisbon   London   Madrid   Mexico City   Milan
Montreal   New Delhi   San Juan   Singapore
Sydney   Tokyo   Toronto

Library of Congress Cataloging-in-Publication Data

Parrette, William A.
    Motif programming in the X Window system environment / William A.
    Parrette.
        p.   cm. — (The UNIX/C series)
    Includes index.
    ISBN 0-07-031722-4 (hard) — ISBN 0-07-031723-2 (soft)
    1. X Window System (Software system)   2. Motif (Software system)
I. Title   II. Series.
QA76.76.W56P37   1993
005.4'3—dc20   92-31210
                                                               CIP

1 2 3 4 5 6 7 8 9 0   DOH/DOH   9 8 7 6 5 4 3 2

ISBN   0-07-031722-4   {HC}
ISBN   0-07-031723-2   {PBK}

*The sponsoring editor for this book was Neil Levine, the editing
supervisor was Kimberly A. Goff, and the production supervisor was
Donald F. Schmidt.*

Printed and bound by R. R. Donnelley & Sons Company.

Contents

Preface

Introduction

¤   This book is another in a series of books that will allow a reader to learn
about the UNIX operating system and its concepts and facilities for data
processing, software development, and database applications.   The series
will cover a number of topics that correspond to ITDC's popular curriculum
of UNIX related courses, including:

```
UNIX for Application Developers
UNIX Shell Programming
The C Programming Language
Programming with the C Libraries
Advanced C Programming under UNIX
C++ for C Programmers
Motif Programming in the X Window System Environment
UNIX System Administration
Advanced UNIX System Administration
UNIX Security
Using UNIX Networks
Unix Network Programming
Unix Network Administration
Unix Networking
UNIX Internals
Informix SQL for Application Developers
Informix 4GL for Application Developers
Informix ESQL SQL/C Interface
```

   The series will be organized so that no matter what job function you may
need to perform in a UNIX-based data-processing organization, there will be
a path through the series that you can follow on your own, or within a
series of ITDC classes, that will allow you to become fluent and competent
with the tools needed for that job. The chart in Figure P.1 will help you
understand the topics you will need to study.

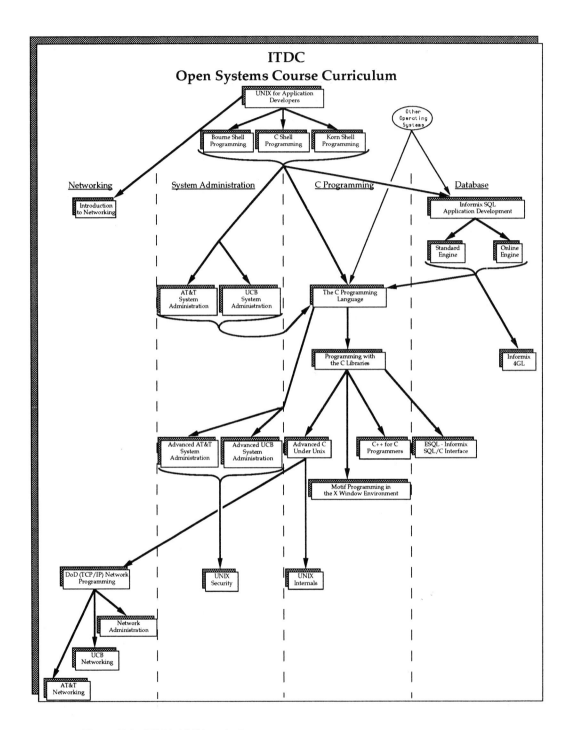

Figure P.1 ITDC's UNIX curriculum.

What You Will and Will Not Learn

◻   This ITDC/McGraw-Hill series of books assumes that the reader has a data-processing background. If you have experience with some other operating system and programming language – either using large mainframe computers or programming a small personal computer – you will be able to use these books to learn about UNIX.

You do need to understand that this series does *not* teach about computer concepts and organization, number systems, data processing, programming, or database concepts. These books are *not* for the computer novice! Although they do try to make learning UNIX topics as simple as possible, you must be familiar with basic computer and data-processing concepts to be able to use them effectively.

Also, please understand that this series cannot teach you *everything* about UNIX. The umbrella term UNIX that we use here covers such a wide variety of topics that it would be difficult to write about all of them. In fact, our experience tells us that typical UNIX users use only about 40 percent of the tools and utilities available to them. And even after years of experience, total usage may approach only 70 percent of what's available. It seems that no one person learns everything there is to know about UNIX and its related systems.

What we will concentrate on in this series are those UNIX topics that we have found useful in getting the UNIX student started on the right path. Once started, we will find that the typical student has the tools needed to start exploring further independently, and this exploration becomes the best UNIX learning process.

Using This Book

◻   Of course, this book and others in this series are intended for use in on-the-job, instructor-led, corporate training programs such as those offered by ITDC (Information Technology Development Corporation). We have used the material in this book for several years to successfully train hundreds of students to use the the OSF (Open Software Foundation)/Motif toolkit with the X Window System for developing user interfaces to data-processing applications. This text can also be used as a college text for a nonintroductory computer course about Motif and X at the sophomore level or above.

◻   To make effective use of this book and others in the series, you must have access to a computer system that runs the X Window System and in which the OSF/Motif toolkit has been installed correctly. One advantage of the X Window System and the OSF/Motif toolkit is that when you learn to use them on one computer, they work the same way on any other computer running X and Motif that you may have access to. Because of this fact, this book makes no assumptions about the particular version of X or OSF/Motif that you may have. What we present should work equally well on X Version 11 Release 3, 4, or 5 with Motif 1.0, 1.1, or 1.2 under AT&T UNIX, BSD, Xenix, Ultrix, AIX, or any other UNIX-compatible system.

While using this book, you will have to understand that computer manufacturers must configure X and Motif for their particular machines. This configuration involves the customizing of some aspects of the operation of the software on their hardware. While this book attempts to show practical or typical examples of techniques, you are cautioned to check all commands and functions against the manufacturer-supplied documentation for compatibility.

Organization of This Book

□   There are only two prerequisites for the study of the material in this book. First, you must have used the underlying operating system (UNIX or others), editors, commands, and tools for some type of data-processing application development. Second, you must be relatively experienced in the use of the C programming language and the functions in the standard C library. All example code in this book is presented in C and assumes familiarity with standard C syntax and things such as structures, unions, pointers, and functions, as well as pointers to these and other things.

This book is designed to be used in a *hands-on* learning environment. As stated previously, this means that you should be studying the material with easy access to a computer terminal with X and Motif. Although you may find just sitting and reading the book useful, you really should be able to try some of the many examples and work on the exercises to benefit the most from the text.

Each chapter in this book is organized to include an introduction, objectives, text, review questions, and exercises. The introduction will give you an overview of the topics being discussed, the objectives will highlight the topics of interest, the text will give you the details, the review questions will let you determine whether you learned the main topics, and the exercises will give you a chance to practice.

Throughout the body of the text, you will see both figures and examples that give you some additional detail on a particular subject in the text. The figures and examples use similar numbering systems that are, in fact, completely separate. A figure is used to show you some type of graphic item or to display a segment of what a terminal screen should look like — in other words, something that you can't type in and try out. On the other hand, an example should contain something that you can type in from your terminal keyboard and see if the output matches that shown in the example. Be careful; the numbers will look very similar, but a figure and an example are completely different.

In the body of the examples you will notice that we use two different types of fonts: boldfaced and lightfaced (or normal). The boldfaced font is intended to show the input that you type to a particular utility program. The normal font represents the output of the utility.

Finally, you will notice a small bullet character appearing in the left margin from time to time. Although it may appear that these bullets appear randomly throughout the text they do serve a purpose. The small bullet characters are used to indicate a change in thought or direction for the topic being discussed in that section.

What Is ITDC?

¤   ITDC (Information Technology Development Corporation) was formed in 1984 to provide training, consulting, and software development services to the emerging UNIX community. We have successfully trained thousands of students in both the government and private sectors on the use of the UNIX operating system, C programming, shell programming, system administration, Motif/X, and many other UNIX-related topics.

This book is the culmination of years of experience in training computer application developers to use the OSF/Motif toolkit with the X Window System for developing user interfaces for their application programs. If you have any questions about ITDC's services or need more information, we can be reached at the address and phone number shown in Figure P.2.

This book is written for the training of software developers. ITDC also offers a wide range of courses that can meet the training needs of everyone from end users who are just beginning to work with a UNIX-based computer to programmers and system administrators who need more detailed technical information.

Agenda

¤   All ITDC courses span five days of study. A typical course starts at 8:30 a.m. and ends at 4:30 p.m., Monday through Friday. What can you expect within one week? Figure P.3 shows a typical agenda for the Motif Programming in the X Window System Environment course.

This, of course, assumes that there will be a 10-minute break every one to two hours and an hour taken out for lunch.

¤   What do you do at the end of the week? We suggest that when you get back to your normal work environment, you come back to this book and try more of the examples and rework some, if not all, the exercises. If you didn't get through all the optional sessions in class, you might take this time to study the rest of them on your own. And finally, *practice!* We can't emphasize this enough! As much as we would like to wave a magic wand over your head at the end of one week and pronounce you a wizard, it just doesn't work that way. We can expect that you will have picked up enough of the concepts and facilities to start to do further explorations on your own. Only with lots of *practice, Practice, PRACTICE* will you become the expert you want and need to be.

```
ITDC
4000 Executive Park Drive, Suite 310
Cincinnati, OH 45241-4007

(513)733-4747: Voice
(513)733-5194: Fax
(513)733-5006: Computer login: guest, Password: guest
```

Figure P.2 Contacting ITDC.

```
Monday:
    Chapter 1    What is a Window System?
    Chapter 2    What is the X Window System?
    Chapter 3    What is the Motif Toolkit?
    Chapter 4    Graphic-User Interface Objects-Widgets
    Chapter 5    X Application Programming Concepts
    Chapter 6    Event-Driven Programming
    Chapter 7    Multiple Widget Programs
    Chapter 8    Passing Data to a Callback Function
Tuesday:
    Chapter 9    Resources
    Chapter 10   Resource Files
    Chapter 11   Motif Primitive Widgets
Wednesday:
    Chapter 12   Motif Manager Widgets
    Chapter 13   Motif Text Widget
    Chapter 14   Common Motif Manager Widgets
    Chapter 15   Graphic-User Interface Design Guidelines
Thursday:
    Chapter 16   X Events
    Chapter 17   Motif Menus
    Chapter 18   Motif Dialog Boxes
Friday:
    Chapter 19   Color
    Chapter 20   X Fonts, Motif Fontlists, and the X Cursor Font
    Chapter 21   A Motif Case Study Example Program
    Chapter 22   Graphics Context
Further study:
    Chapter 23   Drawing Graphics Objects
    Chapter 24   Pixmaps and Bitmaps
    Chapter 25   Motif Window Manager
    Chapter 26   X11R4, X11R5, and Motif 1.1 & 1.2
```

Figure P.3 Motif Programming in the X Window System Environment course agenda.

ITDC hopes that you will find this book a useful piece of reference material after you have finished your study. However, you must understand that the organization and layout of the text was designed with teaching, not referencing, in mind. Therefore, it is important that in addition to this text, you obtain the appropriate manuals from your hardware and software vendors to use for reference.

If you are attempting to use this book on your own as an independent-study tool, we have the following suggestions. For each chapter, read the introduction to get an overview of what is to be covered. Next, read through and try to understand the objectives so that you know the specific topics that you are expected to learn about. Following that, read the text and try as many of the examples as you feel comfortable with. Finally, answer the review questions and work through the exercises. Answers to the exercises are available from ITDC.

If you follow this outline for each chapter and try to stick to the previous agenda, you should be able to get through most of the material within the same one-week time frame. However, we would like to point out that you can, and will, learn much more with the ability to ask questions and participate in the group dynamics of an instructor-led class.

Trademark Notices

¤ Throughout this book there may be at least one reference to corporate names or product names that may be protected as trademarks. One of the necessary evils that we must then perform is to notify you of who the trademark owner is.

A/UX is a trademark of Apple Computer, Inc.; Ada is a trademark of the U.S. Department of Defense; AIX is a trademark of IBM Corporation; AT&T is a trademark of American Telephone and Telegraph Corporation; BBN is a trademark of Bolt, Beranek, and Newman; BSD is a trademark of the University of California at Berkeley; CAE is a trademark of X/Open; CDC is a trademark of Control Data Corporation; CP/M is a trademark of Digital Research, Inc.; DEC is a trademark of Digital Equipment Corporation; DoD is a trademark of the U.S. Department of Defense; DOMAIN/IX is a trademark of Apollo Computer Corporation; GECOS is a trademark of Honeywell Corporation; HP-UX is a trademark of Hewlett-Packard Company; IBM is a trademark of International Business Machines Corporation; Informix is a trademark of Informix Corporation; Macintosh is a trademark of Apple Computer, Inc.; Motif is a trademark of the Open Software Foundation; MP/M is a trademark of Digital Research Corporation; MS/DOS is a trademark of MicroSoft Corporation; Multics is a trademark of Honeywell Corporation; MVS is a trademark of IBM Corporation; NOS and NOS/VE are trademarks of CDC; OS/2 is a trademark of IBM Corporation; OS/MFT is a trademark of IBM Corporation; OS/MVT is a trademark of IBM Corporation; OSF is a trademark of the Open Software Foundation; PDP-7 is a trademark of DEC; PL/I is a trademark of IBM Corporation; SunOS is a trademark of Sun Microsystems, Inc.; TOS is a trademark of IBM Corporation; UI is a trademark of UNIX International; Ultrix is a trademark of DEC; UNIX is a trademark of USL; USL is a trademark of UNIX Software Laboratories; VM/370 is a trademark of IBM Corporation; VMS is a trademark of DEC; Xenix is a trademark of MicroSoft Corporation; X Window System is a trademark of the Massachusetts Institute of Technology X Consortium; X is a trademark of the Massachusetts Institute of Technology X Consortium; ZEUS is a trademark of Zilog, Inc.; Z-80 is a trademark of Zilog, Inc.

Acknowledgments

¤ As the author, I would like to thank everyone who made this book possible. First, the current staff at ITDC: instructors — Jim Adams, Dwayne Backhus, Doug Lee, Jim Lees, John Reynolds, Glenn Stafford, and Vicki Sweda; sales and marketing staff — Steve Kastner, Dave Knight, and Sheri Schraivogel; office staff — Linda Fowler, Dick Frederick, and Barbara Young; and executives — Derek Arnold, Mike Harrington, and Mary Kay Murlas.

Also, special thanks go to the staff at McGraw-Hill: Neil Levine, Kimberly Goff, Cathy Hertz, and Midge Haramis.

I would also like to express my appreciation to Bruce Schuchardt for his xgrabsc program on uunet, which was used to grab X screen images for use as illustrations within this book; Jerry Smith for his excellent Xhibition '92 presentation on Xt/Motif program design; and Donald L. McMinds for his thorough and complete discussion of the the differences between OSF/Motif 1.0 and 1.1 in his book *Mastering OSF/Motif Widgets*.

What Is a
Window
System?

Introduction

◻ Programming for a graphic-user interface to a computer system is significantly different from programming for a command-line interface. There are many new concepts and facilities that a programmer must become familiar with. In this chapter you will learn about these concepts and facilities and how they depend on a computer-based windowing system. A brief history of windowing systems also will be presented.

Objectives

◻ After completing this chapter, you will be able to:

◻ Describe the difference between batch processing, command line processing, and processing using a graphic-user interface.

◻ Explain the acronym *GUI*.

◻ Describe how a window system is used like a desktop.

◻ Explain the type of terminal that is required for a window system.

◻ Define the term *input focus*.

◻ List four different types of input devices that can be used with a window system.

◻ Explain why a GUI is easy to learn to use.

❑ Describe why it is more difficult to write code for a GUI program than for a command-line, prompt-based program.

❑ Name the programming methodology required for programming a window system.

❑ Explain how an event loop works.

❑ List three different types of events that can occur in a window system.

❑ Describe how the X Window System is related to the Xerox Star computer system.

Data-Processing: Batch vs. Command-Line vs. Graphic-User Interfaces

❑ Over the years, data processing has gone through a variety of changes. In the early days, computers were very large machines that needed their own special air-conditioned rooms and a large staff of specially trained people to operate and program the machines to do their data processing. More recently, computers have shrunk enough in size to fit on almost anyone's desktop and more and more people are learning to operate and program these machines to perform data-processing tasks.

On the early computers, programmers wrote their instructions to the computer by hand, on paper, and gave them to a keypunch operator for transfer to punched cards. The programmer then took the deck of punched cards to the computer operator, who read them into the computer with a "batch" of card decks from other programmers. The results of the data processing were printed out on paper and sent to the program's users. This *batch processing* was one of the original methods developed for communication between computers and people.

Soon afterward, someone figured out that a much more efficient use of the computer could be realized if the programmers and users could enter the data-processing programs and commands themselves. A modified television set (or monitor) and a typewriter keyboard were combined to create a device called a *video-display terminal.* People could enter a "line of commands" from the keyboard and watch the results of the data-processing being displayed on the screen. This *command-line processing* could be used by people with less specialized training to communicate with a computer.

More recently, small but very powerful desktop computers have been appearing everywhere. A larger number of people with little computer training want to use these machines to perform data-processing tasks. The batch interface and the command-line interface used successfully on earlier machines were no longer adequate for these untrained users — a new interface to the computer was needed.

❑ A great deal of research has been performed to determine what type of user interface would be the most useful to the widest variety of people from computer programmers to computer users. One of the most common conclusions of these research efforts was that a *graphic-user interface* should be used to allow users to manipulate objects on the screen in much the same way they manipulate objects around their office and on their desks. With the proper design, these *GUI* (pronounced "gooey") processing systems would be more intuitive and easier to learn and use. Figure 1.1 shows what a typical GUI for a program would look like.

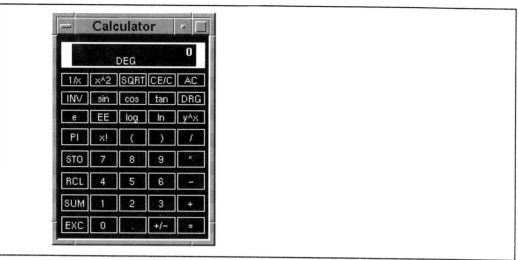

Figure 1.1 GUI (graphic-user interface) to a computer system.

Almost all graphic-user interfaces are built on top of a *window system*.

Window System Concepts

     One key feature of a window system is that it allows the user to run more than one program at a time. Similar in concept to the idea that you may have many projects going on at once—with different stacks of paper on your desk for each project, several different trains of thought working at the same time, and trying to get each one of many related and unrelated tasks completed at the same time—a windowing system gives you the ability to run several different programs on your computerized desktop all at the same time. When you need to run another program to accomplish some data-processing, task you just open another window on the screen for it to run in.

     Windowing systems usually require some type of *graphic-display terminal*. This is because the windows of the windowing system are drawn, just like their real-life namesakes, as a rectangular graphical element on the display screen. At the minimum, a window will have a border and a background color that distinguishes it from the other windows on the screen.

     Similar to the stacks of paper that lie around on your desktop at work, some of these windows can overlap each other. One window may be on top of the stack obscuring all or a portion of a window that lies below it in the stack. The window system usually allows you to restack the windows or move them in such a way as to cause some other window to become visible.

     Since you can, in fact, work on only one thing at a time, a windowing system will let you work with only one window at a time. The window that you are currently working with is often called the *input focus* window because it is the "focus" of your current work and it is the only window receiving "input" from the terminal at that time. The windowing system will allow you to move the input focus from one window to another depending on which task, or program, you want to work on at that time. Figure

1.2 shows how a windowed graphic-display terminal would look with several windows open at once, but with only one window having input focus.

Types of Input to a Window System

□   A window system will require two types of input to perform the operations described above. Keyboard input will be needed to respond to the prompts for input data that an application running in a window will require. However, another type of input will be needed to manipulate and activate objects on the graphic screen. This type of input is usually provided by a device called a *mouse.*

A mouse is a small rectangular box that is attached to the keyboard or terminal display by a cable. The mouse is designed so that it can roll or slide along the desktop near the terminal. As the mouse is moved, a small window called a pointer, or mouse cursor, moves a corresponding direction

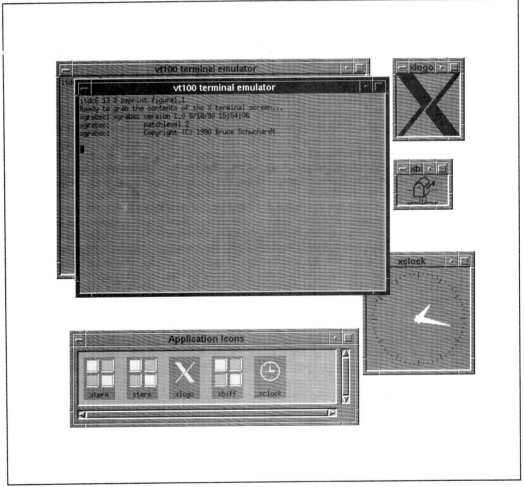

Figure 1.2   Typical windowed graphic-display terminal screen.

and distance on the screen. The mouse is moved so that the pointer will move on the screen from one window to another.

Input is provided from the mouse by way of one or more buttons located on top of the mouse. The press or release of a mouse button with the pointer positioned within a window on the screen is another type of input to the windowed program. Depending on which button is pressed and which window the pointer is in will cause some action to take place on the graphic-display terminal. Figure 1.3 shows a typical mouse and the corresponding pointer on the screen.

In addition to the mouse device, there are a number of other alternate input devices that could be configured to provide input to a window system:

trackball | A trackball is essentially an upside-down mouse. Instead of rolling a little box around on the table, the trackball stays stationary while you use your hand to roll a ball within the box to move the mouse cursor. Buttons are provided, as on the mouse, to provide input once the pointer is correctly positioned.

touch screen | A touch screen is a special surface that can be applied to the screen of a graphic-display terminal. You use your finger to specify the X/Y-coordinate for the mouse pointer. Instead of pressing a button for input to the window, the contact between your finger and the screen is used to activate the window at that coordinate position.

graphics tablet | A graphics tablet basically takes the idea of the touch screen and lays it out on a large flat surface next to the terminal. Instead of using your finger for input, a pencil-like stylus is used to touch the tablet at some specific X/Y-coordinate location and provide input to the window located there.

Figure 1.3 Typical mouse and screen pointer.

The only requirements for this type of input device is that it be able to move a pointer window to some specific X/Y-coordinate location on the screen and to provide one or more distinct types of binary input —press/release, on/off, true/false, or similar.

Advantages of a Graphic-User Interface

▢   There are at least four advantages to using a GUI with a computer system:

  ▢ Easy to learn

  ▢ Easy to use

  ▢ Intuitive operation

  ▢ Better screen management and the ability to easily switch between tasks

▢   It is difficult to teach a user how, why, and when to enter a command such as:

```
awk -F: '/^[^s-v].*csh$/{print $1, "--", $7}' /etc/passwd
```

Although this command could be hidden in a command or batch file, it is much easier to teach someone to move the mouse, position the pointer on an object on the screen, and press a mouse button to accomplish some data-processing task. It is a well-known fact that users trained to operate a graphic-user interface learn to work with the interface sooner and more effectively than an equivalent command-line interface.

▢   The use of a command-line interface usually requires that you memorize a large number of commands whose syntax resembles Greek more than English. The commands may have a number of variations that cause the command to act in special ways in certain situations. If you can't memorize the commands, then you must have access to large and equally complex reference manuals in which you can look up the proper command syntax needed for a particular operation. With a GUI it is so much simpler to point and click to accomplish some task.

▢   If you sit someone down in front of a graphic-user interface system, show that person the basic operation of the mouse, and encourage him or her to just try things out to see what happens—chances are that the user will learn to operate that system on the basis of nothing more than intuition. Since the GUI is a more consistent interface, when users try one operation and see that it works the same way in many different contexts, they are more apt to be confident in trying other similar operations just to see if it works. There is absolutely no way that you can intuitively know what commands, or syntax of commands, are available in a command line-interface.

▢   The graphic-user interface typically allows the user to execute multiple programs all at the same time just like most modern operating systems allow for multiple background processes to run at the same time. However, one of the biggest advantages to the GUI is that each program or process executes in a separate window that the user can move, resize, reorder, or restack in any order for complete control over and management of the visual appearance of the screen. Still a bigger advantage, unlike running multiple background processes, is that the user can switch input focus to any of the processes running in any of the windows to work with that particular program and then switch input focus to another window later to work with a different program. With a graphic-user interface, users are in complete control of what they do and when they do it.

Disadvantages of a Graphic-User Interface

¤ Although the use of a GUI does offer some powerful advantages, there are also some disadvantages that you must be aware of, revolving around two main issues:

¤ Efficiency

¤ Programming

¤ In order to allow the average programmer to create applications that use the features of a window system, the window system developer will create a library of prewritten functions that can be called to perform the most typical tasks. Functions are usually available to create, move, resize, and destroy windows; to watch the mouse for movement and cause the mouse pointer to move appropriately on the screen in response; to handle input requests from both the mouse and the keyboard; to draw a variety of graphics objects such as lines, circles, and rectangles; and much, much more.

These functions that the programmer can call will, in turn, call lower-level functions that perform the more primitive operations required to accomplish some windowing task. These functions may also call other functions. This is not untypical—so what may have originally looked like a relatively small program that calls a few functions to perform some basic windowing operations can turn out to be a very large program that has hundreds of function calls linked in. A "small" windowing program can turn out to be hundreds of thousands of bytes long!

¤ Programming in a windowed environment is radically different from programming in a command-line environment. A command-line-oriented program will display some text on the screen to prompt the user for some type of input data, read the data, perform some process on the data, and repeat the process until it reaches the end of its input. Whether you were processing a menu option, trying to get a filename for input data, or just reading numbers to perform some arithmetic operation, the data-processing method was basically the same. With the programmer in control of processing the data, the program can be written with standard modular top-down block-structured programming techniques.

Programming in a windowed environment requires a different programming model. Instead of top-down block-structured programming, a window system programmer must use an *event-driven* programming model.

Application Programming for a Window System

◻ In a windowed environment the programmer no longer has control over what the user will do next. Because the user can move the mouse to literally any position on the screen and provide input at the mouse pointer location at any time, it is the user who controls the program's operation, and not the program.

Because the user can provide any type of input at any time, the program must be much more careful about managing those inputs and making sure that they make sense in the current context before it acts on them. For example, if the user has a text window to enter a filename in and a button window to click the mouse in to open the file, the program must make sure that the filename text data has been entered first before the user clicks on the open button. If the proper sequence of inputs is not followed, then the program must handle the "error situation" in a meaningful and useful way. The programmer has a great deal more to worry about in a window-oriented program than in a command-line-oriented program.

Because these user inputs can occur at any time and at any location on the screen, a new terminology has evolved to describe them. Instead of calling them *inputs,* window system programmers call them *input events* — or simply *events*. Programming a window system application is termed *event-driven programming*.

◻ A non-event-driven program starts executing and follows a specific sequence of logical steps, based on the inputs provided, to a specific ending point and terminates its execution. An event-driven program starts executing and enters an infinite loop. Inside the loop the program will ask for the next input event from the window system and, according to the type of event, call some function to process it. When the function returns, control goes back to the infinite loop, which receives and processes the next event. Figure 1.4 shows a C language-like pseudocode segment that outlines the typical event-driven model.

The event loop continues to process input events until a program-defined exit event occurs. When the program sees this exit event, it can do whatever cleanup is needed and return control to the window system. Typical types of window events include the following:

keyboard events	Whenever the user presses (or releases) a key on the terminal keyboard an event is generated that describes which key was pressed and when and where it was pressed.
mouse button events	Whenever the user presses (or releases) a button on the mouse an event is generated that describes which button was pressed and when and where it was pressed.
pointer motion events	The act of sliding the mouse across the table top, moving the mouse pointer on the screen also generates an event which describes when and where the pointer moved to.
window exposure events	When one window that was stacked beneath another window is moved to the top of the window stack, it will cause some portion of

```
main()
    {
    InputEvent event;

    Initialize();
    OpenWindows();
    while(1)
        {
        event = GetNextEvent();
        switch(event)
            {
            EventType1:
                Process1();
                break;
            EventType2:
                Process2();
                break;
            EventType3:
                Process3();
                break;
            ...
            ExitEvent:
                exit();
            }
        }
    }
Process1()
    {
    ...
    }
Process2()
    {
    ...
    }
...
```

Figure 1.4 Event-driven programming style in pseudocode.

the window that was hidden to become visible, generating an event that describes which portion of the window was exposed.

input focus events   When input focus is transferred from one application window to another, an event is generated that describes which window received the input focus.

These, and other events, are stored in an event queue (from the British: a line, as of persons waiting to be served) in first-in/first-out (FIFO) order. When the program requests an event, the window system gets the next event off of the top of the queue (the oldest event) and returns it to the program.

A Brief History of Window Systems

◻ Although window systems have only recently gained wide acceptance in the data-processing community, they have a long and involved history that dates back to the late 1960s and early 1970s. Most of the initial research into computer-user interfaces was done at the Xerox Palo Alto Research Center (PARC) in Palo Alto, California. Although the goals of that research were fairly lofty (to design and build an easy-to-use notebook-sized computer, without a keyboard interface, called the DynaBook), the results were actually incorporated into a Xerox product called the *Star*.

The Xerox Star computer had most of the features found in today's graphic-user interface window-based systems. It was easy to use, fairly intuitive in operation, and (unfortunately) way ahead of its time. The Star was so radically new and different from any other computer on the market that very few organizations wanted to buy it. Using this new technology was too much of a risk for most people.

◻ Late in the development of the Star computer, some people from Apple Computer toured the Xerox PARC facility to see what new technologies were being developed. Soon thereafter, Apple started working on what was to become known as the *Lisa* and *Macintosh* computers. The goals for the Macintosh were similar to the goals for the Star—to be easy to learn, easy to use, and intuitive in operation. Another goal was to make the Macintosh as much of an "appliance" computer as possible so that no computer or data-processing knowledge would be required for its operation.

Again, the Macintosh was just a little ahead of its time. Although it sold much better than the Xerox Star computer, Apple's Apple II line of computers still sold much better. It wasn't until IBM and MicroSoft "legitimized" the windowed environment with its MS/Windows product for MS/DOS that the Macintosh really started to take off.

◻ Around the same time that the Macintosh and MS/Windows were starting to show that window systems were in fact useful interfaces for data processing on computers, the Laboratory for Computer Science at the Massachusetts Institute of Technology (MIT) was working on a project called Argus. The Argus project was intended to create a programming language that could be used in a networked, distributed computing environment.

Bob Scheifler, who was in charge of debugging the Argus software, decided that a window system would be a very useful tool in his debugging efforts. In the distributed environment there could be many different related processes running on many of the nodes in the network. If each process could be run and controlled from separate windows on a single terminal, the debugging process would be much simpler.

◻ At the same time that the Argus research was under way, MIT also was working on a project called Athena. The Athena project was intended to build a large heterogeneous (composed of dissimilar parts) computing environment and was supported by both IBM and DEC. With a wide variety of workstations installed throughout the campus and a wide variety of users trying to use these workstations for data processing, an early goal of Athena was to develop a hardware-independent and consistent user interface. One of the people assigned to Athena by DEC was an engineer by the name of Jim Gettys.

Scheifler started talking to Gettys to see if he knew of any windowing software that was already available which could be used for the Argus project. While looking around, they found that Paul Asente and Brian Reid had created a prototype of a window system at Stanford University that they called W. Asente and Reid gave a copy of the W system to Scheifler and Gettys which they turned around and developed into the *X Window System.*

Like any other piece of software the X Window System, or simply X, has been through a number of versions in its lifetime. In 1990 and 1991 the most recent and widespread version of X was Version 11, Release 3 (X11R3), with X11R4 just starting to become available from some vendors. Throughout 1992 R3 was still the most prominent version of X available across a wide variety of systems, but R4 was getting a lot of "press" and was starting to appear on an increasing number of machines. In 1993 R4 will be the dominant version with R5 (available in September 1991) starting to become available from some vendors.

With the popularity of window systems in general and X in particular, MIT had to create a new organization to control the future development of the X Window System. The MIT X Consortium was created as a membership organization that would allow interested hardware and software vendors to suggest new directions for X. The X Consortium releases a new version of X about once a year with production versions starting to become available from vendors about six months after release. Another six months to a year after initial availability, the new version of X then starts to become prominent in use throughout the industry. Development is currently under way for R6, while plans are certainly being made for R7.

The X Window System is currently the most popular window system available running on workstations from a wide variety of manufacturers. Versions of X run on computers from DEC, Hewlett-Packard, Apollo, Data General, IBM, Siemens, Sony, and many others. Even personal computer manufacturers such as IBM and Apple are getting into the act by allowing the IBM PC and Macintosh to access and display X programs running on another computer in a network. X is quickly becoming a standard in windowing system software.

Review Questions

Please write down the answers to the following questions:

1. What is the difference between batch processing, command-line processing, and processing using a graphic-user interface?

2. What is the meaning of the acronym GUI?

3. How is a window system used like a desktop?

4. Which type of terminal is required for a window system?

5. What is the meaning of the term input focus?

6. List four different types of input devices that can be used with a window system.

7. Why is a GUI is easy to learn to use?

8. Why is it more difficult to write code for a GUI program than for a command-line, prompt-based program?

9. What is the name the programming methodology required for programming a window system?

10. How does an event loop work?

11. List three different types of events that can occur in a window system.

12. How is the X Window System related to the Xerox Star computer system?

2

What Is the X Window System?

Introduction

¤ The X Window System is a computer-based windowing system that allows you to write programs that employ a graphic-user interface. In this chapter you will learn about the facilities available in the X Window System which allow you to write GUI programs. You will also learn some of the terminology that is specific to X, how to start X, and the purpose of an X window manager.

Objectives

¤ After completing this chapter, you will be able to:

☐ Define the term *pixel*.

☐ Explain the difference between an X client program and an X server program.

☐ Describe what the X Protocol is used for.

☐ Define the term *language bindings* and how these bindings are related to your X application program.

☐ Explain the the differences between Xlib, the X Toolkit, and an X widget set.

☐ Define the term *look-and-feel*.

◻ Describe what a root window is.

◻ Explain the coordinate system used to place X windows on the screen.

◻ Describe the workings of an X application window hierarchy.

◻ Explain what happens when a window is mapped or realized.

◻ Describe what a mouse is and what it is used for.

◻ List four new defined X data types and describe what they are used for.

◻ Explain the differences in starting X with the xinit and xdm commands.

◻ List three different window managers.

◻ Describe the purpose of a window manager.

The X Window System

◻ The X Window System operates with a bitmapped graphic-display terminal. This special type of terminal allows each individual *pixel* (picture element) on the screen to be accessed and used to display a specific color or shade of gray. The pixels are the elements used to construct a graphic image such as a window on the screen.

Communication between an X Window-based application (called a *client*) and the bitmapped graphic-display terminal is accomplished through a special piece of software called the X *server*. The X clients make requests to the X server to receive input from the terminal mouse and keyboard or to produce output on the terminal screen. The X server is a true server program in that it acts as an intermediary for any client application that wants to use the resources of a graphic-display terminal.

Communication between the client and the server is accomplished with a special messaging system called the *X Protocol*. This protocol is a network-transparent protocol that is used to send data between the X clients and an X server. The two transport mechanisms that are currently supported are TCP/IP and DECnet with others under development. Through the X Protocol an X client application can send requests to any server running on any computer connected to the network and cause its outputs and inputs to be sent to and received from any terminal to which that server is connected.

From the X client application developer's point of view the X Protocol is implemented as a series of *language bindings* or function libraries. Function libraries for X currently exist for Ada, Lisp, and C with others under development. The library that implements the X Protocol for the C programming language is called *Xlib*. Figure 2.1 shows the relationship between the various parts of the X Window System.

Xlib contains nearly 300 functions that have been preprogrammed to create, move, resize, stack, and destroy windows; to draw lines, rectangles, arcs, and polygons; to use fonts, colormaps, graphic images, and cursors; and to execute a wide variety of other operations.

As can be seen from Figure 2.1, the Xlib library is not the only library that is used to create an X Window client application. Programming with only Xlib has been compared to programming in Assembler language. You can get the basic tasks accomplished in Xlib, but the amount of code needed for producing a simple window with some text on the screen can amount to

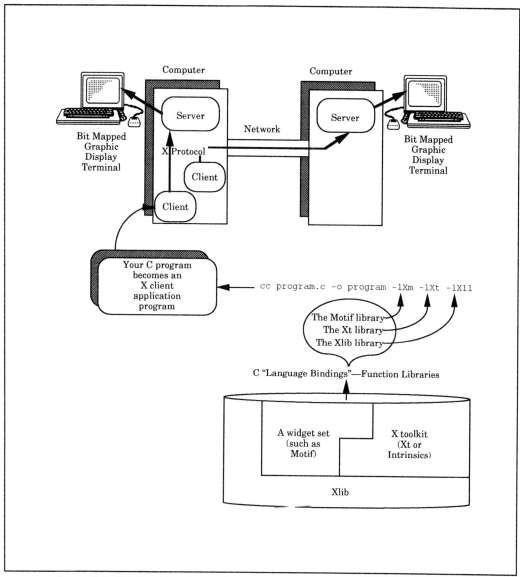

Figure 2.1 Relationship between the components of the X Window System.

hundreds of lines. Because of this complexity another, higher-level, library is sometimes used in combination with Xlib.

◻   The *X Toolkit,* or Xt for short (sometimes referred to as the *Intrinsics*), is a set of preprogrammed functions that the X programmer can use to write X Window applications from a higher level. Usually, one Xt function call will translate into several Xlib function calls. In fact, most of the more common standard Xlib function sequences have had an Xt function written for them.

There are hundreds of Xt functions to perform the standard X initializations, communicate input events from specific windows back to the client application, deal with events in the event queue, handle interclient communication, and create and manage user interface objects called *widgets*.

A widget is a collection of one or more windows that are laid out in such a way as to form a graphics object. A widget definition also contains a set of procedures or functions that are invoked as a result of user input in the widget's windows. If you have ever used a GUI on any computer, you have seen examples of what Xt refers to as widgets. Push buttons, scroll bars, text boxes, menus, and dialog boxes are all examples of widgets. Widgets are not just windows.

The X toolkit provides only a few specific widgets to use in a client application. So, when using Xt, the application developer will usually use a set of separately developed widgets referred to as a *widget set*.

Widget sets are simply a collection of preprogrammed graphics objects that are common to many GUI programs. Widget sets are not a part of the X Window System. If you want to use a set of widgets in your X client application, you must obtain (buy) them from some other vendor. Widget sets are available from MIT (the Athena widget set), AT&T (the Open Look widget set), the Open Software Foundation (the Motif widget set), and other vendors.

Each widget set will provide the same basic types of functionalities. Almost all widget sets provide some kind of push button, label, text box, scroll bar, drawing area, menu, and so on. The main differences in the widget sets is in the form of their *look-and-feel*.

All widget sets will provide a push-button-type widget, but each widget set vendor's idea of what a push button should look like will be different. The "look" of the push button will be different depending on which vendor's push button you decide to use. Also, what happens when the push button is pressed using some type of mouse or keyboard input will make the button "feel" different depending on which widget vendor's push button you decide to use.

Some people have said that X uses the terms *client* and *server* backward from or in reverse to their normal usage. This is not true. The X server is a true terminal server that accepts requests from its clients and responds to those requests through the terminal screens and keyboards it controls. However, X does give a slightly different meaning to some other common data-processing terms.

Whenever X refers to a display, it is not talking about one of the screens on the terminal it controls. X uses the term *display* as another name for the server. When you write to the display (as you would in any other computer context), you are actually sending an X Protocol message to the X server.

Whenever X refers to a screen, it is talking about one of the physical screens on the terminal that a server controls. When the server draws on the screen, it is satisfying an X Protocol request from some X client application to cause some type of graphics object to appear on a terminal screen. Figure 2.2 illustrates these concepts.

Again, in X, your client application sends X Protocol requests to the display. In response, the display causes the graphic-user interface to be drawn on a screen. When the user enters input to the screen from the

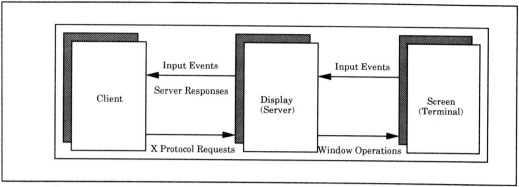

Figure 2.2 Client, server, display, and screen are used differently in X.

mouse or keyboard, input events are sent from the screen to the display and the display sends the events to the appropriate client application.

The client application sits in an infinite loop requesting services from the display and waiting for input events from the screen. The server responds to the requests for services and passes the input events to the clients.

X Windowing Concepts

❑ An X window is a graphical element constructed as a rectangular section of a terminal screen. A window is defined by a border, a background color or pattern, an X/Y-coordinate for its origin, a height, and a width. Whenever the X server takes control of a particular terminal, it installs a special window called the *root window* on the terminal screen.

The root window has a border that is 0 pixels wide and a background color defined by the specific server. The origin of the root window (its upper-left-hand corner) is installed at the upper-left-hand corner of the terminal screen (X = 0, Y = 0). The root window will be as tall and wide as the maximum number of pixels available in the height and width of the screen. In other words, the root window is the terminal screen.

Any new windows that you create will be installed on top of the root window as a *child* of the root window. This child window will be located with its upper-left-hand corner at some specific X/Y location with respect to the origin of the root window. The X values increase from 0 at the left side of the screen to the maximum number of pixels to the right in the width of the screen; the Y values increase from 0 at the top of the screen to the maximum number of pixels to the bottom in the height of the screen. Windows are created with some specific X/Y-coordinate origin, border width, border color, background color, height, and width.

❑ A child of the root window can be a simple window as described above or a more complex window with children of its own. In fact, windows displayed on a particular screen in an X window client application form a hierarchy as shown in Figure 2.3.

A window is actually allocated as a data structure within the X server. The X client holds an identifier for a particular window data structure. The window does not actually become visible on the terminal screen until the client tells the server to *map* the window.

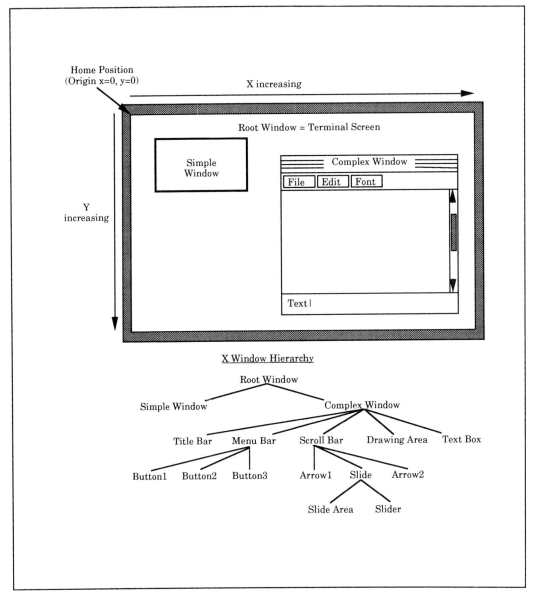

Figure 2.3 Typical X window tree hierarchy.

▫   When the client requests that a window be mapped (or "realized," as it is sometimes called), the server issues the proper drawing instructions to cause a graphic representation of the data in the structure to appear on the screen.

However, if the window that is being mapped is the child of some other window in the window hierarchy, it will not become visible itself until its parent has been mapped. Every ancestor to a window must be mapped and visible before the child window can become visible. A window can be mapped in such a way that it will partially or completely obscure another window on the screen.

If a child window is mapped completely outside the bounds of its parent, it cannot become visible on the screen. For a child window to be visible on the screen, some portion of the window must be located within the bounds of its parent. If a child window is mapped so that part of the window is inside the parent and part is outside the parent, then only the portion inside the parent will be visible and we say that the child is *clipped by the parent*.

X Window Pointer Concepts

¤ All X client applications depend on a pointing device — typically a mouse. A mouse is a small rectangular box that can roll or slide on a flat surface near the terminal and is connected to the terminal by a cable. The mouse will have anywhere from one to five buttons on top of it that can be used to provide input to an X client.

As the mouse is moved around on the desktop a *cursor*, commonly called the *mouse pointer* (or simply *pointer*), moves a corresponding distance and direction on the screen. When the pointer enters a particular window on the screen, one or more of the mouse buttons can be pressed to provide input to the window.

The pointer is really just another X window and can assume a variety of different shapes. Standard shapes include a variety of arrows pointing in different directions, a variety of hand shapes with a finger pointing in different directions, a coffee mug, a watch, a skull and crossbones, a heart, and even Gumby. No matter what shape the cursor takes, there is always one particular X/Y-coordinate within the cursor's window that defines the exact location of the cursor. This cursor coordinate is called the *hot spot*.

¤ The movement of the pointer, the pointer entering a window, the pointer leaving a window, and mouse button clicks are all events that an X client application can watch for and take action on. The pointing device is one of the primary means of input to an X Window program.

X and Xt Data Types

¤ In addition to their functions, both the Xlib and Xt libraries have defined a series of new data types that are used to define the parameters and return values for their functions. Although standard C types are used where appropriate in some cases, in many cases the newly defined data types give a more accurate description of the data being used and provide for portability across multiple hardware platforms. Of course, these new data types are defined with the preprocessor #define directive or the C language typedef statement in one of the many header files used with X.

The following is a list of some of the new X-specific data types:

Boolean   A data type to indicate True (1) or False (0)

Cardinal   A data type used to specify an unsigned integer value

Cursor   An identifier used to reference a particular cursor shape stored in the server

Dimension	A data type used to specify the height or width of a window
Display	An identifier used to reference a particular server to communicate with
Position	A data type used to specify an X- or Y-coordinate
Region	An identifier used to reference an arbitrary set of pixels on the screen
String	A data type that is equivalent to a character pointer
Time	A data type used to hold time values as some specific number of milliseconds
Widget	An identifier used to reference a particular user interface object
Window	An identifier used to reference a particular X window on the screen
XEvent	A data type used to describe an input event from a terminal

Many other data types also are defined. Some of these data types translate directly into equivalent C data types such as int, float, or char *, while others are defined over a structure or union definition. The X application programmer should use the defined types just as if they were real C data types.

Starting X

Depending on how X is being run on your system, the way you log in can be slightly different. Before you can start using X, three things must happen. Depending on how X is set up on your system, some or all of these steps may be performed automatically.

◻ Start an X server process running.

◻ Start at least one instance of a terminal emulator program.

◻ Start a window manager.

If everything is started automatically for you, as a result of the login process, the screen will be cleared, the root window will be installed and a window will appear with some type of decorations around it. Inside the window you will see the standard command interpreter prompt for your system. At this point you can start using the system as if you were seated in front of a standard ASCII (American Standard Code for Information Interchange)-based terminal connected to your computer.

Some system administrators go so far as to have X installed when the system is brought up. Instead of running the standard login process to get your login information, they can run a special X client called xdm. The xdm process acts just like a standard login process prompting you for all the necessary login information, but it does it from an X-based window.

If your initial window does not have any special decorations around it — if it is just a rectangle with a border and a background color — then you do not have a window manager process. Although one is not required in X11R3 (it will be in X11R4), it will make your X life a lot easier if you can get a window manager up and running.

To get a window manager running, simply type its name at the command interpreter prompt and *make sure you run it in the background*. Several window managers are available, and you may have one of the following:

uwm   The universal window manager

awm   The Athena window manager

twm   Tom's window manager

mwm   The Motif window manager

If X starts up, but a terminal emulator window does not appear — you're in big trouble! Call your system administrator and get some help.

If, after logging in, X doesn't start up and all you get is the standard command interpreter prompt, you will need to start X manually. To do this, you have two options:

xdm   You can execute the xdm command yourself from the prompt. Xdm will, of course, prompt you for your login information again. Once the information is successfully entered, however, xdm should start X, a window manager, and a terminal emulator for you.

xinit   The xinit command also can be entered from the prompt. It will not prompt you for any login information but should start X, a window manager, and a terminal emulator for you.

If neither one of these commands works, then again — you're in big trouble! Call your system administrator and get some help.

Window Manager Concepts

The window manager is an important part of any X Window System. It is the window manager's responsibility to "manage" the terminal screen "real estate." This means, essentially, that it is up to the window manager program to decide where and how new windows are placed on the root window.

Typically, window managers also give you some additional controls to manipulate the windows on the screen. Most window managers allow you to move windows from one location to another, change the size of a window, and move input focus from one window to another. Many window managers also allow you to change the stacking order of the windows on the screen to cause some previously hidden window to become visible again.

A window manager is just another X client. However, this client is given special privileges that allow it to intercept certain Xlib calls and deal with them internally itself. The window manager uses the same Xlib calls that any other client does but is usually developed to complement and work with a specific widget set.

So, in general, the Athena window manager is used with the Athena widget set and the Motif window manager is used with the Motif widget set. However, there is absolutely nothing in the window manager code that keeps you from running, for example, an Open Look widget program under the control of Tom's window manager. The only thing the window manager does is control the size, placement, movement, and input focus for the other client windows being placed on the root window.

❏   A *Special Note about the Term "Data-Processing:"* Throughout this book
you will see this term used a number of times. There may be some
disagreement about the meaning of this term with respect to business,
scientific, statistical, publishing, and other applications. However, when
used in this book, the term *data-processing* is used in its generic sense,
which refers to using a computer to process some data regardless of whether
the data is business, scientific, statistical, publishing, or any other type of
data. When you see this term in this book you should read it literally as
"data" "processing" — no other meaning is expressed or implied.

Review Questions

❏   Please write down the answers to the following questions.

1. What is the meaning of the term pixel?

2. Explain the difference between an X client program and an X server
    program.

3. What is the X Protocol is used for?

4. Define the term language bindings. How are these bindings related to
    your X application program?

5. What are the differences between Xlib, the X Toolkit, and an X
    widget set?

6. What is the meaning of the term look-and-feel?

7. Explain what a root window is.

8. Describe the coordinate system used to place X windows on the screen.

9. What is the purpose of an X application window hierarchy?

10. What happens when a window is mapped or realized?

11. What is a mouse, and what it is used for?

12. List four new defined X data types and what they are used for.

13. What is the difference between starting X with the xinit and xdm com-
    mands?

14. List three different window managers.

15. What is the purpose of a window manager?

Exercises

❏   The following exercises are designed to give you the opportunity to practice
the concepts and facilities presented in this chapter.

1. Start the X Window System running from your terminal with xinit,
    xdm, or whatever program is appropriate for your computer system.

2. Run the standard X client application named xclock. Can you do any-

thing in the xterm window? Why or why not?

3. Double-click (click mouse button 1 twice in rapid succession) in the push button in the upper-left-hand corner of the xclock window – the push button with the horizontal bar in it. What happened?

4. Run the standard X client application named xclock in the background. Can you do anything in the xterm window now? Why or why not?

5. Click and release mouse button 1 in the push button in the upper-left-hand corner of the xclock window – the push button with the horizontal bar in it. Choose the close option from the menu that appears by pointing to it and clicking mouse button 1 on it. What happened?

6. There are two types of input focus: pointer and explicit. Pointer focus allows input to be sent to whichever window the pointer happens to be in. Explicit focus requires you to click mouse button 1 in a window to move input focus. Try moving the mouse pointer to different windows on the screen to see if you can determine which type of input focus is currently in effect on your system.

7. Run the standard X client application named xlogo in the background.

8. Within the window of the xlogo client, using the mouse, point to the title bar push button in the top center of the xlogo window, click mouse button 1 and hold it down, then drag the mouse across the table. What happened?

9. Start another xterm client application running in the background.

10. Position the mouse pointer anywhere in the root window (outside all client windows). Click and hold mouse button 1. What happened?

11. With the root window menu displayed, try experimenting with some of the options.

3

What Is the
Motif
Toolkit?

Introduction

¤ The Open Software Foundation provides an X-based toolkit, or widget set, called Motif. In this chapter you will learn the purpose of OSF and how Motif is related to it. You will also learn about the Motif window manager and how to use it to move and resize windows as well as manage input focus.

Objectives

¤ After completing this chapter, you will be able to:

☐ Explain why OSF was formed.

☐ List the three key user needs addressed by OSF software products.

☐ Describe what Motif is and how it relates to OSF.

☐ List three features that the Motif library provides.

☐ List two new data types provided by Motif.

☐ Explain the purpose of the Motif window manager.

☐ List three of the client decoration push buttons provided for all client windows by the Motif window manager.

☐ Describe the difference between pointer input focus and explicit input focus.

◻ Explain the relationship between X and Motif.

◻ Describe which part of the X/Motif system is responsible for the operation of the window mechanism and which part is responsible for the window visual appearance and action policies.

◻ List four of the programs that are usually running in a typical X/Motif session.

The Open Software Foundation

◻ In May 1988 Apollo Computer Inc., DEC, Groupe Bull, Hewlett-Packard, IBM Corp., Nixdorf Computer AG, N.V., and Siemens AG banded together to sponsor the formation of a nonprofit corporation to be a neutral supplier of open-system software technologies. This corporation was the Open Software Foundation.

OSF's mission is to be the leading supplier of complete, innovative, and equitable open-systems environments to the worldwide computer industry. OSF provides software that addresses three key user needs:

1. Portability—allowing application software to run on multiple vendors' systems

2. Interoperability—allowing different systems from different vendors to work together transparently

3. Scalability—allowing a software environment to be hosted on the entire range of hardware platforms from desktop devices to supercomputers

OSF provides several services to its membership. Educational services allow members to learn about OSF software products. Consulting services allow members access to OSF's engineering staff for technical consulting. Members also have access to OSF's software products, which include the OSF/1 operating system and the OSF/Motif graphic-user interface for the X Window System.

OSF/Motif

◻ Motif is a widget set that is available for the X Window System from OSF. The Motif *user environment* provides a graphic user interface that offers user-oriented, PC-style behavior and screen appearance for applications running on any system which can support the X Window System.

The OSF/Motif environment offers:

◻ A common user interface across a wide variety of platforms

◻ A widely available application-programming interface

◻ An X-based development environment with a set of extensible development tools

◻ Easy-to-use Presentation Manager-style interactive behavior

◻ A distinctive three-dimensional (3-D) appearance

Motif provides advanced application portability designed to preserve software and user training investments. It is designed to allow transparent interoperability in the heterogeneous, networked computing environments of today.

The components of OSF/Motif include an extensible user interface toolkit, an applications programming interface (API or widget set), a user interface language, a window manager, and a complete set of documentation. The documentation includes a Style Guide which contains a specification of how a well-behaved Motif application should operate. Your application must follow the suggestions in the Style Guide to be considered Motif-compliant and accepted by OSF.

Motif Toolkit Library

◻ Just like the Xlib and Xt libraries, the Motif library provides hundreds of functions that allow you to work with the widgets provided in the Motif widget set. The Motif toolkit includes the following:

◻ 3 new widget classes used to group related widgets together

◻ 10 primitive widgets used as GUI interface objects

◻ 6 gadgets which are also interface objects but don't have their own window

◻ 2 shell widgets for handling menus and dialog boxes

◻ 13 manager widgets to control the layout of primitive widgets for an application

◻ 18 composite widgets predefined as a manager with specific primitive children

The Motif library contains functions that allow for the creation of each specific type of widget or gadget in the toolkit. There are also functions that allow you to interface with the Motif window manager and the Motif resource manager. Functions are provided to allow Motif client applications to work with the X clipboard for cut-and-paste features. Also, dozens of other functions are provided to allow an easier interface to working with the widgets themselves.

Motif Data Types

◻ Just like the Xlib and Xt libraries, the Motif library provides several new data types that are defined or typedefed in the Motif header files for you. Again, these data types are provided for documentation, convenience, and portability. These data types are usually somewhat more descriptive of what the data actually is than the underlying C data type would show. Some of the new Motif data types are:

XmFontList	A data type used for font-related information
XmString	A data type used to hold character strings and internationalization data
XmString Direction	A data type used to specify the printing direction for a string

Motif Window Manager

The Motif window manager is a special X client program provided by OSF that is designed to manage the layout of other client application windows on the root window of an X Window terminal screen. The operation of a Motif-based application does not depend on the Motif window manager or any other window manager at all. However, with a window manager running, using the X Window System is a much more pleasant experience.

The Motif window manager's primary purpose is to provide for the initial placement of a client application's main window somewhere on the root window of the screen. The Motif window manager places a border around the main client window that contains *client decorations*. These decorations allow for the movement and resizing of the client application window independent of the application itself.

The client decorations are really a series of special Motif PushButtons that include:

minimize button	This button allows you to shrink the application window into an icon. Shrink the window when you aren't using it and it is getting in the way of your using other windows on the screen.
maximize button	This button allows you to expand the application window to fill the entire screen. Expand the window when an application gives you a work area that is too small to work in and you need more room.
title bar button	This button allows you to move the application window. Simply click, hold, and drag in this button, and the window manager lets you drag the window to a new location on the screen.
window manager menu button	This button allows you to communicate with the window manager more directly. Clicking this button pops up a menu with several options that allow you to manipulate the window using the keyboard instead of the mouse. One option should be a "close" option that lets you close the client application window and kill the application.

resize handle buttons

There are a total of eight resize handles located around the outside edge of the client application window. As the name implies, you can resize the window using these buttons. Simply click, hold, and drag in any one of these buttons, and the window will enlarge or shrink in the direction that you drag the mouse.

Figure 3.1 shows a typical client application window being managed by the Motif window manager identifying the location of the different client decorations.

One other feature of the Motif window manager is its ability to direct input focus to a particular client application window. Two styles of focus policy are available: pointer and explicit. Pointer focus policy specifies that whatever window the mouse pointer happens to be in is the window that has focus. Explicit focus policy specifies that you must click mouse button 1 in a window to have it receive input focus.

No matter which focus policy you choose, the policy simply specifies which client application window will receive input from the keyboard and the mouse. Only one application can have input focus at a time.

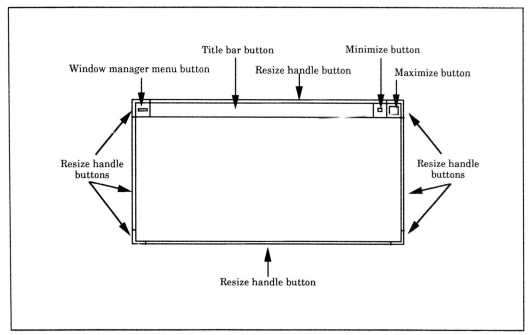

Figure 3.1 Motif window manager client decorations.

The Relationship between X and Motif

◻ Motif is a vendor-specific (OSF) widget set. It is not a stand-alone system. Like all widget sets, Motif requires the base X Window System, including the Xlib and Xt libraries. Typically, when you buy Motif from a computer vendor you will also get a copy of the X Window System.

One of the most important concepts that you need to understand at this point is that the base X layers provide a *mechanism* for displaying windows on a bitmapped graphic-display terminal. X does *not* specify a policy regarding how those windows should look or how they should operate in response to input.

It is up to a widget set, such as Motif, to implement these policies. Motif defines what a PushButton will look like and what happens to that look when you use the mouse pointer or the keyboard to "push" the button. The action that is performed in response to a button being pushed is again defined by Motif. The policy of what happens when a button is pressed is specific to Motif and is not directly related to the base X Window System.

This policy is often referred to as a *look-and-feel*. The purpose of the different widget sets such as Motif, Open Look, and Athena is to allow the programmer to provide a different look-and-feel among different programs while using the same basic window mechanisms that are provided by the MIT X Window system.

A Typical X/Motif Terminal Session

◻ In a typical X/Motif terminal session you will have the X server, the Motif window manager, a command interpreter, a terminal emulator, and several other clients running at the same time. Figure 3.2 shows the generic relationships that exist between each of these individual processes as the X Window System is in operation. Note that all the programs are running asynchronously.

Output from and Input to a Motif Application

◻ This book assumes that you will be writing X/Motif programs using the C programming language. All the example code in this book uses C and the C language bindings for X and Motif. You must be familiar with the basic C syntax—especially dealing with functions, arrays, structures, and pointers—to be able to read the examples in this book. You should also be familiar with the Standard C Library and many of the functions it contains.

◻ Experienced C programmers will soon find themselves asking: "Where does the output from printf() go to in a Motif program? Where does scanf() read its input from?"

Remember—the <stdio.h> include file defines three standard files. Stdin is the standard file that input is read from and is usually assigned to the terminal keyboard. Stdout and stderr are the standard output files that you write output and error messages to, respectively, and are usually assigned

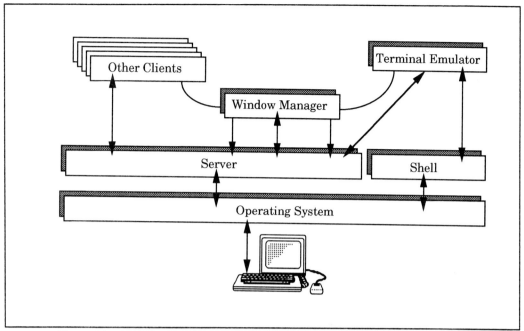

Figure 3.2 Relationship between processes in a typical X/Motif session.

to the terminal screen. Printf() writes to stdout, while scanf() reads from stdin.

In many operating systems a C program (or process) that is executed will inherit the file information for these three standard files from the process that started it running (its parent process). From Figure 3.2, it can be seen that the xterm terminal emulator program is where you, as a user, start an X client running. It should be obvious, then, that the client will inherit its stdin, stdout, and stderr file information from the xterm. This, of course, means that anything you printf() will be displayed in the text of the xterm window and anything you read with scanf() will have to be entered from the xterm window (after it receives input focus).

Review Questions

◻ Please write down the answers to the following questions:

1. Why was OSF formed?

2. List the three key user needs addressed by OSF software products.

3. What is Motif, and how does it relate to OSF?

4. List three features that the Motif library provides.

5. List two new data types provided by Motif.

6. What is the purpose of the Motif window manager?

7. List three of the client decoration push buttons provided for all client

windows by the Motif window manager.

8.   How do pointer input focus and explicit input focus differ?

9.   What is the relationship between X and Motif?

10. Which part of the X/Motif system is responsible for the operation of the window mechanism, and which part is responsible for the window visual appearance and action policies?

11. List four programs that are usually running in a typical X/Motif session.

Exercises

¤   The following exercises are designed to give you the opportunity to practice the concepts and facilities presented in this chapter:

1.   For one or more of any of the client applications that you currently have running, manipulate the various Motif Window Manager buttons that make up the client decorations surrounding the client window. For example:

     ¤   The Motif Window Manager button on the left

     ¤   The title bar button in the middle

     ¤   The minimize button on the right

     ¤   The maximize button on the right

     ¤   Any of the eight resize handle buttons around the outside edge of the window

     A maximized window can be "restored" to its original size by clicking on the maximize button a second time. A minimized window (iconified window) can be "restored" to its original size by double-clicking on its icon.

Graphic-User Interface Objects – Widgets

Introduction

◻ To make programming with X a little easier, the X Toolkit provides a data abstraction called a *widget*. In this chapter you will learn what a widget is and how widgets provide for a type of object-oriented programming with X. You will also learn about several different widget types and how they fit into a widget class tree.

Objectives

◻ After completing this chapter, you will be able to:

◻ Define an object with respect to object-oriented programming.

◻ List two goals of object-oriented programming.

◻ List the three main features of object-oriented programming.

◻ Explain what an abstract data type is.

◻ Describe the process of encapsulation.

◻ Explain how inheritance works.

◻ Relate the X concept of a widget to object-oriented programming concepts.

◻ List five Motif widgets and what they are used for.

◻ List two Xt widgets and what they are used for.

◻ Explain the purpose of the Motif widget class tree.

X and Object-Oriented Programming

◻ With widgets, X and Motif use some *object-oriented programming* techniques to organize and classify the widgets in a way that will make them more useful to the application developer. The object (a widget in this case) is a piece of code that can be thought of as a "black box." It will accept specific inputs, perform a process on those inputs, and produce a related output in response.

Some of the goals of any object-oriented technology are:

1. To improve productivity by increasing software extensibility. Although the objects in X are predefined for a specific purpose, there are *hooks* into the object which allow you to "extend" its basic operation with code of your own.

2. To improve productivity by increasing software reusability. The purpose of predefined objects is so that the programmer doesn't have to "reinvent the wheel." Predefined objects are created for the most common functions needed in a typical program.

3. To control the complexity of software. To meet the demands of today's data-processing requirements, software systems have become more complex than ever before—especially with the needs of graphic-user interfaces and database systems. This complexity must be controlled so that the cost of software maintenance can be kept to a minimum.

4. To control the cost of software maintenance. Implementation of a software system is actually less than half of the problem in today's software development environment. Finding or training someone who can understand, change, and fix these systems is a more difficult problem.

◻ The features of an object-oriented programming system that address the above problem areas include:

◻ Data abstraction

◻ Encapsulation

◻ Inheritance

◻ Abstract data types are not the data types defined in your programming language. An abstract data type is a *defined data type*. A GUI push button is an example of an abstract data type. It is actually a data structure defining how the button will look on the screen as well as a set of procedures that will determine how it operates. Data (inputs and outputs) and a set of operations (processes) define an abstract data type.

◻ Encapsulation is the process of defining an *instance*, or occurrence, of an item (a variable) of a particular abstract data type. Having the abstract data type "PushButton" available is one thing—but to use it in your program, you must encapsulate the data and the process into an instance of a PushButton as an object your program can work with. In the C programming language type int with addition, subtraction, multiplication, and division defined on it is similar to an abstract data type. The statement "int i;" encapsulates an instance of that data type into the variable i that can have those operations performed on it. For those of you involved with object-oriented programming, please note that this is not a complete or exact definition of encapsulation as you may be familiar with it.

Inheritance is an aspect of abstract data types that defines how related data types are grouped together into *classes* that share another common data type as a parent in a hierarchy. Figure 4.1 shows an example of an abstract data type class hierarchy that could be used for geometric objects.

In Figure 4.1 an instance of an object of type square will inherit its own local copy of all the features of square (such as side length) as well as features of type parallelogram (such as parallel sides), type quadrangle (such as four sides and four angles), and type geometric object (such as line width, style, and color). If an instance of an object of type geometric object has specific attributes, an instance of an object of square will inherit the same attributes.

Widget Concepts

What is a widget? A widget is an object – an abstract data type. It is a collection of one or more X windows held together with a geometry for a specific look and a set of procedures that implement its operation. Both Motif and Xt have abstract data types (widgets) for a wide variety of user interface objects that can be used to accept input or supply output in a graphic-user interface program. Figure 4.2 shows some examples of user interface component widgets.

To use a widget in your program, you have to encapsulate an instance of the widget data type as an object that your program can use. You can define as many instances of a widget as you need for the purposes of your application program. But each individual instance of the widget is a separate occurrence of an object of that widget data type. Each one has its own appearance and purpose, which is completely separate and different from every other occurrence of that widget type in your program.

Each widget belongs to a class of related widgets that is organized into a hierarchy. When you define an instance of a widget, it inherits attributes from all of its parents, grandparents, and others all the way up to the root

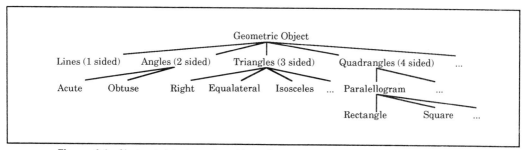

Figure 4.1 Abstract-data-type class hierarchy.

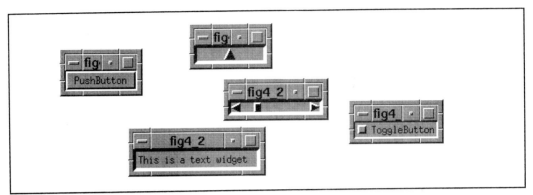

Figure 4.2 Widget examples.

of the hierarchy. These attributes, of course, have default values. You can stick with the defaults in a particular instance, or you can change the attributes to suit some other needs before you create the instance of the object or after it has been created and displayed on the screen.

Motif Widgets

□ A number of widgets defined in the Motif widget set can be instantiated into an object in your X program. These widget data types are encapsulated into an object in your program with a specific look-and-feel:

ArrowButton	Used as a push-button-type widget with an arrow head drawn on the button
CascadeButton	Used as a push button with an indication that a menu can be poped up from it
DrawnButton	Used as a push button with some graphic object or picture drawn on it
Label	Used to display noneditable text as a label for another object
List	Used to present a list of options from which one or more items can be selected
PushButton	Used as a simple push button
ScrollBar	Used to page, or scroll, through a larger work area with a small viewport
Separator	Used to visually separate two objects or areas from one another
Text	Used to display or enter ASCII text data
ToggleButton	Used as a push button that has a state associated with it—pressed in or popped out
BulletinBoard	Used to manage one or more other widgets according to specific X/Y-coordinates for each one

DrawingArea	Used as a drawing space to draw graphics objects in
Form	Used to manage one or more other widgets with attachments specified as to how they should be positioned with respect to the form or other widgets within the form
Frame	Used as a picture frame to surround some other widget and make its appearance stand out
PanedWindow	Used to manage one or more other widgets in individually resizable window panes
RowColumn	Used to manage one or more other widgets in equally sized and spaced rows or columns
Scale	Used to indicate a specific numeric value that falls into a specified range of values; operates similar to a scroll bar
ScrolledWindow	Used to manage some other large widget by placing a smaller scrollable viewport over it
FileSelectionBox	Used to prompt for and receive a specific filename from a list of possibilities
MainWindow	Used as the Motif Style Guide-compliant application "shell" with areas defined for a menu bar, two scroll bars, a command or message area, and a work area
MessageBox	Used to display some type of message to an application user
SelectionBox	Used to prompt for and receive some type of text data from a user

Several other widgets are defined in the Motif widget set. All of the widgets can be classified as belonging to one of three widget groupings. *Primitive widgets* are those widgets with which the user interacts to provide input to a Motif program and accept output from the program. *Manager widgets* are those widgets that have no input or output semantics but, instead, are used to manage the layout (or geometry) of the other primitive and manager widgets in a Motif application. Finally, *composite widgets* are a predefined collection of a manager and primitive widgets that have been designed for a special purpose. Composite widgets are provided for several types of menus, dialog boxes, and scrollable work areas.

Xt Widgets

Only four widgets defined in the Xt widget set can be instantiated into an object in your X application program. These widgets, called *shell widgets*, are of a special type that have no physical appearance on the screen:

| OverrideShell | Used for windows that completely bypass the window manager, such as popup and pulldown menus |
| TransientShell | Used for windows that can be manipulated by the window manager but cannot be iconified separately, such as dialog boxes |

TopLevelShell   Used for normal windows that can be manipulated by
                       the window manager

ApplicationShell   Used by the window manager to define a separate appli-
                       cation instance

The X/Motif Widget Class Tree

◻ Figure 4.3 shows the organization of the X/Motif widget class tree. This
tree shows how widgets are organized into related classes. From the previous discussion you should be able to understand that when an instance of a
particular widget is encapsulated into an occurrence of a specific object in
your program, it inherits attributes and features from all the widget classes
that appear above it in the widget class tree. That is, in fact, the reason
and purpose for organizing the widgets in this way.

Purpose of this Book

◻ Before we get down to the "nuts and bolts" of programming a widget-based
program, it is important to take note of what we will and will not be talking about on the following pages. This book is intended to be an introduction to Motif programming in the X Window System environment. It is
intended to lead the student through all the steps necessary in order to
write a complete and functional Motif client program to perform some data-
processing task in the X Window System environment. It is not intended to
be a complete and detailed reference manual for Motif.

This book also is not intended to introduce the student to everything there
is to know about the X Window System. Therefore, although there are
features of X (besides graphic-user interfaces) that make it useful in other
areas, we will cover only those aspects that are generally useful in simple
Motif client applications. Specifically, X was developed for use in a
networked environment and has some interesting interclient communication
facilities. These two topics will not be discussed in any great detail.

This book will also not discuss any of the new interactive development
tools (IDTs) or, as they are sometimes called, GUI builders. There are
many good products on the market that do an acceptable job of generating
X/Motif C code and can be useful tools for prototyping the user interface to
an application in the initial design processes for a project. However, just
like Motif's UIL (User Interface Language) and any other "high-level
language," IDTs have to take the generic case of each widget into account
and cannot write the C code for the widget as efficiently as the programmer
can "by hand."

When through with this book, the student with typical C programming
skills will be able to design, develop, and run Motif widget-based applications using the X Window System and the C programming language.
Learning to take full advantage of all the capabilities of OSF/Motif and the
X Window System will require more to be written in future books.

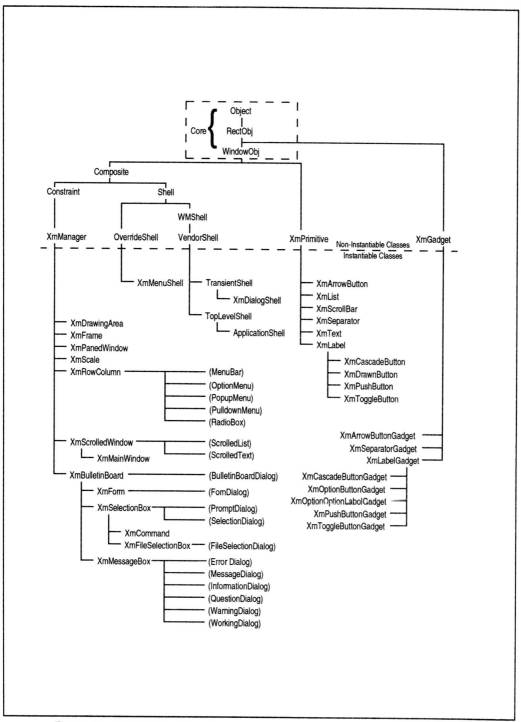

Figure 4.3 X/Motif widget class tree.

Review Questions

¤   Please write down the answers to the following questions:

1. What is the purpose of an object with respect to object-oriented programming?

2. List two of the goals of object-oriented programming.

3. List the three main features of object-oriented programming.

4. What is an abstract data type?

5. How does the process of encapsulation work?

6. How does inheritance work?

7. How is the concept of a widget related to object-oriented programming concepts?

8. List five Motif widgets and what they are used for.

9. List two Xt widgets and what they are used for.

10. What is the purpose of the Motif widget class tree?

X Application
Programming
Concepts

Introduction

¤ All X/Motif application programs have similar structures. There are specific functions that must be called in a specific order to implement the event-driven, object-oriented features in a widget-based program. In this chapter you will learn about these functions and construct a simple single-widget program with them.

Objectives

¤ After completing this chapter, you will be able to:

☐ Explain why an X/Motif programmer must have a good set of reference documentation.

☐ Describe the function and macro naming conventions used in X, Xt, and Motif.

☐ List some of the header files required by an X program.

☐ Describe the function used to perform required initializations in an X/Motif client application and its return value.

☐ Explain how to detect and handle errors when calling X/Motif functions.

☐ Describe the function used to create a Motif PushButton widget and its return value.

- Explain why each and every widget in your client application has two "names."
- Describe what happens when you manage a widget.
- List two functions that can be used to manage widgets.
- Explain which function causes your application to finally be mapped, or realized, to the screen.
- Describe how to implement an event loop with the Xt Intrinsics.
- Explain the options needed to compile an X/Motif client application program.
- Describe how to run an X/Motif client application program.

Documentation

Unfortunately, with hundreds of functions available in Xlib, hundreds of functions available in Xt, and hundreds of functions available in a widget set like Motif, no one person will be able to memorize all there is to know about the X Window System! You must have a good set of documentation readily available if you are going to start programming in X.

If you have installed X yourself from a distribution tape from MIT, the tape also contains a lot of documentation on Xlib, Xt, and a variety of other X-related topics. You will want to print these out and have them available before you start writing code.

If you bought a computer system with X installed on it, there will undoubtably be an X manual among the documentation that you received from your hardware vendor. Make sure that it covers both the Xlib and the Xt functions and have it close by before you begin programming.

If both options fail, there are a number of good books available on the market that cover the X Window System. One set of books that many people have found useful are the books from O'Reilly and Associates, Inc.:

Volume 0: *X Protocol Reference Manual,*
ISBN 0-937175-50-1, $30.00
Volume 1: *Xlib Programming Manual,*
ISBN 0-937175-27-7, $34.95
Volume 2: *Xlib Reference Manual,*
ISBN 0-937175-28-5, $34.95
Volume 3: *X Window System User's Guide,*
ISBN 0-937175-36-6, $30.00
Volume 4: *X Toolkit Intrinsics Programming Manual,*
ISBN 0-937175-56-0, $30.00
Volume 5: *X Toolkit Intrinsics Reference Manual,*
ISBN 0-937175-57-9, $30.00
X Window System in a Nutshell,
ISBN 0-937175-24-2, $24.95

If you are using the Motif widget set, there is still more documentation that you need. If you bought Motif direct from OSF, there is a set of manuals that come with the product. If you bought a computer system with

Motif installed on it there will undoubtably be a Motif manual among the documentation that you received from your hardware vendor. If both these options fail, OSF has published a set of trade books that you will find invaluable:

OSF/Motif User's Guide,
  ISBN 0-13-640509-6, $16.00
OSF/Motif Style Guide,
  ISBN 0-13-640491-X, $16.00
OSF/Motif Programmer's Guide,
  ISBN 0-13-640525-8, $32.00
OSF/Motif Programmer's Reference,
  ISBN 0-13-640517-7, $40.00

Obviously, to get all these documents would require a substantial investment on anybody's part. However, it can't be stressed enough that you must have adequate documentation to get started with X programming. Learning the basics is easy—that's what this book is about. But once you get going, you will want to be able to use some of the advanced capabilities and techniques. To do this you will have to know what functions are available in which libraries, which means that you will absolutely need a good set of reference documentation.

Function Naming Conventions

Each set of library functions uses a particular naming convention to help the programmer remember which functions belong to which library. In the Xlib library all function names will begin with an uppercase X and will use a mixed-case convention in the letters that follow. If the function name consists of more than one word, then subsequent words in the function name will start with an uppercase letter and be followed by lowercase letters. All Xlib macros follow the same mixed-case convention but do not begin with an uppercase X.

The Xt Intrinsics library uses a similar naming convention. All functions and macros in the Xt library follow the same mixed-case convention that the Xlib functions do but begin with the letters Xt. The Intrinsics library does not distinguish between function and macro names.

The Motif library uses the same mixed-case naming convention that both Xlib and Xt use. But all Motif function names will begin with the letters Xm. Figure 5.1 shows some examples of function and macro names from each of the three libraries.

Header Files

In the C language, when you use specific functions from some function library, there are usually one or more "header" files that you must #include through the preprocessor. All X Window programs require include files called <X11/Xlib.h> and <X11/X.h>. The <X11/Xlib.h> file contains most of the structure declarations that an Xlib program will need and

```
Xlib Function Name Examples:
    XAllocNamedColor()          XDefineCursor()
    XDrawRectangles()           XCheckTypedWindowEvent()
    XSetClipRectangles()        XChangeKeyboardMapping()
Xlib Macro Name Examples:
    DefaultColormapOfScreen()   DefaultScreenOfDisplay()
    QLength()                   WhitePixelOfScreen()
Xt Function Name Examples:
    XtInitialize()              XtAddCallback()
    XtMainLoop()                XtNameToWidget()
    XtRemoveInput()             XtSetSensitive()
Xt Macro Name Examples:
    XtSetArg()                  XtNumber()
    XtClass()                   XtIsRealized()
Motif Function Name Examples:
    XmCreatePushButton()        XmMessageBoxGetChild()
    XmConvertUnits()            XmListDeselectPos()
    XmRemoveWMProtocols()       XmStringExtent()
```

Figure 5.1 Function naming conventions.

includes <X11/X.h> for you. The <X11/X.h> file contains most of the defined constants used within X programs.

If you are programming with the Intrinsics, <X11/Intrinsic.h> will also need to be included. This file contains declarations and structure definitions required by many of the Xt functions. The <X11/Intrinsic.h> file is also included for you when you include <X11/Xlib.h>.

Some other include files you may want to be aware of are:

<X11/Xutil.h>   Additional structure types and constant definitions for miscellaneous Xlib functions

<X11/Xatom.h>   The predefined atoms for properties, types, and font characteristics

<X11/cursorfont.h>   The constants used to select a cursor shape from the standard cursor font

<X11/keysym.h>   Predefined key symbols corresponding to keycodes

<X11/resource.h>   Resource manager structure definitions and function declarations

Initializing and Creating a Shell Widget

The first things that any widget-based program must do include initializing the Intrinsics, creating an application context, opening a connection to the X server, and creating a special type of widget called a *top-level shell widget*. All these functions have been included together in a single function called XtInitialize(). Figure 5.2 shows the parameters and return type for XtInitialize().

```
Widget XtInitialize(shell_instance_name, application_class,
                    options, num_options, address_of_argc, argv)

String              shell_instance_name; /*unused in X11R3 */
String              application_class;
XrmOptionDescRec    options[];
Cardinal            num_options;
Cardinal            *address_of_argc;
String              argv[];
```

Figure 5.2 XtInitialize() syntax.

Initializing the Intrinsics involves giving initial values to the many data structures that the Xt toolkit uses in its operation with the widgets. Because of these initializations, you can call Xt Initialize() only once in any X program.

Application contexts allow for multiple logical applications to exist in the same address space. Each context corresponds to one application that has its own independent event loop and display connection. Each logical application performs its own independent processing for some data-processing task separate from all other contexts. Each X client must have at least one application context.

Your program must open a display connection to a server in order for you to communicate with the server using the X Protocol. This connection also allows the server to interact with the terminal on your behalf. The display connection is added to the application context so that your "logical" application has a way of communicating with your terminal.

Another important aspect of XtInitialize is the creation of an instance of a TopLevelShell widget. All X widget programs must have a shell widget because it is through the shell widget that the window manager communicates with your program. When the window manager lets a user do something like move a window by dragging on its title bar, the window manager must have a way of notifying all the widgets in your program of the new location so that they can redraw themselves there. This communication is done through a shell widget.

XtInitialize() creates an TopLevelShell widget for you and returns you its widget id. If the function failed in any of its operations for any reason, it will return you an invalid widget id. The invalid value that is returned is NULL, which should be tested for to ensure successful completion of the function. Figure 5.3 shows an actual example of how XtInitialize() would be called.

By convention argv[0] is passed as the shell widget instance name. The class name is a completely arbitrary string of characters that you choose to describe what type of application this is – there are no standards. You could choose "Edit" if this were a text editor program, or "Db" if this were a database program, but whatever you choose, pick a useful and appropriate name because you will be using it later. Note that the class name usually starts with an uppercase letter

The third and fourth parameters are set to NULL and 0 because we will not be using them in this book. These two parameters implement some

```
#include <stdio.h>
main(argc, argv)
Cardinal argc;
String argv[];
    {
    Widget topShell;

    topShell = XtInitialize(argv[0], "Edit", NULL, 0, &argc, argv);
    if(topShell == NULL)
        {
        fprintf(stderr, "Could not initialize.\n");
        exit(-1);
        }
    ...

        --OR--
#include <stdio.h>
main(argc, argv)
Cardinal argc;
String argv[];
    {
    Widget topShell;

    if((topShell=XtInitialize(argv[0], "Edit", NULL, 0, &argc, argv)) == NULL)
        {
        fprintf(stderr, "Could not initialize.\n");
        exit(-1);
        }
    ...
```

Figure 5.3 Calling XtInitialize().

advanced features that let you determine how the command line used to invoke your client is scanned and searched for special options to control your application's operation.

The last two parameters are your command line argument variables: argc and argv. Note that you must pass the address of argc to this function. XtInitialize(), like any other function that gets an address passed to it, has the ability to access and modify your command-line arguments. Argv is already an address so we do not need the address operator on it. More will be presented on this feature later.

□   The XtInitialize() function has been superseded by XtAppInitialize() in Release 4 of Version 11 of the X Window System. Both functions do essentially the same thing but XtAppInitialize() takes some additional parameters that give it some added functionality.

Error Handling

□   As in the standard C library, there are two types of functions in the X and Motif libraries. There are those functions that return a value to you and there are those functions that don't return a value to you. These two types of functions, just as with the standard C library, must be handled differently.

If a function is designed to return some piece of data to you, then that piece of data will be important somewhere in your program. If it wasn't important, then the function wouldn't bother returning anything at all. These same functions must also have a way of telling your program that they couldn't perform their operation successfully.

Most of the functions in the X and Motif libraries handle this problem in much the same way that the functions from the standard C library handle the problem. If the function is returning you some type of useful data, then it will be some nonzero value. If the function is trying to inform you of an error condition then it will return the constant NULL. This error condition, should always be checked for with any X or Motif function that returns a value to you. The use of XtInitialize in Figure 5.3 shows two typical methods for checking a function's return value for errors.

◻   How do you tell which functions return a value and which ones do not? Again, just as with the standard C library, if a function is declared to return type void, it does not return anything to you. All the X and Motif functions have their return type declared in their respective header files, which are described in the X and Motif documentation.

You must be cautious, though! Remember that X and Motif have declared a number of their own unique data types to make things a little more readable and descriptive within your program. Some of the declared function return types that you see in the documentation are actually typedefed in a way you might not expect. For example, if you use the data type XtCallbackProc, which is defined as a return type for a special type of function called a *callback function*, it is really a typedef for void! If you tried to check the return value for a function declared as XtCallbackProc, it wouldn't work.

Here, then, is one of the finer points of X programming: As soon as possible, you need to be aware of the underlaying C data type for most of the more common X and Motif data types. If you aren't at least aware of this possible problem, you could spend many hours (days?... weeks?...) trying to track down a problem that doesn't really exist.

How do you find out about the underlaying C data types? Read the documentation and scan through the header files. Just about every experienced X programmer that you talk to will tell you to read through the header files — there's lots to learn there.

Creating a Motif PushButton Widget

◻   Once you have a shell widget created in your program, you can start creating the user interface widgets that your program will need. You can, for example, create a Motif PushButton widget. Each widget in the Motif toolkit has its own unique create function. Figure 5.4 shows the parameters and return type for XmCreatePushButton().

This function will create an instance of a PushButton widget as an interface object in your program. All the appearance and action attributes will be encapsulated into a new and unique instance. The look-and-feel of the PushButton widget will result from the attribute inheritance that occurs for this class of widget from the widget class tree.

```
#include <Xm/PushB.h>

Widget XmCreatePushButton(parent_id, instance_name, arg_list, arg_count)

Widget        parent_id;
String        instance_name;
ArgList       arg_list;
Cardinal      arg_count;
```

Figure 5.4 XmCreatePushButton() syntax.

Although this instance will have some definite visual behaviors, when you click on it with the mouse and the mouse pointer, it will not cause any of *your* programming to execute – yet! We have to hook the widget into your specific data-processing code through something called the callback mechanism. Figure 5.5 shows an actual example of how XmCreatePushButton() would be called.

Each and every Motif widget has its own unique and different header file defined for it. If you are going to create a Motif PushButton widget, you must include <Xm/PushB.h>. It will include all the necessary data and function declarations for the proper use of this function. It will also contain all the necessary Xlib and Xt includes! *In a Motif-based widget program the only includes you need are the Motif widget includes – all basic X and Xt include files are included for you.* Other include files will be required for special functions such as defining a new cursor and working with keysyms.

Every X widget-based program forms an instance tree with the widgets defined in the program. The shell widget forms the base of the tree with all other widgets spreading out below it in a hierarchy. (However, a shell widget can, itself, have only one child because shell widgets have no *geometry management policy* which would allow them to position children.) The first parameter to every Motif widget creation function is the widget id (returned from a create function) of the widget above this instance in the program's instance tree – its *parent widget.*

Because a widget within your program can be referenced from outside your program (through something called a *resource file*), it is important that each widget in your program have a unique name. The second

```
#include <stdio.h>
#include <Xm/PushB.h>
...
Widget myButton;
...
if((myButton = XmCreatePushButton(topShell, "hello", NULL, 0)) == NULL)
        {
        fprintf(stderr, "Could not create push button.\n");
        exit(-1);
        }
...
```

Figure 5.5 Creating a Motif PushButton.

parameter to every Motif widget creation function is a character string that you create and define for that widget's *instance name*. Instance names do not have to be unique within a program, but if they are not unique, you will have trouble referencing them as separate widgets from a resource file. By default, the instance name is used as the label that appears on the Motif PushButton when it is mapped to the screen.

The last two parameters have to do with changing the default look-and-feel of the widget before the instance is actually created. Until we find out what attributes define the look-and-feel and what values they can take on, we will pass NULL and 0 as the last two parameters of any widget creation function. This essentially means that we want the default look-and-feel.

The result of the processing of this function is to create a new instance of a Motif PushButton widget. The function returns the widget id for the instance which is your internal reference point for the newly created Push-Button widget. Each widget you create will have two "names:" its instance name, which is used externally to your program to reference the widget inside your program; and the widget id, which is used internally to your program to reference the widget from within your program code.

Managing Nonshell Widgets

¤   Because of the heirarchial nature of windows in X, each parent window must be told about its children. The children may request a specific initial X/Y-coordinate position within the parent along with a specific height and width. However, the parent window can override these requests and change the position and size of any of its children. The ability that a parent window has to change the characteristics of its children is called *geometry management*.

Every time that you add a new child widget to your program's instance tree, you must notify its parent that you want the widget added to the parent's managed children list. Once on the list, if the parent gets mapped to the terminal screen (becomes visible), it will cause all its managed children to become visible, too. Every nonshell widget in your program's instance tree that you want to be visible on the screen must be *managed*. Two functions are available as described in Figure 5.6. Either one can be used to add a child to its parent's managed children list.

```
void XtManageChildren(children, num_children)

WidgetList   children;
Cardinal     num_children;


    --OR--


void XtManageChild(child)

Widget       child;
```

Figure 5.6 XtManageChildren() and XtManageChild() syntax.

The first of these two functions takes an array of Widget ids as its first parameter (WidgetList is typedefed to an array of, or pointer to, type Widget) and a count of the number of widget ids in the array as the second parameter. Every widget specified in the widget list array must be the child of some common parent. If the children in the array have different parents, an error will be generated.

The second of these two functions is a convenience function. It takes the single widget id supplied as a parameter and constructs a widget list of length 1 with it. XtManageChild() then calls XtManageChildren() with the newly constructed widget list and a count of 1.

◻   Both of these functions will check to see if the parent of the children being managed is being destroyed and will return immediately if this is true. If the parent is not being destroyed then it marks each child as viewable if it is not already being managed and is not in the process of being destroyed itself. Finally, if the parent is already visible, it notifies the parent about the new children so that it can make room on the screen within the geometry of the children that are already displayed and then maps the children to the screen.

Managing children widgets is independent of their ordering on the screen, their order of creation, or their deletion. The parent will only lay out children widgets on the screen that have been managed according to its own geometry management policy and ignore all others. Figure 5.7 shows an example of how these management functions would be called.

◻   In Figure 5.7 the call to XtNumber() simply determines the number of elements in the array. This is a convenience macro that programmatically returns a count of the number of elements in the array parameter by dividing the total size of the array by the size of the first element of the array (a common C technique). If you are not using all the elements in the array, do not use this macro; hard-code the count in the XtManageChildren() call yourself.

Making the Shell Widget Visible

◻   The shell widget has no parent—it is the top-level widget in any X program's widget instance hierarchy. Because of this fact there is no reason to manage the shell widget. Instead, we just want to make the shell widget visible on the screen so that all of the windows below the shell will become visible and the user can start interacting with our program. Figure

```
Widget pushButtons[10];
Widget aPushButton;
...
XtManageChildren(pushButtons, XtNumber(pushButtons));
...
XtManageChild(aPushButton);
...
```

Figure 5.7 Managing widgets with XtManageChildren() and XtManageChild().

5.8 shows the syntax for the XtRealizeWidget() function which performs this operation for us.

Of course, the widget id that you pass to XtRealizeWidget() is usually the widget id that was returned from XtInitialize(). XtRealizeWidget() descends the widget instance tree for the program and creates the actual X windows for each widget. This function also causes these windows to set their attributes on the basis of class information in the widget class tree and performs some final initializations. Finally, for all managed children, the windows for the widgets become realized, or mapped, to the screen.

The reason that you don't have to realize the children widgets themselves is that XtManageChild() and XtManageChildren() call this function for you as part of the process they perform. The children widgets don't become visible, however, until their parent becomes visible. Since the "great-grandparent" of all widgets is the shell widget (the widget at the top of the instance tree), then none of your application widgets will become visible until the shell has been realized. Figure 5.9 shows how the XtRealizeWidget() function would be used in an X program.

Entering an Event Loop

▫ The last thing that the main function of any X program must do is enter the event loop and wait for input events from the application user. The Xt Intrinsics library provides us with another convenience function to handle the event loop of a widget-based program. Instead of coding an infinite loop

```
void XtRealizeWidget(widget_id)

Widget  widget_id;
```

Figure 5.8 XtRealizeWidget() syntax.

```
#include <stdio.h>
main(argc, argv)
Cardinal argc;
String argv[];
    {
    Widget topShell;

    if((topShell=XtInitialize(argv[0], "Edit", NULL, 0, &argc, argv)) == NULL)
        {
        fprintf(stderr, "Could not initialize.\n");
        exit(-1);
        }
    ...
    XtRealizeWidget(topShell);
    ...
```

Figure 5.9 Calling XtRealizeWidget().

with a large switch statement for acting on every possible input event a widget-based program need only call XtMainLoop(). Figure 5.10 shows the syntax for this function.

If you want a specific input event on a specific widget to cause some code you write to be executed, you must register a function with the Intrinsics to be executed when that input event is seen. This type of function execution, called a *callback*, will be discussed in more detail a little later. Once you have registered your data-processing function with the Intrinsics, however, the XtMainLoop() function will then be able to call your function when the specified input event occurs.

XtMainLoop() does not know about any specific exit events. It is up to you and your application-specific programming to decide which input event will cause your application to terminate and return control to X. If you don't define an exit event, you will have to use some other command from your terminal emulator to kill the process for your program.

Just as an event loop is supposed to do, XtMainLoop() watches the input events coming from the terminal, decides which window the event occurred in, and passes the event off to the appropriate widget-specific code or the application-specific code that you write to do your data processing. XtMain-Loop takes no parameters, does not return, and is used only in widget-based programs. Figure 5.11 shows how the XtMainLoop() function would be used in a program.

¤   The XtMainLoop() function has been superseded by XtAppMainLoop() in Release 4 of Version 11 of the X Window System. Both functions do essentially the same thing but XtAppMainLoop() gives some added functionality.

```
void XtMainLoop()
```

Figure 5.10 XtMainLoop() syntax.

```
#include <stdio.h>
main(argc, argv)
Cardinal argc;
String argv[];
    {
    Widget topShell;

    if((topShell=XtInitialize(argv[0], "Edit", NULL, 0, &argc, argv)) == NULL)
        {
        fprintf(stderr, "Could not initialize.\n");
        exit(-1);
        }
    ...
    XtRealizeWidget(topShell);
    XtMainLoop();
    }
```

Figure 5.11 Calling XtMainLoop().

A Complete X/Motif Client Application

◻ Using all the concepts and techniques presented in this chapter, we can put together a simple, but complete, X/Motif-based client application. Example 5.1 shows the code for a program that has a shell widget and a single PushButton widget in it. The program won't do anything yet — we have to tell the Intrinsics what to do for us when the PushButton is pressed. But it is a complete program: it will run and will display something on the terminal screen. Figure 5.12 shows what the result of this simple program would look like on a typical terminal screen.

```c
#include <stdio.h>
#include <Xm/PushB.h>

main(argc, argv)
Cardinal argc;
String argv[];
    {
    Widget topShell;
    Widget myButton;

    /* Initialize  the Intrinsics and create a top Shell widget */
    if((topShell=XtInitialize(argv[0], "Edit", NULL, 0, &argc, argv)) == NULL)
        {
        fprintf(stderr, "Could not initialize.\n");
        exit(-1);
        }

    /* Create the user interface widgets */
    if((myButton = XmCreatePushButton(topShell, "hello", NULL, 0)) == NULL)
        {
        fprintf(stderr, "Could not create push button.\n");
        exit(-1);
        }

    /* Make the program visible on the screen */
    XtManageChild(myButton);
    XtRealizeWidget(topShell);

    /* Wait for input events */
    XtMainLoop();
    }
```

Example 5.1   Single-widget X/Motif application program.

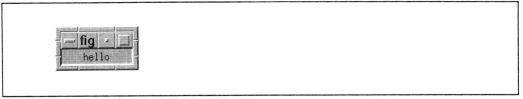

Figure 5.12 Output of the simple single-widget X/Motif application program.

Compiling and Executing X Programs

¤   Once you have finished writing the C source code to your X windows program, you can compile it with a fairly standard invocation for your C compiler. Figure 5.13 shows a typical command line that would be used to compile an X/Motif program contained within a file called myprog.c.

   This command can be typed from the operating system prompt each time
you want to compile another X/Motif program. However, you may find it
more convenient to set it up as a command alias in your command interpreter or even as a batch file or command procedure. Whatever method you
choose, the end result will be an executable object file ready to be run in
the X Window System Environment.

   Some operating systems have broken their networking functions out into a
separate library. Since X uses networking protocols for its basic client-
server communications, you may need to include the networking library.
Figure 5.14 shows the syntax for a typical PC based X/Motif compile line.

   Although these figures show the most common compile command lines,
there may be systems that require still other options. Some compilers must
be told about the networking protocol to use, while others may need to be
told about what type of processor that code is being compiled for or the

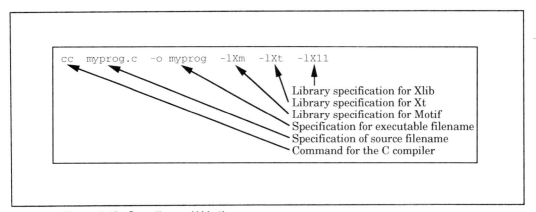

Figure 5.13 Compiling an X/Motif source program.

```
cc  myprog.c  -o myprog  -lXm  -lXt  -lX11  -linet
```

Figure 5.14 Compiling an X/Motif source program with networking.

version of the operating system being used. In fact, one of the more convoluted X/Motif compile command lines in use is shown in Figure 5.15.

Depending on the compiler implementation, the order of the library specifications may have an impact on the compilation of a program. The order shown in these figures seems to be the most common. If your compilation produces some "Unresolved external references," check the order of the libraries on the compile command line.

Another common difference is that the X and Motif include files may not be stored in the standard include directory on your system. If this is the case, then you will have to either specify a different name in your source code or supply a compiler directive to tell the compiler which directory to look to find additional includes. The -I option is a common directive used for this purpose on many C compilers.

◻ When you are ready to run your program, make sure the X server is running and connected to your terminal. Also, make sure that you have a terminal emulator running. One should have been started for you when you started the X server with the xinit command or the xdm command. From the prompt in the terminal emulator window, simply enter the name of your executable object file. Make sure you run your program in the background.

Running your X client application in the background is not necessary. But if you don't run it in the background, your command interpreter and the terminal emulator will fall asleep until your client application terminates. Running clients in the background frees up your command interpreter and terminal emulator so that you can start and run other X clients as needed.

Review Questions

◻ Please write down the answers to the following questions:

1. Why does an X/Motif programmer have to have a good set of reference documentation?

2. What are the function and macro naming conventions used in X, Xt, and Motif?

3. List two of the header files required by an X program.

4. Which function is used to perform required initializations in an X/Motif client application? What is its return value?

```
cc  myprog.c  -o myprog  -DLAI_TCP  -Di386  -DSYSV  \
                         -lXm  -lXt  -lX11  \
                         -ltlisock  -lsocket  -lnsl_s
```

Figure 5.15 Compiling an X/Motif source program with other options.

5. How do you detect and handle errors when calling X/Motif functions?

6. Which function is used to create a Motif PushButton widget? What is its return value?

7. Why does each and every widget in your client application have two "names?"

8. What happens when you manage a widget?

9. List two functions that can be used to manage widgets.

10. Which function causes your application to finally be mapped, or realized, to the screen?

11. How do you implement an event loop with the Xt Intrinsics?

12. What options are needed to compile an X/Motif client application program?

13. How do you run an X/Motif client application program?

Exercises

□ The following exercises are designed to give you the opportunity to practice the concepts and facilities presented in this chapter:

1. Using one of the editors supplied with your operating system, enter the source code for the single-widget X/Motif client application that was presented near the end of this chapter. Place the code in a file called pushme.c.

2. Compile the pushme.c source program into an executable object file called pushme using the C compile command and options appropriate to your operating system.

3. Run the pushme client application in the background.

4. Try adding a second Motif PushButton under the shell widget so that your client will have two PushButtons. Recompile the source code and rerun it as you did in the previous three exercises. What happened? Why?

6

Event-Driven
Programming

Introduction

¤ Because of the event-driven nature of X programming, the programmer must use a different approach for handling input through the widgets of the program. In this chapter you will learn what a callback is and how it is used for receiving input from a widget.

Objectives

¤ After completing this chapter, you will be able to:

◻ Explain what X does when an input event is received for a window in your client.

◻ Describe what callback functions are used for in an X/Motif client.

◻ List the three callbacks available to a Motif PushButton widget.

◻ Describe the function required to register a callback function with the Intrinsics and its return value.

◻ List the components and structure of a callback function.

◻ Describe the functions that are used to remove a callback function from use.

◻ Explain how an X/Motif client application will terminate and exit.

Handling Input through the Widgets

◻ Remember – programming with the X Window System is event-driven programming. As we have already stated, your X program sits in an infinite
event loop waiting for input events to occur. What happens on the terminal
screen is the responsibility of the server, and the server is a separate program that is running at the same time that your application is executing.
The server passes any input events that occur in your windows back to your
client application.

Your program asks XtMainLoop() to watch for specific input events for
you. XtMainLoop() then sits in an infinite loop waiting for notification that
one of the events you wanted has occurred. The server, meanwhile, obtains
the input events from the terminal and stores them in the event queue for
XtMainLoop(). The event loop inside the XtMainLoop() function figures out
which window in your application the event belongs to and *calls you back* to
let you know that one of the events that you wanted has just occurred.

Through the Intrinsics one of the functions that you have written can be
invoked as a result of a specific input event. Before this can happen, you
have to tell the Intrinsics which function you want called for which input
event on which widget. In X terminology, you have to register a *callback
function*.

Callback Function Concepts

◻ A callback function is simply one of the functions that you write within the
code of your application program. However, the function will never be executed in sequential order as it would in a non-event-driven program.
Instead, you tell the Intrinsics to tell the server that when a specific event
occurs in a specific widget that you have created, it should call your callback function for you.

If you want some specific type of action to occur when an input event is
received on some widget in your program, you must register one or more
callback functions for it. *It is in the callback functions of your program that
you perform the application-specific data processing that your program was
written for.* Your program will only process your application-specific data in
response to an input event that has invoked a callback function to do the
data processing your client program was intended to do.

Although other event-handling features are available in X, the callback
mechanism is the primary method for handling input events in a widget-
based program. Each and every widget in the Xt and Motif toolkits has one
or more specific callback events that it can watch for. You cannot watch for
just any type of event in a widget as a callback. You must look through the
documentation for the widget and determine which callbacks have been
defined for the widget.

◻ The Motif PushButton widget, for example, has three different input
events that it can watch for as callbacks. From the Motif documentation we
find that following callbacks are defined:

XmNactivateCallback   If you register a callback for the activate event on
                           a specific PushButton, your callback function will
                           be called when the user positions the mouse
                           pointer in that PushButton, presses mouse button

1, and releases the mouse button without moving the mouse pointer outside the button.

XmNarmCallback   If you register a callback for the arm event on a specific PushButton, your callback function will be called when the user positions the mouse pointer in that PushButton and presses mouse button 1.

XmNdisarmCallback   If you register a callback for the disarm event on a specific PushButton, and if the PushButton has been previously armed, your callback function will be called when the user releases the mouse button.

Again, it is very important that you have an adequate set of reference documentation handy before you begin programming an X- or Motif-based application. For the callback mechanism you must know which callback events are available for which widgets. Not all widgets recognize the same callbacks and the documentation will specify which callbacks are available for a specific type of widget.

▫   You should have noticed that the Motif PushButton widget does not recognize keyboard key press events or any other type of input event. The callback mechanism for widgets recognizes only those events that are defined as callback events for a specific widget type. If you need to watch for input events that are not defined as a callback event for a specific type of widget, you will have to use a different type of event handler.

You should also have noticed that these callback definitions have overlapping functionality. Both the activate and the arm callbacks will be invoked when the user presses mouse button 1 while the mouse pointer is positioned within the Motif PushButton widget; and both the activate and the disarm callbacks can be called when the user releases mouse button 1. You can watch for any of these callback events — or all three. You can also choose to ignore specific input events by not setting up a callback for them.

Registering a Callback Function

▫   In order to set up a callback function for a specific instance of a widget in your client application you must register the function with the Intrinsics. The process of registering a function tells the Intrinsics which widget you want to watch for an event in, which type of callback event you want to watch for, and which function to call in response to the event. Registering a callback function with the Intrinsics is accomplished with a call to XtAddCallback(). Figure 6.1 shows the syntax for the XtAddCallback() function.

```
void XtAddCallback(widget_id, callback_name, function_ptr, client_data)

Widget          widget_id;
String          callback_name;
XtCallbackProc  function_ptr;
XtPointer       client_data;
```

Figure 6.1 XtAddCallback() syntax.

In order for a function to be invoked in response to an input event on a widget, the function must be added to the widget's callback list. XtAdd-Callback() adds a function name to the end of a specified widget's callback list. More than one function can be registered as a callback for a single instance of a widget, and a function can appear more than once on a widget's callback list. When the specific callback event occurs in the widget, the Intrinsics will invoke all the functions on the widget's callback list in the order that they were added.

◻ Callbacks are not actually events—they are a more abstract concept. Callbacks are defined by the widget writer (as opposed to the client application developer) and are defined to occur for some specific combination of conditions within the widget. These conditions may or may not involve actual input events. Figure 6.2 shows how XtAddCallback() would be used in an X program.

The first parameter to XtAddCallback() identifies the widget that the Intrinsics are to watch for a callback event in. The second parameter identifies the callback name as defined in the widget documentation. The third parameter is a pointer to the function that you want invoked in response to the callback and the fourth parameter defines data that you want passed to the callback function when it is invoked. For the time being the fourth parameter will be NULL, indicating that no data will be passed to the function.

Coding a Callback Function

◻ The function that is to be invoked in response to a callback must assume a specific form. There is no flexibility in the design of a callback—all callbacks take the same three parameters and return the same data type. Figure 6.3 shows the required structure of a callback function.

All callback functions return type XtCallbackProc. This data type is defined in one of the X header files as void. This, of course, means that callback functions cannot return a value anywhere. The return statement (if used) must not contain any expression to be returned.

All callback functions take the same three parameters. The first parameter is the widget id of the widget that invoked this callback function. This means that you can register the same function with more than one widget and have the callback function determine which widget invoked it by comparing this parameter to a list of known widget ids.

```
#include <Xm/PushB.h>
...
Widget aButton;
...
aButton = XmCreatePushButton(topShell, "hello", NULL, 0);
XtAddCallback(aButton, XmNactivateCallback, ButtonPushed, NULL);
...
```

Figure 6.2 Calling the XtAddCallback() function.

```
XtCallbackProc function_name(widget_id, client_data, call_data)
Widget      widget_id;
caddr_t     client_data;
caddr_t     call_data;
    {
    /* Your application specific data processing code goes here */

    return;
    }
```

Figure 6.3 Structure of a callback function.

The last two parameters are caddr_t types. (In Release 4 these will be XtPointer.) This data type is defined in <sys/types.h>, a standard C header file, as a generic pointer — usually a character or a void pointer. Client_data is data that is passed to this function from the last parameter of XtAddCallback() and is the data that the client application writer decided to send to the callback function when the specified callback occurs. Call_-data, on the other hand, is data that is passed to this function from the widget and is the data that the widget writer decided to send to the callback function when the specified callback occurs. Figure 6.4 shows how a callback function would be coded in an X/Motif program.

□ *A Special Note about the XtCallbackProc Data Type:* In older versions of the X Window System, the data type XtCallbackProc was simply typedefed as the C language return type void. With this typedef an X programmer could use XtCallbackProc both in the function return type declaration for a callback function and in the actual definition of the callback function. This is the style that is used throughout this book.

With the advent of ANSI C, function return type declarations have been replaced with prototype declarations. To stay current with changes in the C language, the X Window System has changed its definition for XtCallback-Proc. More recent versions of X typedef XtCallbackProc as a pointer to a function that returns void, or, in an ANSI compiler, to a prototype for a pointer to a function that returns void. This change makes XtCallbackProc an unsuitable data type for the definition of a function as shown in Figure 6.4.

If your compiler produces warning or error messages during the compilation of your Motif program that complain about the return type in a function definition, you will want to change the return type of your callback functions to void. This will fix the "error."

Removing a Callback

□ You can change your mind about callbacks "on the fly" within your client application program. If you don't need a specific function/client_data combination on a widget's callback list, you can remove it. Or you may decide to remove all callback functions from a widget's callback list. Figure 6.5 shows the syntax for XtRemoveCallback() and XtRemoveAll-Callbacks() — two functions that can be called to delete functions from a widget's callback list.

```
#include <stdio.h>
#include <Xm/PushB.h>

XtCallbackProc ButtonPushed();

main(argc, argv)
Cardinal argc;
String argv[];
    {
    ...
    Widget aButton;
    ...
    aButton = XmCreatePushButton(topShell, "hello", NULL, 0);
    XtAddCallback(aButton, XmNactivateCallback, ButtonPushed, NULL);
    ...
    }
XtCallbackProc ButtonPushed(widget_id, client_data, call_data)
Widget widget_id;
caddr_t client_data;
caddr_t call_data;
    {
    printf("You just pressed the hello button...\n");
    sleep(3);
    printf("Good Bye!\n");
    exit(0);
    }
```

Figure 6.4 Coding a callback function.

```
void XtRemoveCallback(widget_id, callback_name, function_ptr, client_data)

Widget          widget_id;
String          callback_name;
XtCallbackProc  function_ptr;
XtPointer       client_data;


    --OR--

void XtRemoveAllCallbacks(widget_id, callback_name)

Widget          widget_id;
String          callback_name;
```

Figure 6.5 XtRemoveCallback() and XtRemoveAllCallbacks() syntax.

If you have a specific function that you want to remove from a widget's callback list, then XtRemoveCallback() is used. Notice that this function has the exact same parameters as XtAddCallback(). The function specified by function_ptr is removed only if both the function and the client_data match a function/data pair on the callback list for the widget specified by widget_id. No warning or error message is produced if the function fails to find a match.

XtRemoveAllCallbacks() removes all entries in the widget's callback list for functions that were specified for the callback event passed as the second parameter to this function. No matching is done at all. All functions registered for the specified callback are simply and quietly removed.

Terminating an X Program and Closing the Display

◻ Just like any other C program, when your X client application is finished it should return control and an exit status to the command interpreter. This is usually done with a call to the C language function exit(). You can pass a parameter to the exit() function, which usually takes the form of an integer number in the range of -128 to +127. This number will be your exit status.

Exiting your program will close any open files that you may have as well as the connection to the X server that was created with the call to XtInitialize(). If you want to close your connection to the X server without terminating your X program, you can call XtCloseDisplay(). Figure 6.6 shows the syntax for this function.

XtCloseDisplay() will close the connection between the client application program and the server specified by the display_ptr parameter. This will be done as soon as it is safe to do so. If XtCloseDisplay() is called from a callback or other event handler, the function will wait until the callback is complete (remember everything is operating asynchronously) before the display connection is closed.

It should be noted that client applications do not need to call XtCloseDisplay(). Display connections are closed when the client terminates — either normally or abnormally. XtCloseDisplay() only needs to be called if the X client wants to continue processing after the display connection is closed. Figure 6.7 shows how this function could (but doesn't have to) be used.

The XtDisplay() function takes a widget id as a parameter and, working through the instance tree, determines which display (server) it is currently visible on. The function returns a pointer to type Display, which identifies the server. The XtCloseDisplay() function takes the display pointer and closes this client's connection to that server.

A Complete X/Motif Client Application

◻ Using all the concepts and techniques presented in this chapter, we can put together a simple, but complete, X/Motif-based client application. Example 6.1 shows the code for a program that has a shell widget and a single Motif PushButton widget in it. The program will wait for an activate event

```
void XtCloseDisplay(display_ptr)

Display     *display_ptr;
```

Figure 6.6 XtCloseDisplay() syntax.

```
#include <stdio.h>
Widget topShell;
...
XtCallbackProc ButtonPushed(widget_id, client_data, call_data)
Widget widget_id;
caddr_t client_data;
caddr_t call_data;
    {
    printf("You just pressed the hello button...\n");
    sleep(3);
    printf("Good Bye!\n");
    XtCloseDisplay(XtDisplay(topShell));
    exit(0);
    }
```

Figure 6.7 Calling XtCloseDisplay().

in the PushButton widget, close the display, and exit in response. Figure 6.8 shows what the program would look like on a typical terminal screen.

Review Questions

☐ Please write down the answers to the following questions:

1. What does X do when an input event is received for a window in your client?

2. What are callback functions used for in an X/Motif client?

3. List the three callbacks available to a Motif PushButton widget.

4. Which function is required to register a callback function with the Intrinsics? What is its return value?

5. List the components and structure of a callback function.

6. Which functions are used to remove a callback function from use?

7. How does an X/Motif client application terminate and exit?

Exercises

☐ The following exercises are designed to give you the opportunity to practice the concepts and facilities presented in this chapter:

1. Modify the single-widget program called pushme.c from the previous chapter. Add the callback functions and register the callbacks as shown in the examples presented in this chapter.

2. Compile and run the modified pushme program.

3. Add a callback for the XmNarmCallback on the PushButton widget in the pushme program. Have the callback code print an appropriate

```
#include <stdio.h>
#include <Xm/PushB.h>

Widget topShell;
XtCallbackProc ButtonPushed();

main(argc, argv)
Cardinal argc;
String argv[];
    {
    Widget myButton;

    /* Initialize  the Intrinsics and create a top Shell widget */
    topShell = XtInitialize(argv[0], "Edit", NULL, 0, &argc, argv);

    /* Create the user interface widgets and set up callbacks */
    myButton = XmCreatePushButton(topShell, "hello", NULL, 0);
    XtAddCallback(myButton, XmNactivateCallback, ButtonPushed, NULL);

    /* Make the program visible on the screen */
    XtManageChild(myButton);
    XtRealizeWidget(topShell);

    /* Wait for input events */
    XtMainLoop();
    }

XtCallbackProc ButtonPushed(widget_id, client_data, call_data)
Widget widget_id;
caddr_t client_data;
caddr_t call_data;
    {

    /* Print something on the screen */
    printf("You just pressed the hello button...\n");
    sleep(3);
    printf("Good Bye!\n");

    /* Return control to the operating system */
    XtCloseDisplay(XtDisplay(topShell));
    exit(0);
    }
```

Example 6.1 Single-widget X/Motif application program with a callback.

message when it is invoked. Compile and run the modified program.

4. Add a callback for the XmNdisarmCallback on the PushButton widget in
    the pushme program. Have the callback code print an appropriate mes-
    sage when it is invoked. Compile and run the modified program.

Figure 6.8 Output of the previous X/Motif application program.

Multiple-Widget Programs

Introduction

Most X/Motif programs will consist of some combination of widgets used to perform some data-processing task. In order to use more than one user interface widget, an X/Motif program must use a new type of widget that manages the layout of the user interface widgets. In this chapter you will learn about the constraint, or manager, widget and construct a simple multiple-widget program with it.

Objectives

After completing this chapter, you will be able to.

- Explain the purpose of a composite widget.
- Explain the purpose of a constraint widget.
- Describe the function required to create a Motif RowColumn widget and its return value.
- Explain the RowColumn widget's management policy.
- Describe why the RowColumn widget must be managed.
- List the functions available to cause a widget to become unmanaged.
- Explain the purpose of an X/Motif client application's widget instance, or widget management, tree.

◻ List the four parameters that are common to every Motif widget creation function.

◻ Describe the basic outline of every X/Motif program.

Composite/Manager Widget Concepts

◻ The X Programs that we have seen to this point are severely limited in one important aspect. It turns out that a shell widget can have only one child widget underneath it in an X client application's widget instance tree. (This is because a shell widget has no geometry management policy.) Even a simple program will need more than one widget to interact with. A variety of widgets are usually used to provide many different combinations of input to cause any number of data-processing functions to be executed.

In order to provide this capability a different type of widget is needed—a widget that can have one or more children widgets below it in an X program's widget instance tree. In X terminology we call this type of widget a *composite widget*. A composite widget allows an X program to be composed of one or more user interface (primitive) widgets.

◻ From the X/Motif widget class tree it can be seen that under the Core widget there are only two other classes of widgets. The XmPrimitive widgets are the Motif widgets that are used as user interface objects in an X/Motif program. The Composite widget class is an Intrinsics widget class that groups together those widgets that can have other widgets below them to form a widget instance tree for a specific client application program.

We have already seen one type of composite widget—the shell widget. But, again, shell widgets can only have one child. Their primary purpose is to be the root of a client's widget instance tree and the means of communication between the client and the window manager. The other type of composite widget is called a *constraint widget*.

◻ Constraint widgets are defined as those widgets that can have one or more other widgets instantiated under them in a client's widget instance tree. They are called constraint widgets because they constrain the visual layout of their children according to some widget-specific geometry management policy. This means that the constraint widgets will cause their children to be placed in some specific position with respect to the constraint widget itself or other children widgets that the constraint widget is already managing.

The Motif toolkit has provided a subclass of the constraint widget called XmManager. The XmManager class is defined to give some Motif-specific attributes to the constraint widgets. *Manager* may be a more descriptive term than *constraint* because the intent of the constraint widgets is to manage the layout of its children.

In the widget class tree, below the XmManager class, Motif has defined a wide variety of manager widgets. Each manager widget provides different geometry management policies, which allow for a wide variety of different user interface look-and-feels. Which one you use depends on what type of visual layout you want your user interface widgets to take on when the application's windows are mapped to the screen.

Creating a Motif RowColumn Manager

◻ One type of Motif manager widget allows you to layout its children in a nice, neat row or column. By default, the Motif RowColumn manager will organize all of its children into a vertical column and insure that each child has the exact same height and width producing a very symmetrical look. The RowColumn has no physical appearance of its own but instead manages its children for a specific visual effect.

Because of this layout policy, the RowColumn widget is not one of the more commonly used manager widgets. Instead, the RowColumn widget is most often used for menus where you want the menu selections placed in identical-sized windows in a nice, neat row or column. Figure 7.1 shows the syntax for the XmCreateRowColumn() function.

This function will create an instance of a RowColumn widget as a manager object in your program. All the appearance and action attributes will be encapsulated into a new and unique instance. The look-and-feel of the RowColumn widget will result from the attribute inheritance that occurs for this class of widget from the widget class tree.

With a RowColumn widget installed in your X program the instance tree for your client can start to spread out and include other interface widgets. If your program is going to have more than one user interface object, then it must contain at least one manager widget like the Motif RowColumn widget. Figure 7.2 shows how XmCreateRowColumn() would be used in an X program.

Don't Forget to Manage the Manager

◻ Because of the hierarchical nature of windows in X, each parent window must be told about its children. The children may request a specific initial X/Y-coordinate position within the parent along with a specific height and width. However, the parent window can override these requests and change the position and size of any of its children. The ability that a parent window has to change the characteristics of its children is called *geometry management.*

Whenever you add a new child widget to your program's instance tree, you must notify its parent that you want the widget added to the parent's managed children list. Once on the list, if the parent gets mapped to the terminal screen (becomes visible), it will cause all its managed children to become visible, too. Every nonshell widget in your program's instance tree

```
#include <Xm/RowColumn.h>

Widget XmCreateRowColumn(parent_id, instance_name, arg_list, arg_count)

Widget       parent_id;
String       instance_name;
ArgList      arg_list;
Cardinal     arg_count;
```

Figure 7.1 XmCreateRowColumn() syntax.

```
#include <Xm/RowColumn.h>
#include <Xm/PushB.h>
...
Widget topShell;
Widget myButton1, myButton2, myButton3;
Widget rcManager;
...
topShell = XtInitialize(argv[0], "Edit", NULL, 0, &argc, argv);
rcManager = XmCreateRowColumn(topShell, "rowcolumn", NULL, 0);
myButton1 = XmCreatePushButton(rcManager, "button1", NULL, 0);
myButton2 = XmCreatePushButton(rcManager, "button2", NULL, 0);
myButton3 = XmCreatePushButton(rcManager, "button3", NULL, 0);
...
```

Figure 7.2 Creating a RowColumn widget.

that you want to be visible on the screen must be managed – this includes any of the constraint, or manager, widgets as well.

The constraint widgets are just another widget that gets instantiated in the client program's widget instance tree. It will be instantiated as the child of some parent widget in your program. Just like every other non-shell widget in your program, it must be managed. One of the more common programming errors for beginning X programmers is to remember to manage the children of a particular manager but forget to manage the manager. If you don't add the manager widget to its parent's managed children list, then when the parent becomes visible the manager and its children will not be visible.

α   During the execution of your program you can, if needed, cause a previously visible widget to become invisible. To do this you must take the widget off its parent's managed children list. Two functions are available as shown in Figure 7.3.

The first of these two functions takes an array of Widget ids as its first parameter (WidgetList is typedefed to an array of, or pointer to, type Widget) and a count of the number of widget ids in the array as the second parameter. Every widget specified in the widget list array must be the child of some common parent. If the children in the array have different parents, an error will be generated.

```
void XtUnmanageChildren(children, num_children)

WidgetList   children;
Cardinal     num_children;


    --OR--


void XtUnmanageChild(child)

Widget       child;
```

Figure 7.3 XtUnmanageChild() and XtUnmanageChildren() syntax.

The second of these two functions is a convenience function. It takes the single widget id supplied as a parameter and constructs a widget list of length 1 with it. XtUnmanageChild() then calls XtUnmanageChildren() with the newly constructed widget list and a count of 1.

◻ Both these functions will check to see if the parent of the children being unmanaged is being destroyed and will return immediately if this is true. If the parent is not being destroyed, it marks each child as visible if it is currently being managed and is not in the process of being destroyed itself. For each visible child, if the child is realized, it makes it invisible by unmapping it. Finally, if the parent is already visible, it notifies the parent about the children being removed so that it can rearrange the visible children on the screen according to the geometry management policy in effect for the parent widget.

Unmanaging children widgets is independent of their ordering on the screen, their order of creation, or their deletion. The parent will lay out only those children widgets on the screen that are still managed according to their own geometry management policies and ignore all others. Unmanaging a widget does not destroy it.

Widget Instance/Management Tree

◻ With the addition of the XmManager class of widgets an X client application program's widget instance tree can become quite a bit more complicated. It is now possible to construct GUI programs that have a variety of user interface objects that a user can use to perform a wider variety of data-processing tasks.

At the root of any widget-based program's widget instance tree will be a shell widget. The first widget below the shell will be some type of manager widget. Below this initial manager widget there will be several other widgets, which can be primitive widgets or other manager widgets. With each new instance of a manager widget there will usually be one or more children widgets below it. Figure 7.4 shows a widget instance tree for a fairly simple Motif program and how involved one of these trees can get.

◻ Don't forget that every instance of a widget will have an instance name that uniquely identifies that widget with respect to all other widgets in the program. *When dealing with a widget instance tree such as the one in Figure 7.4 you would use the instance names instead of the class names as shown.* It is particularly important to document the instance names of the widgets and your widget instance tree so that users of your program can add their own unique look-and-feel.

Remember, if you allow it, a user can change some of the visual attributes of the widgets in your program to suit their own tastes. These attributes can be changed with something called an *external resource file*. But to successfully use a resource file to change the look-and-feel for a program, the user absolutely must know the instance names of the widgets in your client program's widget instance tree.

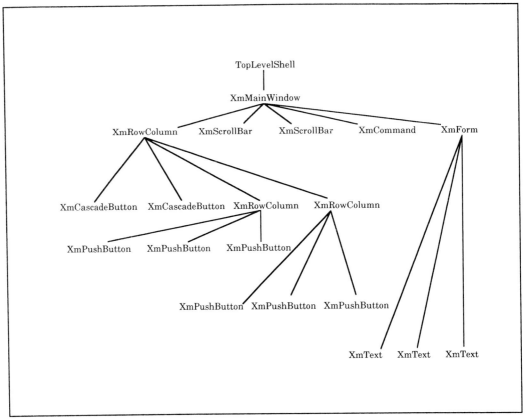

Figure 7.4 Typical Motif widget instance tree.

Parameters for Motif Widget Creation Functions

◻   Although you have seen only two Motif widget creation functions, both of
them have something in common with all other widget creation functions in
the Motif toolkit. Every Motif widget creation function takes the exact
same four parameters. Figure 7.5 reminds you what these four parameters
are for the XmCreatePushButton() and XmCreateRowColumn() functions.

```
Widget XmCreatePushButton(parent_id, instance_name, arg_list, arg_count)
Widget XmCreateRowColumn(parent_id, instance_name, arg_list, arg_count)

Widget      parent_id;
String      instance_name;
ArgList     arg_list;
Cardinal    arg_count;
```

Figure 7.5 Motif widget creation function parameters.

The first parameter is always the widget id of the parent of the widget you are currently creating. It is this parameter that is used to create a widget instance tree for your program. If the widget you are creating is a manager widget, it can have children of its own and its widget id will be specified in some subsequent widget creation function. The hierarchy of widgets within your program is specified by the parent widget id parameter.

The second parameter is always the instance name for the widget you are currently creating. It is this parameter that allows you or your user to reference this specific widget from an external resource file. Using the widget name in a resource file allows you to change the visual appearance of the widget, such as its color, its size, its border, and so on, without recompiling the program.

The last two parameters are used to specify specific visual attributes that are different from the defaults for the widget you are currently creating. Up until now these two parameters have been NULL and 0, respectively. Soon we will see how to construct an attribute list containing one or more visual attributes. This list and a count of the number of elements in the list are always passed as the last two parameters in any widget creation function.

Outline of a Basic X/Motif Program

We now have a firm foundation on which to start building nontrivial X/Motif GUI programs. With everything that has been presented so far, we can say that almost every X/Motif client application program that you write will have the exact same form:

- Include appropriate header files — #include <Xm/PushB.h>, etc.
- Initialize the Intrinsics and create a top-level shell — XtInitialize()
- Create any other needed top-level shells
- Set up an attribute list for the manager widget
- Create the composite/manager widget — XmCreateRowColumn(), etc.
- For each widget:
    - Set up an attribute list for the child widget
    - Create the child widget — XmCreatePushButton(), etc.
    - Add callback routines for the child widget — XtAddCallback()
    - Manage the child widget — XtManageChildren() & XtManageChild()
- Realize the top-level widgets — XtRealizeWidget()
- Enter the event loop — XtMainLoop()

A Complete X/Motif Client Application

◻   Using all the concepts and techniques presented in this chapter, we can put together a simple, but complete, X/Motif-based client application. Example 7.1 shows the code for a program that has a shell widget, a RowColumn manager widget, and six PushButton widgets in it. The program will wait for an activate event in the last PushButton widget and close the display and exit in response. It will print a message to standard output in response to any other push button being activated. Figure 7.6 shows what the result of this program would look like on a typical terminal screen.

Review Questions

◻   Please write down the answers to the following questions:

1. What is the purpose of a composite widget?

2. What is the purpose of a constraint widget?

3. Which function is required to create a Motif RowColumn widget? What is its return value?

4. How does the RowColumn widget manage its children?

5. Why does the RowColumn widget have to be managed?

6. List the functions available to cause a widget to become unmanaged.

7. What is the purpose of an X/Motif client application's widget instance, or widget management, tree?

8. List the four parameters that are common to every Motif widget creation function.

9. What is the basic outline for any X/Motif program?

Exercises

◻   The following exercises are designed to give you the opportunity to practice the concepts and facilities presented in this chapter:

1. Using one of the editors supplied with your operating system, enter the source code for the multiple widget X/Motif client application that was presented at the end of this chapter. Place the code in a file called multibutton.c.

2. Compile the multibutton.c source program into an executable object file called multibutton using the C compile command and options appropriate to your operating system.

3. Run the multibutton client application in the background. Interact with the buttons displayed by multibutton to verify its operation.

4. Try adding another PushButton under the RowColumn widget so that your client will have seven PushButtons. Recompile the source code and

```
#include <stdio.h>
#include <Xm/RowColumn.h>
#include <Xm/PushB.h>

Widget topShell;

XtCallbackProc ExitApplication();
XtCallbackProc PrintMesg();

main(argc, argv)
Cardinal argc;
String argv[];
    {
    Widget rcManager;
    Widget myButton[5];
    Widget exitButton;
    Cardinal i;
    static char labels[][8] = {"button1", "button2", "button3",
                               "button4", "button5", "exit"};

    /* Initialize  the Intrinsics and create a top Shell widget */
    topShell = XtInitialize(argv[0], "Edit", NULL, 0, &argc, argv);

    /* Create the manager widget */
    rcManager = XmCreateRowColumn(topShell, "rcmanager", NULL, 0);

    /* Create the user interface widgets */
    for(i = 0; i < XtNumber(myButton); ++i)
        {
        myButton[i] = XmCreatePushButton(rcManager, labels[i], NULL, 0);
        XtAddCallback(myButton[i], XmNactivateCallback, PrintMesg, NULL);
        }
    exitButton = XmCreatePushButton(rcManager, labels[5], NULL, 0);

    /* Set up callbacks for the widgets */
    XtAddCallback(exitButton, XmNactivateCallback, ExitApplication, NULL);

    /* Make the program visible on the screen */
    XtManageChildren(myButton, XtNumber(myButton));
    XtManageChild(exitButton);
    XtManageChild(rcManager);
    XtRealizeWidget(topShell);

    /* Wait for input events */
    XtMainLoop();
    }
```

Example 7.1 Multiple widget X/Motif application program, part 1.

```
XtCallbackProc PrintMesg(widget_id, client_data, call_data)
Widget widget_id;
caddr_t client_data;
caddr_t call_data;
    {

    /* Print something on the screen */
    printf("You pressed one of my buttons...\n");

    /* Return control to the calling function */
    return;
    }

XtCallbackProc ExitApplication(widget_id, client_data, call_data)
Widget widget_id;
caddr_t client_data;
caddr_t call_data;
    {

    /* Print something on the screen */
    printf("You just pressed the exit button...\n");
    sleep(3);
    printf("Good Bye!\n");

    /* Return control to the operating system */
    XtCloseDisplay(XtDisplay(topShell));
    exit(0);
    }
```

Example 7.2 Multiple widget X/Motif application program, part 2.

Figure 7.6 Output of the previous X/Motif application program.

rerun it as you did in the previous exercises. What happened? Why?

5. Add callbacks for one or more of the XmNactivateCallback, XmNarm-
   Callback, or XmNdisarmCallback lists on your new PushButton. Have

the callback function print an appropriate message in the terminal emulator window when it is invoked.

8

Passing Data
to a
Callback Function

Introduction

¤ Because of the way functions are invoked as the result of input on a widget, passing parameters to the function becomes a little more of a challenge. In this chapter you will learn the mechanism used by an X/Motif program to pass data to a callback function. You will also learn about the widget-specific data that is passed to a callback function.

Objectives

¤ After completing this chapter, you will be able to:

◻ Describe the purpose of client_data in a callback function.

◻ Explain what type of data client_data should be.

◻ Describe the purpose of call_data in a callback function.

◻ Explain what type of data call_data is.

◻ Describe the type of structure passed to a callback function for a callback on a Motif PushButton widget.

◻ Describe the type of structure passed to a callback function for a callback on a Motif RowColumn widget.

◻ List and describe the first two common members of all callback structures.

Function Parameters

◻   When you call a function in the C programming language, you have the
ability to pass one or more parameters to it. The syntax of C specifies that
a function name can be followed by comma-separated, parenthesized list of
data items which will be copied into the function's formal parameters. This,
of course, provides more flexibility in programming functions since the
function's operation can depend on and be guided by inputs provided
through these parameters.

The event-driven nature of X does not allow us to invoke a callback function in the normal way. Instead, we pass a function pointer to the XtAdd-
Callback() routine, which will use the pointer to call the function indirectly
for us when a specific input event occurs. This precludes the use of a
comma-separated, parenthesized list of parameters in the function call.
Another method must be used.

Client__data

◻   The fourth parameter to XtAddCallback() solves this problem for us. This
parameter, called *client__data,* is passed as a parameter to the callback
function for us when a specified input event occurs. There is only one
client__data parameter – if you need to pass more than one item, then you
must pass some type of data aggregate (such as an array or structure)
through the client__data.

The XtAddCallback() function will attempt to pass the client__data to the
callback function as an address type. You can pass an int, a char, a float, a
struct – any type. However, to ensure that the data gets passed to the callback function correctly, you should pass some type of pointer through
client__data. This means that if you really want to pass an int, float, or
similar, you should type cast it to a caddr__t (in Release 4 this will be an
XtPointer) first.

If you pass a pointer to the callback function, then the function will run a
little more quickly and efficiently because it does not have to copy the
client__data from the main function into the formal parameter of the callback function. Also, whenever you pass a pointer to a function, the called
function now has the ability to manipulate and modify the data back in the
calling function directly. Since the return type of a callback function does
not allow you to return a value to its caller, this effectively gives a callback
function the ability to return values to its caller through the client__data.

◻   You should remember that the definition of a callback function requires
three parameters: widget id, client__data, and call__data. The client__data
parameter to the callback function is the parameter that receives a copy of
the data specified as the fourth parameter to XtAddCallback(). When the
input event specified in XtAddCallback() occurs within the widget identified
in its first parameter, the Intrinsics will invoke the callback function for
you after copying the fourth parameter from XtAddCallback() to the second
parameter of the callback function.

This parameter must be declared as, or typecast to, an appropriate type
before the callback function can access it correctly. Client application writers know what data type they are passing to the callback function when
they are writing the program. Application writers will know what data

type the client_data must be. Since the callback function can be invoked from many different widgets, the programmer usually passes a pointer to some type of data structure and then typecasts it to the appropriate type according to which widget invoked the function. This method gives the callback function the maximum flexibility. Figure 8.1 shows an example of how client_data is typically implemented.

Call_data

¤ In addition to the client_data sent by the programmer, each callback function receives an additional parameter in the form of a pointer that comes from the widget. The third parameter to any callback function is called *call_data* and is a pointer to a structure that contains information that the widget writer thought that the client application would need about the input event that invoked the callback. Each widget type has its own callback call_data structure type.

The X and Motif documentation will tell you what the call_data data type is for each different type of widget. Call_data is always a pointer to a C structure that contains widget-specific information. Since one callback function can be invoked from several different types of widgets, the call_data parameter is usually received as a generic pointer and then typecast to the appropriate type according to which widget invoked the function. This method gives the callback function the maximum flexibility. Figure 8.2 shows an example of how call_data is typically accessed.

```
...
int i = 42;
...
exitButton = XmCreatePushButton(rcManager, labels[5], NULL, 0);
XtAddCallback(exitButton, XmNactivateCallback, ExitApplication, &i);
XtManageChild(exitButton);
XtRealizeWidget(topShell);
XtMainLoop();
}

XtCallbackProc ExitApplication(widget_id, client_data, call_data)
Widget widget_id;
caddr_t client_data;
caddr_t call_data;
    {
    printf("You just pressed the exit button...\n");
    printf("Client_data was = %d\n", *((int *) client_data));
    sleep(3);
    printf("Good Bye!\n");
    XtCloseDisplay(XtDisplay(topShell));
    exit(0);
    }
...
```

Figure 8.1 Passing client_data to a callback function.

```
...
int i = 42;
...
exitButton = XmCreatePushButton(rcManager, labels[5], NULL, 0);
XtAddCallback(exitButton, XmNactivateCallback, ExitApplication, &i);
XtManageChild(exitButton);
XtRealizeWidget(topShell);
XtMainLoop();
}

XtCallbackProc ExitApplication(widget_id, client_data, call_data)
Widget widget_id;
caddr_t client_data;
caddr_t call_data;
    {
    XmAnyCallbackStruct *cdPtr = (XmAnyCallbackStruct *) call_data;

    printf("You just pressed the exit button...\n");
    printf("Client_data was = %d\n", *((int *) client_data));
    printf("Widget's reason for invoking callback = %d\n", cdPtr->reason);
    sleep(3);
    printf("Good Bye!\n");
    XtCloseDisplay(XtDisplay(topShell));
    exit(0);
    }
...
```

Figure 8.2 Accessing call_data in a callback function.

Call_data for a PushButton

◻   The Motif PushButton widget defines three callbacks:

XmNactivateCallback

If you register a callback for the activate event on a specific PushButton, your callback function will be called when the user positions the mouse pointer in that PushButton, presses mouse button 1, and releases the mouse button without moving the mouse pointer outside the button.

XmNarmCallback

If you register a callback for the arm event on a specific PushButton, your callback function will be called when the user positions the mouse pointer in that PushButton and presses mouse button 1.

XmNdisarmCallback

If you register a callback for the disarm event on a specific PushButton, then if the PushButton has been previously armed, your callback function will be called when the user releases the mouse button.

For each of these callback events a pointer to a structure of type XmAny-CallbackStruct is passed as the call_data parameter to the callback function that is invoked in response. The structure has the following members:

```
typedef struct
    {
    int     reason;
    XEvent  *event;
    } XmAnyCallbackStruct;
```

reason   Indicates why the callback was invoked. It can contain any of the defined values XmCR_ACTIVATE, XmCR_ARM, or XmCR_DISARM.

event   Pointer to a union of type XEvent, which contains information about the actual X event that triggered the callback. This structure type will be discussed in more detail later.

Call_data for a RowColumn

¤ The Motif RowColumn widget defines three callbacks:

XmNentryCallback   If you register a callback for this event, it will disable, or "revector" the activate callbacks for any ToggleButton, PushButton, and CascadeButton widget contained within the RowColumn. With this callback an application can override the activate callbacks of buttons contained within the RowColumn to a RowColumn supplied activate callback function.

XmNmapCallback   If you register a callback for this event, the function will be invoked when the window associated with the RowColumn widget gets mapped to the screen.

XmNunmapCallback   If you register a callback for this event, the function will be invoked when the window associated with the RowColumn widget gets unmapped from the screen.

For each of these callback events a pointer to a structure of type XmRowColumnCallbackStruct is passed as the call_data parameter to the callback function that is invoked in response. The data contained within the structure is specific to the RowColumn widget that caused the callback − not with respect to any of the widgets that are children of the RowColumn. The structure has the following members:

```
typedef struct
    {
    int     reason;
    XEvent  *event;
    Widget  widget;
    char    *data;
    char    *callbackstruct;
    } XmRowColumnCallbackStruct;
```

reason   Indicates why the callback was invoked. It can contain any of the defined values XmCR_ACTIVATE, XmCR_MAP, or XmCR_UNMAP.

event   Pointer to a union of type XEvent which contains information about the actual X event that triggered the callback. This structure type will be discussed in more detail later.

widget   Widget id of child widget of the RowColumn widget that was activated. This field is valid only when the reason is XmCR_ACTIVATE on an XmNentryCallback for the RowColumn.

data   Contains the client_data value that was supplied to XtAddCallback() when the callback function was registered for the child widget that was activated. This field is valid only when the reason is XmCR_ACTIVATE on an XmNentryCallback for the RowColumn.

callbackstruct   Points to the call_data structure for the activated child of the RowColumn. This field is valid only when the reason is XmCR_ACTIVATE on an XmNentryCallback for the RowColumn.

Although the Motif documentation states that the XmNentryCallback "revectors" the XmNactivateCallbacks for any of its Button children, you must be careful how you register the callbacks to get the effect of "revectoring." *If the XmNentryCallback for the RowColumn is registered first and the XmNactivateCallbacks for the Button children are registered second, the Button callbacks will be revectored to the RowColumn callback. However, if the Button callbacks are registered first, both the Button and the RowColumn callbacks will be invoked.* Although the order in which the callbacks will be invoked cannot be guaranteed, the order that you register the callbacks can be important – be careful.

A Complete X/Motif Client Application

¤ The following example program is the same as the one presented in the previous chapter. The only difference is that the callback functions are passed, then access, their client_data. Also, the functions reference their widget-specific call_data. Example 8.1 shows the code. Figure 8.3 shows what the program would look like on a typical terminal screen.

Review Questions

¤ Please write down the answers to the following questions:

1. What is the purpose of client_data in a callback function?

2. What type of data should client_data be?

3. What is the purpose of call_data in a callback function?

```
#include <stdio.h>
#include <Xm/RowColumn.h>
#include <Xm/PushB.h>

Widget topShell;

XtCallbackProc ExitApplication();
XtCallbackProc PrintMesg();

main(argc, argv)
Cardinal argc;
String argv[];
    {
    Widget rcManager;
    Widget myButton[5];
    Widget exitButton;
    Cardinal i;
    static int data[] = {1, 2, 3, 4, 5};
    static char labels[][8] = {"button1", "button2", "button3",
                                "button4", "button5", "exit"};

    /* Initialize  the Intrinsics and create a top Shell widget */
    topShell = XtInitialize(argv[0], "Edit", NULL, 0, &argc, argv);

    /* Create the manager widget */
    rcManager = XmCreateRowColumn(topShell, "rcmanager", NULL, 0);

    /* Create the user interface widgets */
    for(i = 0; i < XtNumber(myButton); ++i)
        {
        myButton[i] = XmCreatePushButton(rcManager, labels[i], NULL, 0);
        XtAddCallback(myButton[i], XmNactivateCallback, PrintMesg, &data[i]);
        }
    exitButton = XmCreatePushButton(rcManager, labels[5], NULL, 0);

    /* Make the program visible on the screen */
    XtManageChildren(myButton, XtNumber(myButton));
    XtManageChild(exitButton);
    XtManageChild(rcManager);
    XtRealizeWidget(topShell);

    /* Set up callbacks for the widgets */
    XtAddCallback(exitButton, XmNactivateCallback, ExitApplication, labels[5]);

    /* Wait for input events */
    XtMainLoop();
    }
```

Example 8.1 X/Motif application program passing data to a callback, part 1.

```
XtCallbackProc PrintMesg(widget_id, client_data, call_data)
Widget widget_id;
caddr_t client_data;
caddr_t call_data;
    {
    XmAnyCallbackStruct *cdPtr = (XmAnyCallbackStruct *) call_data;

    /* Print something on the screen */
    printf("You pressed one of my buttons...\n");
    printf("In fact,  you pressed button #%d!\n", *((int *) client_data));
    printf("Widget's reason for invoking callback = %d\n", cdPtr->reason);

    /* Return control to the calling function */
    return;
    }


XtCallbackProc ExitApplication(widget_id, client_data, call_data)
Widget widget_id;
caddr_t client_data;
caddr_t call_data;
    {
    XmAnyCallbackStruct *cdPtr = (XmAnyCallbackStruct *) call_data;

    /* Print something on the screen */
    printf("You just pressed the %s button...\n", (char *) client_data);
    printf("Widget's reason for invoking callback = %d\n", cdPtr->reason);
    sleep(3);
    printf("Good Bye!\n");

    /* Return control to the operating system */
    XtCloseDisplay(XtDisplay(topShell));
    exit(0);
    }
```

Example 8.2   X/Motif application program passing data to a callback, part 2.

Figure 8.3   Output of the previous X/Motif application program.

4. What type of data is call_data?

5. Which structure type is passed to a callback function for a callback on a PushButton widget?

6. Which structure type is passed to a callback function for a callback on a RowColumn widget?

7. List and describe the first two common members of all callback structures.

Exercises

¤   The following exercises are designed to give you the opportunity to practice the concepts and facilities presented in this chapter:

1. Modify the multiple-widget program called multibutton.c from the previous chapter. Add the callback functions and register callbacks for the XmNactivateCallback on each Motif PushButton. Have each PushButton call a different callback function which prints a unique and appropriate message. Pass the button number or name as the client_data to the callback functions to be printed as part of its message.

2. Compile and run the modified multibutton program.

3. Add a callback for the XmNarm- and XmNdisarmCallback on the exit PushButton widget in the multibutton program. Have the callback code print an appropriate message when it is invoked. Compile and run the modified program.

4. Revector the XmNactivateCallback for all the PushButton widgets in the multibutton program. Have them all ignore their own XmNactivateCallback and call a RowColumn callback function instead. Compare the widget id that comes into the callback function to the widget id for the exit button to determine when the program should exit.

9

Resources

Introduction

◻ Each widget in an X/Motif program has attributes associated with it that define its look-and-feel. These attributes, called *resources,* are one of the main object-oriented features of a widget based-program. In this chapter you will learn what resources are and how to use them to alter a widget's look-and-feel. You will also learn how to query a widget for its resource values as well as a Motif-specific resource type called a *compound string.*

Objectives

◻ After completing this chapter, you will be able to:

◻ Explain the feature of X and Motif that gives them an object-oriented programming feeling.

◻ Describe what a widget resource is.

◻ List some common widget attributes that are implemented as a resource.

◻ Explain the purpose of widget classes.

◻ Describe what a widget instance is.

◻ Explain resource inheritance.

◻ Explain the purpose of the Core widget class.

◻ List some of the resources in the Core widget class.

◻ Explain the purpose of the XmPrimitive widget class.

◻ List some of the resources in the XmPrimitive widget class.

◻ Explain the purpose of the Composite widget class.

◻ List some of the resources in the Composite widget class.

◻ Explain the purpose of the XmManager widget class.

◻ List some of the resources in the XmManager widget class.

◻ List some of the resources for the PushButton widget.

◻ List some of the resources for the RowColumn widget.

◻ Describe the use of the XtSetArg() function to create an argument list.

◻ Explain the contents and purpose of an argument list.

◻ Describe how an argument list is used with a widget creation function.

◻ Explain how XtSetValues() is used to set resources after a widget has been created.

◻ Describe how XtGetValues() can be used to get resource values from a widget.

◻ List some widget-specific resource convenience functions.

◻ Explain what a compound string is used for.

◻ Describe the difference between a compound string and a C character string.

◻ Explain the use of XmStringCreateLtoR() to convert a C character string into a compound string.

◻ Explain the use of XmStringGetLtoR() to convert a compound string into a C character string.

◻ Describe what the XmStringFree() function is used for.

X and Object-Oriented Programming

◻ One of the main object-oriented features of programming with widgets in X is the widget class tree. As stated previously, this tree structure is intended to organize all the available widgets into related classes. Related widgets are grouped together into the same class when they have some attributes in common.

As can be seen from the widget class tree, repeated in Figure 9.1, all widgets will have certain attributes in common. These attributes are stored in the Core widget class, which is at the root of the widget class tree. Composite widgets are different from primitive widgets, so X and Motif divide these widgets up into two more classes. All the manager widgets have some common attributes which they share, so they all appear under the XmManager widget class. All primitive widgets have some common attributes which they share, so they all appear under the XmPrimitive widget class.

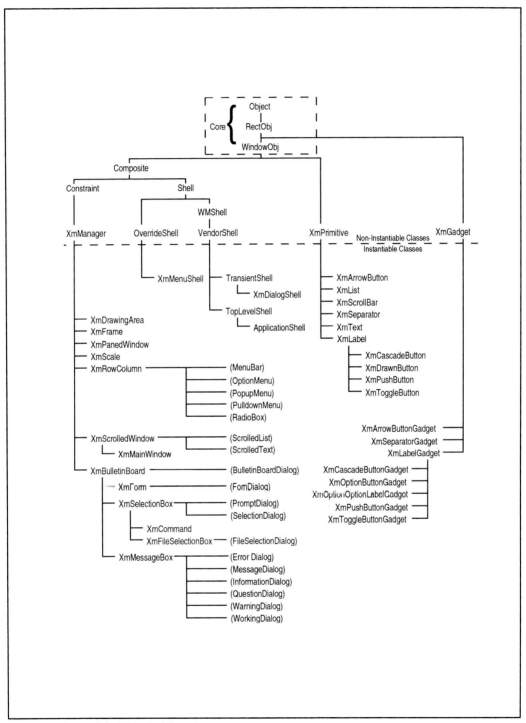

Figure 9.1 X/Motif widget class tree.

Whenever an instance of a particular widget is created, it gets a copy of all the attributes that are related to it. These attributes will define the look-and-feel of this specific instance of the widget, which can be different from the look-and-feel of any other widget in the program because each widget has its own local copy of the attributes. These attributes can be changed either before or after the widget is created, or from data that is stored in a special file located externally to the program.

The attributes that define the look-and-feel for an instance of a widget are called *resources*.

Resource Concepts

□   Every widget has a set of attributes called *resources* that define its look (visual appearance on the screen) and feel (how it operates in response to input events). There are resources that are specific to each widget type as well as resources that are common to all widgets that belong to the same class. There are also resources that are common to all widgets no matter what type they are or what class they are in.

For example, a Motif PushButton widget has (among others) resources such as:

X-coordinate for origin	The X-coordinate that defines the pixel position of the upper-left-hand corner of the widget with respect to the upper-left-hand corner of its parent.
Y-coordinate for origin	The Y-coordinate that defines the pixel position of the upper-left-hand corner of the widget with respect to the upper left-hand-corner of its parent.
width	The width of the widget specified in pixels.
height	The height of the widget specified in pixels.
foreground color	The color used for the text that appears as the label on the widget.
background color	The color used for area underneath the label in the widget not including the shadow area.
top-shadow color	The color used for a thin area around the top and left sides of the widget to give it a three-dimensional appearance.
bottom-shadow color	The color used for a thin area around the bottom and right sides of the widget to give it a three-dimensional appearance.
shadow thickness	The width of the shadow area specified in pixels.
highlight color	The color used for a thin area around the entire perimeter of the widget called the *highlight area,* which is used to show that the widget has input focus.
highlight thickness	The width of the highlight area specified in pixels.

Figure 9.2 shows how these resources are related to a PushButton widget in a pictorial form.

Classes, Instances, and Inheritance

❑   The widget class tree is used to group related sets of resources together. Each particular type of widget has its own class that contains resources that are specific to that type of widget. The widget will also have a *superclass,* or parent class, above it in the widget class tree that contains resources that are specific to several similar widgets. This parent-child-type relationship continues all the way up to the root of the widget class tree, which is called the *Core class.* The Core class contains resources that are common to all widgets.

Every time you create an instance of a particular widget, it will get its own local copy of its class-specific resources to work with. These local resource copies will define the look-and-feel of that particular instance of the widget, which may be completely different from the look-and-feel of any other instance of the same type of widget.

In addition to its own class resources, an instance of a widget will inherit its own local copy of the resources of its parent class as defined in the widget class tree. This inheritance will continue for each widget all the way up to the Core class, which every instance of any type of widget will inherit a copy of. You must understand how this resource inheritance applies to widgets in order to understand how a particular instance of a widget gets its look-and-feel.

❑   For example, from the widget class tree, you can see that an instance of a PushButton widget will receive all the attributes for the XmPushButton class. Since this is a subclass of the XmLabel class, any PushButton instance will also receive a copy of the XmLabel class resources. As you work your way up the tree, you will see that a PushButton will also inherit resources from the XmPrimitive class and the Core class.

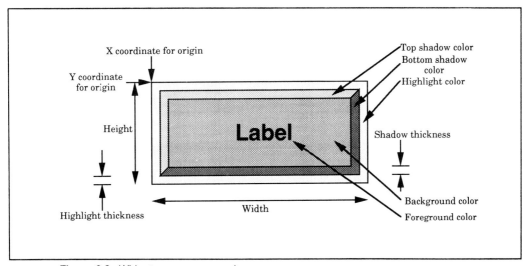

Figure 9.2 Widget resource example.

Doing the same for the RowColumn widget, we see that an instance of a RowColumn will receive all the attributes for the XmRowColumn class. Since this is a subclass of the XmManager class, any RowColumn instance will also receive a copy of the XmManager class resources. As you work your way up the tree, you will see that a RowColumn will also inherit resources from the Constraint class, the Composite class, and the Core class.

It is interesting to note that you cannot create an instance of an XmManager widget, an XmPrimitive widget, or any other widget above these in the widget class tree. The only reason these widgets are defined is to hold related resources together in one place for the widget classes that appear below them in the widget class tree—they are resource holders. When you create an instance of any instantiable widget, it will inherit its own local copy of all the applicable resources starting with its own widget class all the way up the class hierarchy to the Core class.

Core Widget and Resources

The Core class is the Xt Intrinsics base class for all windowed widgets. All widget instances inherit the Core resources. Motif has broken the Core class into three subclasses to support windowless widgets called *gadgets*. These classes are Object, RectObj, and WindowObj. Figure 9.3 shows the Core resources.

Each available resource has a name. The name lets you reference the resource for a widget. There are actually three names. The Motif name (XmN prefix as used in Figure 9.3) is the name that the Motif widget

Name	Type (Default Value)	Access
XmNaccelerators	XtTranslations (NULL)	CSG
XmNancestorSensitive	Boolean (True)	G
XmNbackground	Pixel (White)	CSG
XmNbackgroundPixmap	Pixmap (XmUNSPECIFIED_PIXMAP)	CSG
XmNborderColor	Pixel (Black)	CSG
XmNborderPixmap	Pixmap (XmUNSPECIFIED_PIXMAP)	CSG
XmNborderWidth	Dimension (1)	CSG
XmNcolormap	Colormap (XtCopyFromParent)	CG
XmNdepth	int (XtCopyFromParent)	CG
XmNdestroyCallback	XtCallbackList (NULL)	C
XmNheight	Dimension (0)	CSG
XmNmappedWhenManaged	Boolean (True)	CSG
XmNscreen	Pointer (XtCopyScreen)	CG
XmNsensitive	Boolean (True)	CSG
XmNtranslations	XtTranslations NULL)	CSG
XmNwidth	Dimension (0)	CSG
XmNx	Position (0)	CSG
XmNy	Position (0)	CSG

Figure 9.3 Core resources.

functions use to access the resource. The Intrinsics name (XtN prefix) is the name used by the Intrinsics functions to access the resource. The X resource manager name (no prefix at all) is used external to the program in a resource file — which will be discussed later.

Each resource name is used to refer to a piece of data. That data has a specific data type. The types used in Figure 9.3 can be used in a C program to define data values that are intended to be used for resources. The access column will be explained a little later.

Each resource "instance" name (XmN...) has a corresponding "class" name (XmC...). The class name allows you to reference similar resources that are in effect for a number of different widgets that may even be of different types. If two or more resources belong to the same class, they all can be changed at the same time using the resource class name — even on different widgets. We do not have room in this book to list all of the class names, the default values, or the meaning and purpose of each resource — that's what the Xt and Motif documentation are for. Please refer to these documents for additional information.

XmPrimitive Widget and Resources

◻ The XmPrimitive class is a Motif supporting superclass for other Motif widget classes. All user interface widget instances inherit the XmPrimitive resources. Figure 9.4 shows the XmPrimitive resources.

Composite Widget and Resources

◻ As we have seen, composite widgets are intended to be containers for other children widgets. Composite widgets can have an arbitrary number of children. Their responsibilities include the management of their children from creation through destruction; the destruction of their descendents when the

Name	Type (Default Value)	Access
XmNbottomShadowColor	Pixel (dynamic)	CSG
XmNbottomShadowPixmap	Pixmap (XmUNSPECIFIED_PIXMAP)	CSG
XmNforeground	Pixel (dynamic)	CSG
XmNhelpCallback	XtCallbackList (NULL)	C
XmNhighlightColor	Pixel (Black)	CSG
XmNhighlightOnEnter	Boolean (False)	CSG
XmNhighlightPixmap	Pixmap (dynamic)	CSG
XmNhighlightThickness	short int (0)	CSG
XmNshadowThickness	short int (2)	CSG
XmNtopShadowColor	Pixel (dynamic)	CSG
XmNtopShadowPixmap	Pixmap (XmUNSPECIFIED_PIXMAP)	CSG
XmNtraversalOn	Boolean (False)	CSG
XmNunitType	unsigned char (XmPIXELS)	CSG
XmNuserData	caddr_t (NULL)	CSG

Figure 9.4 XmPrimitive resources.

composite widget is destroyed; and the geometry management (physical arrangement), mapping, and unmapping of their displayable managed children. All Motif manager widget instances inherit the Composite resources. Figure 9.5 shows the Composite resources.

XmManager Widget and Resources

□   The XmManager class is a Motif supporting superclass for other Motif widget classes. All manager widget instances inherit the XmManager resources. Figure 9.6 shows the XmManager resources.

Important Resource Concepts

□   Although an instance of a widget will inherit values for all the resources in all superclasses defined above it in the widget class tree, not all the resources may have meaning for a particular instance of that widget. For example, the XmRowColumn class defines a resource called XmNmenu-HelpWidget which is meaningful only if the RowColumn widget has been configured as a menu. Also, for example, the XmBulletinBoard class defines a resource called XmNautoUnmanage which is meaningful only if the BulletinBoard widget has been configured as a dialog box. Be aware.

□   You cannot assume that just because the Core class is common to both the XmPushButton class and the XmRowColumn class that the default values for all the Core resources for an instance of a RowColumn widget and an instance of a PushButton will be the same! From the Motif documentation you can find that the default value for the XmNborderWidth resource (a

```
Name                              Type (Default Value)                    Access
------------------------------    ------------------------------------    ------
XmNinsertPosition                 XmRFunction (NULL)                      CSG
```

Figure 9.5 Composite resources.

```
Name                              Type (Default Value)                    Access
------------------------------    ------------------------------------    ------
XmNbottomShadowColor              Pixel (dynamic)                         CSG
XmNbottomShadowPixmap             Pixmap (XmUNSPECIFIED_PIXMAP)            CSG
XmNforeground                     Pixel (dynamic)                         CSG
XmNhelpCallback                   XtCallbackList (NULL)                   C
XmNhighlightColor                 Pixel (Black)                           CSG
XmNhighlightPixmap                Pixmap (dynamic)                        CSG
XmNshadowThickness                short int (0)                           CSG
XmNtopShadowColor                 Pixel (dynamic)                         CSG
XmNtopShadowPixmap                Pixmap (XmUNSPECIFIED_PIXMAP)            CSG
XmNunitType                       unsigned char (XmPIXELS)                CSG
XmNuserData                       caddr_t (NULL)                          CSG
```

Figure 9.6 XmManager resources.

Core resource) on a PushButton widget is 0. However, the default value
for the same resource on a RowColumn widget is specified as dynamic!

☐   Make sure you have a copy of all pertinent documentation at hand before
you start writing X and Motif programs. The X, Xt, and Motif reference
documentation is absolutely essential for the task of writing widget-based
X/Motif programs. The reference documents are the final word on how a
specific widget will look and feel.

Resources for PushButtons

☐   The XmPushButton class is a Motif class for instances of PushButton widgets. A PushButton widget is a user interface object that is used to issue
commands from within an application. By default, mouse button 1 is used
to interact with the PushButton. Figure 9.7 shows the XmPushButton
resources and the inherited XmLabel resources.

Resources for RowColumns

☐   The XmRowColumn class is a Motif class for instances of RowColumn widgets. A RowColumn widget is a manager widget that is used to organize its
children in a nice, neat row or column. Children windows are forced to be
the same size. RowColumn widgets were primarily created for Motif menus.
Figure 9.8 shows the XmRowColumn resources.

Setting Resources at Widget Creation

☐   There will be times when you will want one PushButton widget to look and
feel different from another PushButton widget defined within the same
X/Motif client application program. Since a widget's look-and-feel are determined by its resources, this means that you have to set up the values for
those resources at the time the widget is created. This is accomplished
through something called an *argument list*.

An argument list is an array of name-value pairs that is passed to the
widget creation function to specify a new value for a named resource. An
argument list can be used only at widget creation time if the widget
resources have C access. There are two methods for creating an argument
list.

An argument list is either an array declared to be of type Arg or type
ArgList which is a pointer to an Arg array. Both of these Xt types are
typedefed on a structure that has two members:

```
typedef struct
    {
    String      name;
    XtArgVal    value;
    } Arg, *ArgList;
```

```
                              XmLabel Resources

Name                          Type (Default Value)                     Access
---------------------------   ---------------------------------------  ------
XmNaccelerator                String (NULL)                            CSG
XmNacceleratorText            XmString (NULL)                          CSG
XmNalignment                  unsigned char (XmALIGNMENT_CENTER)       CSG
XmNfontList                   XmFontList ("Fixed")                     CSG
XmNlabelInsensitivePixmap     Pixmap (XmUNSPECIFIED_PIXMAP)            CSG
XmNlabelPixmap                Pixmap (XmUNSPECIFIED_PIXMAP)            CSG
XmNlabelString                XmString (NULL)                          CSG
XmNlabelType                  unsigned char (XmSTRING)                 CSG
XmNmarginBottom               short int (0)                            CSG
XmNmarginHeight               short int (2)                            CSG
XmNmarginLeft                 short int (0)                            CSG
XmNmarginRight                short int (0)                            CSG
XmNmarginTop                  short int (0)                            CSG
XmNmarginWidth                short int (2)                            CSG
XmNmnemonic                   char ('\0')                              CSG
XmNrecomputeSize              Boolean (True)                           CSG
XmNstringDirection            XmStringDirection                        CSG
                                (XmSTRING_DIRECTION_L_TO_R)


                            XmPushButton Resources

Name                          Type (Default Value)                     Access
---------------------------   ---------------------------------------  ------
XmNactivateCallback           XtCallbackList (NULL)                    C
XmNarmCallback                XtCallbackList (NULL)                    C
XmNarmColor                   Pixel (dynamic)                          CSG
XmNarmPixmap                  Pixmap (XmUNSPECIFIED_PIXMAP)            CSG
XmNdisarmCallback             XtCallbackList (NULL)                    C
XmNfillOnArm                  Boolean (True)                           CSG
XmNshowAsDefault              short int (0)                            CSG
```

Figure 9.7 XmLabel and XmPushButton resources.

The argument list can be formed as a static initialized array or a preallo-cated array that can be filled in with calls to a function called XtSetArg(). Figure 9.9 shows both methods of creating an argument list.

With the static argument list you will have to have a separate list declared for each widget you want to create. If you use XtSetArg() you will only need one argument list which can be refilled and reused for each widget creation function.

If XtSetArg() is used the technique shown is the preferred method of using the function. Using an index variable instead of hard-coding array element numbers will make the task of adding or deleting resources much easier. The separate increment of the index variable is required because XtSetArg() is actually a macro that dereferences the subscript parameter twice within its definition. Also note that by using XtSetArg() the typecast

```
Name                            Type (Default Value)                    Access
------------------------------  --------------------------------------  ------
XmNadjustLast                   Boolean (True)                          CSG
XmNadjustMargin                 Boolean (True)                          CSG
XmNentryAlignment               unsigned char (dynamic)                 CSG
XmNentryBorder                  short int (dynamic)                     CSG
XmNentryCallback                XtCallbackList (NULL)                   C
XmNentryClass                   WidgetClass (dynamic)                   CSG
XmNisAligned                    Boolean (True)                          CSG
XmNisHomogeneous                Boolean (dynamic)                       CSG
XmNlabelString                  XmString (NULL)                         C
XmNmapCallback                  XtCallbackList (NULL)                   C
XmNmarginHeight                 Dimension (dynamic)                     CSG
XmNmarginWidth                  Dimension (3)                           CSG
XmNmenuAccelerators             String (dynamic)                        CSG
XmNmenuCursor                   String ("arrow")                        C
XmNmenuHelpWidget               Widget (NULL)                           CSG
XmNmenuHistory                  Widget (NULL)                           CSG
XmNmnemonic                     char (dynamic)                          CSG
XmNnumColumns                   short int (dynamic)                     CSG
XmNorientation                  unsigned char (dynamic)                 CSG
XmNpacking                      unsigned char (dynamic)                 CSG
XmNpopupEnabled                 Boolean (True)                          CSG
XmNradioAlwaysOne               Boolean (True)                          CSG
XmNradioBehavior                Boolean (False)                         CSG
XmNresizeHeight                 Boolean (True)                          CSG
XmNresizeWidth                  Boolean (True)                          CSG
XmNrowColumnType                unsigned char (XmWORK_AREA)             CG
XmNshadowThickness              int (dynamic)                           CSG
XmNspacing                      short int (dynamic)                     CSG
XmNsubMenuId                    Widget (NULL)                           CG
XmNunmapCallback                XtCallbackList (NULL)                   C
XmNwhichButton                  unsigned int (dynamic)                  CSG
```

Figure 9.8 XmRowColumn resources.

of the value member is unnecessary because the macro does the casting for you.

The last two parameters to any Motif widget creation function are an argument list and an argument count. It doesn't matter which method of creating the argument list that you use. Just create the list containing the resource names and values that you want to use for your new widget instance and pass the list and a count of the number of elements in the list as the last two parameters to the widget creation function.

```
...
Cardinal n = 4;
static Arg argList[] =
    {
        {XmNheight, (XtArgVal) 100},
        {XmNwidth, (XtArgVal) 200},
        {XmNx, (XtArgVal) 5},
        {XmNy, (XtArgVal) 30}
    };
ArgList argPtr = argList;

    --OR--

Cardinal n;
Arg argList[10];
...
n = 0;
XtSetArg(argList[n], XmNheight, 100); n++;
XtSetArg(argList[n], XmNwidth, 200); n++;
XtSetArg(argList[n], XmNx, 5); n++;
XtSetArg(argList[n], XmNy, 30); n++;

    --Once the argList is created--

...
XmCreatePushButton(bbManager, "button1", argList, n);

    --OR--

XmCreatePushButton(bbManager, "button1", argPtr, n);
...
```

Figure 9.9 Creating a resource argument list.

Setting and Getting Resources After Widget Creation

You can, if you want, set the values for the resources in a widget instance after the widget has been created. If the resource that you want to set has S access then you can use the XtSetValues() function to give that resource a value without using an argument list on the widget creation function. Figure 9.10 shows the syntax for the XtSetValues() function.

Notice that the last two parameters to the XtSetValues() function are the same argument list and argument count that you supply to a widget creation function. To use this function you must create an argument list using either one of the two techniques presented previously and pass the argument list and an argument count as the last two parameters. The first parameter is the widget id of the widget whose resources you are trying to change. Figure 9.11 shows how the XtSetValues() function would be used.

```
void XtSetValues(widget_id, arg_list, arg_count)

Widget        widget_id;
Arg           *arg_list;
Cardinal      arg_count;
```

Figure 9.10 XtSetValues() syntax.

```
...
Cardinal n = 4;
Widget aPushButton;
static Arg argList[] =
    {
        {XmNheight, (XtArgVal) 100},
        {XmNwidth, (XtArgVal) 200},
        {XmNx, (XtArgVal) 5},
        {XmNy, (XtArgVal) 30}
    };
...
aPushButton = XmCreatePushButton(bbManager, "button1", NULL, 0);
XtSetValues(aPushButton, argList, n);


    --OR--

Cardinal n;
Widget aPushButton;
Arg argList[10];
...
aPushButton = XmCreatePushButton(bbManager, "button1", NULL, 0);
...
n = 0;
XtSetArg(argList[n], XmNheight, 100); n++;
XtSetArg(argList[n], XmNwidth, 200); n++;
XtSetArg(argList[n], XmNx, 5); n++;
XtSetArg(argList[n], XmNy, 30); n++;
XtSetValues(aPushButton, argList, n);
```

Figure 9.11 Setting resources programmatically with XtSetValues().

You can set a widget's resources to a particular value with an argument list at widget creation time and then change those resources with a call to XtSetValues() later. For example, you may want a PushButton's background color to be green when it is created but want it to turn red as soon as it has been activated. This can be accomplished with a call to XtSet-Values().

With G access on a widget resource you can also get, or query, the current value for that resource on a particular widget. The XtGetValues() function is used to determine the current setting, or value, for one or more resources in a particular widget instance.

For example, the Motif text widget has, as one of its resources, the current value for the ASCII text being displayed within the text widget. If this text were the name of a file or some other text data that was input by the program's user, you would need to "get" that data from within the widget for use in the data processing of your program. Figure 9.12 shows the syntax for the XtGetValues() function.

Although the parameters for XtGetValues() are the same as those for XtSetValues(), there is a *big* difference in how the argument list is used. With XtSetValues() we had a value, possibly in a variable, that we wanted to *give* to a widget for one of its resources. With XtGetValues() we have a place we want to put a value that we want to *get* from a widget for one of its resources.

For XtSetValues() we simply pass the constant or variable that represents the value we want to set in a widget's resource. For XtGetValues() we pass the *address of a variable* we want the function to put a resource value in. The argument list for XtGetValues() will contain name-address pairs instead of the name-value pairs that we passed to XtSetValues(). Figure 9.13 shows how this function would be used.

```
void XtGetValues(widget_id, arg_list, arg_count)

Widget        widget_id;
Arg           *arg_list;
Cardinal      arg_count;
```

Figure 9.12 XtGetValues() syntax.

```
#include <stdio.h>
...
Cardinal n;
Dimension height, width;
Position x, y;
...
Widget aPushButton;
Arg argList[10];
...
aPushButton = XmCreatePushButton(bbManager, "button1", NULL, 0);
...
n = 0;
XtSetArg(argList[n], XmNheight, &height); n++;
XtSetArg(argList[n], XmNwidth, &width); n++;
XtSetArg(argList[n], XmNx, &x); n++;
XtSetArg(argList[n], XmNy, &y); n++;
XtGetValues(aPushButton, argList, n);
...
printf("The height and width of the button are: %d & %d\n", height, width);
printf("The origin of the push button is at: x=%d & y=%d\n", x, y);
...
```

Figure 9.13 Calling XtGetValues() to get resource values.

It is important to note that there is *no relationship* between the XtSetArg() macro and any of the widget creation functions, XtSetValues(), or XtGetValues(). The *only* thing the XtSetArg() macro does is to set name-value pairs of data items into a data structure called an *argument list* —and that is all it does. What you do with the argument list after that is up to you and has absolutely nothing to do with the XtSetArg() macro any more.

Resource Convenience Functions

¤ Because argument lists usually take up a lot of room in an X client C program source code, Motif has provided a number of convenience functions that allow you to set and get the values for some of the more common resources on the most frequently used widgets. Not all widgets have these resource convenience functions, but if one is available, it is much easier to use. Here, then, is another reason for having a complete set of X and Motif reference documentation available before you begin programming—many times convenience functions are provided to make X and Motif much easier to use.

Figure 9.14 shows some of the Motif convenience functions that are available. Note that in most cases there is a "set" and a "get" version of the function available. The "set" function allows you to set a resource, while the "get" function allows you to get a resource without having to construct an argument list and calling XtSetValues() or XtGetValues().

```
Motif Scale Widget:
    XmScaleGetValue()
    XmScaleSetValue()
        To get/set the value of the slider in a scale widget with
        respect to the minimum/maximum values of the scale.
Motif ScrollBar Widget:
    XmScrollBarGetValues()
    XmScrollBarSetValues()
        To get/set the value of the slider in a scrollbar widget with
        respect to the minimum/maximum values of the scrollbar.
Motif Text Widget:
    XmTextGetString()
    XmTextSetString()
        To get/set the value of the text string in a text widget.
Motif ToggleButton Widget:
    XmToggleButtonGetState()
    XmToggleButtonSetState()
        To get/set the state of a togglebutton widget.
```

Figure 9.14 Motif resource convenience functions.

Motif Compound Strings

◻ In addition to the widgets and functions of the Motif widget set, OSF has defined a new data type specifically for the text resources on every Motif widget. This resource type was created to allow for easy internationalization of Motif applications where different countries might use different character sets and print directions for character strings. The resource type is called XmString, which Motif refers to as the *compound string* data type.

Compound strings are designed to allow text to be displayed without hard-coding language-dependent attributes within a string. The XmString data type is actually a pointer to a data structure that contains three components:

character set	The mapping between the string of characters that make up a text item and the font in which the text will be displayed
direction	The relationship between the keyboard entry order and the display order of the characters in the string
text	The actual characters to be displayed

Compound strings are not the same thing as C language character strings. Characters such as \n and \t that have special meaning in a C character string have no meaning in an XmString. The XmNlabelString of the Label widget which is inherited by the CascadeButton, PushButton, and ToggleButton, XmNitems of the List widget, and the XmNtitleString of the Scale widget are all examples of resources that must be set with compound strings.

We will not attempt to describe the process of writing an X/Motif application to be used in other countries — that could take a separate book in itself. However, you do need to know how to create and manipulate compound strings within your programs. Because the XmString data type is widely used throughout the Motif widget set, several functions are provided to create, manipulate, and destroy compound strings.

◻ The XmStringCreateLtoR() function is used to convert a C language character string into a Motif compound string. Figure 9.15 shows the syntax for this function.

The first parameter is the C language, null-terminated, character string that is to be converted into a Motif compound string. The second parameter is a constant that determines the mapping that occurs between the characters of the input string and the characters of the output font. Motif supplies one constant that can be used when you do not know which character sets

```
XmString XmStringCreateLtoR(c_string, character_set)

String              c_string;
XmStringCharSet     character_set;
```

Figure 9.15 XmStringCreateLtoR() syntax.

are available at the time the compound string is being created. This constant is XmSTRING__DEFAULT__CHARSET and is the character set that will be used for all examples in the next few chapters.

The function returns type XmString, which is a pointer to the actual compound string data structure. This pointer can then be used as the value for any widget resource whose type is listed as XmString. Figure 9.16 shows how the XmStringCreateLtoR() function would be used in a Motif program.

¤   When the compound string is created, Motif allocates new memory in which to store the XmString data structure. Remember that a compound string is not the same thing as a C character string and, in fact, has a lot more information stored with it. Because they take up more memory, you do not want a lot of compound strings laying around in your program when the memory could be used for other things.

When a compound string is installed as a resource in a Motif widget, the widget makes its own local copy of the compound string in the widget data structure. Two copies of the compound string will exist in your program. If you will not be using the compound string as an XmString resource for some other widget, you should get rid of it. Destroying the compound string releases the memory associated with the XmString and allows the memory to be used for other things. Figure 9.17 shows the syntax for the XmString-Free() function.

```
#include <Xm/PushB.h>
...
Cardinal n;
Arg argList[3];
Widget myButton;
Widget topShell;
XmString labelString;
...
topShell = XtInitialize(argv[0], "Edit", NULL, 0, &argc, argv);
n = 0;
labelString = XmStringCreateLtoR("Push me to exit", XmSTRING_DEFAULT_CHARSET);
XtSetArg(argList[n], XmNlabelString, labelString); n++;
XtSetArg(argList[n], XmNheight, 50); n++;
XtSetArg(argList[n], XmNwidth, 90); n++;
myButton = XmCreatePushButton(topShell, "hello", argList, n);
...
```

Figure 9.16   Creating a compound string with XmStringCreateLtoR().

```
void XmStringFree(compound_string)

XmString     compound_string;
```

Figure 9.17   XmStringFree() syntax.

The only parameter to this function is the XmString value that was returned from some previous call to XmStringCreateLtoR(). The memory that was previously allocated for the compound string will be freed and available for subsequent allocations. There is no return value from this function. Figure 9.18 shows how the XmStringFree() function would be used in a program.

□   If you have retrieved an XmString resource from some widget in your program and you want to work with it as a C character string, then another conversion must take place. Motif provides another function called XmStringGetLtoR() which converts a compound string into a standard, null-terminated, C character string. Figure 9.19 shows the syntax for this function.

The first parameter is the compound string that you want to convert into a C character string. The second parameter is the character set to use in the conversion, which can be XmSTRING_DEFAULT_CHARSET. The third parameter is being used as a return value for the resulting C character string.

The third parameter to this function is usually the address of a character pointer that you have declared within your program. XmStringGetLtoR() will convert the XmString into a character string in a static data area that it creates. The address of the resulting string is stored in the character

```
#include <Xm/PushB.h>
...
Cardinal n;
Arg argList[3];
Widget myButton;
Widget topShell;
XmString labelString;
...
topShell = XtInitialize(argv[0], "Edit", NULL, 0, &argc, argv);
n = 0;
labelString = XmStringCreateLtoR("Push me to exit", XmSTRING_DEFAULT_CHARSET);
XtSetArg(argList[n], XmNlabelString, labelString); n++;
XtSetArg(argList[n], XmNheight, 50); n++;
XtSetArg(argList[n], XmNwidth, 90); n++;
myButton = XmCreatePushButton(topShell, "hello", argList, n);
XmStringFree(labelString);
...
```

Figure 9.18 Freeing a compound string after use.

```
Boolean XmStringGetLtoR(motif_string, character_set, c_string);

XmString            motif_string;
XmStringCharSet     character_set;
char                **c_string;
```

Figure 9.19 Syntax for XmStringGetLtoR().

pointer whose address you pass as the third parameter. Figure 9.20 shows the most common technique for using this function.

XmStringGetLtoR returns a boolean value. It will return True if the function was successful and False otherwise.

¤ Motif provides several other functions that can be used to manipulate compound strings. Just as in the C language, there are functions provided to copy, concatenate, and compare XmStrings as well as other operations. Figure 9.21 lists some of the compound string functions that are available.

A Complete X/Motif Client Application

¤ Using all the concepts and techniques presented in this chapter, we can put together a simple, but complete, X/Motif-based client application. Example 9.1 shows the code for a program that has a shell widget and a single PushButton widget in it. The program will wait for an activate event in the PushButton widget and close the display and exit in response. Resources are used to change the visual appearance of the PushButton. Figure 9.22 shows what the program would look like on a typical terminal screen.

Review Questions

¤ Please write down the answers to the following questions:

   1. What feature of X and Motif gives them an object-oriented programming feeling?

```
#include <stdio.h>
...
Cardinal n;
XmString labelString;
String cString;
...
Widget aPushButton;
Arg argList[10];
...
aPushButton = XmCreatePushButton(bbManager, "button1", NULL, 0);
...
n = 0;
XtSetArg(argList[n], XmNlabelString, &labelString); n++;
XtGetValues(aPushButton, argList, n);
XmStringGetLtoR(labelString, XmSTRING_DEFAULT_CHARSET, &cString);
...
printf("The label for the button reads: %s\n", cString);
...
```

Figure 9.20 Using XmStringGetLtoR().

```
XmString s1, s2;

Boolean XmStringByteCompare(s1, s2);
    /*
     * Performs  a byte-by-byte  comparison of the data  contained
     * within the two  XmString structures.   Returns True if they
     * are equal and False if they are not.
     */

Boolean XmStringCompare(s1, s2);
    /*
     * Performs a  "semantic"  comparison of the text,  direction,
     * and separators within the two XmString structures.  Returns
     * True if they are equal and False if they are not.
     */

XmString XmStringConcat(s1, s2);
    /*
     * Appends compound string s2  onto the end of compound string
     * s1 and returns the resulting XmString.
     */

XmString XmStringCopy(s1);
    /*
     * Makes a copy of the compound string s1 and returns it.
     */

Boolean XmStringEmpty(s1);
    /*
     * Determines  whether  the  text component  of  the  compound
     * string  s1 is  empty or null.  Returns True  if the  string
     * is empty and False otherwise.
     */

int XmStringLength(s1);
    /*
     * Returns the actual byte count of all the data stored in the
     * compound string s1.
     */
```

Figure 9.21 Compound string functions.

2. What is a widget resource?

3. List some common widget attributes that are implemented as a resource.

4. Why do X and Motif have widget classes?

```
#include <stdio.h>
#include <Xm/PushB.h>

Widget topShell;
XtCallbackProc ButtonPushed();

main(argc, argv)
Cardinal argc;
String argv[];
    {
    Widget myButton;
    Arg argList[9];
    XmString labelString;
    Cardinal n;

    /* Initialize  the Intrinsics and create a top Shell widget */
    topShell = XtInitialize(argv[0], "Edit", NULL, 0, &argc, argv);

    /* Create the user interface widgets */
    n = 0;
    labelString =
        XmStringCreateLtoR("Push me to exit", XmSTRING_DEFAULT_CHARSET);
    XtSetArg(argList[n], XmNlabelString, labelString); n++;
    XtSetArg(argList[n], XmNalignment, XmALIGNMENT_CENTER); n++;
    XtSetArg(argList[n], XmNshadowThickness, 6); n++;
    XtSetArg(argList[n], XmNheight, 50); n++;
    XtSetArg(argList[n], XmNwidth, 120); n++;
    XtSetArg(argList[n], XmNforeground, 9); n++;
    XtSetArg(argList[n], XmNbackground, 10); n++;
    XtSetArg(argList[n], XmNtopShadowColor, 11); n++;
    XtSetArg(argList[n], XmNbottomShadowColor, 12); n++;
    myButton = XmCreatePushButton(topShell, "hello", argList, n);
    XmStringFree(labelString);

    /* Set up callbacks for the widgets */
    XtAddCallback(myButton, XmNactivateCallback, ButtonPushed, NULL);

    /* Make the program visible on the screen */
    XtManageChild(myButton);
    XtRealizeWidget(topShell);

    /* Wait for input events */
    XtMainLoop();
    }
```

Example 9.1 X/Motif application program using resources, part 1.

```
XtCallbackProc ButtonPushed(widget_id, client_data, call_data)
Widget widget_id;
caddr_t client_data;
caddr_t call_data;
    {

    /* Print something on the screen */
    printf("You just pressed the hello button...\n");
    sleep(3);
    printf("Good Bye!\n");

    /* Return control to the operating system */
    XtCloseDisplay(XtDisplay(topShell));
    exit(0);
    }
```

Example 9.2   X/Motif application program using resources, part 2.

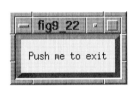

Figure 9.22   Output of the previous X/Motif application program.

   5.   What is a widget instance?

   6.   How does resource inheritance work?

   7.   What is the purpose of the Core widget class?

   8.   List some of the resources in the Core widget class.

   9.   What is the purpose of the XmPrimitive widget class?

 10.   List some of the resources in the XmPrimitive widget class.

 11.   What is the purpose of the Composite widget class?

 12.   List some of the resources in the Composite widget class.

 13.   What is the purpose of the XmManager widget class?

 14.   List some of the resources in the XmManager widget class.

 15.   List some of the resources for the PushButton widget.

 16.   List some of the resources for the RowColumn widget.

 17.   How is the XtSetArg() function used to create an argument list?

18. What is in an argument list, and what is it used for?

19. How do you use an argument list with a widget creation function?

20. How do you use XtSetValues() to set resources after a widget has been created?

21. How do you use XtGetValues() to get resource values from a widget?

22. List some widget-specific resource convenience functions.

23. What is a compound string used for?

24. How is a compound string different from a C character string?

25. How do you use XmStringCreateLtoR() to convert a C character string into a compound string?

26. How do you use XmStringGetLtoR() to convert a compound string into a C character string?

27. What is the XmStringFree() function used for?

28. List some other Motif compound string functions.

Exercises

□ The following exercises are designed to give you the opportunity to practice the concepts and facilities presented in this chapter:

1. Modify the single-widget program called pushme.c from one of the previous chapters. Set up an argument list for the PushButton widget to modify the following resources:

```
XmNshadowThickness          8
XmNlabelString              Push Me
XmNheight                   50
XmNwidth                    100
```

2. Modify the multiple-widget program called multibutton.c from one of the previous chapters. Set up an argument list for the RowColumn widget to modify the following resources:

```
XmNnumColumns               2
XmNpacking                  XmPACK_COLUMN
XmNspacing                  8
```

Set up an argument list for the PushButton widgets to modify the following resources:

```
XmNmarginHeight             20
XmNmarginWidth              40
XmNlabelString              First Button
                            . . .
                            Fifth Button
                            Push Me to Exit
```

Chapter 10

Resource
Files

Introduction

¤   The X Toolkit allows the resources for a widget to be specified in the source code at the time the program is compiled or at execution time from within a resource file. With a resource file, the user can override the default look-and-feel of some of the widgets in an X/Motif program. In this chapter you will learn about resource files – what goes in them, their syntax, and where to place them within the file system.

Objectives

¤   After completing this chapter, you will be able to:

   ¤   Explain the purpose of a resource file.

   ¤   Describe the type of data contained within a resource file.

   ¤   Explain what you must know about an X/Motif client to use a resource file.

   ¤   Describe the syntax for a resource specification in a resource file.

   ¤   Explain how a class name and an instance name are different in a resource file.

   ¤   Describe the difference between tight bindings and loose bindings.

   ¤   Explain how the resource attribute name is specified differently in a resource file than it is in source code.

❑ Describe how comments are placed in a resource file.

❑ List some of the precedence rules that apply to resource files.

❑ List some of the locations that X looks for resource files.

❑ List some of the advantages of using resource files.

❑ List some of the disadvantages of using resource files.

❑ Explain the purpose and use of the xrdb program.

Resource File Concepts

In the previous chapter, you learned the basic ideas behind the use of resources. In this chapter you will learn that resources do not have to be set from within the source code of your X/Motif client application. X gives some additional flexibility by allowing resources to be specified for your client in a text file that is separate from your source program. These files can be created or modified before or after your source program is compiled and are referred to in the X and Motif documentation as *resource files*.

A resource file is an ASCII text file that can be created with any text editor. Within the resource file you can specify the resources for one or more widgets within one or more X/Motif client application programs. Using a very simple syntax, you enter lines in the resource file that specify a resource name for a widget instance in a particular client along with a value for that resource.

The only requirement for the use of a resource file is this: *You must know the instance names and instance hierarchy of the widgets in the client's widget instance tree.* For every Motif widget creation function the second parameter specified that widget's instance name while the first parameter specified its parent widget id. It is absolutely essential that you know the instance name of a widget to use a resource file to change its resources. You must also know that widget's parent so you know where the widget fits into the widget instance tree.

Using a resource file can clean up your C source code and make it a little more readable by removing the argument lists and all of the calls to XtSetArg() that fill them in. Resource files also give you the ability to put off resource definitions until after you have coded the logic of your client application – even after it has been compiled! Using resource files, you have a great deal more flexibility in the specification of resources and their values with your X/Motif client application programs. In earlier versions of X, resource files were called *defaults files*.

Syntax for Resource Files

Each line within a resource file can specify a resource value for a particular instance of a widget, a group of widgets that all have the same instance name, a group of widgets that belong to the same class, or a group of widgets that all have the same resource class. The resource specification in the resource file must conform to a simple syntax as shown in Figure 10.1.

```
object(.|*)subobject[(.|*)subobject...](.|*)attribute:value
```

Figure 10.1 Resource specification syntax in a resource file.

The parenthesis (( )) indicate that a choice must be made from one of the items separated by the vertical bars (|). The square brackets ([ ]) indicate an optional item, while the ellipsis (...) indicates that the previous item can be repeated any number of times. The rest of the syntax is explained in the following paragraphs.

The object in a resource specification can be one of two things. With the object we can specify either a specific client program or a class of similar, related programs. To code a resource for a specific client, use the program name [the same as you usually pass as the first parameter to XtInitialize()] as the object. To code a resource for a class of related applications use the class name [the name you pass as the second parameter to XtInitialize()] as the object.

The subobjects in a resource specification show the path through the widget instance tree that you must follow to gain access to a particular widget. The subobjects can be either the widget instance name (the second parameter to the widget creation function) or a class name. For example, in previous programs, we had Motif PushButton widgets with instance names like hello, button1, button2, button3, button4, button5, and exit. However, no matter what the instance name was, since these were all PushButton widgets, they all have a common class name of XmPushButton.

Whether you are working with the object name or the subobject name, there is one important point to remember: *Instance names always start with a lowercase letter, and class names always start with an uppercase letter.* The rest of the letters in the in a class name are specified exactly as they are defined in the documentation for the specific widget. The rest of the letters in an instance name are specified exactly as they were defined when the widget instance was created.

❏   The object and subobjects in a resource specification can be separated from one another by either a period (.) or an asterisk (*). Using a period separator is called a *tight binding* and requires that you know the exact parent instance or class name on the left and the exact child instance or class name on the right. Using tight binding requires that you know the exact instance hierarchy in the client's widget instance tree.

Using an asterisk separator is called a *loose binding* and allows you to specify that any number of widgets may appear between the parent instance or class on the left and the child instance or class on the right. Using loose bindings gives you a "wildcard" capability in a resource specification.

❏   The last item in a resource specification, the attribute, is the resource name of the resource you are supplying a value for in the last subobject on the line. The resource file is read and processed by X — not Motif or the Intrinsics. As such, the resource name is not the Motif name, nor is it the Intrinsic name. Instead, you must use the X name. The X name for a resource is the same as the Motif or Intrinsic name with the XmN or XtN prefix taken off the front.

The resource name is followed by a colon, optional white space, and the value that is to be used for the resource. Another advantage to resource files is that for resources that have special types, you don't have to call any functions to do conversions to that type for you. For example, compound strings can be specified as simple character strings, and colors can be specified using color names (from /usr/lib/X11/rgb.txt – the X color database). Assuming that the simple one-button client from the previous chapters had been compiled into an executable client called pushme, Figure 10.2 shows several different ways that the background color could be changed to red using a resource file.

◻   Any line that starts with an exclamation point (!) in a resource file is a comment line and will be ignored. You can use the exclamation point to "comment out" lines from a resource file during your testing procedures.

◻   Assuming that the multiple button client from the previous chapters had been compiled into an executable client called multibutton, Figure 10.3 shows several different ways that the resources could be changed using a resource file.

```
pushme.hello.background:                  red
Edit.hello.background:                    red
pushme.XmPushButton.background:           red
Edit.XmPushButton.background:             red
pushme.hello.Background:                  red
Edit.hello.Background:                    red
pushme.XmPushButton.Background:           red
Edit.XmPushButton.Background:             red
*hello.background:                        red
*XmPushButton.background:                 red
*hello.Background:                        red
*XmPushButton.Background:                 red
*background:                              red
*Background:                              red
pushme*background:                        red
Edit*background:                          red
pushme*Background:                        red
Edit*Background:                          red
```

Figure 10.2 Examples of resource file resource specifications.

```
multibutton.rcmanager.button1.background:       green
Edit.rcmanager.XmPushButton.foreground:         yellow
*XmRowColumn.orientation:                       horizontal
multibutton*numColumns:                         2
multibutton*packing:                            pack_column
Edit*XmRowColumn*spacing:                        10
```

Figure 10.3 Examples of resource file resource specifications.

In Figure 10.3 the first line will apply to any client named multibutton. Within that program there must be a composite widget named rcmanager. One of the children below rcmanager must be a primitive widget named button1. The background resource for this widget will be set to green.

The second line will apply to any client that belongs to the Edit client class. Within a program from that class there must be a composite widget named rcmanager. Any child below that belonging to the XmPushButton widget class will have its foreground color set to yellow.

In the third line any client that uses a widget from the RowColumn widget class will have its orientation set to XmHORIZONTAL. The fourth and fifth lines will apply to the multibutton client and set the numColumns and packing resources to 2 and XmPACK_COLUMN, respectively.

Finally, in the last line, any client that belongs to the Edit class of clients and uses a RowColumn widget will have its spacing resource set to 10.

◻ Because there are so many different ways to specify a resource in a resource file — with tight bindings, loose bindings, instance names, class names, and so on — two or more resource specifications in a resource file can apply to the same resource on the same widget. If this is the case, then which one will be applied to the widget?

X has established a set of *precedence rules* to mediate the potential conflict between resource specifications that are trying to set the same resource on the same widget. These rules determine which resource specification will "win" when there is a resource conflict. The following rules apply in ascending order:

1. The hierarchy of the instance and class names in a resource specification must match a clients hierarchy *exactly* or the line is *ignored.*

2. Tight bindings take precedence over loose bindings.

3. Instance names take precedence over class names.

4. Explicit instance or class names take precedence over omitted instance or class names. The line "*scrollbar*background" takes precedence over the line "*background."

5. Left components carry more weight than right components. The line "xterm*background" takes precedence over "*scrollbar*background."

6. If two resource specifications have the exact same precedence, the physical ordering of the lines will determine which takes effect. The line that appears later will have precedence.

Sources for Resources

◻ When your client program starts executing, one of the first things that XtInitialize() does is to create a *resource database* from resource files in several different locations. Although users will typically place their resources in a file in their home directory called .Xdefaults (resources used to be called defaults in older versions of the X Window System), XtInitialize() actually looks in a number of other locations for resource information. The following is a list of places that are consulted, in ascending order, for resource information:

1. /usr/lib/X11/${LANG}app-defaults/<class>. <class> is the class name supplied as the second parameter to XtInitialize(). If this file does not exist, it looks for the file /usr/lib/X11/app-defaults/<class>. The $LANG environment variable is intended for use by clients that will have different resources for different languages and specifies a subdirectory name (with a trailing slash) for a specific language.

2. ${XAPPLRESLANGPATH}<class>. <class> is the class name supplied as the second parameter to XtInitialize(). If this file does not exist, it looks for the file ${XAPPLRESDIR}<class>. Both the $XAPPLRESLANGPATH and the $XAPPLRESDIR environment variables contain a directory name with a trailing slash.

3. RESOURCE_MANAGER property of the root window. This is a special data area that can be manipulated by the xrdb utility program. If this data area does not exist, it looks for the $HOME/.Xdefaults file. The xrdb utility will be discussed later.

4. $XENVIRONMENT. This environment variable contains a full or relative path name or a simple file name for a resource file. If this environment variable is not set, look for $HOME/.Xdefaults-<host>, where <host> is the name of the machine that the client is running on.

5. -xrm command-line arguments. One or more -xrm options can be specified on the command line when starting any X/Motif client. These options have the form -xrm "resource-specification," where the resource-specification uses the exact same syntax as used for lines in a resource file and is quoted to keep the command interpreter from interpreting any asterisks or other special characters it might contain.

6. Your widget's argument lists. The resources that have the "final say" are the ones that are specified in the argument lists of the widget creation and XtSetValues() functions in the source code of your program. These cannot be overridden.

Advantages and Disadvantages of Resource Files

Using resources is absolutely essential when programming with X and Motif. You now know that there are two ways of setting resources for your X/Motif clients. It is important, then, to understand the advantages and disadvantages of each method.

When you use a resource file to supply resources for an X/Motif program you are providing additional flexibility for yourself and the users of your client application. Any user can specify resource settings in their own resource files that override standard settings and reflect personal preferences. The system administrator can create an "app-defaults" file for systemwide customization.

Using a resource file causes the programmer to loose some control. Specifying resources in the client source code gives the programmer greater control. When you specify resources in the argument lists of the widget creation functions they cannot be overridden by any resource specification in any resource file.

However, using resource files can speed client application development. To change a resource value while testing your client, you simply edit and change the resource file and then rerun the program. With hard-coded argument lists you must also recompile the program after a change.

Specifying resources in the argument lists in your source code will provide more efficient operation. The process of searching for, reading, and parsing the resource files adds processing overhead to your program. With the argument lists your program will have less work to do.

Using resource files can simplify your program. Resources in resource files are specified as strings. Coding the same resources in the source code for your client may require calls to one or more functions to compute the value for the resource before you can place it in an argument list. Compound strings, colors, and cursor shapes are examples of resources that are simpler to code in a resource file.

xrdb Program

◻ There is a special data area attached to the root window of every X terminal screen. This data area is used to store resource values for X client application programs and is called the RESOURCE_MANAGER property of the root window. Although we will not describe what a property is here, there is a standard X client application program that can be used to view, load, or modify the resources stored in this data area.

The xrdb program is part of the standard X release from MIT. Its purpose is to work with the resources stored in the RESOURCE_MANAGER property. Remember that XtInitialize() looks to see if this property has been created and if it exists, the function will read the resources from the property *instead* of the $HOME/.Xdefaults file. Figure 10.4 shows the syntax for the xrdb program.

The options specify what type of operation you want to perform on the RESOURCE_MANAGER property of the root window, while the filename is the name of a file that contains resource specifications that will modify the contents of the property. Three of the several options that are available will be discussed here: -load, -merge, and -query.

◻ With the -query option you are telling xrdb that you want to see the contents of the RESOURCE_MANAGER property of the root window. Xrdb will read the property and then display its contents on standard output. Example 10.1 shows what you would expect to see when using this option.

◻ The -load option requires the use of a filename with the xrdb program. The filename will be the name of a resource file whose contents you want loaded into the RESOURCE_MANAGER property of the root window. This load will replace anything that might have already been in the property. Example 10.2 shows how you would use the -load option.

◻ Finally, the -merge option requires the use of a filename with the xrdb program. Instead of replacing the contents of the RESOURCE_MANAGER property, this option specifies that the data from the file should be

```
xrdb [options] [filename]
```

Figure 10.4 Xrdb syntax.

```
$ xrdb -query
multibutton.rcmanager.button1.background:    green
multibutton.rcmanager.button2.background:    red
multibutton.rcmanager.button3.background:    blue
multibutton.rcmanager.button4.background:    firebrick
multibutton.rcmanager.button5.background:    brown
$ _
```

Example 10.1 Using xrdb with the -query option.

```
$ xrdb -query
multibutton.rcmanager.button1.background:    green
multibutton.rcmanager.button2.background:    red
multibutton.rcmanager.button3.background:    blue
multibutton.rcmanager.button4.background:    firebrick
multibutton.rcmanager.button5.background:    brown
$ cat resfile1
Edit.rcmanager.XmPushButton.foreground:           yellow
*XmRowColumn.orientation:                         horizontal
multibutton*numColumns:                           2
$ xrdb -load resfile1
$ xrdb -query
*XmRowColumn.orientation:    horizontal
Edit.rcmanager.XmPushButton.foreground: yellow
multibutton*numColumns: 2
$ _
```

Example 10.2 Using xrdb with the -load option.

merged with the data already in the property. Example 10.3 shows how you would use the -merge option.

□   If a filename is not specified with the -load or -merge options, then xrdb can read its standard input for resource specifications. This allows you to add resources directly from the terminal keyboard. Some versions of xrdb also support a -remove option to remove the RESOURCE_MANAGER property of the root window. There are some additional capabilities of the xrdb program that have not been discussed here.

A Complete X/Motif Client Application

□   Using all the concepts and techniques presented in this chapter, we can put together a simple, but complete, X/Motif-based client application. Example 10.4 shows the code for a program that has a shell widget and a single PushButton widget in it. The program will wait for an activate event in the PushButton widget and close the display and exit in response. This is the same as the example from the previous chapter; however, a resource file is used to change the visual appearance of the PushButton instead of hardcoding the resource values in the source code of the program.

```
$ xrdb -query
*XmRowColumn.orientation:    horizontal
Edit.rcmanager.XmPushButton.foreground: yellow
multibutton*numColumns: 2
$ cat resfile2
multibutton*packing:                        pack_column
Edit*XmRowColumn*spacing:                   10
$ xrdb -merge resfile2
$ xrdb -query
*XmRowColumn.orientation:    horizontal
Edit*XmRowColumn*spacing:    10
Edit.rcmanager.XmPushButton.foreground: yellow
multibutton*numColumns: 2
multibutton*packing:    pack_column
$ _
```

Example 10.3 Using xrdb with the -merge option.

Example 10.5 shows what the resource file for the previous program would look like. Note that these resource specifications could go in a $HOME/.Xdefaults file, a file called Edit in a directory pointed to by the $XAPPLRESDIR environment variable, a file pointed to by the $XEN-VIRONMENT environment variable, or any number of other places that resource files can exist. Notice how the class name for the application is being used as the first element in each resource specification instead of the application instance name. Figure 10.5 shows what the program would look like on a typical terminal screen.

Review Questions

◻ Please write down the answers to the following questions:

1. What is the purpose of a resource file?
2. What type of data is contained within a resource file?
3. How is an X/Motif client's widget instance tree related to a resource file?
4. What is the syntax for a resource specification in a resource file?
5. How are class names and instance names different in a resource file?
6. How do you specify tight bindings and loose bindings in a resource file?
7. What is the difference between a resource attribute name as specified in a resource file and in source code?
8. How are comments placed in a resource file?

```
#include <stdio.h>
#include <Xm/PushB.h>

Widget topShell;
XtCallbackProc ButtonPushed();

main(argc, argv)
Cardinal argc;
String argv[];
    {
    Widget myButton;

    /* Initialize  the Intrinsics and create a top Shell widget */
    topShell = XtInitialize(argv[0], "Edit", NULL, 0, &argc, argv);

    /* Create the user interface widgets */
    myButton = XmCreatePushButton(topShell, "hello", NULL, 0);

    /* Set up callbacks for the widgets */
    XtAddCallback(myButton, XmNactivateCallback, ButtonPushed, NULL);

    /* Make the program visible on the screen */
    XtManageChild(myButton);
    XtRealizeWidget(topShell);

    /* Wait for input events */
    XtMainLoop();
    }

XtCallbackProc ButtonPushed(widget_id, client_data, call_data)
Widget widget_id;
caddr_t client_data;
caddr_t call_data;
    {

    /* Print something on the screen */
    printf("You just pressed the hello button...\n");
    sleep(3);
    printf("Good Bye!\n");

    /* Return control to the operating system */
    XtCloseDisplay(XtDisplay(topShell));
    exit(0);
    }
```

Example 10.4 X/Motif application program using a resource file.

```
Edit.hello.labelString:          Push me to exit
Edit.hello.alignment:            alignment_center
Edit.hello.shadowThickness:      6
Edit.hello.height:               50
Edit.hello.width:                120
Edit.hello.foreground:           wheat
Edit.hello.background:            forestgreen
Edit.hello.topShadowColor:       red
Edit.hello.bottomShadowColor:    aquamarine
```

Example 10.5 Resource file for the previous X/Motif application program.

Figure 10.5 Output of the previous X/Motif application program.

9. List some of the precedence rules that apply to resource files.

10. List some of the locations that X looks for resource files.

11. List some of the advantages of using resource files.

12. List some of the disadvantages of using resource files.

13. What is the purpose of the xrdb program? How is it used?

Exercises

□ The following exercises are designed to give you the opportunity to practice the concepts and facilities presented in this chapter:

1. Create a .Xdefaults file in your home directory. Within your .Xdefaults file, put the resource specifications necessary to change the attributes of the PushButton widget in the pushme program to the following values:

    ```
    XmNforeground              thistle
    XmNbackground              forestgreen
    XmNarmColor                red
    XmNfillOnArm               True
    ```

2. Within your .Xdefaults file, put the resource specifications necessary to change the attributes of the PushButton widgets in the multibutton program to the following values:

```
XmNforeground-all buttons    wheat
XmNbackground-button 1       blue
XmNbackground-button 2       navyblue
XmNbackground-button 3       midnightblue
XmNbackground-button 4       lightblue
XmNbackground-button 5       cadetblue
XmNbackground-exit button    aquamarine
XmNarmColor                     red
XmNfillOnArm                    True
```

Also remove the XmNnumColumns and XmNpacking resources from the source code for the RowColumn widget. Add the resource specifications to your .Xdefaults file necessary to change the attributes of the RowColumn widget to the following values:

```
XmNorientation               horizontal
```

3. Make a new directory in your home directory called Resources. Set the XAPPLRESDIR environment variable to the full path name of the Resources directory. Move your .Xdefaults file to the Resources directory and rename it to Edit (the class name from XtInitialize() in both the pushme and multibutton programs). Rerun your pushme and multibutton programs to see if the resource specifications still take effect.

4. Unset the XAPPLRESDIR environment variable and create a new environment variable called XENVIRONMENT. Place the full path name of the Edit file in the Resources directory in this environment variable. Rerun your pushme and multibutton programs to see if the resource specifications still take effect.

5. Unset the XENVIRONMENT environment variable and use the xrdb program to load the resource specifications from your Edit resource file into the WINDOW_MANAGER property of the root window. Use the -query option to verify that the operation was successful. Rerun your pushme and multibutton programs to see if the resource specifications still take effect.

Motif
Primitive
Widgets

Introduction

¤ The Motif widget set provides a number of different user interface widgets that you can use to interact with your user in an X/Motif client application program. In this chapter you will learn about the Motif primitive widgets that can be used to get input from your program's user.

Objectives

¤ After completing this chapter, you will be able to:

¤ Use the Motif ArrowButton widget.

¤ Use the Motif CascadeButton widget.

¤ Use the Motif DrawnButton widget.

¤ Use the Motif Label widget.

¤ Use the Motif List widget.

¤ Use the Motif ScrollBar widget.

¤ Use the Motif Separator widget.

¤ Use the Motif ToggleButton widget.

¤ Use Motif gadgets.

Primitive Widget Concepts

¤ Motif primitive widgets are the user interface components of an X/Motif-based program. These widgets are the ones that are manipulated by the user to provide input to your program or to receive output from your program. To get your program to do something, the user will interact with the primitive widgets that you provide.

There are widgets that allow you to issue a command (button widgets) and are available in a variety of different styles, widgets that allow you to choose one item from a list of possibilities (list widget), widgets that allow you to choose a value from a range (scroll bar widget), widgets that allow you to visually separate two areas within your client area (separator widget), and widgets that allow you to input and output textual data (text widget).

The following sections define these primitive widgets – their creation functions, resources, and callback data structures. For more detailed information about possible resource values, resource class information, and so forth, please consult your Motif reference documentation.

Motif ArrowButton

¤ The ArrowButton is a type of push-button widget that consists of a directional arrow surrounded by a border shadow. When it is activated or armed, the shadow moves to give the appearance that the arrow button has been pressed in. When it is disarmed, the shadow reverts to its normal appearance which looks as if it is popped out. Figure 11.1 shows the syntax for the XmCreateArrowButton() function.

The ArrowButton widget inherits resources from the Core and XmPrimitive classes. Its class name is XmArrowButton. Figure 11.2 shows what an ArrowButton widget would look like.

The XmArrowButton widget class defines a set of resources that are inherited by an instance of an ArrowButton widget. Figure 11.3 lists these new resources and their type and access.

When a callback occurs for an ArrowButton widget for any one of the callback resources listed in Figure 11.3, a pointer to a structure of type XmAnyCallbackStruct is passed as the call_data parameter to the callback function that is invoked in response. The structure has the following members:

```
#include <Xm/ArrowB.h>

Widget XmCreateArrowButton(parent_id, instance_name, arg_list, arg_count)

Widget      parent_id;
String      instance_name;
ArgList     arg_list;
Cardinal    arg_count;
```

Figure 11.1 XmCreateArrowButton() syntax.

Figure 11.2 Visual appearance of an ArrowButton widget.

```
Name                           Type (Default Value)                  Access
------------------------------ ------------------------------------- ------
XmNactivateCallback            XtCallbackList (NULL)                  C
XmNarmCallback                 XtCallbackList (NULL)                  C
XmNarrowDirection              unsigned char (XmARROW_UP)             CSG
XmNdisarmCallback              XtCallbackList (NULL)                  C
```

Figure 11.3 XmArrowButton resources.

```
typedef struct
    {
    int     reason;
    XEvent  *event;
    } XmAnyCallbackStruct;
```

reason   Indicates why the callback was invoked. It can contain any of
            the defined values XmCR_ACTIVATE, XmCR_ARM, or
            XmCR_DISARM.

event   Pointer to a union of type XEvent which contains information
            about the actual X event that triggered the callback.

Motif CascadeButton

口   The CascadeButton is normally used in a menu system. When installed in a
     MenuBar, this button can be used to activate a PulldownMenu. When
     installed in any MenuPane, this button can be used to activate a Cas-
     cadeMenu. The visual appearance for the CascadeButton differs depending
     on what type of widget is its parent and how it is used.
         The submenu that is displayed with this widget can be activated when the
     CascadeButton is installed in a MenuBar, a PopupMenu, or a Pulldown-
     Menu. The visual appearance of the button can include a label or a pixmap
     and cascading indicator. The default behavior of the CascadeButton
     depends on what type of menu it is installed in. By default, mouse button
     1 interacts with this button when it is in a MenuBar or a PulldownMenu.
     Mouse button 3 interacts with the CascadeButton in a PopupMenu. Figure
     11.4 shows the syntax for the XmCreateCascadeButton() function.
         The CascadeButton widget inherits resources from the Core, XmPrimi-
     tive, and XmLabel classes. Its class name is XmCascadeButton. Figure
     11.5 shows what a CascadeButton widget would look like.

```
#include <Xm/CascadeB.h>

Widget XmCreateCascadeButton(parent_id, instance_name, arg_list, arg_count)

Widget      parent_id;
String      instance_name;
ArgList     arg_list;
Cardinal    arg_count;
```

Figure 11.4 XmCreateCascadeButton() syntax.

Figure 11.5 Visual appearance of a CascadeButton widget.

The XmCascadeButton widget class defines a set of resources that are inherited by an instance of a CascadeButton widget. Figure 11.6 lists these new resources and their type and access.

When a callback occurs for a CascadeButton widget for any one of the callback resources listed in Figure 11.6, a pointer to a structure of type XmAnyCallbackStruct is passed as the call_data parameter to the callback function that is invoked in response. The structure has the following members:

```
typedef struct
    {
    int      reason;
    XEvent   *event;
    } XmAnyCallbackStruct;
```

reason   Indicates why the callback was invoked. It can contain any of
                the defined values XmCR_ACTIVATE, XmCR_ARM, or
                XmCR_DISARM.

Name	Type (Default Value)	Access
XmNactivateCallback	XtCallbackList (NULL)	C
XmNcascadePixmap	Pixmap ("menu-cascade")	CSG
XmNcascadingCallback	XtCallbackList (NULL)	C
XmNmappingDelay	int (100)	CSG
XmNsubMenuId	Widget (0)	CSG

Figure 11.6 XmCascadeButton resources.

event   Pointer to a union of type XEvent which contains information about the actual X event that triggered the callback.

Motif DrawnButton

¤   The DrawnButton widget consists of an empty widget window surrounded by a shadow border. The empty window can be used as a graphics area where the application writer can draw things. The DrawnButton has Push-Button input semantics. Figure 11.7 shows the syntax for the XmCreateDrawnButton() function.

The DrawnButton widget inherits resources from the Core, XmPrimitive, and XmLabel classes. Its class name is XmDrawnButton. Figure 11.8 shows what a DrawnButton widget would look like.

The XmDrawnButton widget class defines a set of resources that are inherited by an instance of a DrawnButton widget. Figure 11.9 lists these new resources and their type and access.

When a callback occurs for a DrawnButton widget for any one of the callback resources listed in Figure 11.9, a pointer to a structure of type XmDrawnButtonCallbackStruct is passed as the call_data parameter to the callback function that is invoked in response. The structure has the following members:

```
#include <Xm/DrawnB.h>

Widget XmCreateDrawnButton(parent_id, instance_name, arg_list, arg_count)

Widget       parent_id;
String       instance_name;
ArgList      arg_list;
Cardinal     arg_count;
```

Figure 11.7 XmCreateDrawnButton() syntax.

Figure 11.8 Visual appearance of a DrawnButton widget.

Name	Type (Default Value)	Access
XmNactivateCallback	XtCallbackList (NULL)	C
XmNarmCallback	XtCallbackList (NULL)	C
XmNdisarmCallback	XtCallbackList (NULL)	C
XmNexposeCallback	XtCallbackList (NULL)	C
XmNpushButtonEnabled	Boolean (False)	CSG
XmNresizeCallback	XtCallbackList (NULL)	C
XmNshadowType	unsigned char (XmSHADOW_ETCHED_IN)	CSG

Figure 11.9 XmDrawnButton resources.

```
typedef struct
    {
    int      reason;
    XEvent   *event;
    Window   window;
    } XmDrawnButtonCallbackStruct;
```

reason   Indicates why the callback was invoked. It can contain any of the defined values XmCR_ACTIVATE, XmCR_ARM, or XmCR_DISARM.

event   Pointer to a union of type XEvent which contains information about the actual X event that triggered the callback.

window   Window id of the X window in which the event occurred.

Motif Label

◻   The Motif Label widget is an instantable widget as well as a superclass for some of the Motif Button widgets. The Label widget does not accept input and inherits only one callback defined for subclass inheritance. The purpose of the Label widget is to allow text labels to be placed in a client area giving a title to some other widget. Figure 11.10 shows the syntax for the XmCreateLabel() function.

The Label widget inherits resources from the Core and XmPrimitive classes. Its class name is XmLabel. Figure 11.11 shows what a Label widget would look like.

```
#include <Xm/Label.h>

Widget XmCreateLabel(parent_id, instance_name, arg_list, arg_count)

Widget       parent_id;
String       instance_name;
ArgList      arg_list;
Cardinal     arg_count;
```

Figure 11.10 XmCreateLabel() syntax.

Figure 11.11 Visual appearance of a Label widget.

The XmLabel widget class defines a set of resources that are inherited by an instance of a Label widget. Figure 11.12 lists these new resources and their type and access.

When a callback occurs for an Label widget, a pointer to a structure of type XmAnyCallbackStruct is passed as the call_data parameter to the callback function that is invoked in response. The structure has the following members:

```
typedef struct
    {
    int      reason;
    XEvent   *event;
    } XmAnyCallbackStruct;
```

reason   Indicates why the callback was invoked. It will contain the defined value XmCR_HELP.

event   Pointer to a union of type XEvent which contains information about the actual X event that triggered the callback.

Name	Type (Default Value)	Access
XmNaccelerator	String (NULL)	CSG
XmNacceleratorText	XmString (NULL)	CSG
XmNalignment	unsigned char (XmALIGNMENT_CENTER)	CSG
XmNfontList	XmFontList ("Fixed")	CSG
XmNlabelInsensitivePixmap	Pixmap (XmUNSPECIFIED_PIXMAP)	CSG
XmNlabelPixmap	Pixmap (XmUNSPECIFIED_PIXMAP)	CSG
XmNlabelString	XmString (NULL)	CSG
XmNlabelType	unsigned char (XmSTRING)	CSG
XmNmarginBottom	short int (0)	CSG
XmNmarginHeight	short int (2)	CSG
XmNmarginLeft	short int (0)	CSG
XmNmarginRight	short int (0)	CSG
XmNmarginTop	short int (0)	CSG
XmNmarginWidth	short int (2)	CSG
XmNmnemonic	char ('\0')	CSG
XmNrecomputeSize	Boolean (True)	CSG
XmNstringDirection	XmStringDirection (XmSTRING_DIRECTION_L_TO_R)	CSG

Figure 11.12 XmLabel resources.

Motif List

¤   The List widget allows a user to select one or more items from a list of possibilities. Items can be selected in a variety of ways using either the mouse
or the keyboard. The list entries are created from an array of compound
strings.

The number of entries in the list is determined by a visibleItemCount
resource. If a larger set of choices is needed with only a few visible at a
time, then a ScrolledList widget should be created. A variety of XmNselectionPolicy values are available:

XmSINGLE_SELECT   Only one item can be selected at a time. A
                      callback is invoked for the selected item.

XmMULTIPLE_SELECT   Multiple items can be selected by clicking on
                      them individually. A callback is invoked each
                      time an new item is selected. Some other
                      method should be used (such as a PushButton)
                      to indicate that the multiple selection is com-
                      plete.

XmEXTENDED_SELECT   A range of items can be selected with a click-
                      hold-drag operation. The range can be modi-
                      fied using the shift key and multiple ranges
                      can be selected using the control key. The
                      callback is controlled by the XmNautomatic
                      Selection resource.

XmBROWSE_SELECT   Only one item can be selected at a time with a
                      click-hold-drag operation. Callbacks can be
                      invoked while traversing the items in the list
                      and is controlled by the XmNautomaticSelec-
                      tion resource.

In all cases selected items have their foreground and background colors
inverted and selected items can be acted on through appropriate callbacks.
The XmNautomaticSelection resource determines whether callbacks are
invoked while traversing items in the list or only invoked when a selection is
committed by releasing the mouse button. Figure 11.13 shows the syntax
for the XmCreateList() function.

```
#include <Xm/List.h>

Widget XmCreateList(parent_id, instance_name, arg_list, arg_count)

Widget      parent_id;
String      instance_name;
ArgList     arg_list;
Cardinal    arg_count;
```

Figure 11.13 XmCreateList() syntax.

The List widget inherits resources from the Core and XmPrimitive classes. Its class name is XmList. Figure 11.14 shows what a List widget would look like.

The XmList widget class defines a set of resources that are inherited by an instance of a List widget. Figure 11.15 lists these new resources and their type and access.

When a callback occurs for a List widget for any one of the callback resources listed in Figure 11.15, a pointer to a structure of type XmListCallbackStruct is passed as the call_data parameter to the callback function that is invoked in response. The structure has the following members:

Figure 11.14 Visual appearance of a List widget.

Name	Type (Default Value)	Access
XmNautomaticSelection	Boolean (False)	CSG
XmNbrowseSelectionCallback	XtCallbackList (NULL)	C
XmNdefaultActionCallback	XtCallbackList (NULL)	C
XmNdoubleClickInterval	int (250)	CSC
XmNextendedSelectionCallback	XtCallbackList (NULL)	C
XmNfontList	XmFontList ("fixed")	CSG
XmNitemCount	int (0)	CSG
XmNitems	XmStringTable (NULL)	CSG
XmNlistMarginHeight	Dimension (0)	CSG
XmNlistMarginWidth	Dimension (0)	CSG
XmNlistSpacing	short int (0)	CSG
XmNmultipleSelectionCallback	XtCallbackList (NULL)	C
XmNselectedItemCount	int (0)	CSG
XmNselectedItems	XmStringTable (NULL)	CSG
XmNselectionPolicy	unsigned char (XmBROWSE_SELECT)	CSG
XmNsingleSelectionCallback	XtCallbackList (NULL)	C
XmNstringDirection	XmStringDirection (XmSTRING_DIRECTION_L_TO_R)	CSG
XmNvisibleItemCount	int (1)	CSG

Figure 11.15 XmList resources.

```
typedef struct
    {
    int         reason;
    XEvent      *event;
    XmString    item;
    int         item_length;
    int         item_position;
    XmString    *selected_items;
    int         selected_item_count;
    int         selection_type;
    } XmListCallbackStruct;
```

reason	Indicates why the callback was invoked.
event	Pointer to a union of type XEvent which contains information about the actual X event that triggered the callback.
item	The single item from the list that was selected as a result of the action that invoked the callback.
item_length	The length of the list item that was selected as a result of the action that invoked the callback.
item_position	The position of the item within the list that was selected as a result of the action that invoked the callback.
selected_items	Pointer to an array of compound strings that will contain those list items that had been selected (highlighted) on the list when the callback was invoked.
selected_item_count	The number of items in the selected_items list.
selection_type	Indicates the type of the most recent extended selection; it can be any one of the defined values XmINITIAL, XmMODIFICATION, or XmADDITION.

There are a wide variety of convenience functions available that let you interact with a List without resorting to resources and calls to XtSet-Values() and XtGetValues(). These functions let you add and delete items from a List, select and deselect items from a List, and manipulate the visible portion of a List. Figures 11.16 and 11.17 show the syntax for many of these functions.

Motif ScrollBar

□   The ScrollBar widget is usually used to allow a user to view a large data area through a smaller viewport. When the user interacts with the ScrollBar, the viewport moves within the larger data area. This scrolling feature is not automatic and must be configured with client application code.

```
void XmListAddItem(widget_id, item, position)
    /*
     * Adds the compound string item to the List at the indicated position.
     * The position is 1-relative with 0 indicating the bottom.  If the new
     * item appears in the XmNselectedItems list it will become selected
     * after it is added.
     */

void XmListAddItemUnselected(widget_id, item, position)
    /*
     * Same as above except that the item will not be selected.
     */

void XmListDeleteItem(widget_id, item)
    /*
     * Deletes the compound string item from the List.
     */

void XmListDeletePos(widget, position)
    /*
     * Same as above except that the item to be deleted is specified by
     * a 1-relative position number.
     */

void XmListDeselectAllItems(widget_id)
    /*
     * Deselect all previously selected items in the List and remove
     * them from the XmNselectedItems list.
     */

void XmListDeselectItem(widget_id, item)
    /*
     * Deselect the previously selected compound string item in the
     * List and remove it from the XmNselectedItems list.
     */

void XmListDeselectPos(widget, position)
    /*
     * Same as above except that the item to be deleted is specified by
     * a 1-relative position number.
     */
Boolean XmListItemExists(widget_id, item)
    /*
     * Determines if the compound string item appears in the List.
     * Returns True if it does and False if it doesn't.
     */
```

Figure 11.16 List convenience functions.

```
void XmListSelectItem(widget_id, item, notify)
    /*
     * Select the compound string item in the List and add it to the
     * XmNselectedItems list.  The Boolean notify parameter is used
     * to specify whether the associated selection callback is invoked.
     */

void XmListSelectPos(widget_id, position, notify)
    /*
     * Same as above except that the item to be selected is specified by
     * a 1-relative position number.
     */

void XmListSetBottomItem(widget_id, item)
    /*
     * Makes the existing compound string item the last visible item in
     * the List.
     */

void XmListSetBottomPos(widget_id, position)
    /*
     * Same as above except that the item to be made last is specified by
     * a 1-relative position number.
     */

void XmListSetItem(widget_id, item)
    /*
     * Makes the existing compound string item the first visible item in
     * the List.
     */

void XmListSetPos(widget_id, position)
    /*
     * Same as above except that the item to be made first is specified by
     * a 1-relative position number.
     */
```

Figure 11.17 List convenience functions.

A ScrollBar consists of two arrows at opposite ends of a long rectangle. The rectangle is called the *trough,* and a smaller rectangle, called the *slider,* is placed within the trough. Interaction with the ScrollBar is accomplished by clicking the arrows, clicking within the trough, or dragging the slider. The ratio of the size of the slider to the size of the scroll area is usually a reflection of the size of the viewport with respect to the larger data area. Figure 11.18 shows the syntax for the XmCreateScrollBar() function.

The ScrollBar widget inherits resources from the Core and XmPrimitive classes. Its class name is XmScrollBar. Figure 11.19 shows what a ScrollBar widget would look like.

```
#include <Xm/ScrollBar.h>

Widget XmCreateScrollBar(parent_id, instance_name, arg_list, arg_count)

Widget      parent_id;
String      instance_name;
ArgList     arg_list;
Cardinal    arg_count;
```

Figure 11.18 XmCreateScrollBar() syntax.

Figure 11.19 Visual appearance of a ScrollBar widget.

The XmScrollBar widget class defines a set of resources that are inherited by an instance of a ScrollBar widget. Figure 11.20 lists these new resources and their type and access.

When a callback occurs for a ScrollBar widget for any one of the callback resources listed in Figure 11.20, a pointer to a structure of type XmScrollBarCallbackStruct is passed as the call_data parameter to the

```
Name                            Type (Default Value)                      Access
----------------------------    ---------------------------------------   ------
XmNdecrementCallback            XtCallbackList (NULL)                      C
XmNdragCallback                 XtCallbackList (NULL)                      C
XmNincrement                    int (1)                                    CSG
XmNincrementCallback            XtCallbackList (NULL)                      C
XmNinitialDelay                 int (250)                                  CSG
XmNmaximum                      int (100)                                  CSG
XmNminimum                      int (0)                                    CSG
XmNorientation                  unsigned char (XmVERTICAL)                 CSG
XmNpageDecrementCallback        XtCallbackList (NULL)                      C
XmNpageIncrement                int (10)                                   C
XmNpageIncrementCallback        XtCallbackList (NULL)                      C
XmNprocessingDirection          unsigned char (XmMAX_ON_BOTTOM)            CSG
XmNrepeatDelay                  int (50)                                   CSG
XmNshowArrows                   Boolean (True)                             CSG
XmNsliderSize                   int (10)                                   CSG
XmNtoBottomCallback             XtCallbackList (NULL)                      C
XmNtoTopCallback                XtCallbackList (NULL)                      C
XmNvalue                        int (0)                                    CSG
XmNvalueChangedCallback         XtCallbackList (NULL)                      C
```

Figure 11.20 XmScrollBar resources.

callback function that is invoked in response. The structure has the following members:

```
typedef struct
    {
    int     reason;
    XEvent  *event;
    int     value;
    int     pixel;
    } XmScrollBarCallbackStruct;
```

reason   Indicates why the callback was invoked.

event   Pointer to a union of type XEvent which contains information about the actual X event that triggered the callback.

value   Contains the new slider location value.

pixel   For horizontal ScrollBars, this is the X-coordinate position of where the mouse button selection occurred. For vertical ScrollBars, this is the Y-coordinate. This value is only for the XmNtoTopCallback and the XmNtoBottomCallback.

Two convenience functions can be used to interact with a ScrollBar: XmScrollBarGetValues(), which retrieves the current state of a ScrollBar, and XmScrollBarSetValues(), which sets the state of a ScrollBar. Figure 11.21 shows the syntax for these two functions.

Notice that addresses are passed as the last four parameters to XmScrollBarGetValues(). These are the addresses of the variables that you have created to hold the returned values. Integer values are passed in the corresponding parameters of XmScrollBarSetValues as the values that you want to set in the ScrollBar. The notify parameter identifies whether the XmNvalueChangedCallback should be invoked (True) or not (False).

```
void XmScrollBarGetValues(widget_id, value_rtn, slider_size_rtn,
                          increment_rtn, pg_increment_rtn)
void XmScrollBarSetValues(widget_id, value, slider_size, increment,
                          pg_increment, notify)

Widget  widget_id;
int     *value_rtn;
int     *slider_size_rtn;
int     *increment_rtn;
int     *pg_increment_rtn;
int     value;
int     slider_size;
int     increment;
int     pg_increment;
Boolean notify;
```

Figure 11.21 ScrollBar convenience functions.

Motif Separator

◻ The Separator widget is a simple widget that is used as a graphic item to separate items in a client display area. The Separator line will be centered in the height or width of its parent depending on its orientation.

The Seperator does not have a shadow. However, the inherited shadowThickness resource is used for the thickness of the Separator widget. Several different graphic styles are available for the Separator. The Separator widget does not accept input. Figure 11.22 shows the syntax for the XmCreateSeparator() function.

The Separator widget inherits resources from the Core and XmPrimitive classes. Its class name is XmSeparator. Figure 11.23 shows what a Separator widget would look like.

The XmSeparator widget class defines a set of resources that are inherited by an instance of a Separator widget. Figure 11.24 lists these new resources and their type and access.

```
#include <Xm/Separator.h>

Widget XmCreateSeparator(parent_id, instance_name, arg_list, arg_count)

Widget       parent_id;
String       instance_name;
ArgList      arg_list;
Cardinal     arg_count;
```

Figure 11.22 XmCreateSeparator() syntax.

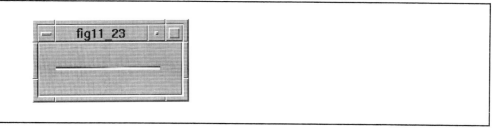

Figure 11.23 Visual appearance of a Separator widget.

```
Name                              Type (Default Value)                    Access
-------------------------------   -------------------------------------   ------
XmNmargin                         short int (0)                           CSG
XmNorientation                    unsigned char (XmHORIZONTAL)            CSG
XmNseparatorType                  unsigned char (XmSHADOW_ETCHED_IN)      CSG
```

Figure 11.24 XmSeparator resources.

There are no callbacks defined for the Separator widget.

Motif ToggleButton

The ToggleButton widget is used to set nontransitory state data within an application. The widget usually consists of a state indicator that can be either square- or diamond-shaped as well as a label. The shape of the indicator is used to indicate whether one of several or any of several related toggle buttons can be set at the same time.

The semantics of the toggle button imply a selected or unselected state. The indicator will be filled when it is selected and not filled when it is deselected. Normally mouse button 1 is used to interact with the ToggleButton. Figure 11.25 shows the syntax for the XmCreateToggleButton() function.

The ToggleButton widget inherits resources from the Core, XmPrimitive, and XmLabel classes. Its class name is XmToggleButton. Figure 11.26 shows what a ToggleButton widget would look like.

The XmToggleButton widget class defines a set of resources that are inherited by an instance of a ToggleButton widget. Figure 11.27 lists these new resources and their type and access.

When a callback occurs for a ToggleButton widget for any one of the callback resources listed in Figure 11.27, a pointer to a structure of type XmToggleButtonCallbackStruct is passed as the call_data parameter to the callback function that is invoked in response. The structure has the following members:

```
#include <Xm/ToggleB.h>

Widget XmCreateToggleButton(parent_id, instance_name, arg_list, arg_count)

Widget      parent_id;
String      instance_name;
ArgList     arg_list;
Cardinal    arg_count;
```

Figure 11.25 XmCreateToggleButton() syntax.

Figure 11.26 Visual appearance of a ToggleButton widget.

```
Name                           Type (Default Value)              Access
------------------------------ --------------------------------- ------
XmNarmCallback                 XtCallbackList (NULL)             C
XmNdisarmCallback              XtCallbackList (NULL)             C
XmNfillOnSelect                Boolean (True)                   CSG
XmNindicatorOn                 Boolean (True)                   CSG
XmNindicatorType               unsigned char (XmN_OF_MANY)      CSG
XmNselectColor                 Pixel (dynamic)                  CSG
XmNselectInsensitivePixmap     Pixmap (XmUNSENSITIVE_PIXMAP)     CSG
XmNselectPixmap                Pixmap (XmUNSENSITIVE_PIXMAP)     CSG
XmNset                         Boolean (False)                  CSG
XmNspacing                     short int (4)                    CSG
XmNvalueChangedCallback        XtCallbackList (NULL)             C
XmNvisibleWhenOff              Boolean (True)                   CSG
```

Figure 11.27 XmToggleButton resources.

```
typedef struct
    {
    int     reason;
    XEvent  *event;
    Boolean set;
    } XmToggleButtonCallbackStruct;
```

reason   Indicates why the callback was invoked.

event   Pointer to a union of type XEvent which contains information about the actual X event that triggered the callback.

set   Reflects the current state of the ToggleButton when the callback occurred.

Two convenience functions can be used to interact with a ToggleButton: XmToggleButtonGetState(), which retrieves the current state of a ToggleButton, and XmToggleButtonSetState(), which sets the state of a ToggleButton. Figure 11.28 shows the syntax for these two functions.

XmToggleButtonGetState() returns True if the ToggleButton is set and False otherwise. The state parameter to XmToggleButtonSetState() can be True to set the ToggleButton and False to unset it. The notify parameter identifies whether the XmNvalueChangedCallback should be invoked (True) or not (False).

```
Boolean XmToggleButtonGetState(widget_id)
void XmToggleButtonSetState(widget_id, state, notify)

Widget  widget_id;
Boolean state;
Boolean notify;
```

Figure 11.28 ToggleButton convenience functions.

Motif Gadgets

◻ Because client programs tend to put a large load on the memory and I/O (input/output) resources of a computer system, X/Motif programmers try to find ways to optimize their applications. OSF has provided one form of optimization through a new class of widgets called *gadgets*. Gadgets are implemented as windowless widgets.

The implementation of the Motif widget set has modified the Intrinsics Core Widget class and subdivided it into three parts: Object, RectObj, and WindowObj. Branching off between the RectObj and WindowObj, from this modified Core class, is the Motif XmGadget class. There are Motif gadgets for an ArrowButton, Separator, Label, CascadeButton, PushButton, and ToggleButton — each of which has a corresponding Motif widget.

The gadgets were created by taking the corresponding widget structure and eliminating some of the members. The gadget does not get its own X windows drawn for it. Instead, it is drawn as a graphics object on its parent and shares its parent's X windows.

The resources that were "lost" by the gadget are gained from its parent. This has two implications:

1. Gadgets will provide much of the same functionality as the corresponding widget, but you will get a dramatic performance improvement. The gadget will give your client a quicker startup time, smaller executable object program size, as well as faster execution speed.

2. Gadgets do not have the ability to support some features that widgets support easily. Gadgets cannot have popup children, translations and actions defined on them (which we haven't talked about), or their own visual resources (foreground, background, top shadow color, bottom shadow color, and so on).

Figure 11.29 shows the resource sets for the Object, RectObj, and WindowObj widget classes. Gadgets will inherit from the Object and the RectObj but *not* from the WindowObj — Gadgets do not have their own X windows.

Gadgets are usually used in menus and dialog boxes. In general, X/Motif application programmers will use gadgets unless there is an overriding reason not to. If, for example, a button must have a different background color than its parent, you are forced to use a widget. Figure 11.30 shows the resource set for the XmGadget class. Notice that there are no color resources for gadgets.

Motif PushButtonGadget

◻ The PushButtonGadget issues commands within an X/Motif client application. The visual appearance consists of a text label or an icon surrounded by a border shadow. When the user interacts with the gadget, the border shadow moves to give the appearance that the button has been pressed in.

```
                                   Object

Name                     Type (Default Value)                    Access
------------------------ --------------------------------------- ------

XmNdestroyCallback       XtCallbackList (NULL)                   C


                                   RectObj

Name                     Type (Default Value)                    Access
------------------------ --------------------------------------- ------

XmNancestorSensitive     Boolean (True)                          G
XmNborderWidth           Dimension (1)                           CSG
XmNheight                Dimension (0)                           CSG
XmNsensitive             Boolean (True)                          CSG
XmNwidth                 Dimension (0)                           CSG
XmNx                     Position (0)                            CSG
XmNy                     Position (0)                            CSG


                                  WindowObj

Name                     Type (Default Value)                    Access
------------------------ --------------------------------------- ------

XmNaccelerators          XtTranslations (NULL)                   CSG
XmNbackground            Pixel (White)                           CSG
XmNbackgroundPixmap      Pixmap (XmUNSPECIFIED_PIXMAP)            CSG
XmNborderColor           Pixel (Black)                           CSG
XmNborderPixmap          Pixmap (XmUNSPECIFIED_PIXMAP)            CSG
XmNcolormap              Colormap (XtCopyFromParent)             CG
XmNdepth                 int (XtCopyFromParent)                  CG
XmNmappedWhenManaged     Boolean (True)                          CSG
XmNscreen                Pointer (XtCopyScreen)                  CG
XmNtranslations          XtTranslations NULL)                    CSG
```

Figure 11.29 Object, RectObj, and WindowObj resources.

```
Name                     Type (Default Value)                    Access
------------------------ --------------------------------------- ------

XmNhelpCallback          XtCallbackList (NULL)                   C
XmNhighlightOnEnter      Boolean (False)                         CSG
XmNhighlightThickness    short int (0)                           CSG
XmNshadowThickness       short int (2)                           CSG
XmNtraversalOn           Boolean (False)                         CSG
XmNunitType              unsigned char (XmPIXELS)                CSG
XmNuserData              caddr_t (NULL)                          CSG
```

Figure 11.30 XmGadget Resources.

Normally, the user will interact with the gadget using mouse button 1. However, if the gadget resides in a popup menu, then mouse button 3 activates and arms the gadget. This can, of course, be controlled with resources. Figure 11.31 shows the syntax for the XmCreatePushButtonGadget() function.

The PushButtonGadget inherits resources from the Object, RectObj, XmGadget, and XmLabelGadget classes. Its class name is XmPushButtonGadget. Figure 11.32 shows what a PushButtonGadget would look like.

The XmPushButtonGadget class defines a set of resources that are inherited by an instance of a PushButtonGadget. Figure 11.33 lists these new resources and their type and access.

When a callback occurs for a PushButtonGadget for any one of the callback resources listed in Figure 11.33, a pointer to a structure of type XmAnyCallbackStruct is passed as the call_data parameter to the callback function that is invoked in response. The structure has the following members:

```
#include <Xm/PushBG.h>

Widget XmCreatePushButtonGadget(parent_id, instance_name, arg_list, arg_count)

Widget      parent_id;
String      instance_name;
ArgList     arg_list;
Cardinal    arg_count;
```

Figure 11.31 XmCreatePushButtonGadget() syntax.

Figure 11.32 Visual appearance of a PushButtonGadget.

Name	Type (Default Value)	Access
XmNactivateCallback	XtCallbackList (NULL)	C
XmNarmCallback	XtCallbackList (NULL)	C
XmNarmColor	Pixel (dynamic)	CSG
XmNarmPixmap	Pixmap (XmUNSPECIFIED_PIXMAP)	CSG
XmNdisarmCallback	XtCallbackList (NULL)	C
XmNfillOnArm	Boolean (True)	CSG
XmNshowAsDefault	short int (0)	CSG

Figure 11.33 XmPushButtonGadget resources.

```
typedef struct
    {
    int     reason;
    XEvent  *event;
    } XmAnyCallbackStruct;
```

reason   Indicates why the callback was invoked.

event   Pointer to a union of type XEvent which contains information about the actual X event that triggered the callback.

¤   Remember — there are gadget versions of each of the following Motif widgets: ArrowButton, Separator, Label, CascadeButton, PushButton, and ToggleButton. The Motif documentation contains a complete description of their features and resources.

A Complete X/Motif Client Application

¤   Using all the concepts and techniques presented in this chapter, we can put together a simple, but complete, X/Motif-based client application. Example 11.1 shows the code for a program that has a shell widget, a RowColumn widget, and several Primitive widgets in it. The program will wait for an activate or a valueChanged event in one of the Primitive widgets and print a message in response. This is similar to examples from the previous chapters; however, it uses many of the Primitive widgets described in this chapter.

Example 11.3 shows what the resource file for the previous program would look like. Note that these resource specifications could go in a $HOME/.Xdefaults file, a file called Edit in a directory pointed to by the $XAPPLRESDIR environment variable, a file pointed to by the $XENVIRONMENT environment variable, or any number of other places that resource files can exist. Notice how the class name for the application is being used as the first element in each resource specification instead of the application instance name. Figure 11.34 shows what the program would look like on a typical terminal screen.

Exercises

¤   The following exercises are designed to give you the opportunity to practice the concepts and facilities presented in this chapter:

1. Create an X/Motif client application that uses a RowColumn widget to manage five Label widgets. Each one of the XmNlabelStrings for the individual Labels should be specified as the following:

```c
#include <stdio.h>
#include <Xm/RowColumn.h>
#include <Xm/ArrowB.h>
#include <Xm/CascadeB.h>
#include <Xm/DrawnB.h>
#include <Xm/Label.h>
#include <Xm/ScrollBar.h>
#include <Xm/Separator.h>
#include <Xm/ToggleB.h>

Widget topShell;
XtCallbackProc WidgetInteraction();

main(argc, argv)
Cardinal argc;
String argv[];
    {
    Widget rcMgr, myPrimitives[7];

    /* Initialize  the Intrinsics and create a top Shell widget */
    topShell = XtInitialize(argv[0], "Edit", NULL, 0, &argc, argv);

    /* Create the manager widget */
    rcMgr = XmCreateRowColumn(topShell, "rcMgr", NULL, 0);

    /* Create the user interface widgets */
    myPrimitives[0] = XmCreateArrowButton(rcMgr, "arw_btn", NULL, 0);
    myPrimitives[1] = XmCreateCascadeButton(rcMgr, "csc_btn", NULL, 0);
    myPrimitives[2] = XmCreateDrawnButton(rcMgr, "drw_btn", NULL, 0);
    myPrimitives[3] = XmCreateLabel(rcMgr, "label", NULL, 0);
    myPrimitives[4] = XmCreateScrollBar(rcMgr, "scr_bar", NULL, 0);
    myPrimitives[5] = XmCreateSeparator(rcMgr, "separator", NULL, 0);
    myPrimitives[6] = XmCreateToggleButton(rcMgr, "tog_btn", NULL, 0);

    /* Set up callbacks for the widgets */
    XtAddCallback(myPrimitives[0],
        XmNactivateCallback, WidgetInteraction, NULL);
    XtAddCallback(myPrimitives[1],
        XmNactivateCallback, WidgetInteraction, NULL);
    XtAddCallback(myPrimitives[2],
        XmNactivateCallback, WidgetInteraction, NULL);
    XtAddCallback(myPrimitives[4],
        XmNvalueChangedCallback, WidgetInteraction, NULL);
    XtAddCallback(myPrimitives[6],
        XmNvalueChangedCallback, WidgetInteraction, NULL);
```

Example 11.1 X/Motif application program with different primitive widgets, part 1.

```
    /* Make the program visible on the screen */
    XtManageChild(rcMgr);
    XtManageChildren(myPrimitives, XtNumber(myPrimitives));
    XtRealizeWidget(topShell);

    /* Wait for input events */
    XtMainLoop();
    }

XtCallbackProc WidgetInteraction(widget_id, client_data, call_data)
Widget widget_id;
caddr_t client_data;
caddr_t call_data;
    {

    /* Print something on the screen */
    printf("You just interacted with one of my widgets...\n");
    sleep(3);

    /* Return control to the operating system */
    return;
    }
```

Example 11.2 X/Motif application program with different primitive widgets, part 2.

```
Edit.rcMgr.arw_btn.arrowDirection:   arrow_down
Edit.rcMgr.csc_btn.labelString:      This is a CascadeButton
Edit.rcMgr.drw_btn.labelType:        pixmap
Edit.rcMgr.drw_btn.labelPixmap:      /usr/include/X11/bitmaps/xlogo32
Edit.rcMgr.label.labelString:        This is a Label
Edit.rcMgr.scr_bar.orientation:      horizontal
Edit.rcMgr.separator.separatorType:  shadow_etched_out
Edit.rcMgr.separator.height:         10
Edit.rcMgr.tog_btn.labelString:      This is a ToggleButton
Edit.rcMgr.tog_btn.set:              true
```

Example 11.3 Resource file for the previous X/Motif application program.

```
        Last Name
        First Name
        Age
        Salary
        Title
```

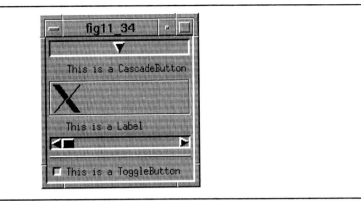

Figure 11.34 Output of the previous X/Motif application program.

Have the label text right justified within each Label widget.

2. Change the previous exercise to use Label gadgets instead of Label widgets.

3. Create an X/Motif client application that uses a RowColumn widget to manage four ArrowButton widgets. Have each of the ArrowButtons point in different directions: up, right, down, and left. Code one or more callback functions that will be invoked for the XmNactivateCallback on the buttons. Have the callback functions print a message that describes which button was pressed.

4. Create an X/Motif client application that uses a RowColumn widget to manage five ToggleButton widgets. Have the XmNlabelString resources for the individual ToggleButtons set to:

        Sight
        Sound
        Touch
        Smell
        Taste

    Code one or more callback functions for the XmNvalueChangedCallback on the ToggleButtons that prints a message describing which ToggleButton has changed state.

5. Change the previous exercise so that the RowColumn widget's XmNradioBehavior resource is set to True. Modify the callback function(s) for the ToggleButtons to access the call_data parameter to retrieve the state of the ToggleButton. Have the message printed from the callback function indicate the current state of the button.

6. Create an X/Motif client application that contains a List widget. The list widget will contain five items:

```
Apple
Banana
Kiwi
Peach
Pear
```

The following resources must be set for the List widget:

```
XmNitemCount                   5
XmNvisibleItemCount            5
XmNitems                       an array of compound strings
```

The XmNitems resource is a pointer to (the address of) an array of compound strings. Each compound string is created with XmString-CreateLtoR() and contains one of the fruit names specified above.

7. Change the previous exercise so that the List's XmNselectionPolicy is set to XmSINGLE_SELECT. Add a callback to the List widget's XmNsingleSelectionCallback list to invoke a function when a list item is selected. Using the call_data parameter to the callback function, print a message that displays the item member from the structure to indicate which item was selected from the list.

Motif
Manager
Widgets

Introduction

◻   The Motif widget set provides more than just a number of user interface, or primitive, widgets. Several types of *manager* widgets are also available to provide a variety of different *layout policies* for the other widgets in your program. If you are constructing a Motif application that contains several other user interface widgets, you will need one of these manager widgets to control the position of the other widgets on the screen.

Objectives

◻   After completing this chapter, you will be able to:

  ◻   Use the Motif BulletinBoard widget.
  ◻   Use the Motif DrawingArea widget.
  ◻   Use the Motif Frame widget.
  ◻   Use the Motif PanedWindow widget.
  ◻   Use the Motif Scale widget.
  ◻   Use the Motif ScrolledWindow widget.

Manager Widget Concepts

◻ Motif manager widgets are the widgets that hold the user interface components of an X/Motif-based program together. These widgets are the ones that control the layout of the primitive widgets in your application and give it its own distinctive appearance. When an X/Motif program needs to use more than one primitive widget for its operation, you will be using one of these manager widgets.

There are widgets that allow you to organize primitive widgets in an X/Y-coordinate system (BulletinBoard widget), perform graphics operations (DrawingArea widget), draw attention to an area in your application with a distinctive border (Frame widget), manage a number of other widgets in individually resizable window panes (PanedWindow widget), choose a numeric value from within an allowable range (Scale widget), and provide a scrollable viewport over a larger work area (ScrolledWindow widget).

The following sections define these manager widgets and their creation functions, resources, and callback data structures. For more detailed information about possible resource values, resource class information, and so on, please consult your Motif reference documentation.

Motif BulletinBoard

◻ The BulletinBoard widget is a composite widget that has a very simple layout policy for its children. All children are placed within an X/Y-coordinate system whose origin is the upper-left-hand corner of the BulletinBoard. The BulletinBoard will size itself so that all of its managed children will be completely visible.

All Motif dialog boxes are implemented with a BulletinBoard. There are a number of resources and callbacks that are particularly useful in both modal and modeless dialog boxes. Figure 12.1 shows the syntax for the XmCreateBulletinBoard() function.

The BulletinBoard widget inherits resources from the Core, Composite, Constraint, and XmManager widget classes. Its class name is XmBulletinBoard. Although there are no specific visual attributes to a BulletinBoard, Figure 12.2 shows what an application that uses a BulletinBoard would look like.

The XmBulletinBoard widget class defines a set of resources that are inherited by an instance of a BulletinBoard widget. Figure 12.3 lists these new resources and their type and access.

```
#include <Xm/BulletinB.h>

Widget XmCreateBulletinBoard(parent_id, instance_name, arg_list, arg_count)

Widget      parent_id;
String      instance_name;
ArgList     arg_list;
Cardinal    arg_count;
```

Figure 12.1 XmCreateBulletinBoard() syntax.

Figure 12.2 Visual appearance of a BulletinBoard widget.

Name	Type (Default Value)	Access
XmNallowOverlap	Boolean (True)	CSG
XmNautoUnmanage	Boolean (True)	CSG
XmNbuttonFontList	XmFontList (NULL)	CSG
XmNcancelButton	Widget (NULL)	SG
XmNdefaultButton	Widget (NULL)	SG
XmNdefaultPosition	Boolean (True)	CSG
XmNdialogStyle	unsigned char (dynamic)	CSG
XmNdialogTitle	XmString (NULL)	CSG
XmNfocusCallback	XtCallbackList (NULL)	C
XmNlabelFontList	XmFontList (NULL)	CSG
XmNmapCallback	XtCallbackList (NULL)	C
XmNmarginHeight	short int (10)	CSG
XmNmarginWidth	short int (10)	CSG
XmNnoResize	Boolean (False)	CSG
XmNresizePolicy	unsigned char (XmRESIZE_ANY)	CSG
XmNshadowType	unsigned char (XmSHADOW_OUT)	CSG
XmNstringDirection	XmStringDirection (XmSTRING_DIRECTION_L_TO_R)	CSG
XmNtextFontList	XmFontList (NULL)	CSG
XmNtextTranslations	XtTranslations (NULL)	C
XmNunmapCallback	XtCallbackList (NULL)	C

Figure 12.3 XmBulletinBoard resources.

When a callback occurs for a BulletinBoard widget for any one of the callback resources listed in Figure 12.3, a pointer to a structure of type XmAnyCallbackStruct is passed as the call_data parameter to the callback function that is invoked in response. The structure has the following members:

```
typedef struct
    {
    int     reason;
    XEvent  *event;
    } XmAnyCallbackStruct;
```

reason   Indicates why the callback was invoked.

event   Pointer to a union of type XEvent which contains information
            about the actual X event that triggered the callback.

Motif DrawingArea

◻   The DrawingArea widget is an empty widget that can be used for a variety
    of graphics or drawing operations. It does not do any drawing itself but
    instead defines a number of callbacks that can be used for drawing pur-
    poses. Callbacks are defined to notify the application that it needs to draw
    something and when the widget receives input from the keyboard or mouse.

    Although the DrawingArea widget is a composite and manager widget, it
    has a very minimal layout policy for any children you may define (similar to
    the BulletinBoard). Its primary purpose is to be a blank slate for you to
    scribble in. Figure 12.4 shows the syntax for the XmCreateDrawingArea()
    function.

    The DrawingArea widget inherits resources from the Core, Composite,
    Constraint, and XmManager widget classes. Its class name is XmDrawing-
    Area. Although there are no specific visual attributes to a DrawingArea,
    Figure 12.5 shows what an application that uses a DrawingArea would look
    like.

    The XmDrawingArea widget class defines a set of resources that are
    inherited by an instance of a DrawingArea widget. Figure 12.6 lists these
    new resources and their type and access.

    When a callback occurs for an DrawingArea widget for any one of the call-
    back resources listed in Figure 12.6, a pointer to a structure of type
    XmDrawingAreaCallbackStruct is passed as the call_data parameter to the
    callback function that is invoked in response. The structure has the follow-
    ing members:

```
typedef struct
    {
    int      reason;
    XEvent   *event;
    Window   window;
    } XmDrawingAreaCallbackStruct;
```

```
#include <Xm/DrawingA.h>

Widget XmCreateDrawingArea(parent_id, instance_name, arg_list, arg_count)

Widget      parent_id;
String      instance_name;
ArgList     arg_list;
Cardinal    arg_count;
```

Figure 12.4 XmCreateDrawingArea() syntax.

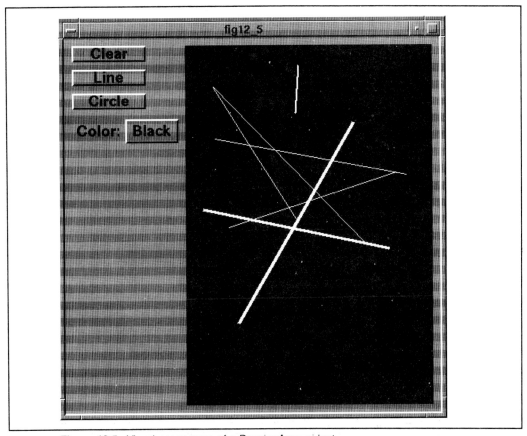

Figure 12.5 Visual appearance of a DrawingArea widget.

Name	Type (Default Value)	Access
XmNexposeCallback	XtCallbackList (NULL)	C
XmNinputCallback	XtCallbackList (NULL)	C
XmNmarginHeight	short int (10)	CSG
XmNmarginWidth	short int (10)	CSG
XmNresizeCallback	XtCallbackList (NULL)	C
XmNresizePolicy	unsigned char (XmRESIZE_ANY)	CSG

Figure 12.6 XmDrawingArea resources.

reason   Indicates why the callback was invoked.

event   Pointer to a union of type XEvent which contains information about the actual X event that triggered the callback.

window   Window id of the widget in which the callback occurred.

Motif Frame

◻   The Frame widget is a very simple manager widget that is used to enclose a single child widget in a graphic visual frame. It uses XmManager class resources for the drawing of the frame and always resizes itself to match the size of its child plus the margins defined for the Frame.

The Frame widget is usually used to enclose another manager widget when you need the manager to have the same border appearance as the other primitive widgets used in the program. The Frame can also be used to enclose a single primitive widget when you want to make it stand out from the other primitive widgets or draw attention to it. Figure 12.7 shows the syntax for the XmCreateFrame() function.

The Frame widget inherits resources from the Core, Composite, Constraint, and XmManager widget classes. Its class name is XmFrame. Figure 12.8 shows what a Frame widget would look like.

The XmFrame widget class defines a set of resources that are inherited by an instance of a Frame widget. Figure 12.9 lists these new resources and their type and access.

There are no callbacks defined for a Frame widget.

```
#include <Xm/Frame.h>

Widget XmCreateFrame(parent_id, instance_name, arg_list, arg_count)

Widget      parent_id;
String      instance_name;
ArgList     arg_list;
Cardinal    arg_count;
```

Figure 12.7 XmCreateFrame() syntax.

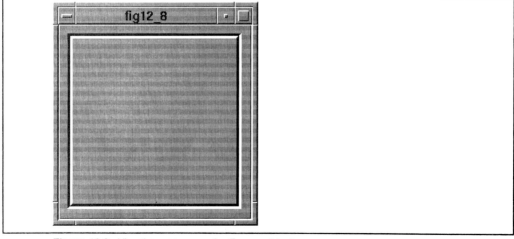

Figure 12.8 Visual appearance of a Frame widget.

```
Name                                Type (Default Value)                      Access
---------------------------------   ------------------------------------      ------
XmNmarginHeight                     short int (10)                            CSG
XmNmarginWidth                      short int (10)                            CSG
XmNshadowType                       unsigned char (XmSHADOW_ETCHED_IN)        CSG
```

Figure 12.9 XmFrame resources.

Motif PanedWindow

¤   The PanedWindow widget is a composite manager widget that lays its children out in a series of vertical window panes. The children of the PanedWindow will appear in the order they are created from top to bottom. The PanedWindow will resize itself to match the width of its widest child and all other children will be forced to the same width. The height of the PanedWindow will be the sum of the heights of its children, plus the amount of spacing between them and their top and bottom margins.

The user can adjust the size of the window panes for each child individually. Each child window will have a sash which can be manipulated with the mouse to vary the child's height. The sash will appear as a small box below and to the right of the child it controls. With the mouse pointer positioned in the sash, pressing mouse button 1, holding it down, and dragging the mouse, will resize the child.

The PanedWindow is also a Constraint widget. This means that there are PanedWindow resources that are not applied to a PanedWindow widget. Instead, the Constraint resources are applied to the children of the PanedWindow and are used to constrain the layout of the children in some way. For the PanedWindow the Constraint resources constrain the size of its children.

The PanedWindow will not allow any of its children to be resized greater than their Constraint maximum size. Also, the PanedWindow will not allow any of its children to be resized less than their Constraint minimum size. If the Constraint minimum and Constraint maximum sizes are the same, the PanedWindow will not display a sash for that child window, and it cannot be resized. Figure 12.10 shows the syntax for the XmCreatePanedWindow() function.

```
#include <Xm/PanedW.h>

Widget XmCreatePanedWindow(parent_id, instance_name, arg_list, arg_count)

Widget      parent_id;
String      instance_name;
ArgList     arg_list;
Cardinal    arg_count;
```

Figure 12.10 XmCreatePanedWindow() syntax.

The PanedWindow widget inherits resources from the Core, Composite, Constraint, and XmManager widget classes. Its class name is XmPanedWindow. Figure 12.11 shows what a PanedWindow widget would look like.

The XmPanedWindow widget class defines a set of resources that are inherited by an instance of a PanedWindow widget. Figure 12.12 lists these new resources and their type and access.

There are no callbacks defined for a PanedWindow widget.

Motif Scale

The Scale widget is a composite widget that is used like a primitive widget. It is used to select a single value from a range of possibilities. The Scale can be used as an input/output widget which the application's user can interact with or as an output only widget (through the XmNsensitive resource) that the application uses to display a value.

The Scale is implemented as a composite widget so that it can have children widgets that it will manage. The Scale supports one or more Label widgets or gadgets as children which will be displayed to one side of the Scale and can be used as "tick marks." The Labels are then used to indicate a relative value at various positions along the Scale. Figure 12.13 shows the syntax for the XmCreateScale() function.

The Scale widget inherits resources from the Core, Composite, Constraint, and XmManager widget classes. Its class name is XmScale. The Scale widget is similar in appearance and operation to the ScrollBar widget. The main difference is that there are no ArrowButtons on the ends. The Scale can have a title and has the ability to display the current value of the Scale within its range. Figure 12.14 shows what a a Scale would look like.

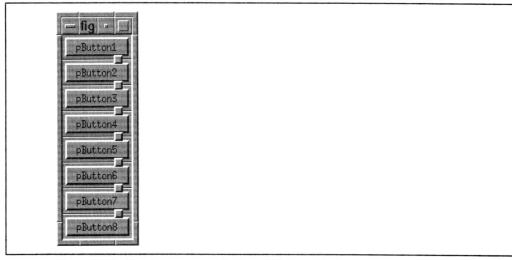

Figure 12.11 Visual appearance of a PanedWindow widget.

```
                        PanedWindow Resources


Name                            Type (Default Value)              Access
------------------------------  --------------------------------  ------
XmNmarginHeight                 short int (3)                     CSG
XmNmarginWidth                  short int (3)                     CSG
XmNrefigureMode                 Boolean (True)                    CSG
XmNsashHeight                   Dimension (10)                    CSG
XmNsashIndent                   Position (-10)                    CSG
XmNsashShadowThickness          int (2)                           CSG
XmNsashWidth                    Dimension (10)                    CSG
XmNseparatorOn                  Boolean (True)                    CSG
XmNspacing                      int (8)                           CSG



                   PanedWindow Constraint Resources


Name                            Type (Default Value)              Access
------------------------------  --------------------------------  ------
XmNallowResize                  Boolean (False)                   CSG
XmNmaximum                      int (1000)                        CSG
XmNminimum                      int (1)                           CSG
XmNskipAdjust                   Boolean (False)                   CSG
```

Figure 12.12 XmPanedWindow resources.

```
#include <Xm/Scale.h>

Widget XmCreateScale(parent_id, instance_name, arg_list, arg_count)

Widget        parent_id;
String        instance_name;
ArgList       arg_list;
Cardinal      arg_count;
```

Figure 12.13 XmCreateScale() syntax.

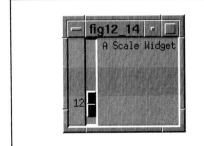

Figure 12.14 Visual appearance of a Scale widget.

The XmScale widget class defines a set of resources that are inherited by an instance of a Scale widget. Figure 12.15 lists these new resources and their type and access.

When a callback occurs for an Scale widget for any one of the callback resources listed in Figure 12.15, a pointer to a structure of type XmScaleCallbackStruct is passed as the call_data parameter to the callback function that is invoked in response. The structure has the following members:

```
typedef struct
    {
    int      reason;
    XEvent   *event;
    int      value;
    } XmScaleCallbackStruct;
```

reason   Indicates why the callback was invoked.

event   Pointer to a union of type XEvent which contains information about the actual X event that triggered the callback.

value   The new slider location value.

There are two convenience functions that can be used to interact with a Scale. XmScaleGetValue() retrieves the current numeric value of a Scale while XmScaleSetValue() sets the numeric value of a Scale. Figure 12.16 shows the syntax for these two functions.

Name	Type (Default Value)	Access
XmNdecimalPoints	short int (0)	CSG
XmNdragCallback	XtCallbackList (NULL)	C
XmNfontList	XmFontList ("Fixed");	CSG
XmNhighlightOnEnter	Boolean (False)	CSG
XmNhighlightThickness	short int (0)	CSG
XmNmaximum	int (100)	CSG
XmNminimum	int (0)	CSG
XmNorientation	unsigned char (XmVERTICAL)	CSG
XmNprocessingDirection	unsigned char (XmMAX_ON_TOP)	CSG
XmNscaleHeight	Dimension (0)	CSG
XmNscaleWidth	Dimension (0)	CSG
XmNshowValue	Boolean (False)	CSG
XmNtitleString	XmString (NULL)	CSG
XmNtraversalOn	Boolean (False)	CSG
XmNvalue	int (0)	CSG
XmNvalueChangedCallback	XtCallbackList (NULL)	C

Figure 12.15 XmScale resources.

```
void XmScaleGetValue(widget_id, value_rtn)
void XmScaleSetValue(widget_id, value)

Widget  widget_id;
int     *value_rtn;
int     value;
```

Figure 12.16 Scale convenience functions.

Motif ScrolledWindow

◻   The ScrolledWindow widget is used to provide a small viewport over a
larger work area. It contains areas for one or two ScrollBars and some type
of work area widget. The ScrollBars are used to scroll the viewport over the
larger work area. The work area widget must be created separately by the
application, and its widget id must be installed as a resource in the ScrolledWindow.

The ScrolledWindow can operate in one of two modes. In the automatic
mode the scrolled window will create two scroll bars and a clipping window
for you. As the user interacts with the ScrollBars, the ScrolledWindow will
use the clipping window to display a portion of the application-defined work
area. ScrollBar callbacks are automatically created for you to move the clipping window over the work area.

The second mode might be called the "application-defined" mode. In this
mode the application is responsible for creating the ScrollBars, installing the
widget ids as resources, and setting up its own callbacks for the operation
of the ScrollBars with respect to the work area. The mode you use must be
decided at the time the ScrolledWindow is created and cannot be changed
afterward.

Sometimes it is practical to create a larger work area with a viewport
over it. In a graphics application you may want a large drawing area of
some specific size. In this case the viewport can be used to display the portion that the user is working on now. Sometimes it is impractical to create
a large work area with a viewport over it. In a text editing application you
may have a large quantity of text data stored in a file that you would like
to view 24 lines at a time. In this case you do not want to read all the data
in – you want to read only the data necessary to fill the viewport. Figure
12.17 shows the syntax for the XmCreateScrolledWindow() function.

In the "application-defined" mode you have to create your own child widgets. Once you have the widgets for the ScrolledWindow created, you must
install them into the ScrolledWindow widget. This is accomplished with a
call to the XmScrolledWindowSetAreas() function. This function identifies
which of the children are to be actively managed by the ScrolledWindow. It
also installs the children widget ids into the ScrolledWindow widget. Figure
12.18 shows the syntax for the XmScrolledWindowSetAreas() function.

The first parameter to this function is the widget id of the ScrolledWindow whose areas you want to install your children widget ids in. The
remaining parameters are the widget ids of those children. If you are not

```
#include <Xm/ScrolledW.h>

Widget XmCreateScrolledWindow(parent_id, instance_name, arg_list, arg_count)

Widget        parent_id;
String        instance_name;
ArgList       arg_list;
Cardinal      arg_count;
```

Figure 12.17 XmCreateScrolledWindow() syntax.

```
void XmScrolledWindowSetAreas(widget, h_scroll, v_scroll, work)

Widget        widget;    /* ScrolledWindow widget id        */
Widget        h_scroll;  /* Horizontal ScrollBar widget id  */
Widget        v_scroll;  /* Vertical ScrollBar widget id    */
Widget        work;      /* Work area widget id             */
```

Figure 12.18 XmScrolledWindowSetAreas() syntax.

supplying all three subareas, you can pass NULL as the value for those children that you are not installing in the ScrolledWindow.

The ScrolledWindow widget inherits resources from the Core, Composite, Constraint, and XmManager widget classes. Its class name is XmScrolledWindow. Figure 12.19 shows what an application that uses a ScrolledWindow would look like.

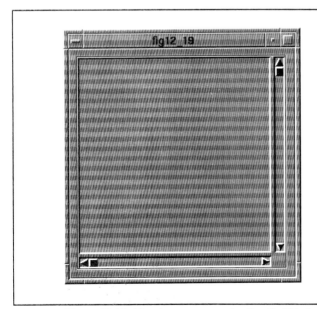

Figure 12.19 Visual appearance of a ScrolledWindow widget.

The XmScrolledWindow widget class defines a set of resources that are inherited by an instance of a ScrolledWindow widget. Figure 12.20 lists these new resources and their type and access.

There are no callbacks defined for a ScrolledWindow widget. When operating in either mode, the application must set up its own callbacks for the ScrollBar widgets if it wants to be notified of user input.

ScrolledWindow Extensions

▫ Motif provides two additional functions that create a ScrolledWindow. These two functions are convenience functions that are actually used to create a Primitive widget with the ScrolledWindow as its parent. In both cases the ScrolledWindow is used to provide a small viewport over a larger display area in the Primitive widget..

▫ The XmCreateScrolledList() function creates an instance of a List widget with a ScrolledWindow as its parent. The function returns the widget id of the child List widget. Figure 12.21 shows the syntax for the XmCreate-ScrolledList() function.

```
Name                                  Type (Default Value)                      Access
-----------------------------------   ------------------------------------      ------

XmNclipWindow                         Widget (NULL)                             G
XmNhorizontalScrollBar                Widget (NULL)                             CSG
XmNscrollBarDisplayPolicy             unsigned char (XmSTATIC)                  CG
XmNscrollBarPlacement                 unsigned char (XmBOTTOM_RIGHT)            CSG
XmNscrolledWindowMarginHeight         Dimension (0)                            CSG
XmNscrolledWindowMarginWidth          Dimension (0)                            CSG
XmNscrollingPolicy                    unsigned char (XmAPPLICATION_DEFINED)    CG
XmNspacing                            Dimension (4)                            CSG
XmNverticalScrollBar                  Widget (NULL)                             CSG
XmNvisualPolicy                       unsigned char (XmVARIABLE)                CG
XmNworkWindow                         Widget (NULL)                             CSG
```

Figure 12.20 XmScrolledWindow resources.

```
#include <Xm/List.h>


Widget XmCreateScrolledList(parent_id, instance_name, arg_list, arg_count)

Widget      parent_id;
String      instance_name;
ArgList     arg_list;
Cardinal    arg_count;
```

Figure 12.21 XmCreateScrolledList() syntax.

    ☐   The XmCreateScrolledText() function creates an instance of a Text widget with a ScrolledWindow as its parent. The function returns the widget id of the child Text widget. Figure 12.22 shows the syntax for the XmCreate-ScrolledText() function.

    ☐   If you need to get the widget id of the ScrolledWindow parent widget in either one of these composite widgets, you must use the XtParent() function. The parent widget id would be needed in those cases where you wanted to attach the scrolled composite widget to some other type of manager widget. The function takes the child widget id as a parameter and returns the child's parent widget id. Figure 12.23 shows the syntax for the XtParent() function.

A Complete X/Motif Client Application

    ☐   Using all the concepts and techniques presented in this chapter, we can put together a simple, but complete, X/Motif-based client application. Example 12.1 shows the code for a program that has a shell widget, a Bulletin-Board widget, and several other Manager and Primitive widgets in it. The program will wait for an activate event in the last PushButton of the PanedWindow then print a message and exit in response. This is similar to examples from the previous chapters; however, it uses many of the Manager widgets described in this chapter.

    Example 12.3 shows what the resource file for the previous program would look like. Note that these resource specifications could go in a $HOME/.Xdefaults file, a file called Edit in a directory pointed to by the $XAPPLRESDIR environment variable, a file pointed to by the $XENVIRONMENT environment variable, or any number of other places that resource files can exist. Notice how the class name for the application is being used as the first element in each resource specification instead of the application instance name. Figure 12.24 shows what the program would look like on a typical terminal screen.

```
#include <Xm/Text.h>

Widget XmCreateScrolledText(parent_id, instance_name, arg_list, arg_count)

Widget        parent_id;
String        instance_name;
ArgList       arg_list;
Cardinal      arg_count;
```

Figure 12.22 XmCreateScrolledText() syntax.

```
Widget XtParent(child_id)

Widget        child_id;
```

Figure 12.23 XtParent() syntax.

```
#include <stdio.h>
#include <Xm/BulletinB.h>
#include <Xm/PanedW.h>
#include <Xm/PushB.h>
#include <Xm/Frame.h>
#include <Xm/ScrolledW.h>
#include <Xm/DrawingA.h>
#include <Xm/Scale.h>

Widget topShell;
XtCallbackProc ExitButton();

main(argc, argv)
Cardinal argc;
String argv[];
    {
    Widget bBoard, pWindow, pButton[8], frame, sWindow, dArea, scale;
    static char *pbNames[8] = {"pButton1", "pButton2", "pButton3", "pButton4",
                               "pButton5", "pButton6", "pButton7", "pButton8"};
    Arg argList[10];
    Cardinal i;

    /* Initialize  the Intrinsics and create a top Shell widget */
    topShell = XtInitialize(argv[0], "Edit", NULL, 0, &argc, argv);

    /* Create the manager widget */
    bBoard = XmCreateBulletinBoard(topShell, "bBoard", NULL, 0);

    /* Create the user interface widgets */
    pWindow = XmCreatePanedWindow(bBoard, "pWindow", NULL, 0);
    for(i = 0; i < XtNumber(pButton); ++i)
        pButton[i] = XmCreatePushButton(pWindow, pbNames[i], NULL, 0);
    frame = XmCreateFrame(bBoard, "frame", NULL, 0);
    XtSetArg(argList[0], XmNscrollingPolicy, XmAUTOMATIC);
    sWindow = XmCreateScrolledWindow(frame, "sWindow", argList, 1);
    dArea = XmCreateDrawingArea(sWindow, "dArea", NULL, 0);
    scale = XmCreateScale(bBoard, "scale", NULL, 0);

    /* Make the program visible on the screen */
    XtManageChild(bBoard);
    XtManageChild(pWindow);
    XtManageChildren(pButton, XtNumber(pButton));
    XtManageChild(frame);
    XtManageChild(sWindow);
    XtManageChild(dArea);
    XtManageChild(scale);
    XtRealizeWidget(topShell);
```

Example 12.1 X/Motif application program with different manager widgets, part 1.

```
    /* Set up callbacks for the widgets */
    XtAddCallback(
        pButton[XtNumber(pButton) - 1], XmNactivateCallback, ExitButton, NULL);

    /* Wait for input events */
    XtMainLoop();
    }

XtCallbackProc ExitButton(widget_id, client_data, call_data)
Widget widget_id;
caddr_t client_data;
caddr_t call_data;
    {

    /* Print something on the screen */
    printf("You just pressed the last paned button...\n");
    sleep(3);

    /* Return control to the operating system */
    XtCloseDisplay(XtDisplay(topShell));
    exit(0);
    }
```

Example 12.2 X/Motif application program with different manager widgets, part 2.

```
Edit.bBoard.pWindow.x:                      0
Edit.bBoard.pWindow.y:                      0
Edit.bBoard.pWindow.XmPushButton.height:    35
Edit.bBoard.pWindow.XmPushButton.width:     80
Edit.bBoard.frame.x:                        100
Edit.bBoard.frame.y:                        0
Edit.bBoard.frame.height:                   300
Edit.bBoard.frame.width:                    300
Edit.bBoard.frame.sWindow.height:           280
Edit.bBoard.frame.sWindow.width:            280
Edit.bBoard.frame.sWindow.dArea.height:     5000
Edit.bBoard.frame.sWindow.dArea.width:      5000
Edit.bBoard*dArea.backgroundPixmap:         /usr/include/X11/bitmaps/woman
Edit.bBoard.scale.x:                        100
Edit.bBoard.scale.y:                        301
Edit.bBoard.scale.height:                   100
Edit.bBoard.scale.width:                    300
Edit.bBoard.scale.orientation:              horizontal
Edit.bBoard.scale.processingDirection:      max_on_right
Edit.bBoard.scale.showValue:                true
Edit.bBoard.scale.titleString:              A Scale widget
```

Example 12.3 Resource file for the previous X/Motif application program.

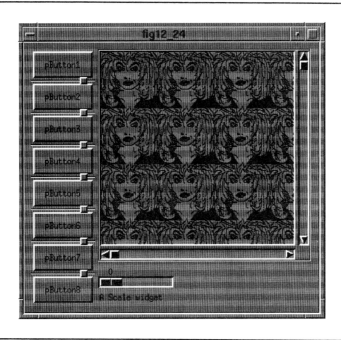

Figure 12.24 Output of the previous X/Motif application program.

Exercises

¤ The following exercises are designed to give you the opportunity to practice the concepts and facilities presented in this chapter:

1. Modify the Exercise from the previous chapter that contained the List widget/fruit list example. Put the List widget and a vertical ScrollBar widget together as children of a BulletinBoard manager. Obtain the height of the List widget and install it as the height of the ScrollBar.

2. Modify the previous Exercise to add 10 more fruit names. Include the following in the List:

Grape	Orange
Lemon	Pineapple
Lime	Plum
Melon	Prune
Nectarine	Strawberry

Connect the ScrollBar to the List widget such that operating the ScrollBar will scroll through the List items. Functions will have to be set up for the increment-, decrement-, pageIncrement-, pageDecrement-, and dragCallbacks on the scrollbar (or, just the valueChanged callback). In the callback functions you can use the XmListSetPos() function to position the list items within the visible portion of the list:

```
#include <Xm/List.h>

/*
 * A List function that makes a specified list item the
 * first visible item in the list.
 */
void XmListSetPos(widget, position);

Widget     widget;     /* Widget id of the List widget to be    */
                       /* positioned                            */
int        position;   /* Array element number of List item to be */
                       /* positioned first in the List.  Number */
                       /* is "1-relative" with 0 meaning bottom. */
```

It is important to notice how the size of the slider contained within the scroll bar can affect the number of items that can be visible in the list. If the slider is too big, you will not be able to view all of the items. If your slider is too small, you may see some empty space at the end of the list.

3. Modify the Exercise from a previous chapter that had four ArrowButtons as children of a RowColumn. Change the RowColumn widget into a PanedWindow widget.

4. Write an X/Motif client application program that displays a Scale widget. Set the title of the Scale to "Warp Factor" and the minimum and maximum values to 1 and 10, respectively. Also set the resource needed to show the current value of the Scale with respect to its minimum and maximum.

5. Modify the previous Exercise so that the Scale widget manages 10 Label widgets as children. The label strings on each of the Label widgets should be "10 -" through "1 -," respectively. Make sure the label strings are right justified.

6. Modify the previous Exercise so that the Scale widget is the child of a Frame widget.

```
*pb1.leftAttachment:            attach_form
*pb1.leftOffset:                10
*pb1.topAttachment:             attach_form
*pb1.topOffset:                 10
*pb1.width:                     100
*pb1.height:                    50
!
!*pb2.leftWidget:               specified in source code
!*pb2.topWidget:                specified in source code
*pb2.leftAttachment:            attach_opposite_widget
*pb2.leftOffset:                0
*pb2.topAttachment:             attach_widget
*pb2.topOffset:                 10
*pb2.width:                     100
*pb2.height:                    50
!
!*draw1.leftWidget:             specified in source code
!*draw1.topWidget:              specified in source code
*draw1.leftAttachment:          attach_widget
*draw1.leftOffset:              10
*draw1.topAttachment:           attach_opposite_widget
*draw1.topOffset:               0
*draw1.rightAttachment:         attach_form
*draw1.rightOffset:             10
*draw1.bottomAttachment:        attach_form
*draw1.bottomOffset:            10
```

Figure 14.10 Resource file entries for typical Form attachments, part 1.

Motif MainWindow

◻   The MainWindow widget is a composite manager widget that provides a
standard layout for a typical Motif client application. It defines five
subareas for a menu, a message area, a work area, and two ScrollBars.
The application is responsible for creating the widgets for these subareas
and installing them in the MainWindow itself. You don't have to use all the
subareas in a MainWindow — they are optional.

   The MainWindow is organized so that a MenuBar widget can be installed
across the top with a Text widget right below it. The Text widget is typically used for commands or messages. Below the Text widget the MainWindow provides space for a ScrolledWindow widget. MainWindow is, in fact,
a subclass of ScrolledWindow.

   The MainWindow widget can also create two Separator widgets that provide a visual separation between its three primary components. Figure
14.13 shows the syntax for the XmCreateMainWindow() function.

   The MainWindow widget inherits resources from the Core, Composite,
Constraint, XmManager, and XmScrolledWindow widget classes. Its class
name is XmMainWindow. Figure 14.14 shows what a MainWindow would

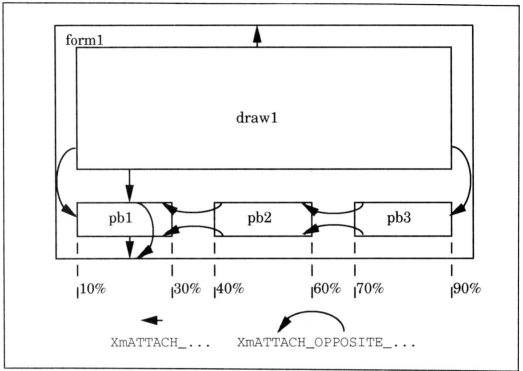

Figure 14.11 Typical Form attachments, part 2.

look like if it was used to construct an OSF/Motif Style Guide-compliant application.

The XmMainWindow widget class defines a set of resources that are inherited by an instance of a MainWindow widget. Figure 14.15 lists these new resources and their type and access.

There are no callbacks defined for a MainWindow widget.

In order to use the MainWindow widget, the application must first create the widgets that will be used in each of the five subareas. Up to five widgets can be created, but none of them are required. Usually you create a MenuBar widget, a Text widget, two ScrollBar widgets, and some type of work area widget such as a DrawingArea, a BulletinBoard, or a Form.

Once you have the widgets for the MainWindow created, you must install them into the MainWindow widget. This is accomplished with a call to the XmMainWindowSetAreas() function. This function identifies which of the children are to be actively managed by the MainWindow. It also installs the children widget ids into the MainWindow widget. Figure 14.16 shows the syntax for the XmMainWindowSetAreas() function.

The first parameter to this function is the widget id of the MainWindow whose areas you want to install your children widget ids in. The remaining parameters are the widget ids of those children. If you are not supplying all five subareas, you can pass NULL as the value for those children that you are not installing in the MainWindow.

```
*form1.width:              360
*form1.height:             250
!
*pb1.leftAttachment:       attach_position
*pb1.leftPosition:         10
*pb1.rightAttachment:      attach_position
*pb1.rightPosition:        30
*pb1.topAttachment:        attach_opposite_form
*pb1.topOffset:            -60
*pb1.bottomAttachment:     attach_form
*pb1.bottomOffset:         10
!
!*pb2.topWidget:           specified in source code
!*pb2.bottomWidget:        specified in source code
*pb2.leftAttachment:       attach_position
*pb2.leftPosition:         40
*pb2.rightAttachment:      attach_position
*pb2.rightPosition:        60
*pb2.topAttachment:        attach_opposite_widget
*pb2.topOffset:            0
*pb2.bottomAttachment:     attach_opposite_widget
*pb2.bottomOffset:         0
!
!*pb3.topWidget:           specified in source code
!*pb3.bottomWidget:        specified in source code
*pb3.leftAttachment:       attach_position
*pb3.leftPosition:         70
*pb3.rightAttachment:      attach_position
*pb3.rightPosition:        90
*pb3.topAttachment:        attach_opposite_widget
*pb3.topOffset:            0
*pb3.bottomAttachment:     attach_opposite_widget
*pb3.bottomOffset:         0
!
!*draw1.leftWidget:        specified in source code
!*draw1.rightWidget:       specified in source code
!*draw1.bottomWidget:      specified in source code
*draw1.leftAttachment:     attach_opposite_widget
*draw1.leftOffset:         0
*draw1.rightAttachment:    attach_opposite_widget
*draw1.rightOffset:        0
*draw1.topAttachment:      attach_form
*draw1.topOffset:          10
*draw1.bottomAttachment:   attach_widget
*draw1.bottomOffset:       10
```

Figure 14.12 Resource file entries for typical Form attachments, part 2.

```
#include <Xm/MainW.h>

Widget XmCreateMainWindow(parent_id, instance_name, arg_list, arg_count)

Widget        parent_id;
String        instance_name;
ArgList       arg_list;
Cardinal      arg_count;
```

Figure 14.13 XmCreateMainWindow() syntax.

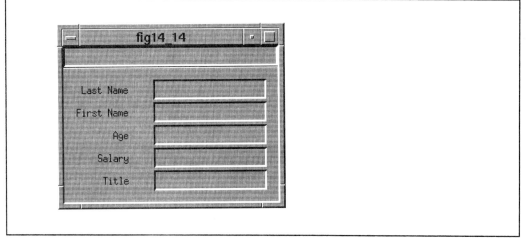

Figure 14.14 Visual appearance of a MainWindow widget.

Name	Type (Default Value)	Access
XmNcommandWindow	Widget (NULL)	CSG
XmNmainWindowMarginHeight	Dimension (0)	CSG
XmNmainWindowMarginWidth	Dimension (0)	CSG
XmNmenuBar	Widget (NULL)	CSG
XmNshowSeparator	Boolean (False)	CSG

Figure 14.15 XmMainWindow resources.

Defined Widget Resource Values

◻   In the discussion of all the different widgets over the last four chapters, we
have seen many different resource sets where one or more of the resources
have used a defined name for their value. To keep the discussion of the

```
#include <Xm/MainW.h>

void XmMainWindowSetAreas(widget, menu, command, h_scroll, v_scroll, work)

Widget      widget;    /* MainWindow widget id          */
Widget      menu;      /* MenuBar widget id             */
Widget      command;   /* Text command area widget id   */
Widget      h_scroll;  /* Horizontal ScrollBar widget id */
Widget      v_scroll;  /* Vertical ScrollBar widget id  */
Widget      work;      /* Work area widget id           */
```

Figure 14.16 XmMainWindowSetAreas() syntax.

individual widgets clear, simple, and to the point we avoided listing these
defined resource values except where it was absolutely necessary for the
understanding of the operation of the widget. In this section (at the end of
the discussion of all of the OSF/Motif widgets) we are going to rectify the
omission.

For example, the ArrowButton widget has an XmNarrowDirection
resource that is set to XmARROW__UP by default; the DrawnButton
widget has an XmNshadowType resource that is set to XmSHADOW__-
ETCHED__IN by default; and, the ScrollBar widget has an XmNprocessingDirection resource that is set to XmMAX__ON__BOTTOM by default.
What other values can these and other resource values take on?

In the file /usr/include/Xm/Xm.h, OSF has defined a number of different
names that can be used for these and other resources on many different
widgets. In Figures 14.17 and 14.18 these resource values have been sum-
marized and alphabetized on a per-widget basis for your easy reference.
The defined names are very descriptive and you will be able to immediately
identify which values go with which resources.

A Complete X/Motif Client Application

□ Using all the concepts and techniques presented in this chapter, we can put
together a simple, but complete, X/Motif-based client application. Example 14.1 shows the code for a program that has a shell widget and a Form
widget in it. The program has a variety of other widgets installed as children of the form. There is no provision for exit.

Example 14.2 shows what the resource file for the previous program
would look like. Note that these resource specifications could go in a
$HOME/.Xdefaults file, a file called Edit in a directory pointed to by the
$XAPPLRESDIR environment variable, a file pointed to by the $XEN-
VIRONMENT environment variable, or any number of other places that
resource files can exist. Notice how the class name for the application is
being used as the first element in each resource specification instead of the
application instance name. Figure 14.19 shows what the program would
look like on a typical terminal screen.

```
Pixmap defined names:                     XmATTACH_POSITION
    XmUNSPECIFIED_PIXMAP                   XmATTACH_SELF
                                          XmATTACH_WIDGET
Compound string defined names:            XmRESIZE_ANY
    XmSTRING_COMPONENT_CHARSET            XmRESIZE_GROW
    XmSTRING_COMPONENT_DIRECTION          XmRESIZE_NONE
    XmSTRING_COMPONENT_END            ArrowButton defined names:
    XmSTRING_COMPONENT_SEPARATOR          XmARROW_DOWN
    XmSTRING_COMPONENT_TEXT               XmARROW_LEFT
    XmSTRING_COMPONENT_UNKNOWN            XmARROW_RIGHT
    XmSTRING_COMPONENT_USER_BEGIN         XmARROW_UP
    XmSTRING_COMPONENT_USER_END       Separator defined names:
    XmSTRING_COMPOUND_STRING              XmDOUBLE_DASHED_LINE
    XmSTRING_DEFAULT_CHARSET              XmDOUBLE_LINE
    XmSTRING_DIRECTION_L_TO_R             XmNO_LINE
    XmSTRING_DIRECTION_R_TO_L             XmPIXMAP
Size policy defined names:                XmSHADOW_ETCHED_IN
    XmCHANGE_ALL                          XmSHADOW_ETCHED_OUT
    XmCHANGE_HEIGHT                       XmSINGLE_DASHED_LINE
    XmCHANGE_NONE                         XmSINGLE_LINE
    XmCHANGE_WIDTH                        XmSTRING
Unit type defined names:              ScrollBar defined names:
    Xm1000TH_INCHES                       XmMAX_ON_BOTTOM
    Xm100TH_FONT_UNITS                    XmMAX_ON_LEFT
    Xm100TH_MILLIMETERS                   XmMAX_ON_RIGHT
    Xm100TH_POINTS                        XmMAX_ON_TOP
    XmPIXELS                          List defined names:
RowColumn defined names:                  XmBROWSE_SELECT
    XmHORIZONTAL                          XmDYNAMIC
    XmMENU_BAR                            XmEXTENDED_SELECT
    XmMENU_OPTION                         XmMULTIPLE_SELECT
    XmMENU_POPUP                          XmSINGLE_SELECT
    XmMENU_PULLDOWN                       XmSTATIC
    XmNO_ORIENTATION                  ScrolledWindow defined names:
    XmNO_PACKING                          XmAPPLICATION_DEFINED
    XmPACK_COLUMN                         XmAS_NEEDED
    XmPACK_NONE                           XmAUTOMATIC
    XmPACK_TIGHT                          XmBOTTOM_LEFT
    XmVERTICAL                            XmBOTTOM_RIGHT
    XmWORK_AREA                           XmCONSTANT
ToggleButton defined names:               XmRESIZE_IF_POSSIBLE
    XmN_OF_MANY                           XmSTATIC
    XmONE_OF_MANY                         XmTOP_LEFT
Form defined names:                       XmTOP_RIGHT
    XmATTACH_FORM                         XmVARIABLE
    XmATTACH_NONE                     Text defined names:
    XmATTACH_OPPOSITE_FORM                XmMULTI_LINE_EDIT
    XmATTACH_OPPOSITE_WIDGET              XmSINGLE_LINE_EDIT
```

Figure 14.17 Defined names for Motif resource values, part 1

```
Label defined names:                      Callback reason defined names:
    XmALIGNMENT_BEGINNING                     XmCR_ACTIVATE
    XmALIGNMENT_CENTER                        XmCR_APPLY
    XmALIGNMENT_END                           XmCR_ARM
Dialog box defined names:                     XmCR_BROWSE_SELECT
    XmDIALOG_APPLICATION_MODAL                XmCR_CANCEL
    XmDIALOG_APPLY_BUTTON                     XmCR_CASCADING
    XmDIALOG_CANCEL_BUTTON                    XmCR_CLIPBOARD_DATA_DELETE
    XmDIALOG_COMMAND                          XmCR_CLIPBOARD_DATA_REQUEST
    XmDIALOG_COMMAND_TEXT                     XmCR_COMMAND_CHANGED
    XmDIALOG_DEFAULT_BUTTON                   XmCR_COMMAND_ENTERED
    XmDIALOG_ERROR                            XmCR_DECREMENT
    XmDIALOG_FILE_SELECTION                   XmCR_DEFAULT_ACTION
    XmDIALOG_FILTER_LABEL                     XmCR_DISARM
    XmDIALOG_FILTER_TEXT                      XmCR_DRAG
    XmDIALOG_HELP_BUTTON                      XmCR_EXECUTE
    XmDIALOG_HISTORY_LIST                     XmCR_EXPOSE
    XmDIALOG_INFORMATION                      XmCR_EXTENDED_SELECT
    XmDIALOG_LIST                             XmCR_FOCUS
    XmDIALOG_LIST_LABEL                       XmCR_HELP
    XmDIALOG_MESSAGE                          XmCR_INCREMENT
    XmDIALOG_MESSAGE_LABEL                    XmCR_INPUT
    XmDIALOG_MODELESS                         XmCR_LOSING_FOCUS
    XmDIALOG_NONE                             XmCR_MAP
    XmDIALOG_OK_BUTTON                        XmCR_MODIFYING_TEXT_VALUE
    XmDIALOG_PROMPT                           XmCR_MOVING_INSERT_CURSOR
    XmDIALOG_PROMPT_LABEL                     XmCR_MULTIPLE_SELECT
    XmDIALOG_QUESTION                         XmCR_NONE
    XmDIALOG_SELECTION                        XmCR_NO_MATCH
    XmDIALOG_SELECTION_LABEL                  XmCR_OK
    XmDIALOG_SEPARATOR                        XmCR_PAGE_DECREMENT
    XmDIALOG_SYMBOL_LABEL                     XmCR_PAGE_INCREMENT
    XmDIALOG_SYSTEM_MODAL                     XmCR_RESIZE
    XmDIALOG_TEXT                             XmCR_SINGLE_SELECT
    XmDIALOG_VALUE_TEXT                       XmCR_TO_BOTTOM
    XmDIALOG_WARNING                          XmCR_TO_TOP
    XmDIALOG_WORKING                          XmCR_UNMAP
    XmDIALOG_WORK_AREA                        XmCR_VALUE_CHANGED
```

Figure 14.18 Defined names for Motif resource values, part 2

Exercises

◻ The following exercises are designed to give you the opportunity to practice
the concepts and facilities presented in this chapter:

1. Create an X/Motif client application that uses a Form widget to manage
the layout of several children. The children will include three

```c
#include <stdio.h>
#include <Xm/Form.h>
#include <Xm/RowColumn.h>
#include <Xm/DrawingA.h>
#include <Xm/PushB.h>
#include <Xm/ToggleB.h>

Widget topShell;

main(argc, argv)
Cardinal argc;
String argv[];
    {
    Widget form, rcLeft, rcRight, draw, ltButton[4], rtButton[4];
    static char *ltbNames[4]={"ltButton1","ltButton2","ltButton3","ltButton4"};
    static char *rtbNames[4]={"rtButton1","rtButton2","rtButton3","rtButton4"};
    Arg argList[10];
    Cardinal i;

    /* Initialize  the Intrinsics and create a top Shell widget */
    topShell = XtInitialize(argv[0], "Edit", NULL, 0, &argc, argv);

    /* Create the manager widget */
    form = XmCreateForm(topShell, "form", NULL, 0);

    /* Create the user interface widgets */
    draw = XmCreateDrawingArea(form, "draw", NULL, 0);
    XtSetArg(argList[0], XmNrightWidget, draw);
    rcLeft = XmCreateRowColumn(form, "rcLeft", argList, 1);
    for(i = 0; i < XtNumber(ltButton); ++i)
        ltButton[i] = XmCreateToggleButton(rcLeft, ltbNames[i], NULL, 0);
    XtSetArg(argList[0], XmNleftWidget, draw);
    rcRight = XmCreateRowColumn(form, "rcRight", argList, 1);
    for(i = 0; i < XtNumber(rtButton); ++i)
        rtButton[i] = XmCreateToggleButton(rcRight, rtbNames[i], NULL, 0);

    /* Make the program visible on the screen */
    XtManageChild(form);
    XtManageChild(rcLeft);
    XtManageChildren(ltButton, XtNumber(ltButton));
    XtManageChild(draw);
    XtManageChild(rcRight);
    XtManageChildren(rtButton, XtNumber(rtButton));
    XtRealizeWidget(topShell);

    /* Wait for input events */
    XtMainLoop();
    }
```

Example 14.1 X/Motif application program with a Form widget.

```
Edit.form.height:                        100
Edit.form.width:                         275
Edit.form.XmRowColumn.topAttachment:     attach_form
Edit.form.rcLeft.leftAttachment:         attach_form
Edit.form.rcLeft.rightAttachment:        attach_widget
Edit.form.rcRight.leftAttachment:        attach_widget
Edit.form.rcRight.rightAttachment:       attach_form
Edit.form.rcRight.radioBehavior:         true
Edit.form.draw.background:               wheat
Edit.form.draw.foreground:               forestgreen
Edit.form.draw.topAttachment:            attach_position
Edit.form.draw.topPosition:              10
Edit.form.draw.bottomAttachment:         attach_position
Edit.form.draw.bottomPosition:           90
Edit.form.draw.leftAttachment:           attach_position
Edit.form.draw.leftPosition:             30
Edit.form.draw.rightAttachment:          attach_position
Edit.form.draw.rightPosition:            70
Edit.form.draw.backgroundPixmap:         /usr/include/X11/bitmaps/wingdogs
```

Example 14.2   Resource file for the previous X/Motif application program.

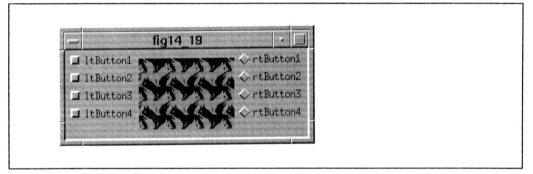

Figure 14.19   Output of the previous X/Motif application program.

PushButton widgets and a DrawingArea widget. Have the PushButtons appear in a vertical column on the left side of the application area and the DrawingArea on the right. When the Form is resized, the buttons should not change their size or position but the DrawingArea should grow or shrink proportionately. The Labels on the PushButtons should be specified as:

```
Clear
Line
Circle
```

2. Modify the program from a previous chapter that had five Label widgets and five Text widgets in RowColumns as children of a BulletinBoard. Install the BulletinBoard as the work area in a MainWindow widget. Also, create a Text widget and install it as the command/message area

in the MainWindow. Do not worry about the MenuBar for now, but cause the Separator widgets to appear between the three areas.

15

Graphic-User Interface Design Guidelines

Introduction

□ One reason for the success of the Motif widget set in the X Window System environment is the Motif Style Guide. This document describes how a "well-behaved" Motif application should look and feel. If a Motif application wants the OSF "stamp of approval" and acceptance by its users, it must follow the guidelines in the Guide. This chapter presents an overview of the information contained within the OSF/Motif Style Guide.

Objectives

□ After completing this chapter, you will be able to:

□ List the four standard components of OSF/Motif.

□ List the three audiences the Style Guide addresses.

□ Explain why Motif applications should give control to their user.

□ Describe the features that make a Motif application consistent.

□ Explain the experience of direct manipulation.

□ Describe the features that make a Motif application flexible.

□ Explain why you should not automatically move windows or warp the mouse pointer.

◻ List three general areas that almost every Motif application will contain.

◻ Explain why grouping related controls is important.

◻ List three common methods of grouping related controls.

◻ List four things to remember when designing client areas.

◻ Explain which Motif manager widget provides for a Style Guide compliant application.

Motif Style Guide

◻ The Motif Style Guide is provided as one of the four standard parts of OSF/Motif:

Toolkit   The OSF/Motif Toolkit contains the wide variety of widgets and gadgets that we have already seen in the preceding chapters and more. The toolkit provides for standard graphic-user interfaces that can be applied to a wide variety of applications. This allows for uniform look-and-feels that allow users to learn to use new applications quickly and more efficiently.

mwm   The Motif Window Manager, as we have already seen, allows the X Window System user to manipulate the application's main windows with a consistent set of user interface objects. The resize handles, title bar, maximize button, minimize button, and the window manager button provide the consistent, intuitive, and easy-to-use tools needed to organize the X terminal screen to suit each user's individual preferences.

UIL   The User Interface Language is a Motif-specific fourth-generation programming language. UIL will not be discussed in this book. It provides the programmer with a tool by which the *initial* state of the user interface for an application can be described. Widgets and their layout, initial resource values, and other items can be specified with UIL. Callbacks, event handlers, and other application-specific items must still be coded in C.

Style Guide   The Motif Style Guide is used by widget writers, window manager developers, and application programmers to ensure that the results of their efforts are consistent in their look-and-feel. If a new widget, window manager, or other Motif application is to get the OSF "stamp of approval," it must follow the guidelines set forth in the Style Guide.

Widget writers use the Style Guide to modify existing widget operations or to write new widgets that are consistent with the OSF/Motif widget set. The look-and-feel of new or modified widgets must have the same three-dimensional appearance of and operate in a manner similar to the existing widgets in the toolkit. This will ensure that the widgets will be readily accepted by the users of the applications in which they will be incorporated.

Window manager developers use the Style Guide to modify existing window manager operation or to write new window managers that are consistent with the OSF/Motif look-and-feel. Acceptance of the standard Motif window manager, mwm, dictates that any new window managers must have a similar and consistent look-and-feel. This will ensure that the new window managers will be accepted by Motif users as an alternative to mwm.

Application programmers use the Style Guide to ensure that their application will operate in a manner similar to all other Motif applications. This usually means that common controls (PushButtons, Menus, DialogBoxes, etc.) are located in similar places, that similar controls have similar meanings, and that the user is in full control at all times. In short, the programmer must write the application to conform to the Style Guide guidelines so that any user who is familiar with any other Motif application can sit down with the new application and understand how to operate it with little or no training.

Giving Power to the User

□   Every Motif application should be written such that the user is in control of its operation. The user should be given the controls needed to accomplish a given task and direct control over them. Users will have a feeling of control over an application if it is consistent and gives them the ability to directly manipulate the controls and other objects in the application themselves. The applications must also be flexible and make the user explicitly decide on an action that will have irreversible effects.

□   Consistency must be one of the highest design goals in any Motif application. All applications that share the same environment (Motif in this case) must be consistent with one another to ensure their success in the marketplace. If your Motif application is not consistent with all other Motif applications, the user feels a loss of control and will probably not use your application for their task or choose a different application that is more consistent.

Consistency means that similar controls will operate in a similar manner and have similar uses. If a PushButton in one application has a Label with an ellipsis (...) after it and clicking that button causes a DialogBox to pop up, any other application that uses the ellipsis on a PushButton Label should do the same thing. Consistency also means that the same action will always produce the same result in many different applications. If you can click-hold-drag the title bar of one application to move its location on the screen, then any other application that has a title bar ought to work the same way.

Another factor in the consistency of an application is placement of the user controls in the application's window. The controls and functions that are used most often should be presented first, at the top of the application, in a logical and straightforward order. This is usually accomplished with some type of MenuBar where the main functions of the application are immediately visible and ready for use.

Those functions that are not used frequently should be hidden from view and only called up on an as-needed basis. A graphics application may need to change the background color of the objects being drawn. Since this function is not used as often as the line-drawing function itself, the button used to draw a line will always be visible and available while the background color function is used by calling up a DialogBox from a Pulldown-Menu off of the MenuBar.

When a Motif application is consistent, the user will have a greater sense of control. A user who feels in control will be more apt to use the application more frequently and experiment with it to try to learn its advanced features. A user who starts using an application frequently will start to tell other users about the application and its capabilities, and it will start to become more successful in the marketplace.

口   The Motif Style Guide also discusses the experience of direct manipulation. The experience of direct manipulation is defined as the connection of a user action in an application with an observable response from the application. In a direct-manipulation user interface, users will experience the immediate visible result of their actions.

Immediate visible response is the most important aspect of the direct manipulation experience. The performance problems of slow hardware or of poor program design and implementation can make it difficult for a user to concentrate on the task for which they are using your Motif application. No matter how pretty an application may look, if it is slow in its operation, it will be practically unusable by a user.

Direct manipulation also implies that the objects that a user manipulates in your Motif application can be acted on directly by the user in a manner similar to objects they manipulate in the real physical world. With the Motif widget set, direct manipulation is supported with things like Push-Buttons that are pushed, ToggleButtons that are toggled, and Scales that you slide to select a value between some minimum and maximum.

Direct manipulation gives the user a sense of power and control with your Motif application. Instead of typing some arcane command syntax on a command line, the user can point and click to manipulate an object on the screen. Giving the users the power to directly manipulate objects on the screen reduces the amount of information they must memorize and gives them a greater sense of control.

口   Motif applications should also be flexible — flexible in the way the user chooses to interact with the application and flexible in allowing the user to configure aspects of the application to fit personal preferences. Flexibility is an important aspect of giving the user the power to control the application.

A Motif application should provide more than one way to get a task accomplished. By doing this, you allow the user to choose the method that is most comfortable to them. An example of this within the Motif widget set is menus. A user may point to a PushButton on a MenuBar, post a PulldownMenu, and select a PushButton to cause some action to take place. However, instead of using the mouse to post a menu, the application can define a keyboard mnemonic character that will post the PullDown and another to activate the desired option. You can even specify some alt- or control-key sequence that will activate the option without posting menus.

A user should also be given a limited amount of control over the visual appearance of their favorite applications. Not all users like a light-blue background; some users may prefer chartreuse PushButtons; other users may like to see pictures instead of Labels on their button widgets. Letting users configure a certain limited number of attributes that reflect personal style and preferences gives then a greater sense of control and encourages them to explore and try to understand the details of your Motif application.

◻   Finally, since the user is in control, make the user control the application. Never do something automatically for the user. Always make the user make a conscious decision about an operation – especially those with irreversible effects. Automatic operations make the user feel that they have lost control.

Never move windows automatically for the user. If a window is to be moved, give the user a control or tool that can be used to move the window. The main window of your Motif application provides this ability with its title bar. However, this is also true of the subwindows created as children of the application main window. Always give the user control over the basic operations of your application.

Never warp the mouse pointer. If your application needs the mouse to be at a specific location on the screen, make the user move it – that's what the mouse is for. If the mouse pointer starts jumping from one location to another in response to actions from within your application, the user will feel that they have lost control over it. Always give the user control over the basic operations of your application.

Explicit control is an especially important issue for those operations within your application that have irreversible effects. Before you allow the user to destroy an object – close a file before saving changes, remove a file, or similar – give the user a chance to think twice about it. In these cases a DialogBox should be popped up to ask "Are you sure you want to...?"-type questions. Make sure the user knows that the effects of a destructive action cannot be reversed. Always give the user control over the basic operations of your application.

Client Areas

◻   All Motif programmers should attempt to keep the visual presentation of their programs simple and to the point. The use of dozens of widgets scattered across a large window space can look confusing to a user. Cluttered applications that are confusing to a user will cause them, again, to feel a loss of control.

To avoid this situation, the Motif Style Guide suggests that almost every application can be organized into a window with as little as three to five main areas:

◻   A MenuBar

◻   One or more scrolled or paned work areas

◻   An optional control panel

◻   A message area

◻   An optional command entry area

Not all applications will fit into a simple user interface like this. However, experience shows that the vast majority of applications can fit and should be structured in this manner to enforce the user's sense of consistency, flexibility, and control.

◻   A MenuBar is a narrow horizontal widget that appears at the top of an application's work space, usually right below the title bar. A series of CascadeButton widgets are located in the MenuBar, and interaction with one of the CascadeButtons causes a PulldownMenu to be posted. The PulldownMenu contains a series of PushButton widgets that give the user access to the main functions of the application.

The PushButtons that invoke the application's main functions are "hidden" in the menus to keep from cluttering the main application window and work space. If a single button interaction is not enough for a specific application function, the PushButton in the PulldownMenu can be used to post another widget such as a CascadingMenu or a DialogBox for more complex user interactions.

Menus are the primary means of communication between a user and an application. Almost every application will require one or more menus and a MenuBar is usually the best means of presenting the functions of an application to a user.

◻   Every application will need a work area of some type to accomplish its main task. A graphics program will use a DrawingArea to create its graphic objects; a data-entry program will use a Form to organize its text fields for data entry in a logical and consistent order; a spreadsheet program will use a RowColumn to display its cells in the standard row/column format.

Whatever the application, there will be some type of primary work area in which to accomplish the task that the program was designed for. There are two main styles within Motif.

The scrolled work area can be used to scroll a small viewport over a larger working area. One or two ScrollBars are provided, horizontal and/or vertical, to move the viewport (called a *clipping window*) over the larger area. Most graphics applications use this technique to let the graphics artist work in a small area of a larger DrawingArea. When ready to move to a different part of the graphic, the artist interacts with the ScrollBars to move the viewport to another area.

A PanedWindow is another alternative that allows multiple work areas to be viewed in individually resizable window panes. The window panes can be organized only in a vertical direction. The size of the panes is controlled by a Sash located on a separator between the panes. A spreadsheet program could use this technique to let an accountant display two or more widely separated areas of the same worksheet. In order to see a little more of one of the areas and a little less of the other, the accountant just grabs the Sash and moves it in the appropriate direction to resize the PanedWindow.

◻   At times, certain functions are used so often that putting them in a menu will make your application difficult to use. In these situations adding a control panel to the work area is sometimes useful. A control panel is nothing more than a RowColumn containing a series of PushButtons and callbacks or Labels and event handlers. Interacting with one of the widgets in the RowColumn causes some function to be invoked just like choosing an option off of a menu.

A graphics program may use a control panel to display a pallet of tools for the artist to use. The line tool, the circle tool, the eraser tool, and other tools can all be placed in a control panel for easy access. A word-processing program may use a control panel to display frequently used formatting options for the writer to use. The right-ragged option, the left-ragged option, the justified option, and the centered option can all be placed in a control panel for easy access.

There are many different reasons for presenting a series of items, controls, or options in a control panel. It is a generally accepted alternate method for presenting a series of options, controls, functions, or other items for a user to select from. For consistency, control panels are usually located at the leftmost side of the work area or right underneath the Menu-Bar.

¤　　Communication with an application's user is typically accomplished through a DialogBox. A DialogBox pops up out of nowhere to notify the user of something or to ask for some kind of input. An alternative to this type of communication is to provide one or two Text widgets as message or command areas.

If they are used, these Text widgets are usually located below the work area at the bottom of the application's main window. One Text widget could be used for both purposes or two Text widgets could be used for a cleaner and clearer operation.

The Message area would be used for very short messages or prompts for input into the command area. The command area is typically used for some type of text input. Whether for responding to requests for input or entering some text based command, a command area can be a useful data-entry area. Figure 15.1 shows what a typical Motif application might look like if it followed the guidelines specified in the Motif Style Guide.

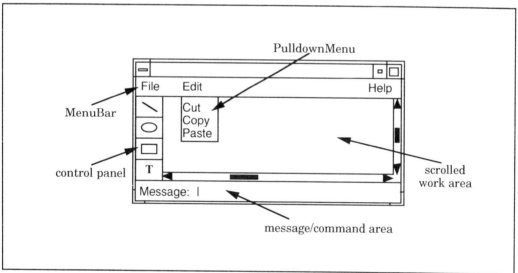

Figure 15.1 Outline of a Style Guide-compliant application area.

Grouping Related Controls

◻ For the proper visual design of an application, any controls that are logically related or have a similar function should be grouped together. Keeping the user interface structured and organized is an important aspect of designing Motif programs that have consistency, flexibility, and user control.

Consistent and flexible applications group controls together to provide a visual cue that they are related to one another. The grouped controls will also usually have a title associated with them to indicate what their related function is. Controls are often grouped in a single row or column or multiple rows or columns to give them an organized and logical look-and-feel.

Since the PushButton and other button widgets are the most common type of interface object in a Motif application, you should use them sparingly. Use PushButtons only for frequently used commands. Unless you are trying to duplicate the physical appearance of existing equipment, PushButtons should be grouped into a row or a column in a Menu, a DialogBox, or a control panel.

◻ PulldownMenus are discussed in detail following event handlers in the next chapter. This type of Menu can contain a series of PushButtons or ToggleButtons configured as a "radio box" (only one item can be active or selected at any one time) or a "check box" (many items can be active or selected at any one time). Selecting an item off of a PulldownMenu can lead to a DialogBox or some other type of control being displayed. Menu items are always presented in a vertical column.

The selections of a PulldownMenu do not appear until the menu is selected. However, the title of the PulldownMenu is always visible and is usually displayed in a MenuBar. PulldownMenus provide a visual cue of their presence along with an efficient use of space. Using PulldownMenus usually requires some minimum amount of mouse movement and interaction.

As an example, most Motif applications will have to deal with data stored in a file in the computer's file system. OSF strongly suggests that every application have a MenuBar with a File PulldownMenu. After posting, the File PulldownMenu will present options for dealing with files. Options such as Open, Close, Save, Save As, and Print are typically available to work with the application data stored in a file.

◻ PopupMenus are discussed along with PulldownMenus in a later chapter. PopupMenus provide the exact same functionality as PulldownMenus. Selecting an item off of a PopupMenu can lead to an action or some other series of controls being displayed. PopupMenu items are also displayed in a vertical column.

The advantage of a PopupMenu is that it can pop up at the current mouse location, provided the widget at the current location has a menu associated with it — no mouse movement required. However, its main disadvantage is that it does not provide any visual cue of its existence — the user has to know where it is.

As an example, consider a graphics application. All graphics applications deal with drawing lines in a variety of geometric shapes on some type of DrawingArea widget. However, you do not want all the objects to be drawn with the same linewidth. So, you could associate a PopupMenu with the DrawingArea such that when the user presses a specific mouse button in the DrawingArea a PopupMenu will appear offering a series of line-width possibilities.

□ DialogBoxes are discussed after Menus in a later chapter. DialogBoxes can contain any of the Button, List, or valuator controls that were discussed previously. However, since the controls do appear in a DialogBox, they should have some related function. If a DialogBox starts looking too crowded or busy, some of the controls should be hidden in Menus or second level DialogBoxes.

There is a lot of flexibility in the design and arrangement of controls within a DialogBox. Just like the main application window, controls can be grouped in boxes or organized into a series of rows or columns. White space should be effectively used to separate controls for better visibility. There are two types of DialogBoxes: MessageBoxes and SelectionBoxes.

MessageBoxes are usually displayed by the application without any explicit action by the user. These types of DialogBoxes are intended to display a message that informs the user of some event or action the application is about to perform. A MessageBox will give the user the ability to respond and say "OK," go ahead with the action, or "Cancel" the action.

SelectionBoxes are usually displayed as the result of some explicit action taken by the user. SelectionBoxes give the user a set of controls such as Buttons, Lists, and Text widgets to supply some type of input data to the application. A SelectionBox will give the user the ability to respond and say "OK," go ahead and apply the data entered in the DialogBox to the application, or "Cancel" the operation.

DialogBoxes, like Menus, use the application window space efficiently because they are not visible until they are displayed. However, like Popup-Menus, they do not provide a visual cue to their existence. This means, of course, that the user must know what action is required to post the Dialog-Box from the application.

As an example, when the user selects the SaveAs option off of the File PulldownMenu from the MenuBar, the application could post a DialogBox. The DialogBox would contain things such as a ScrolledList of the names of the files in the current directory, an OptionMenu that would allow the user to change directories, a PushButton that allowed the user to switch disk devices, and a Text widget for the entry of a new filename. These would be the typical types of controls needed by a user to save the data from one file into a different file in the computer's file system.

□ Control panels provide the exact same functionality as a DialogBox. They can contain all of the same types of controls and provide the same flexibility of arrangement. Since a control panel is permanently displayed, it allows the most frequently used controls to be always visible and available. And, since they are always visible, they offer a strong visual cue to their existence but do take up screen space.

For example, a word-processing application might contain what is commonly referred to as a *ruler control panel* right underneath the MenuBar. The ruler would be graduated using inches, centimeters, or some other measurement unit (perhaps chosen from a DialogBox). Within the ruler control panel would be controls for the right and left margin definition as well as for the placement of tabulator (tab) stops. By pointing the mouse in the ruler and clicking or dragging controls the user is able to set margins and tabs easily — some of the most common operations needed in a word-processing application.

◻ OSF does not restrict how controls are combined to the combinations described within the OSF/Motif Style Guide — it only suggests some common configurations. The criterion for developing control combinations should always be consistency, flexibility, and user control. The control combination should allow the people who use the application to work more efficiently and more effectively and become more productive. Figure 15.2 shows a typical combination of controls within a DialogBox.

Designing a Client Area

◻ When beginning the design of a client area, either the main area, a control panel, or a DialogBox, there are several things to keep in mind:

◻ Arrange controls in natural scanning order.

◻ Arrange controls in the sequence people use them.

◻ Choose appropriate controls.

◻ Make decisions between PushButtons and PopupMenus.

◻ Make decisions between Menus and DialogBoxes.

◻ Align columns of controls.

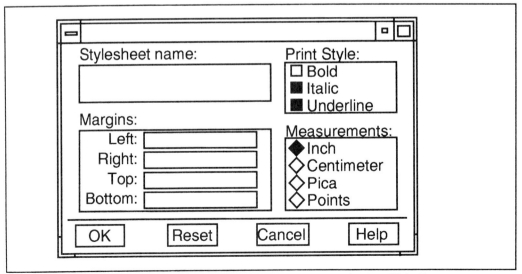

Figure 15.2 Outline of a Style Guide-compliant control grouping in a DialogBox.

❑ Use defaults.

❑   Always design the layout of your Motif application windows and controls according to the natural scanning order of the people who will be using the application. For users in the United States, this will normally be from left to right and from top to bottom. However, for users in other countries this may be different. This is a perfect reason for putting as many positioning resources as possible into resource files so that different resource files can be used for different countries.

Related to the natural scanning order is the arrangement of controls. Always arrange the controls in the order in which people will use them. The scanning order gives position, while the sequence gives priority. As an example, you might have a DialogBox that allows the user to change some application specific-settings. The DialogBox also presents a series of Push-Buttons to accept the settings (OK), to test the settings (Apply), to restore the original values (Reset), and to cancel the settings without changing anything (Cancel). Since the OK button is the one used most often, it should appear farthest to the left. The Apply button is the next most frequently used so it appears next. The least frequent usage occurs with the Reset and Cancel so they appear last.

❑   Choose the right control (tool or widget) for the right job. As an example, ToggleButtons in a RadioBox, ToggleButtons in a CheckBox, OptionMenus, and List widgets can all be used to choose one item from a list of possibilities. When you need to choose one item from a small, mutually exclusive list of possibilities, the RadioBox is easy to operate. For more options, an OptionMenu may be a better choice because it takes up a smaller amount of space and is almost as easy to operate. For many options, the List widget is usually the easiest to use. Both the List widget and the CheckBox allow multiple items to be chosen at one time.

Since a wide variety of different widget combinations can be used for the same purpose, some care must be used when selecting which widgets to use for a particular job. Don't choose a control just because it's cute or unique or because you just wanted to try something different this time. Use the control that's consistent and flexible, gives the user control, and makes sense.

❑   The two Motif user interface objects that give quick access to frequently used application functions are the control panel and the PopupMenu. In general, a PopupMenu is preferred when the application has the user focused on the work area most of the time. In these types of applications moving the mouse between a control panel and the work area would be distracting.

A control panel with a series of PushButtons is preferred when the user is not constantly focused on the work area. Whenever the user needs to make frequent selections from a list or several selections at the same time, or when the user is manipulating the mouse outside of the work area for other operations, a control panel makes more sense. But also remember, some combination of Menus and control panels can also provide an efficient and flexible set of tools for the user.

❑   As the design of your Motif application proceeds, you will find many cases where a function can be accomplished with a Menu or a DialogBox.

Since you must strive to make your application consistent with other Motif applications, you must know when it is appropriate to use a Menu and when it is appropriate to use a DialogBox. Menu selections act like the controls used in DialogBoxes — but there are differences.

Menus are modal. The user must act to cause the Menu to be posted, and until the user makes a selection from the menu, he or she can't interact with any other part of the application. Therefore, Menus are relatively short-lived. They come and go as needed, taking up space on the screen only when in use.

On the other hand, DialogBoxes can be modal or modeless. A modeless DialogBox can be displayed and will stay visible until the user tells it to go away. This, of course, means that it takes up more screen work space but allows the user to make several selections and see their effects in the main work area immediately.

If you want a user to browse a list of current settings or make a single selection from a list of possibilities, a Menu is faster. When several selections must be made, a DialogBox is the better choice.

❑ Alignment of controls is an important issue. PushButtons are usually placed in a row along the bottom of a DialogBox. ToggleButtons configured as either RadioBoxes or CheckBoxes are usually aligned in a column. No matter which manager you use to lay out your application space, make sure columns of controls are aligned straight up and down. (The RowColumn does this for you automatically.)

Proper alignment ensures that the user won't have to move back and forth between controls to make a selection of one item from a related list. Proper alignment also ensures a clean and organized visual appearance for the user. Both these items will increase the application user's sense of control and gain their acceptance.

❑ Whenever your user has a choice between a number of alternatives, always make one of the alternatives the default. The default alternative is the one that most users select when using a particular function. Having a default selection makes the application easier to use.

For ToggleButtons in a RadioBox or a CheckBox, having a default selection is simple. When the ToggleButtons are displayed, simply have the default ToggleButton(s) already set. This way, there is nothing extra the user has to do. They simply accept the settings and continue on with the application.

For a series of PushButtons, the default Button is usually indicated with an extra border. (DialogBoxes do this automatically.) The user then has a visual cue as to which Button is the default. To select the default Button the user either double-clicks in the area that contains the default Button or presses the Return/Enter key on the keyboard.

Motif's MainWindow Widget

❑ The OSF/Motif Toolkit provides a widget that allows the application developer to put together a Style Guide-compliant client program quickly and easily. As we have already seen, the MainWindow widget provides three of the five suggested standard application areas:

◻ A MenuBar

◻ A work area

◻ A message Text widget

The other two optional areas can be configured into these three. The optional control panel and the actual work area widget could both be a children of a Form, and the Form could then be installed as the work area of the MainWindow. The optional command Text widget could be child of a RowColumn along with the message Text widget, and the RowColumn could then be installed as the message area of the MainWindow.

Once you learn about Menus in a later chapter, it will become easy to install the MenuBar and its associated PulldownMenus into the MainWindow widget. The Motif Style Guide suggests that, at a minimum, every Motif application should have a File, Edit, View, Options, and Help PulldownMenu available from the MenuBar. These PulldownMenus will contain a variety of PushButtons that give the user access to the main functions of your program.

Once you learn about DialogBoxes in a later chapter, you will be able to provide even more functionality to your application's users. By selecting items off of one of the PulldownMenus or from an optional control panel, you can pop up a DialogBox to give your user access to additional functions and features. Usually, a PushButton in a PulldownMenu that has an ellipsis (...) following its Label indicates that selecting that menu item will post a DialogBox.

◻ This chapter was intended as a brief overview of the OSF/Motif Style Guide. However, with a good understanding of the material actually contained in the Style Guide, you should be able to start developing applications that are OSF-compliant and will be readily accepted by a wide variety of Motif users.

Review Questions

◻ Please write down the answers to the following questions:

1. List the four standard components of OSF/Motif.

2. List the three audiences the Style Guide addresses.

3. Why should a Motif application give control to its user?

4. What features make a Motif application consistent?

5. Explain the experience of direct manipulation.

6. What features make a Motif application flexible?

7. Why shouldn't you automatically move windows or warp the mouse pointer?

8. List three general areas that almost every Motif application will contain.

9. Why is grouping related controls important?

10. List three common methods of grouping related controls.

11. List four things to remember when designing client areas.

12. Which Motif manager widget provides for a Style Guide-compliant application?

X
Events

Introduction

◻ The preceding chapters have given you all the basic information needed to start developing X client applications using the Motif widget set — with one exception. In order to support *popup children*, like menus and dialog boxes, you must know about another event-handling mechanism. In this chapter we will leave the Motif topics and concentrate on how the Xt Intrinsics can be used to help you handle events beyond the widget callback mechanism.

Objectives

◻ After completing this chapter, you will be able to:

◻ Describe the basic means of communication between an X client application and a user.

◻ Explain where events are stored.

◻ Describe how events are usually accessed.

◻ Explain the difference between a callback and an event.

◻ Describe which mechanism a widget writer uses to implement callbacks.

◻ List four different event types and the events that generate them.

◻ Describe how to register an event-handling function.

◻ Explain what an event mask is.

◻ Describe the difference between a maskable event and a nonmaskable event.

◻ Explain how to code an event-handling function.

◻ List the three parameters to an event-handling function and their types.

◻ Describe the function needed to remove an event handler.

◻ Explain the purpose of an event data structure.

◻ Describe what all event structures have in common.

◻ Explain the purpose of the XEvent union.

◻ Describe how to dereference an XEvent union member to access data in an event-specific data structure.

◻ Explain what motion, expose, button, and key events are.

◻ Use the XQueryPointer() function to get the position of the mouse pointer.

◻ Use the XLookupString() function to translate key codes into ASCII characters.

◻ Code a timeout function.

◻ Code a workproc function.

Event Concepts

◻ As we have said previously, X events are the basic means of communication between an application user sitting in front of an X terminal and the X client application. X events are generated as a result of user input from the keyboard or the mouse and state changes on the X terminal screen.

When an event is received from the terminal, the X server stores it in an event queue. Each client application has its own event queue to hold its events in first-in/first-out (FIFO) order. When the client application needs the next input event from the user, it gets it from the queue, decides which window (not widget) it belongs to, and notifies the window-specific code about the occurrence of the event. At this point, your application-specific code takes over to do its data-processing. Figure 16.1 illustrates this type of event processing.

◻ There are a number of different event types available in the X Window System. Each one of these event types generates a variety of different information concerning the details of the event: the time it occurred, the screen position at which it occurred, the window id of the window in which it occurred, whether it was a real event or a user-generated event, and so on. This event information is bundled together into a data structure that is passed to the code you wrote to handle the event.

◻ Although there are Xlib functions that allow you to access events from your event queue in a nonsequential manner, events are generally retrieved from the top of the queue and processed in order. Remember, X client application programs are event-driven — they sit in an infinite loop, wait for an input event, and then take some action on it. In an X application the

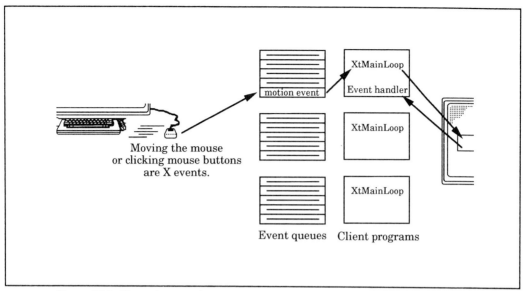

Figure 16.1 X event processing.

programmer no longer decides on the order of processing in the program. Instead, the user is in control and will decide what happens next.

Differences between Callbacks and Event Handlers

❑   When you first look at events you might get the impression that event handlers are the same thing as callback functions. Although events and callbacks give you similar functionalities they are different. In fact, the callback mechanism uses the event mechanism to implement its operations.

   When a widget writer creates a new widget, they must make many decisions about its use and operation. One of the most important decisions is which combinations of a widget's internal states and user input will be accepted and allow the widget to change to a different state. These combinations are defined and implemented as a callback. So a callback function is not just an event handler; it is an event handler for a specific type of widget for a specific combination of widget state and user input.

   Of course, the widget writer uses the Xt Intrinsics event-handling mechanism to look for the events for a callback. But the widget has to be in a specific state for the event to make sense and generate the callback.

❑   The Xt Intrinsics event-handling mechanism is a more generic event-handling mechanism. Although an event handler is associated with a specific widget, it does not depend on the widget being in a special state for the event to be handled. In fact, you can watch for any type of an event in any widget with an appropriate Xt event handler. Figure 16.2 illustrates these differences.

   Remember that in a PushButton widget there were only three callbacks defined: an activate callback (click mouse button 1 in the PushButton window), an arm callback (press mouse button 1 in the PushButton window), and a disarm callback (release mouse button 1 after an arm callback in a

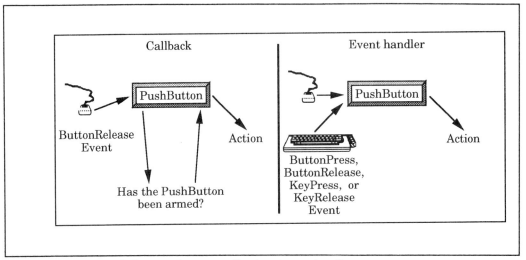

Figure 16.2 Differences between callback and event handling.

PushButton window). With an event handler you could watch for keyboard keys being pressed in a PushButton window, input focus moving into a PushButton window, the mouse pointer moving through a PushButton window, and much more.

Event Types

In X11R3, 29 different types of events are defined. Each event type will have one or more physical events defined to generate that event type. The following is a list of some of the event types you may be concerned with while writing an X/Motif client application:

XButtonEvent   Generated by ButtonPress events and Button-Release events, the XButtonEvent type is created when a button on the mouse is pressed or released.

XClientMessageEvent   Generated by ClientMessage events, the XClient-MessageEvent type is created when a client application calls XSendEvent() to send a client manufactured event type to another application.

XColormapEvent   Generated by ColormapNotify events, the XColor-mapEvent type is created when a change occurs to a colormap associated with a particular client window.

XConfigureEvent   Generated by ConfigureNotify events, the XConfigureEvent type is created when changes occur to a window's size, position, border, stacking order, and so on — in other words, its configuration.

XCreateWindowEvent   Generated by CreateNotify events, the XCreate-WindowEvent type is created when windows are created.

XDestroyWindowEvent	Generated by DestroyNotify events, the XDestroyWindowEvent type is created when windows are destroyed.
XCrossingEvent	Generated by EnterNotify and LeaveNotify events, the XCrossingEvent type is created when the mouse pointer enters or leaves a window.
XExposeEvent	Generated by Expose events, the XExposeEvent type is created when a window becomes visible or a previously hidden portion of a window becomes visible on the screen.
XFocusChangeEvent	Generated by FocusIn and FocusOut events, the XFocusChangeEvent type is created when the keyboard focus window changes.
XNoExposeEvent	Generated by NoExpose events, the XNoExpose type is created when the source area for an XCopyArea() or an XCopyPlane() is completely available.
XGraphicsExposeEvent	Generated by GraphicsExpose events, the XGraphicsExposeEvent type is created when the source area for an XCopyArea() or an XCopyPlane() is not available or is partially obscured by another window.
XGravityEvent	Generated by GravityNotify events, the XGravityEvent type is created when a window is moved because of the change in size of its parent.
XKeymapEvent	Generated by KeymapNotify events, the XKeymapEvent type is created immediately after EnterNotify or FocusIn events as a way for an application to read the keyboard state as it is "awakened," since these two events usually indicate that the application is about to receive user input.
XKeyEvent	Generated by KeyPress and KeyRelease events, the XKeyEvent type is created when *any* key on the keyboard is pressed or released. This even applies to modifier keys like shift, alt, and control.
XMapEvent	Generated by MapNotify events, the XMapEvent type is created when a window is mapped to the screen.
XUnmapEvent	Generated by UnmapNotify events, the XUnmapEvent type is created when a window gets unmapped from the screen.
XMappingEvent	Generated by MappingNotify events, the XMappingEvent type is created when any change occurs in the physical to logical mapping of the keyboard keys or mouse buttons through calls to one of several Xlib functions.

XMotionEvent   Generated by MotionNotify events, the XMotionEvent type is created when the user moves the mouse pointer or when the client application warps the mouse pointer to a new location.

XVisibilityEvent   Generated by VisibilityNotify events, the XVisibilityEvent type is created when a change occurs in the visibility of a window.

Registering an Event Handler

☐   As stated previously, there are many similarities between callbacks and events. Just as with callbacks, if you are going to use the Intrinsics to watch for events, you must register which events you want to watch for on which widgets. This is accomplished with a call to XtAddEventHandler(). Figure 16.3 shows the syntax for the XtAddEventHandler() function.

For a function to be invoked in response to an input event on a widget, the function must be added to the widget's event-handler list. XtAddEventHandler() adds a function name to the end of a specified widget's event-handler list. More than one function can be registered as an event handler for a single instance of a widget, and a function can appear more than once on a widget's event-handler list. When the specific event occurs in the widget the Intrinsics will invoke all the functions on the widget's event-handler list for that event. Figure 16.4 shows how XtAddEventHandler() would be used in an X program.

The first parameter to XtAddEventHandler() identifies the widget that the Intrinsics are to watch for an event in. The second parameter identifies the bitwise OR of the event masks appropriate for all the event types you

```
void XtAddEventHandler(widget_id, event_mask, nonmaskable,
                    function_ptr, client_data)

Widget          widget_id;
XtEventMask     event_mask;
Boolean         nonmaskable;
XtEventHandler  function_ptr;
XtPointer       client_data;
```

Figure 16.3 XtAddEventHandler() syntax.

```
#include <Xm/PushB.h>
...
Widget aButton;
...
aButton = XmCreatePushButton(topShell, "hello", NULL, 0);
XtAddEventHandler(aButton, ButtonPressMask | ButtonReleaseMask,
                False, BPressEventFunc, NULL);
...
```

Figure 16.4 Calling the XtAddEventHandler() function.

want a particular function to be invoked for. The third parameter is either the constant True or the constant False and identifies whether you want this function invoked for nonmaskable events (ClientMessage, MappingNotify, SelectionNotify, etc.). Nonmaskable events are those events that there are no masks for and are sent to every client whenever they occur. The fourth parameter is a pointer to the function that you want invoked in response to the event, and the fifth parameter defines data that you want passed to the event-handler function when it is invoked.

Notice the similarities in the parameters between this function and the XtAddCallback() function. Except for the nonmaskable parameter, they are almost identical and, in fact, are used for much the same purpose. Figure 16.5 shows a chart of the X event types listed previously, the corresponding event name, and the event mask name which is used in the call to XtAddEventHandler().

Coding an Event Handler

◻ The function that is to be invoked in response to an event must assume a specific form. There is no flexibility in the design of an event handler – all event handlers take the same three parameters and return the same data type. Figure 16.6 shows the required structure of an event-handler function.

All event-handler functions return type XtEventHandler. This data type is defined in one of the X header files as void. This, of course, means that event-handler functions cannot return a value anywhere. The return statement (if used) must not contain any expression to be returned.

All event-handler functions take the same three parameters. The first parameter is the widget id of the widget that invoked this event-handler function. This means that you can register the same function with more than one widget and have the event-handler function determine which widget invoked it by comparing this parameter to a list of known widget ids.

The second parameter is a caddr__t type. (In Release 4 this will be an XtPointer.) This data type is defined in <sys/types.h>, a standard C header file, as a generic pointer – usually a character or a void pointer. Client__data is data that is passed to this function from the last parameter of XtAddEventHandler() and is the data that the client application writer decided to send to the event-handler function when the specified event occurs.

The third parameter, on the other hand, is data that is passed to this function from the event-handling mechanism. The data type of call__data is usually defined as a pointer to XEvent and is the data that X decided to send to the event-handling function when the specified event occured. Figure 16.7 shows how an event-handler function would be coded in an X/Motif program.

◻ *A Special Note about the XtEventHandler Data Type:* In older versions of the X Window System, the data type XtEventHandler was simply typedefed as the C language return type void. With this typedef an X programmer could use XtEventHandler both in the function return type declaration for a event-handler function and in the actual definition of the event-handler function. This is the style that is used throughout this book.

```
      Event Types                Event Names              Event Mask Names
---------------------        ------------------        -------------------------
  XButtonEvent               ButtonPress               ButtonPressMask
  XButtonEvent               ButtonRelease             ButtonReleaseMask
  XClientMessageEvent        ClientMessage             *
  XColormapEvent             ColormapNotify            ColormapChangeMask
  XConfigureEvent            ConfigureNotify           StructureNotifyMask
  XCreateWindowEvent         CreateNotify              SubstructureNotifyMask
  XDestroyWindowEvent        DestroyNotify             SubstructureNotifyMask
  XCrossingEvent             EnterNotify               EnterNotifyMask
  XCrossingEvent             LeaveNotify               LeaveNotifyMask
  XExposeEvent               Expose                    ExposureMask
  XFocusChangeEvent          FocusIn                   FocusChangeMask
  XFocusChangeEvent          FocusOut                  FocusChangeMask
  XNoExposeEvent             NoExpose                  *
  XGraphicsExposeEvent       GraphicsExpose            *
  XGravityEvent              GravityNotify             StructureNotifyMask
  XKeymapEvent               KeymapNotify              KeymapStateMask
  XKeyEvent                  KeyPress                  KeyPressMask
  XKeyEvent                  KeyRelease                KeyReleaseMask
  XMapEvent                  MapNotify                 StructureNotifyMask
  XUnmapEvent                UnmapNotify               StructureNotifyMask
  XMappingEvent              MappingNotify             *
  XMotionEvent               MotionNotify              PointerMotionMask
  XMotionEvent               MotionNotify              PointerMotionHintMask
  XMotionEvent               MotionNotify              ButtonMotionMask
  XMotionEvent               MotionNotify              Button1MotionMask
  XMotionEvent               MotionNotify              Button2MotionMask
  XMotionEvent               MotionNotify              Button3MotionMask
  XMotionEvent               MotionNotify              Button4MotionMask
  XMotionEvent               MotionNotify              Button5MotionMask
  XVisibilityEvent           VisibilityNotify          VisibilityChangeMask


* - indicates a nonmaskable event
```

Figure 16.5 Event types, event names, and corresponding event mask names.

```
XtEventHandler function_name(widget_id, client_data, call_data)
Widget       widget_id;
caddr_t      client_data;
XEvent       *call_data;
    {
    /* Your application specific data processing code goes here */

    return;
    }
```

Figure 16.6 Structure of an event-handler function.

```
#include <stdio.h>
#include <Xm/PushB.h>

main(argc, argv)
Cardinal argc;
String argv[];
    {
    ...
    Widget aButton;
    ...
    aButton = XmCreatePushButton(topShell, "hello", NULL, 0);
    XtAddEventHandler(aButton, ButtonPressMask | ButtonReleaseMask,
                    False, BPressEventFunc, NULL);
    ...
    }
XtEventHandler BPressEventFunc(widget_id, client_data, call_data)
Widget widget_id;
caddr_t client_data;
XEvent *call_data;
    {
    printf("You just pressed the hello button...\n");
    sleep(3);
    printf("Good Bye!\n");
    exit(0);
    }
```

Figure 16.7 Coding an event-handler function.

With the advent of ANSI C, function return type declarations have been replaced with prototype declarations. To stay current with changes in the C language, the X Window System has changed its definition for XtEvent-Handler. More recent versions of X typedef XtEventHandler as a pointer to a function that returns void, or, in an ANSI compiler, to a prototype for a pointer to a function that returns void. This change makes XtEventHandler an unsuitable data type for the definition of a function as shown in Figure 16.7.

If your compiler produces warning or error messages during the compilation of your Motif program that complain about the return type in a function definition, you will want to change the return type of your event-handler functions to void. This will fix the "error."

Removing an Event Handler

◻ You can change your mind about event handlers "on the fly" within your client application program. If you don't need a specific function/client_data combination on a widget's event-handler list, you can remove it. Figure 16.8 shows the syntax for XtRemoveEventHandler()—a function that can be called to delete functions from a widget's event-handler list.

```
void XtRemoveEventHandler(widget_id, event_mask, nonmaskable,
                          function_ptr, client_data)

Widget          widget_id;
XtEventMask     event_mask;
Boolean         nonmaskable;
XtEventHandler  function_ptr;
XtPointer       client_data;
```

Figure 16.8 XtRemoveEventHandler() syntax.

If you have a specific function that you want to remove from a widget's event-handler list, then use XtRemoveEventHandler(). Notice that this function has the exact same parameters as XtAddEventHandler(). The function specified by function_ptr is removed only if both the function and the client_data match a function/data pair on the event-handler list for the widget specified by widget_id. No warning or error message is produced if the function fails to find a match.

If the widget is realized, this function will call Xlib to prevent the windows of the widget from receiving further events of the specified type. To keep any event handler from being called at all, call XtRemoveEventHandler() with an event_mask of XtAllEvents, with a nonmaskable parameter of True, and passing the client_data registered in some previous call to XtAddEventHandler().

X Event Data Structures

□   With the callback mechanism, the widget writer sent some widget-specific data to the callback function through its third parameter, which we called call_data. For each widget, there was a widget-specific pointer to a data structure passed through call_data to the callback function. It was then up to the application programmer to typecast the pointer to point to the appropriate structure type according to the type of widget that invoked the callback.

We have a similar situation with event handlers. Each type of event generates a pointer to a data structure that contains some event-specific data that is passed to the event-handler function through its call_data parameter. However, since event handlers are more generic, there is a more generic method we can use to access the call_data event-specific data structure.

□   The third parameter to an event-handler function should always be declared as a pointer to an XEvent. The XEvent data type is actually a C language union that contains members for each and every event type available in X. The following code shows you the definition of the XEvent union:

```
typedef union _XEvent {
        int type;                /* must not be changed; first element */
        XAnyEvent                xany;
        XButtonEvent             xbutton;
        XCirculateEvent          xcirculate;
        XCirculateRequestEvent   xcirculaterequest;
        XClientMessageEvent      xclient;
        XColormapEvent           xcolormap;
        XConfigureEvent          xconfigure;
        XConfigureRequestEvent   xconfigurerequest;
        XCreateWindowEvent       xcreatewindow;
        XCrossingEvent           xcrossing;
        XDestroyWindowEvent      xdestroywindow;
        XErrorEvent              xerror;
        XExposeEvent             xexpose;
        XFocusChangeEvent        xfocus;
        XGraphicsExposeEvent     xgraphicsexpose;
        XGravityEvent            xgravity;
        XKeyEvent                xkey;
        XKeymapEvent             xkeymap;
        XMapEvent                xmap;
        XMapRequestEvent         xmaprequest;
        XMappingEvent            xmapping;
        XMotionEvent             xmotion;
        XNoExposeEvent           xnoexpose;
        XPropertyEvent           xproperty;
        XReparentEvent           xreparent;
        XResizeRequestEvent      xresizerequest;
        XSelectionClearEvent     xselectionclear;
        XSelectionEvent          xselection;
        XSelectionRequestEvent   xselectionrequest;
        XUnmapEvent              xunmap;
        XVisibilityEvent         xvisibility;
        long                     pad[24];
} XEvent;
```

You will remember that a C language union allocates enough memory for its largest member and then maps all the remaining members over the top of that memory space. In an XEvent, this allows the event data structure to be read into the memory space allocated and, no matter what type it actually is, to be accessed correctly (according to its event type — always the first member of the event structure) through the appropriate event type union member.

As an example, if you were coding an event-handler function for a ButtonPress event from the mouse using the ButtonPressMask in the call to XtAddEventHandler(), you would need to access the xbutton XEvent union member which is declared to be of type XButtonEvent. The data stored in the xbutton data structure would contain information specific to the event that your event-handler function is handling. The following code shows you what the XButtonEvent data structure looks like:

```
typedef struct {
    int          type;        /* of event */
    unsigned long serial;      /* # of last rqst. processed by server */
    Bool         send_event;  /* true if this came from a SendEvent() */
    Display      *display;     /* Display the event was read from */
    Window       window;      /* window event reported relative to */
    Window       root;        /* root window that event occured on */
    Window       subwindow;   /* child window */
    Time         time;        /* milliseconds */
    int          x, y;        /* pointer x,y coord. in event window */
    int          x_root, y_root; /* coordinates relative to root */
    unsigned int state;       /* key or button mask */
    unsigned int button;      /* detail */
    Bool         same_screen; /* same screen flag */
} XButtonEvent;
typedef XButtonEvent XButtonPressedEvent;
typedef XButtonEvent XButtonReleasedEvent;
```

As you become more experienced with these event data structures, you will start to notice that they have some common members. In fact, the first five members of each and every structure in the XEvent union are the same. This commonality is one reason why you can determine which data structure was loaded into the union and which structure map to use to access its members.

Accessing Members of X Event Data Structures

◻   Once you know what the XEvent union looks like and what the data structure for the event you are processing looks like, then accessing the event structure members becomes a fairly standard C language structure or union pointer dereferencing operation. Figure 16.9 shows how the dereferencing might be accomplished in a typical event-handling function.

In Figure 16.9, notice the use of the structure/union pointer dereferencing operator (->) to access the xbutton structure member of the call_data union. Once the appropriate union member is accessed, accessing the member of the structure is simply a matter of using the structure member reference operator (.). Using this XEvent union type definition, it is easy to access any member of any event structure passed as call_data to any event-handling function.

Other Common Event Structure Definitions

◻   There is a different structure definition for each and every structure member in the XEvent union definition. Remember that the first five members of all of these structure definitions are the same but, after that, there are many differences. Several of the more common event structure definitions have been listed here for your convenience in working some of the exercises in this book. However, because of the number of different structures available, we cannot list all of them in this book! It must be

```
#include <stdio.h>
#include <Xm/PushB.h>

main(argc, argv)
Cardinal argc;
String argv[];
    {
    ...
    Widget aButton;
    ...
    aButton = XmCreatePushButton(topShell, "hello", NULL, 0);
    XtAddEventHandler(aButton, ButtonPressMask | ButtonReleaseMask,
                    False, BPressEventFunc, NULL);
    ...
    }
XtEventHandler BPressEventFunc(widget_id, client_data, call_data)
Widget widget_id;
caddr_t client_data;
XEvent *call_data;
    {
    if(call_data->type == ButtonPress)
        if(call_data->xbutton.button == 3)
            {
            printf("You just pressed button 3...\n");
            sleep(3);
            printf("Good Bye!\n");
            exit(0);
            }
        else
            {
            printf("You just pressed button %d...\n",
                    call_data->xbutton.button);
            sleep(3);
            return;
            }
    }
```

Figure 16.9 Accessing members of an event structure in an event handler.

emphasized again — you must have a good set of documentation readily available if you are going to start programming in X.

◻ Expose events are generated any time any portion of a window that was previously hidden becomes visible. This might occur because of the movement of one window over the top of another, restacking of the windows, or similar. No matter how little or how much of a window becomes visible, at least one expose event will be generated. And, depending on the number of windows that were on top of the window being exposed, there may be one or more expose events generated.

The XExposeEvent data structure contains members that describe the exposed region. The X/Y-coordinates of the origin of the exposed region along with its width and height are returned. An expose event can occur in which a single rectangle is not enough to describe the exposed region, in which case multiple expose events are generated.

Normally, in a widget-based program, you do not need to worry about expose events too much. All the widgets know how to redraw themselves when they become exposed. However, if you are doing some drawing or working with graphics objects called *pixmaps,* these do not automatically get redrawn if hidden and exposed. Depending on the availability of *backing store* (discussed later), you may have to handle the redrawing of these graphics objects yourself when your application receives an expose event. The XExposeEvent data structure is defined as follows:

```
typedef struct {
    int             type;      /* of event */
    unsigned long serial;      /* # of last rqst. processed by server */
    Bool            send_event;/* true if this came from a SendEvent() */
    Display         *display;  /* Display the event was read from */
    Window          window;    /* "event" window reported relative to */
    int             x, y;      /* coord. of origin of exposed region */
    int             width, height;  /* size of exposed region */
    int             count;     /* if non-zero, at least this many more */
} XExposeEvent;
```

□   Motion events are those events that are generated by the movement of the mouse pointer on the screen. There are two classifications — motion without a mouse button being pressed and motion with a mouse button being pressed.

For motion without buttons being pressed, you can watch for each pixel of movement on the screen with PointerMotionMask. As you might imagine, this can be a very large number of events. X allows you to trim this number of events down by asking for hints with the PointerMotionHintMask modifier. With motion hints only one event is generated each time the mouse is moved and in order to determine the actual mouse pointer location, you must make a call to XQueryPointer().

For motion with a mouse button pressed, you can watch for motion with any button pressed with ButtonMotionMask. The XMotionEvent data structure has a member which describes which mouse button was pressed while the mouse was moving. However, the Button1MotionMask, Button2MotionMask, Button3MotionMask, Button4MotionMask, and Button5MotionMask mask values will let you specifically select which button motion events you want to watch for. The XMotionEvent data structure is defined as follows:

```
typedef struct {
    int            type;        /* of event */
    unsigned long  serial;      /* # of last rqst. processed by server */
    Bool           send_event;  /* true if this came from a SendEvent() */
    Display        *display;     /* Display the event was read from */
    Window         window;      /* window event reported relative to */
    Window         root;        /* root window that event occured on */
    Window         subwindow;   /* child window */
    Time           time;        /* milliseconds */
    int            x, y;        /* pointer x,y coord. in event window */
    int            x_root, y_root; /* coordinates relative to root */
    unsigned int   state;       /* key or button mask */
    char           is_hint;     /* detail */
    Bool           same_screen; /* same screen flag */
} XMotionEvent;
typedef XMotionEvent XPointerMovedEvent;
```

The PointerMotionHintMask cannot be used by itself. This mask value is a modifier and must be OR'ed together with some other mask value. For example, you could use the bitwise OR of ButtonPressMask and PointerMotionHintMask to watch for ButtonPress events or PointerMotion events. In the event-handler function that is called in response you can compare the event type to MotionNotify and call XQueryPointer() to determine the actual location of the mouse pointer.

Key events are generated every time a key on the keyboard changes state. On hardware that supports it, key events are generated when a key is pressed or a key is released. Some keyboards cannot generate KeyRelease events, and only the main keys (a-z, A-Z, 0-9), the Shift key, and the Control key are guaranteed to be available.

Keyboard events are very similar to mouse button events. There are, of course, many more keys on a keyboard than there are buttons on a mouse. The data structures for the two types of events are very similar. One major difference is that the key that was pressed to generate the event is returned as a server dependent key code. In order to translate the encoded key value to an ASCII character value, you must pass the keycode to the function XLookupString(). The XKeyEvent data structure is defined as follows:

```
typedef struct {
    int            type;        /* of event */
    unsigned long  serial;      /* # of last rqst. processed by server */
    Bool           send_event;  /* true if this came from a SendEvent() */
    Display        *display;     /* Display the event was read from */
    Window         window;      /* "event" window reported relative to */
    Window         root;        /* root window that event occured on */
    Window         subwindow;   /* child window */
    Time           time;        /* milliseconds */
    int            x, y;        /* pointer x,y coord. in event window */
    int            x_root, y_root; /* coordinates relative to root */
    unsigned int   state;       /* key or button mask */
    unsigned int   keycode;     /* detail */
```

```
     Bool             same_screen;/* same screen flag */
} XKeyEvent;
typedef XKeyEvent XKeyPressedEvent;
typedef XKeyEvent XKeyReleasedEvent;
```

Determining the Actual Mouse Pointer Location

❑ Using the PointerMotionHintMask to receive only one event instead of hundreds of events for mouse movement provides an interesting problem. The event structure is just a hint – an indication that the pointer is moving – and cannot contain any actual X/Y-coordinates for the actual location of the pointer. Because of this problem, another method must be used to access the mouse pointer location on the screen.

From within the event-handling function you can determine the actual mouse pointer location by calling XQueryPointer(). This function uses a window id to determine which screen the pointer position is returned for and then returns the position as well as a wide variety of other information about the current pointer location. Figure 16.10 shows the syntax for XQueryPointer().

The first parameter is a display pointer. From a discussion of the XtCloseDisplay() in a previous chapter, you should remember that this can be obtained by calling the function XtDisplay() and passing it any widget id. The second parameter is a window id, and, although we haven't talked about this yet, either, can be obtained with a call to the function XtWindow() and passing it any widget id. Both these parameters are passed to this function to identify which display connection and which screen on the display connection are to be accessed for the pointer information.

The remaining parameters are addresses to memory locations that you define in your client application. After the call to XQueryPointer(), these memory locations will be filled in with information about the current location of the mouse pointer. The root parameter will contain the id of the root window the pointer is currently on, while the child parameter will contain the window id of the child of window_id (passed as the second parameter) the pointer is currently in. If the pointer is not currently in a child of window_id, the child parameter will contain a zero.

```
Bool XQueryPointer(display, window_id,
                 root, child, root_x, root_y, win_x, win_y, keys_buttons)

Display       *display;
Window        window_id;
Window        *root;         /* Returned */
Window        *child;        /* Returned */
int           *root_x;       /* Returned */
int           *root_y;       /* Returned */
int           *win_x;        /* Returned */
int           *win_y;        /* Returned */
unsigned int *keys_buttons; /* Returned */
```

Figure 16.10 XQueryPointer() syntax.

The root_x and root_y parameters will contain the X/Y-coordinates of the pointer relative to the root's origin. The win_x and win_y parameters will contain the X/Y-coordinates of the pointer relative to the origin of window_id (passed as the second parameter). The keys_buttons parameter will contain the bitwise OR of one or more of ShiftMask, LockMask, ControlMask, Mod1Mask, Mod2Mask, Mod3Mask, Mod4Mask, Mod5Mask, Button1Mask, Button2Mask, Button3Mask, Button4Mask, and Button5-Mask.

This function returns a boolean value — either True or False. If True is returned, the pointer is on the same screen as window_id (passed as the second parameter) and all return values are valid. If False is returned, the pointer is not on the same screen as window_id and only the root, root_x, and root_y parameters are valid. Figure 16.11 shows how the XQueryPointer() function would be used in an event-handling function.

◻ *A Special Note about the XtWindow() Function:* It is important to understand that the XtWindow() function returns a window id. This id is a unique number that is assigned to every X window that the server creates and displays on the screen. If your client application does not have a window displayed on the screen, XtWindow() cannot return a valid window id. Remember — until your client code invokes the XtRealizeWidget() function to realize your top-level Shell widget, there are no windows on the screen. This means that XtWindow cannot return a valid window id until after the XtRealizeWidget() function has been called and your client's windows have been realized! If you must have a window id before you call XtRealizeWidget(), X supplies a macro called RootWindowOfScreen(), which takes a screen pointer as a parameter and returns the window id of the root window. The root window is realized as soon as the X server starts up and is always available.

Translating Keypress Events into Characters

◻ When using the KeyPressMask in XtAddEventHandler(), the event-handler function gets passed an XKeyEvent data structure that contains a lot of information about the KeyPress or KeyRelease event. One thing that the structure does not contain is the ASCII value of the key that changed state. Instead, it contains something called a *keycode*.

The keycode is a server-dependent code for the key that just changed its state. You must translate the keycode into some other form before you can use it in your client application code. The XLookupString() function translates the keycode from the XKeyEvent structure into something called a keysym as well as into its printable ASCII value. Figure 16.12 shows the syntax for XLookupString().

The first parameter is the pointer to the XKeyEvent data structure passed to the event-handler function used to process the KeyPress or KeyRelease event. The function will access the keycode from the structure, perform the conversions on it, and return the converted data through the remaining parameters.

The second and third parameters describe a buffer that will be used to store the printable ASCII characters converted by XLookupString(). The buffer parameter is a character array that you set up and pass to the

```
#include <stdio.h>
#include <Xm/DrawingA.h>

main(argc, argv)
Cardinal argc;
String argv[];
    {
    ...
    Widget aDrawingArea;
    ...
    aDarea = XmCreateDrawingArea(topShell, "draw", NULL, 0);
    XtAddEventHandler(aDarea, ButtonPressMask | PointerMotionHintMask,
                   False, PointerEventFunc, NULL);
    ...
    }

XtEventHandler PointerEventFunc(widget_id, client_data, call_data)
Widget widget_id;
caddr_t client_data;
XEvent *call_data;
    {
    Window root, child;
    Position root_x, root_y;
    Position win_x, win_y;
    unsigned int keys_buttons;

    if(XQueryPointer(XtDisplay(widget_id), XtWindow(widget_id),
                   &root, &child, &root_x, &root_y, &win_x, &win_y,
                   &keys_buttons))
        {
        printf("With respect to the current window: ");
        printf("x = %d, y = %d\n", win_x, win_y);
        }
    printf("With respect to the root window: ");
    printf("x = %d, y = %d\n", root_x, root_y);
    return;
    }
```

Figure 16.11 Using the XQueryPointer() function.

```
int XLookupString(event, buffer, length, keysym, status)

XKeyEvent       *event;
char            *buffer;        /* Returned */
int             length;
KeySym          *keysym;        /* Returned */
XComposeStatus  *status;        /* Returned */
```

Figure 16.12 XLookupString() syntax.

function. The length of your buffer is passed as the third parameter. The length of the buffer is usually 1 since one keystroke usually corresponds to one ASCII character. However, if you have mapped one particular keystroke into multiple characters (a possibility with other Xlib function calls), you will have to make the buffer big enough to hold the maximum number of characters that can be returned from a KeyPress or KeyRelease event.

The keysym parameter is another return value from XLookupString() and contains yet another translation of the original keycode. The keysym, or key symbol, can contain one of a series of defined names that are defined through <X11/keysym.h>. There is a keysym defined for every possible keystroke from the keyboard as well as other characters from other languages. Figure 16.13 shows some of the defined keysym names.

A discussion of the last parameter to XLookupString() is beyond the scope of this book and will not be discussed here. Suffice it to say that this parameter is another return value for something called the *compose key*

```
XK_BackSpace                              XK_plus
XK_Tab                                    XK_comma
XK_Return                                 XK_minus
XK_Escape                                 XK_period
XK_Delete        /* Delete, rubout */     XK_slash
XK_Left          /* Left arrow */         XK_0            /* digits */
XK_Up            /* Up arrow */              ...
XK_Right         /* Right arrow */        XK_9
XK_Down          /* Down arrow */         XK_colon
XK_F1            /* Function keys */       XK_semicolon
   ...                                    XK_less
XK_F35                                    XK_equal
XK_Shift_L       /* Left shift */         XK_greater
XK_Shift_R       /* Right shift */        XK_question
XK_Control_L     /* Left control */       XK_at
XK_Control_R     /* Right control */      XK_A            /* Upper case */
XK_Caps_Lock     /* Caps lock */            ...
XK_Shift_Lock    /* Shift lock */         XK_Z
XK_Alt_L         /* Left alt */           XK_bracketleft
XK_Alt_R         /* Right alt */          XK_backslash
XK_space                                  XK_bracketright
XK_exclam                                 XK_asciicircum
XK_quotedbl                               XK_underscore
XK_numbersign                             XK_quoteleft
XK_dollar                                 XK_a            /* Lower case */
XK_percent                                  ...
XK_ampersand                              XK_z
XK_quoteright                             XK_braceleft
XK_parenleft                              XK_bar
XK_parenright                             XK_braceright
XK_asterisk                               XK_asciitilde
```

Figure 16.13 Keysym names.

state information. For our purposes we will specify this parameter as NULL.

The function returns an integer value which is the actual length of the converted ASCII string that was stored in your buffer parameter. This value cannot be greater than the length value that was passed as the third parameter. Figure 16.14 shows how the XlookupString() function would be used.

Timeouts

☐ The Xt Intrinsics provide for another type of event — a pseudoevent called a timeout. A timeout allows you to set up what amounts to an alarm clock to wait for some time interval to pass. As soon as the time interval passes, one of your functions will be called for you.

```
#include <stdio.h>
#include <Xm/DrawingA.h>

main(argc, argv)
Cardinal argc;
String argv[];
    {
    ...
    Widget aDrawingArea;
    ...
    aDarea = XmCreateDrawingArea(topShell, "draw", NULL, 0);
    XtAddEventHandler(aDarea, KeyPressMask,
                    False, KeyEventFunc, NULL);
    ...
    }

XtEventHandler KeyEventFunc(widget_id, client_data, call_data)
Widget widget_id;
caddr_t client_data;
XEvent *call_data;
    {
    char buffer[1];
    KeySym keysym;
    int actual;

    actual = XLookupString(call_data, buffer, 1, &keysym, NULL);
    if(actual != 1)
        fprintf(stderr, "XLookupString() conversion error\n");
    else
        printf("ASCII character entered =>%c<=\n", buffer[0]);
    return;
    }
```

Figure 16.14 Using the XLookupString() function.

Just as with callbacks and event handlers, you have to register your timeout with the Intrinsics. This is accomplished with a call to XtAddTimeOut(). Figure 16.15 shows the syntax for this function.

The first parameter specifies the length of the time interval you want to wait before the function is called. The value is given in milliseconds. The second parameter is the name of the function that you want called when the interval passes. And the third parameter is your client-specific data that will be passed to the timeout function when it is called. The Release 4 Intrinsics have a new version of this function called XtAppAddTimeOut() — different parameters, same functionality.

¤   XtAddTimeOut() returns an identifier that will uniquely identify the pending timeout pseudoevent. If you need to remove the timeout before it expires and calls your function, you can make a call to XtRemoveTimeOut(). Figure 16.16 shows the syntax for this function.

The only parameter to this function is an XtIntervalId that was returned from a previous call to XtAddTimeOut(). The id identifies which timeout you want to remove. Timeouts are automatically removed after they have expired and called the timeout function. XtRemoveTimeOut() is needed only when the timeout is to be removed before it expires.

¤   The function that is called in response to a timeout must take on a specific form. Since a timeout is not associated with a widget, there is no widget id to pass to the function. Also, since there is no specific event or callback associated with the timeout, there is no call_data parameter. The only parameter that gets passed to a timeout function is the client_data you specify in the call to XtAddTimeOut(). Figure 16.17 shows the outline for a typical timeout function.

Work Procedures

¤   The Xt Intrinsics provide for another type of event — a pseudoevent called a workproc. A workproc allows you to set up a procedure to do some work when there are no input events to process. When there are no events in your event queue, then one of your workprocs will be called for you. In effect, a workproc is a nonevent event handler.

```
XtIntervalId XtAddTimeOut(interval, function_ptr, client_data)

unsigned long       interval;
XtTimerCallbackProc function_ptr;
XtPointer           client_data;
```

Figure 16.15 XtAddTimeOut() syntax.

```
void XtRemoveTimeOut(id)

XtIntervalId id;
```

Figure 16.16 XtRemoveTimeOut() syntax.

```
XtTimerCallbackProc function_name(client_data)
caddr_t    client_data;
    {
    /* Your application specific data processing code goes here */

    return;
    }
```

Figure 16.17 Timeout function structure.

Just as with callbacks, event handlers, and timeouts, you have to register your workproc with the Intrinsics. This is accomplished with a call to XtAddWorkProc(). Figure 16.18 shows the syntax for this function.

The first parameter is the name of the function that you want called when there are no input events. The second parameter is your client-specific data that will be passed to the work procedure when it is called. The Release 4 Intrinsics have a new version of this function called XtAppAddWorkProc() – different parameters, same functionality.

□   XtAddWorkProc() returns an identifier that will uniquely identify the pending workproc pseudoevent. If you need to remove the workproc before it expires and calls your function, you can make a call to XtRemoveWorkProc(). Figure 16.19 shows the syntax for this function.

The only parameter to this function is an XtWorkProcId that was returned from a previous call to XtAddWorkProc(). The id identifies which workproc you want to remove.

□   The function that is called when there are no input events must assume a specific form. Since a workproc is not associated with a widget, there is no widget id to pass to the function. Also, since there is no specific event or callback associated with the workproc, there is no call_data parameter. The only parameter that gets passed to a workproc function is the client_data you specify in the call to XtAddWorkProc(). Figure 16.20 shows the outline for a typical workproc function.

Notice that the work procedure returns a Boolean value. This is the first time that any callback or event-handler-type function has ever returned anything and the return value has special significance. If the function returns True, the work procedure will be removed after it completes. If it

```
XtWorkProcId XtAddWorkProc(function_ptr, client_data)

XtWorkProc function_ptr;
XtPointer   client_data;
```

Figure 16.18 XtAddWorkProc() syntax.

```
void XtRemoveWorkProc(id)

XtWorkProcId id;
```

Figure 16.19 XtRemoveWorkProc() syntax.

```
Boolean function_name(client_data)
caddr_t     client_data;
    {
    /* Your application specific data processing code goes here */

    return True;
    }
```

Figure 16.20 Workproc function structure.

returns False, the work procedure will remain and be called again the next
time there are no input events to process.
   An important feature of workprocs that you must understand is that they
are not interruptible! That is to say, *when a work procedure begins executing, it will execute to completion.* If any input events occur while the
workproc is executing, *they will not be processed until the workproc is done.*
Because of this, you should not perform a lot of work in a work
procedure—let it do only small units of work at a time. If workprocs are
allowed to do large amounts of data processing, the application user will
notice a serious degradation in performance.

A Complete X/Motif Client Application

□ Using all the concepts and techniques presented in this chapter, we can put
   together a simple, but complete, X/Motif-based client application. Example 16.1 shows the code for a program that has a shell widget and a
   DrawingArea widget in it. An event handler is installed that watches for a
   variety of events dealing with the mouse buttons.
      Figure 16.21 shows what the program would look like on a typical termi-
   nal screen.

Review Questions

□ Please write down the answers to the following questions:

   1. What is the basic means of communication between an X client appli-
       cation and a user?

   2. Where are events stored?

   3. How are events usually accessed?

   4. What is the difference between a callback and an event?

   5. What mechanism does a widget writer use to implement callbacks?

   6. List four different event types and the events that generate them.

   7. How do you register an event-handling function?

   8. What is an event mask?

   9. What is the difference between a maskable event and a nonmaskable

```
#include <stdio.h>
#include <Xm/DrawingA.h>

XtEventHandler BPressEventFunc();
Widget topShell;

main(argc, argv)
Cardinal argc;
String argv[];
    {
    Widget draw;
    Arg argList[10];
    Cardinal i;

    /* Initialize  the Intrinsics and create a top Shell widget */
    topShell = XtInitialize(argv[0], "Edit", NULL, 0, &argc, argv);

    /* Create the manager widget */
    i = 0;
    XtSetArg(argList[i], XmNheight, 200); i++;
    XtSetArg(argList[i], XmNwidth, 200); i++;
    draw = XmCreateDrawingArea(topShell, "draw", argList, i);

    /* Set up event handlers for the widgets */
    XtAddEventHandler(draw,
                    ButtonPressMask | ButtonReleaseMask | ButtonMotionMask,
                    False, BPressEventFunc, NULL);

    /* Make the program visible on the screen */
    XtManageChild(draw);
    XtRealizeWidget(topShell);

    /* Wait for input events */
    XtMainLoop();
    }

XtEventHandler BPressEventFunc(widget_id, client_data, call_data)
Widget widget_id;
caddr_t client_data;
XEvent *call_data;
    {

    /* Print something on the screen */
    printf("For the drawing area widget,  you just ");

    /* Determine which event invoked this function */
    switch(call_data->type)
        {
```

Example 16.1 X/Motif application program with an event handler, part 1.

```
        case ButtonPress:

            /* Print something on the screen */
            printf("pressed button %d at x=%d/y=%d\n",
                    call_data->xbutton.button, call_data->xbutton.x,
                    call_data->xbutton.y);
            break;
        case ButtonRelease:

            /* Print something on the screen */
            printf("released button %d at x=%d/y=%d\n",
                    call_data->xbutton.button, call_data->xbutton.x,
                    call_data->xbutton.y);

            /* Determine which button invoked this function */
            if(call_data->xbutton.button == 3)
                {

                /* Return control to the operating system */
                printf("Good Bye!\n");
                sleep(3);
                exit(0);
                }
            break;
        case MotionNotify:

            /* Print something on the screen */
            printf("moved with a button down to x=%d/y=%d\n",
                    call_data->xbutton.x, call_data->xbutton.y);
            break;
        default:

            /* Print something on the screen */
            printf("received some unknown kind of event!\n");
            break;
        }

/* Return control to the calling function */
return;
}
```

Example 16.2 X/Motif application program with an event handler, part 2.

event?

10. How do you code an event-handling function?

11. List the three parameters to an event-handling function and their types.

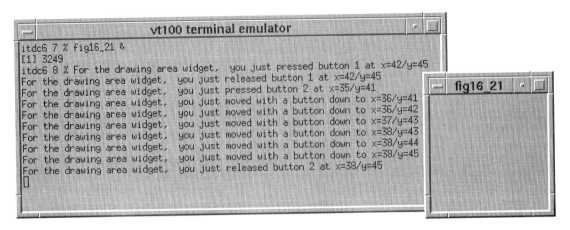

Figure 16.21 Output of the previous X/Motif application program.

12. Which function is used to remove an event handler?

13. What is the purpose of an event data structure?

14. What do all event structures have in common?

15. What is the purpose of the XEvent union?

16. How do you dereference an XEvent union member to access data in an event-specific data structure?

17. What is a motion event? An expose event? A button event? A key event?

18. What is the XQueryPointer() function for?

19. What is the XLookupString() function for?

20. How do you code a timeout function?

21. How do you code a workproc function?

Exercises

The following exercises are designed to give you the opportunity to practice the concepts and facilities presented in this chapter:

1. Create a simple X/Motif client application that has a DrawingArea widget in it similar to the one presented at the end of the text in this chapter. Set up an event handler to watch for mouse button events, and print out some of the members of the XButtonEvent data structure that gets passed through your call_data parameter. You should try printing things like the X/Y-coordinates with respect to the active window in which the button event occurred, the X/Y-coordinates with respect to the root window, and the button number of the button that caused the event.

2. Modify the previous program to also watch for button motion events.

Have an event handler print an appropriate message when they occur.

3. Modify the previous program to also watch for keyboard key events and print out some members of the XKeyEvent data structure that is passed through your call_data parameter. You should try printing things like the X/Y-coordinates with respect to the active window in which the button event occurred, the X/Y-coordinates with respect to the root window, and the actual ASCII character for the key that was pressed or released.

4. Modify the previous program to also watch for expose events and print out some members of the XExposeEvent data structure that is passed through your call_data parameter. You should try printing things like the X/Y-coordinates of the origin of the exposed area with respect to the active window, the width and the height of the exposed area, and the count of the number of other expose events left in the event queue.

17

Motif
Menus

Introduction

¤ Everybody knows what a menu is. A menu lets you chose one or more items from a list of possibilities. Whether you are choosing food items from a restaurant menu, a television show from a menu called a "television guide," a name and phone number from a menu called a "telephone directory," or a program to execute from a menu of alternatives on a computer terminal screen, everyone has used a menu at one time or another. Menus are probably one of the most common types of user interface components in modern data-processing applications. Motif supports three different styles of menus which are discussed in this chapter.

Objectives

¤ After completing this chapter, you will be able to:

  ¤ Describe which widget class is the foundation of the Motif menu systems.

  ¤ Explain why Motif menus are contained within their own Shell widget.

  ¤ Explain the purpose of a menu.

  ¤ List two ways to interact with a menu.

  ¤ Describe the purpose of a mnemonic and an accelerator.

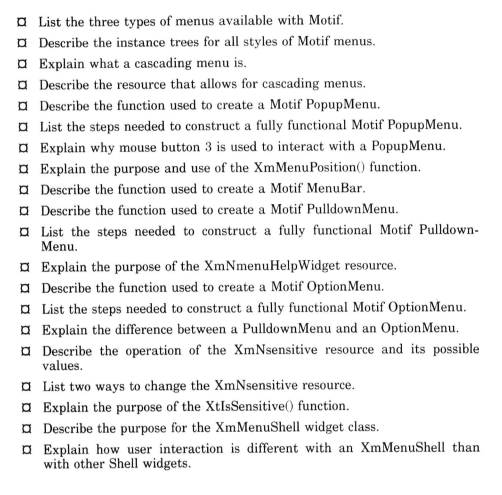

❑ List the three types of menus available with Motif.

❑ Describe the instance trees for all styles of Motif menus.

❑ Explain what a cascading menu is.

❑ Describe the resource that allows for cascading menus.

❑ Describe the function used to create a Motif PopupMenu.

❑ List the steps needed to construct a fully functional Motif PopupMenu.

❑ Explain why mouse button 3 is used to interact with a PopupMenu.

❑ Explain the purpose and use of the XmMenuPosition() function.

❑ Describe the function used to create a Motif MenuBar.

❑ Describe the function used to create a Motif PulldownMenu.

❑ List the steps needed to construct a fully functional Motif Pulldown-Menu.

❑ Explain the purpose of the XmNmenuHelpWidget resource.

❑ Describe the function used to create a Motif OptionMenu.

❑ List the steps needed to construct a fully functional Motif OptionMenu.

❑ Explain the difference between a PulldownMenu and an OptionMenu.

❑ Describe the operation of the XmNsensitive resource and its possible values.

❑ List two ways to change the XmNsensitive resource.

❑ Explain the purpose of the XtIsSensitive() function.

❑ Describe the purpose for the XmMenuShell widget class.

❑ Explain how user interaction is different with an XmMenuShell than with other Shell widgets.

Menu Concepts

❑ The first thing that every Motif programmer should know about Motif menus is that they are not separate widgets. All Motif menus are specially configured RowColumn widgets that have some type of Button children for the menu choices. Menus are, in fact, the main reason for the existence of the RowColumn widget. The RowColumn's XmNrowColumnType resource determines how the RowColumn will be configured.

The second thing that every Motif programmer should know about Motif menus is that a menu has its own separate Shell widget. Whenever you use one of the Motif convenience functions to create a RowColumn configured as a menu, it is also configured as a child of an XmMenuShell widget. The Shell widget allows the menu to pop up out of nowhere without any effect on the other widgets in your program. If you didn't have a separate shell widget the menus would have to be squeezed between the other user interface widgets already visible in your program.

◻   Just like any other menu, the Motif menus allow you to pick one item from a list of possibilities. Posting a menu (causing it to become visible) is accomplished by pressing one of the mouse buttons on a specific widget. On all Motif menus, you can press to post the menu, hold, and drag to a menu selection (some type of button), and when you release the mouse button, the item the mouse pointer was on will be selected. Another type of interaction available on some Motif menus lets you also click to post the menu and, when visible, you can click on one of the options (without dragging) to select it. The type of menu you are interacting with will determine which mouse button you use and the type of interaction available.

Motif also supports keyboard interaction with menus through the use of *mnemonics* and *accelerators*. A mnemonic is a single character which, when typed from the keyboard in combination with the Alt or Meta key, will post an associated menu. Mnemonics are usually used with a menu that is already visible to select a menu item. The mnemonic is usually one of the letters contained within the label of the Motif PushButton on the posted menu. For this reason, mnemonics must be unique within a particular menu. Motif will underline the letter in the PushButton label that has been designated as a mnemonic.

Accelerators are a special key sequence that are used to select a menu item directly. You do not have to post a menu to use the accelerator for one of its options. Simply entering the accelerator key sequence from the keyboard causes the associated menu option to be selected and acted on immediately. Usually, some combination of Alt, Ctrl, or Meta and some function key will form an accelerator. Motif will list the accelerator key sequence for a menu option to the right of the option's label.

◻   Motif supports three styles of menus:

PopupMenu   PopupMenus pop up out of nowhere. You can attach a PopupMenu to literally any other widget in your application. When the user interacts with that widget with the mouse, the menu will pop up with its list of options. By default, mouse button 3 interacts with a PopupMenu.

PulldownMenu   PulldownMenus consist of a MenuBar widget and a series of PulldownMenu widgets. The MenuBar has several CascadeButton widgets visible in it. When you interact with one of the CascadeButtons, an associated PulldownMenu will pop down below the Cascade-Button with its list of options. By default, mouse button 1 interacts with a PulldownMenu.

OptionMenu   OptionMenus are a special type of menu that is based on a CascadeButton. When the user interacts with the CascadeButton, the OptionMenu will pop up with its list of options. After the user selects one of the options, the label of the selected option will replace the label on the CascadeButton. With an OptionMenu, the last selected option is always visible in the Cas-cadeButton associated with the OptionMenu.

Figure 17.1 shows what these three types of menus would look like.

Menu Instance Trees

❑ Perhaps the most difficult thing to understand about Motif menus is their
instance trees. PopupMenu instance trees are fairly simple and straightforward, but PulldownMenus and OptionMenus are not. These last two menu
styles have some different parenting requirements for proper operation.

❑ PopupMenus are simple. Any widget in your Motif application can have a
PopupMenu attached to it. The widget that has the PopupMenu attached
to it may, or may not, be the parent of the menu depending on its ability
to support popup children. The options on the PopupMenu are some type of
Button widget or gadget and are children of the PopupMenu. You then set
up some type of callback or event handler for the buttons to do your menu-

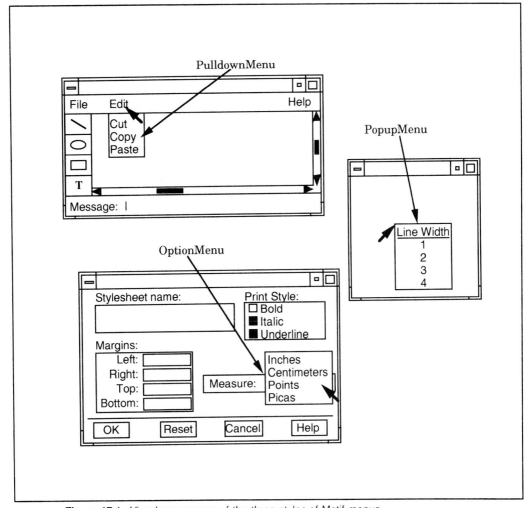

Figure 17.1 Visual appearance of the three styles of Motif menus.

specific data processing. Figure 17.2 shows what the instance tree for a PopupMenu would look like.

When the user interacts with the parent of the PopupMenu with the mouse, then the PopupMenu will pop up. This interaction is usually accomplished with mouse button 3.

□   Pulldown menus are the most common type of GUI menu system. In a Motif PulldownMenu, a MenuBar widget is created as the child of some other parent widget. The MenuBar then becomes the parent of one or more CascadeButton widgets, which become the options within the MenuBar. When a CascadeButton is configured as the child of a MenuBar, it will not display its cascading indicator (->). A Motif PulldownMenu is then created for each CascadeButton, but the PulldownMenus are also children of the MenuBar. An association is made between a CascadeButton and a PulldownMenu through the CascadeButton's XmNsubMenuId resource.

The options on the PulldownMenu are some type of Button widget or gadget and are children of the PulldownMenu. You then set up some type of callback or event handler for the buttons to do your menu-specific data processing. Figure 17.3 shows what the instance tree for a PulldownMenu system would look like.

When the user interacts with one of the CascadeButtons in the MenuBar using the mouse, the associated PulldownMenu will appear below the CascadeButton. This interaction is usually accomplished with mouse button 1.

□   The Motif OptionMenu is somewhat similar to the PulldownMenu. A Motif OptionMenu widget is created as the child of some other parent widget. The OptionMenu automatically creates (you do not do this yourself) a CascadeButton and a Label widget for you. When a CascadeButton is created as part of an OptionMenu, it will not display its cascading indicator (->). At the same time, you create a PulldownMenu as the child of the same parent. An association is made between the OptionMenu and the PulldownMenu through the OptionMenu's XmNsubMenuId resource.

The options on the PulldownMenu are some type of Button widget or gadget and are children of the PulldownMenu. You then set up some type of callback or event handler for the buttons to do your menu-specific data processing. Figure 17.4 shows what the instance tree for a OptionMenu system would look like.

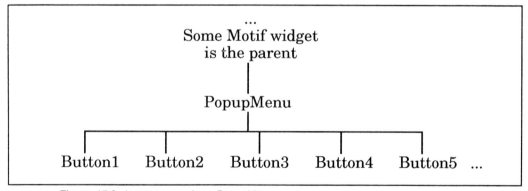

Figure 17.2 Instance tree for a PopupMenu.

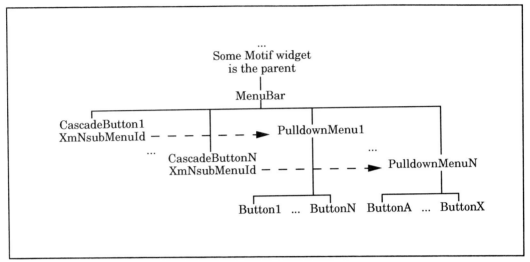

Figure 17.3 Instance tree for a PulldownMenu.

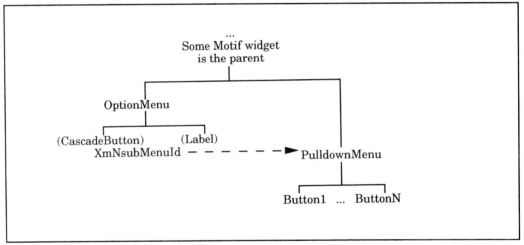

Figure 17.4 Instance tree for a OptionMenu.

When the user interacts with the CascadeButton in the OptionMenu using the mouse, the associated PulldownMenu will appear over the top of the CascadeButton. The Button that contained the last option chosen from the OptionMenu will be aligned with the CascadeButton. This interaction is usually accomplished with mouse button 1.

Any of the menu types can be cascading menus. A cascading menu is one where, when an option is chosen from the primary menu, a secondary menu pops up to indicate additional choices. The secondary menu may have a tertiary cascading menu and so on. Cascade menus will make menu instance trees even more complex.

To implement a cascade menu in a menu pane simply use a CascadeButton widget or gadget. A CascadeButton, when used in this way, will display a cascading indicator (->) to the right of its label. This indicator is used to visually locate a menu option that has a submenu attached to it. The submenu is attached to the CascadeButton through its XmNsubMenuId resource. Figure 17.5 shows what a cascade menu would look like.

Whenever you interact with a cascading menu the associated CascadeButton automatically positions and displays the menu whose widget id is in its XmNsubMenuId resource. Cascade menus also have different parenting requirements. *The cascading PulldownMenu pane's parent is the menu pane that contained the CascadeButton and not the CascadeButton itself.*

Motif PopupMenus

◻ As stated before, PopupMenus can be attached to any other widget in your X/Motif client application program. To create a PopupMenu, use the XmCreatePopupMenu() convenience function. This function will create an instance of a RowColumn widget configured as a PopupMenu. Figure 17.6 shows the syntax for XmCreatePopupMenu().

◻ To create a PopupMenu you will typically go through the following steps:

1. Create the popup menu pane as the child of some other widget in your

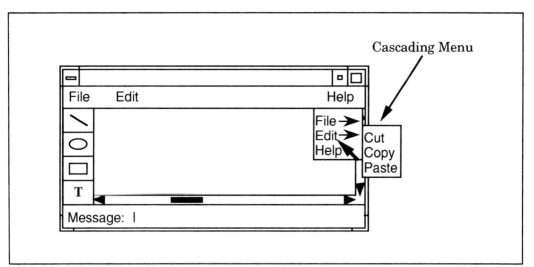

Figure 17.5 Visual appearance of a cascading menu.

```
#include <Xm/RowColumn.h>


Widget XmCreatePopupMenu(parent_id, instance_name, arg_list, arg_count)

Widget      parent_id;
String      instance_name;
ArgList     arg_list;
Cardinal    arg_count;
```

Figure 17.6 XmCreatePopupMenu() syntax.

program with a call to XmCreatePopupMenu(). *Do not* manage the PopupMenu.

2. Create the Button widgets or gadgets as children of the PopupMenu using the appropriate XmCreate...Button() function call. Manage the Buttons.

3. Attach an event handler to the parent of your PopupMenu with a call to XtAddEventHandler(). In the event-handler function you will make a call to XtManageChild() to cause the PopupMenu to become visible. The event-handler function should manage the PopupMenu on a ButtonPress event for mouse button 3.

Since the PopupMenu becomes visible because of an explicit call to XtManageChild() in an event-handling function, literally any event can cause a PopupMenu to become visible. By default, mouse button 3 is used, but it can just as easily be a KeyPress on some specific key, a MotionNotify across some other widget, or an Expose for another window – any event at all.

The reason why mouse button 3 is used instead of mouse button 1 is that the PopupMenu can be attached to any other widget – even other widgets that attach special meanings to mouse button 1 themselves. For example, you could attach a PopupMenu to a PushButton widget. However, the PushButton widget takes a the ButtonPress event from mouse button 1 as an XmNarmCallback and an XmNactivateCallback. If the same mouse button is used to activate the posting PushButton and the PushButtons within the menu, the menu grabs the event and selects the first item in the PopupMenu. This is a bug in Motif 1.0, which will be fixed in 1.1.

□   Because the PopupMenu is enclosed in its own Shell widget, the window for the menu will appear independent and separate from the client application window that the popup was attached to. In fact, if you do nothing else, the window for the PopupMenu will appear at X=0/Y=0 with respect to the root window. For this reason Motif supplies another convenience function that allows you to position a PopupMenu at the location of a ButtonPress event. Figure 17.7 shows the syntax for the XmMenuPosition() function, which performs this processing for you.

The first parameter is the widget id of the PopupMenu that you are about ready to post (manage). The second parameter is the pointer to the XButtonEvent (or XEvent) from the mouse button press event used to post the menu. XmMenuPosition does not return a value.

```
#include <Xm/RowColumn.h>

void XmMenuPosition(menu, event)

Widget        menu;
XButtonEvent *event;
```

Figure 17.7 XmMenuPosition() syntax.

This function will access the event parameter to get the X/Y-coordinates of the event and install them as the XmNx and XmNy resources for the Shell widget surrounding the PopupMenu. This will cause the menu to pop up exactly at the point where the user mouse-downed within the parent widget of the PopupMenu — not at the origin of the root window. Figure 17.8 shows a code segment that uses a PopupMenu.

```
...
#include <Xm/BulletinB.h>
#include <Xm/RowColumn.h>
#include <Xm/PushB.h>
...
XtEventHandler BPressFunc();
...

    Widget bbManager;
    Widget popUp;
    Widget popPBs[5];
    char buffer[20];
    ...
    bbManager = XmCreateBulletinBoard(mwManager, "bbmanager", argList, i);
    ...
    popUp = XmCreatePopupMenu(bbManager, "popUp", NULL, 0);
    for(i = 0; i < XtNumber(popPBs); ++i)
        {
        sprintf(buffer, "Popup Choice #%d", i + 1);
        popPBs[i] = XmCreatePushButton(popUp, buffer, NULL, 0);
        }
    XtAddEventHandler(bbManager, ButtonPressMask, False, BPressFunc, popUp);
    ...
    XtManageChild(bbManager);
    ...
XtEventHandler BPressFunc(widget_id, client_data, call_data)
Widget widget_id;
caddr_t client_data;
XEvent *call_data;
    {
    Widget menu;

    if(call_data->xbutton.button == 3)
        {
        XmMenuPosition(client_data, call_data);
        XtManageChild(client_data);
        }
    return;
    }
```

Figure 17.8 Coding a PopupMenu in a Motif application.

Motif PulldownMenus

☐   PulldownMenus are the most complicated type of Motif menu simply because they usually involve so many widget instances. All Motif Pulldown-Menus start off with a RowColumn widget configured as a MenuBar. Figure 17.9 shows the syntax for the XmCreateMenuBar() function.

The MenuBar will contain a series of CascadeButtons that contain your choices for the PulldownMenus. For every menu that you want to pull down from the MenuBar, you must create a RowColum widget configured as a PulldownMenu and attach it to a CascadeButton. Figure 17.10 shows the syntax for the XmCreatePulldownMenu() function.

☐   To create a PulldownMenu you will typically go through the following steps:

1. Create the MenuBar as the child of some other widget in your program with a call to XmCreateMenuBar(). Manage the MenuBar widget.

2. Create all the PulldownMenus as children of the MenuBar with calls to XmCreatePulldownMenu(). *Do not* manage the PulldownMenu widgets.

3. Create the CascadeButtons for the menu choices in the MenuBar as children of the MenuBar with calls to XmCreateCascadeButton(). Set the

```
#include <Xm/RowColumn.h>

Widget XmCreateMenuBar(parent_id, instance_name, arg_list, arg_count)

Widget       parent_id;
String       instance_name;
ArgList      arg_list;
Cardinal     arg_count;
```

Figure 17.9 XmCreateMenuBar() syntax.

```
#include <Xm/RowColumn.h>

Widget XmCreatePulldownMenu(parent_id, instance_name, arg_list, arg_count)

Widget       parent_id;
String       instance_name;
ArgList      arg_list;
Cardinal     arg_count;
```

Figure 17.10 XmCreatePulldownMenu() syntax.

XmNsubMenuId resource for each CascadeButton to the widget id of the PulldownMenu that you want to be associated with that button. Manage the CascadeButton widgets.

4. Create the Button widgets or gadgets as children of the PulldownMenus using the appropriate XmCreate...Button() function calls. Manage the Buttons.

Notice that with a PulldownMenu system you manage everything except the PulldownMenus themselves. When you interact with one of the CascadeButtons in the MenuBar (using mouse button 1), it will automatically position and manage the PulldownMenu pane whose widget id is in its XmNsubMenuId resource. There is no need to call XtMenuPosition() or XtManageChild() on the PulldownMenu as you did with the PopupMenu. Figure 17.11 shows a code segment that uses a PulldownMenu.

With a RowColumn widget configured as a MenuBar there is an additional resource that you can take advantage of. The Motif Style Guide specifies that MenuBars should contain a Help menu and that the Help menu should be positioned at the far-right-hand side of the MenuBar. To help you accomplish Style Guide compliance with a Help menu, the RowColumn widget supplies a XmNmenuHelpWidget resource.

Your Help menu is created in the exact same way as any other PulldownMenu following the exact same steps as listed above. The only difference is that once the CascadeButton for the Help menu has been created, its widget id is placed in the MenuBar's XmNmenuHelpWidget resource. The RowColumn that has been configured as a MenuBar will ensure that the widget whose widget id appears in this resource will appear at the right-most side of the MenuBar.

Motif OptionMenus

An OptionMenu is a special kind of PulldownMenu without the MenuBar. All Motif OptionMenus are created from a RowColumn widget configured as an OptionMenu. The main difference being that an OptionMenu automatically creates the two main operating widgets for you. Figure 17.12 shows the syntax for the XmCreateOptionMenu() function.

Within the OptionMenu this function creates a Label widget and a CascadeButton widget. The Label widget lets you provide a title for the OptionMenu, which you have access to through the XmNlabelString resource. The CascadeButton lets you associate a PulldownMenu with with the OptionMenu through the RowColumn's XmNsubMenuId resource.

To create an OptionMenu you will typically go through the following steps:

1. Create a PulldownMenu as a child of the same parent as the OptionMenu with a call to XmCreatePulldownMenu(). *Do not* manage the PulldownMenu widget.

2. Create the OptionMenu as a child of some other widget in your program with a call to XmCreateOptionMenu(). Set the XmNsubMenuId

```
...
#include <Xm/BulletinB.h>
#include <Xm/RowColumn.h>
#include <Xm/PushB.h>
#include <Xm/CascadeB.h>
...
    Widget bbManager;
    Widget mBar;
    Widget mbCBs[2];
    Widget mbPull[2];
    Widget pull1PBs[5];
    Widget pull2PBs[5];
    char buffer[30];
    ...
    bbManager = XmCreateBulletinBoard(mwManager, "bbmanager", argList, i);
    ...
    mBar = XmCreateMenuBar(mwManager, "menubar", NULL, 0);
    mbPull[0] = XmCreatePulldownMenu(mBar, "pulldown1", NULL, 0);
    mbPull[1] = XmCreatePulldownMenu(mBar, "pulldown2", NULL, 0);
    XtSetArg(argList[0], XmNsubMenuId, mbPull[0]);
    mbCBs[0] = XmCreateCascadeButton(mBar, "cascade1", argList, 1);
    XtSetArg(argList[0], XmNsubMenuId, mbPull[1]);
    mbCBs[1] = XmCreateCascadeButton(mBar, "cascade2", argList, 1);
    for(i = 0; i < XtNumber(pull1PBs); ++i)
        {
        sprintf(buffer, "Pulldown #1 Choice #%d", i + 1);
        pull1PBs[i] = XmCreatePushButton(mbPull[0], buffer, NULL, 0);
        }
    for(i = 0; i < XtNumber(pull2PBs); ++i)
        {
        sprintf(buffer, "Pulldown #2 Choice #%d", i + 1);
        pull2PBs[i] = XmCreatePushButton(mbPull[1], buffer, NULL, 0);
        }
    ...
    XtManageChild(mBar);
    XtManageChildren(pull1PBs, XtNumber(pull1PBs));
    XtManageChildren(pull2PBs, XtNumber(pull2PBs));
    XtManageChildren(mbCBs, XtNumber(mbCBs));
    XtManageChild(bbManager);
    ...
```

Figure 17.11 Coding a PulldownMenu in a Motif application.

resource for the OptionMenu to the widget id of the PulldownMenu that you created in the first step. Manage the OptionMenu widget.

3. Create the Button widgets or gadgets as children of the PulldownMenu using the appropriate XmCreate...Button() function calls. Manage the Buttons.

```
#include <Xm/RowColumn.h>

Widget XmCreateOptionMenu(parent_id, instance_name, arg_list, arg_count)

Widget       parent_id;
String       instance_name;
ArgList      arg_list;
Cardinal     arg_count;
```

Figure 17.12 XmCreateOptionMenu() syntax.

Notice that with an OptionMenu system you manage everything except the PulldownMenu itself. When you interact with the CascadeButton in the OptionMenu (using mouse button 1), it will automatically position and manage the PulldownMenu pane whose widget id is in its XmNsubMenuId resource. There is no need to call XtMenuPosition() or XtManageChild() on the PulldownMenu as you did with the PopupMenu.

When you work with the OptionMenu widget, the label on the Cascade-Button will always show the label of the last Button widget you selected from the PulldownMenu pane. When the menu gets posted, Motif will cause the position of the menu to be such that the last selected Button widget will be positioned over the top of the underlying CascadeButton. When you drag to a new selection on the menu, the label on the Cascade-Button will be replaced with the label from the selection. Figure 17.13 shows a code segment that uses an OptionMenu.

Making Menu Options Unavailable

There will be certain instances within the operation of your X/Motif client application when you will want to make one or more menu options unavailable for selection by a user. As an example, in a File menu from a menu bar you may want the Save option to be unavailable until some change has occurred in the application data. Or, in an Edit Menu, you may not want the user to use the Paste option unless something has been Cut or Copied first. To make a menu option unavailable, you must render it insensitive.

One of the core resource values that is inherited by each and every widget instance you create in your application is called the XmNsensitive resource. This resource is a Boolean value that determines whether a widget is sensitive to user input. When a Menu option (a Button widget) has its XmNsensitive resource set to True (the default), it operates normally – as you are used to seeing it.

When a Button widget's XmNsensitive resource is set to False, it becomes insensitive. This means that it will not respond to KeyPress, KeyRelease, ButtonPress, ButtonRelease, MotionNotify, EnterNotify, LeaveNotify, FocusIn, or FocusOut events. With a Menu option Button widget, this means that it will not allow that option to be picked off the menu. So, to make a Menu option unavailable, you set its XmNsensitive resource to False.

```
...
#include <Xm/BulletinB.h>
#include <Xm/RowColumn.h>
#include <Xm/PushB.h>
...
    Widget bbManager;
    Widget optMenu;
    Widget optPull;
    Widget optPBs[5];
    Arg argList[10];
    XmString xmString;
    char buffer[20];
    Cardinal i;
    ...
    bbManager = XmCreateBulletinBoard(mwManager, "bbmanager", argList, i);
    ...
    optPull = XmCreatePulldownMenu(bbManager, "optpulldown", NULL, 0);
    xmString = XmStringCreateLtoR("option menu: ", XmSTRING_DEFAULT_CHARSET);
    i = 0;
    XtSetArg(argList[i], XmNx, 15); ++i;
    XtSetArg(argList[i], XmNy, 60); ++i;
    XtSetArg(argList[i], XmNsubMenuId, optPull); ++i;
    XtSetArg(argList[i], XmNlabelString, xmString); ++i;
    optMenu = XmCreateOptionMenu(bbManager, "option", argList, i);
    for(i = 0; i < XtNumber(optPBs); ++i)
        {
        sprintf(buffer, "Option Choice #%d", i + 1);
        optPBs[i] = XmCreatePushButton(optPull, buffer, NULL, 0);
        }
    XtManageChild(optMenu);
    XtManageChildren(optPBs, XtNumber(optPBs));
    XtManageChild(bbManager);
    ...
```

Figure 17.13 Coding a OptionMenu in a Motif application.

The visual appearance of a Button widget is supposed to change when it is insensitive. In the Motif widget set, when a Button has its XmNsensitive resource set to False, the label of the Button will get "grayed out" using a pixmap specified by the XmNinsensitivePixmap resource. In X terminology, we say that it gets *stippled*.

☐   You can, of course, use XtSetValues() to change a widget's sensitivity as we have seen before. However, the Xt Intrinsics provide a convenience function that can do the work for you. The XtSetSensitive() function can set the XmNsensitive resource on either a Primitive or a Composite widget. Figure 17.14 shows the syntax for this function.

The first parameter is the widget id of the widget whose XmNsensitive resource we want to change. The second parameter is one of the two Boolean values True or False. The function does not return a value.

```
void XtSetSensitive(widget_id, sensitive)

Widget      widget_id;
Boolean     sensitive;
```

Figure 17.14 XtSetSensitive() syntax.

XtSetSensitive() calls XtSetValues() on the specified widget using an argument list containing the XmNsensitive resource and the new sensitive value. If the specified widget is a Composite widget, it recursively descends the widget instance tree propagating the new sensitive value down to each child in the tree with more calls to XtSetValues().

□ You can also check to see if a particular widget is currently sensitive. The Intrinsics provide another function that allows you to determine the setting of a particular widget's XmNsensitive resource. This function is called XtIsSensitive(). Figure 17.15 shows its syntax.

The only parameter is the widget id of the widget whose XmNsensitive resource you are checking. This function will return True if the widget is sensitive to user input or False if the widget is insensitive.

Motif MenuShells

□ Each one of the XmCreate...Menu() functions creates an XmMenuShell widget to support the popup nature of the menus. Although you don't usually deal with the Shell widgets that are created for you to parent a menu, it is a good idea to know a little more about them to be able to make effective use of them.

The XmMenuShell class is subclassed off of the Intrinsics OverrideShell widget class. An OverrideShell bypasses the window manager when displaying itself. This, of course, means that it will not have its own window decorations. OverrideShells are specifically designed to contain Popup or PullDownMenu panes.

The XmMenuShell widget class inherits resources from the Core, Composite, Shell, and OverrideShell widget classes. Its class name is XmMenuShell, and it does not define any new resources for itself. It does, however, override the XmNallowShellResize resource that it inherits from the Shell widget class.

When an XmMenuShell is posted, it grabs all user input. This means that the user must finish interacting with the menu before going on to do anything else with the application. To complete interaction with the menu the user simply chooses one of the options off the menu which causes it to become unposted.

```
Boolean XtIsSensitive(widget_id)

Widget      widget_id;
```

Figure 17.15 XtIsSensitive() syntax.

Buttons are armed as the mouse pointer moves into them and are disarmed as the pointer moves out. When the user releases the mouse button with the pointer inside a Button window, that Button becomes activated. If you need to unpost a menu without selecting a menu option, simply drag or click the mouse pointer anywhere outside the bounds of the menu.

◻ When referencing the children Button widgets of any of the Menus discussed in this section (except a MenuBar) in a resource file, you have to be careful. Because an XmMenuShell widget is created as the parent of your menu for you, there is no way to determine its instance name. This means that you cannot reference a Menu Button widget with a completely tight binding. In a resource file you will be forced to use some type of loose binding to reference the children Button widgets of the Menu.

A Complete X/Motif Client Application

◻ Using all the concepts and techniques presented in this chapter, we can put together a simple, but complete, X/Motif-based client application. Example 17.1 shows the code for a program that has a MainWindow widget, BulletinBoard, a Text message area widget, and a MenuBar widget in it. The MenuBar has two PulldownMenus attached to it with five options on each one. The BulletinBoard has an OptionMenu installed on it with five choices, also. Finally, the BulletinBoard also has an event-handler function attached to it to watch for ButtonPress events on mouse button 3 for a PopupMenu with another five choices on it.

Figure 17.16 shows what the program would look like on a typical terminal screen.

Review Questions

◻ Please write down the answers to the following questions:

1. Which widget class is the foundation of the Motif menu systems?

2. Why are Motif menus contained within their own Shell widget?

3. What is the purpose of a menu?

4. List two ways to interact with a menu.

5. What is the purpose of a mnemonic? An accelerator?

6. List the three types of menus available with Motif.

7. What is a typical instance tree for a PopupMenu? A PulldownMenu? An OptionMenu?

8. What is a cascading menu?

9. Which resource allows for cascading menus?

10. Which function is used to create a Motif PopupMenu?

```
#include <stdio.h>
#include <Xm/BulletinB.h>
#include <Xm/MainW.h>
#include <Xm/RowColumn.h>
#include <Xm/Text.h>
#include <Xm/PushB.h>
#include <Xm/CascadeB.h>

XtEventHandler BPressFunc();
Widget topShell;

main(argc, argv)
Cardinal argc;
String argv[];
    {
    Widget mwManager;
    Widget bbManager;
    Widget msgArea;
    Widget popUp;
    Widget popPBs[5];
    Widget mBar;
    Widget mbCBs[2];
    Widget mbPull[2];
    Widget pull1PBs[5];
    Widget pull2PBs[5];
    Widget optMenu;
    Widget optPull;
    Widget optPBs[5];
    Arg argList[10];
    XmString xmString;
    char buffer[30];
    Cardinal i;

    /* Initialize  the Intrinsics and create a top Shell widget */
    topShell = XtInitialize(argv[0], "Edit", NULL, 0, &argc, argv);

    /* Create the manager widget */
    mwManager = XmCreateMainWindow(topShell, "mwmanager", NULL, 0);

    /* Create the user interface widgets */
    i = 0;
    XtSetArg(argList[i], XmNwidth, 200); ++i;
    XtSetArg(argList[i], XmNheight, 200); ++i;
    bbManager = XmCreateBulletinBoard(mwManager, "bbmanager", argList, i);
    msgArea = XmCreateText(mwManager, "msgarea", NULL, 0);
```

Example 17.1 X/Motif application program with menus, part 1.

```
    mBar = XmCreateMenuBar(mwManager, "menubar", NULL, 0);
    mbPull[0] = XmCreatePulldownMenu(mBar, "pulldown1", NULL, 0);
    mbPull[1] = XmCreatePulldownMenu(mBar, "pulldown2", NULL, 0);
    XtSetArg(argList[0], XmNsubMenuId, mbPull[0]);
    mbCBs[0] = XmCreateCascadeButton(mBar, "cascade1", argList, 1);
    XtSetArg(argList[0], XmNsubMenuId, mbPull[1]);
    mbCBs[1] = XmCreateCascadeButton(mBar, "cascade2", argList, 1);
    for(i = 0; i < XtNumber(pull1PBs); ++i)
        {
        sprintf(buffer, "Pulldown #1 Choice #%d", i + 1);
        pull1PBs[i] = XmCreatePushButton(mbPull[0], buffer, NULL, 0);
        }
    for(i = 0; i < XtNumber(pull2PBs); ++i)
        {
        sprintf(buffer, "Pulldown #2 Choice #%d", i + 1);
        pull2PBs[i] = XmCreatePushButton(mbPull[1], buffer, NULL, 0);
        }
    optPull = XmCreatePulldownMenu(bbManager, "optpulldown", NULL, 0);
    xmString = XmStringCreateLtoR("option menu: ", XmSTRING_DEFAULT_CHARSET);
    i = 0;
    XtSetArg(argList[i], XmNx, 15); ++i;
    XtSetArg(argList[i], XmNy, 60); ++i;
    XtSetArg(argList[i], XmNsubMenuId, optPull); ++i;
    XtSetArg(argList[i], XmNlabelString, xmString); ++i;
    optMenu = XmCreateOptionMenu(bbManager, "option", argList, i);
    for(i = 0; i < XtNumber(optPBs); ++i)
        {
        sprintf(buffer, "Option Choice #%d", i + 1);
        optPBs[i] = XmCreatePushButton(optPull, buffer, NULL, 0);
        }
    popUp = XmCreatePopupMenu(bbManager, "popUp", NULL, 0);
    for(i = 0; i < XtNumber(popPBs); ++i)
        {
        sprintf(buffer, "Popup Choice #%d", i + 1);
        popPBs[i] = XmCreatePushButton(popUp, buffer, NULL, 0);
        }
    XmMainWindowSetAreas(mwManager, mBar, msgArea, NULL, NULL, bbManager);

    /* Set up event handlers for the widgets */
    XtAddEventHandler(bbManager, ButtonPressMask, False, BPressFunc, popUp);

    /* Make the program visible on the screen */
    XtManageChild(mBar);
    XtManageChildren(pull1PBs, XtNumber(pull1PBs));
    XtManageChildren(pull2PBs, XtNumber(pull2PBs));
    XtManageChildren(mbCBs, XtNumber(mbCBs));
    XtManageChild(optMenu);
    XtManageChildren(optPBs, XtNumber(optPBs));
```

Example 17.2 X/Motif application program with menus, part 2.

```
    XtManageChildren(popPBs, XtNumber(popPBs));
    XtManageChild(msgArea);
    XtManageChild(bbManager);
    XtManageChild(mwManager);
    XtRealizeWidget(topShell);

    /* Wait for input events */
    XtMainLoop();
    }

XtEventHandler BPressFunc(widget_id, client_data, call_data)
Widget widget_id;
caddr_t client_data;
XEvent *call_data;
    {
    Widget menu;

    /* Determine which button invoked this function */
    if(call_data->xbutton.button == 3)
        {
        XmMenuPosition(client_data, call_data);
        XtManageChild(client_data);
        }
    return;
    }
```

Example 17.3 X/Motif application program with menus, part 3.

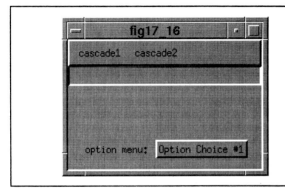

Figure 17.16 Output of the previous X/Motif application program.

11. List the steps needed to construct a fully functional Motif PopupMenu.

12. Why is mouse button 3 used to interact with a PopupMenu?

13. What is the purpose and use of the XmMenuPosition() function?

14. Which function is used to create a Motif MenuBar?

15. Which function is used to create a Motif PulldownMenu?

16. List the steps needed to construct a fully functional Motif Pulldown-Menu.

17. What is the purpose of the XmNmenuHelpWidget resource?

18. Which function is used to create a Motif OptionMenu?

19. List the steps needed to construct a fully functional Motif OptionMenu.

20. What is the difference between a PulldownMenu and an OptionMenu?

21. How do you use the XmNsensitive resource? What are its possible values?

22. List two ways to change the XmNsensitive resource.

23. What is the purpose of the XtIsSensitive() function?

24. What is the purpose of the XmMenuShell widget class?

25. How does user interaction with an XmMenuShell differ from that with other Shell widgets?

Exercises

The following exercises are designed to give you the opportunity to practice the concepts and facilities presented in this chapter:

1. Modify the program from a previous chapter that had three PushButton widgets on the left and a DrawingArea widget on the right of a Form widget. The buttons were labeled Clear, Line, and Circle. Add an OptionMenu below the PushButtons. The label on the OptionMenu should read Color and the options on the menu should be:

```
Black
Blue
Violet
Green
Yellow
Red
White
```

2. Modify the previous program to add a PopupMenu to the DrawingArea. The PopupMenu will have a title Label widget, a Separator widget, and five PushButton widgets. The Label's XmNlabelString will be "Line Width" and the PushButtons will be for widths of 1, 2, 3, 4, or 5 pixels.

3. Modify the program from a previous chapter that had a MainWindow widget that contained a Text message area widget and a BulletinBoard work area widget. The BulletinBoard had two RowColumn widgets with five Label widgets in one and five Text widgets in the other. Add a MenuBar widget that contains three PulldownMenus as follows:

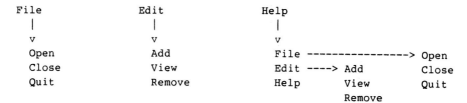

The Help menu will have three buttons — two CascadeButtons and one
PushButton. The two CascadeButtons will pop up PulldownMenu panes
with the options indicated.

18

Motif
Dialog
Boxes

Introduction

◻   In older data-processing applications, if you wanted to ask the user a question or prompt them for some type of input data, you would print a message to the screen and then read their response from the keyboard. In X and other GUI systems, this is no longer possible. Instead of requiring that every X application have one Text widget available for the output of messages and another for the input of responses, another method is available. In this chapter you will learn about dialog boxes to perform this type of user interaction.

Objectives

◻   After completing this chapter, you will be able to:

◻   Explain what dialog boxes are used for.

◻   Describe the two different styles of dialog boxes.

◻   List the two widget classes on which dialog boxes are based.

◻   Explain what a MessageBox is used for.

◻   List the typical children widgets of a MessageBox.

◻   Explain what a SelectionBox is used for.

◻   List the typical children widgets of a SelectionBox.

◻ Explain when a dialog box should be created.

◻ Describe how and when a dialog box is posted.

◻ Explain how long a dialog box remains on the screen.

◻ Describe the use of the XmNautoUnmanage resource in a dialog box.

◻ Describe the use of the XmNdialogStyle resource in a dialog box.

◻ Explain how to get your application to execute some code in response to user interaction with a dialog box.

◻ List the six different styles of preconfigured MessageBox dialogs and how they differ.

◻ Explain why you should reuse dialog widgets instead of creating one widget for each user interaction.

◻ List the three different styles of preconfigured SelectionBox dialogs and how they differ.

◻ List the two functions available to create a customized dialog box.

◻ Describe how to access and change the resources associated with the children widgets of the preconfigured dialog boxes.

◻ Explain why dialog boxes can pop up out of nowhere and then disappear.

Dialog Box Concepts

◻ With what we know about X and Motif so far, if we wanted to display a message to our application's user, we would have two choices. First, we could hope that an xterm is running and fprintf(stdout,...) to display our message there. Unfortunately, it is not required that an xterm be running for any other X/Motif client application to execute. Also, it would be a little awkward to have our application running in one set of windows with messages being displayed in some other window.

Second, We could include a Text widget in our client application space to display our messages in. You might remember that the Motif MainWindow widget takes this approach. In some situations, though, an extra Text widget hanging around may tend to clutter the visual appearance of our application. We have a similar problem with input.

What, then, is an application programmer to do? We don't want to depend on an xterm being available, and we don't want to clutter our application area with Text widgets that are used only once in a while. The answer to these problems is to use a dialog box.

◻ A dialog box is a special type of composite widget that has been preconfigured with a number of different children widgets to allow for some sort of user interaction. There are two styles of Motif dialog boxes. The first lets you display a message and then wait for some type of yes/no answer when the user clicks on a button. The other style lets the user pick an item from a list of possibilities or to type a response into a text widget.

Dialog boxes are designed to pop up when you need them (do you remember what "popping up" implies?) and to go away when you are done. When you want to interact with a user, you put a message into an

appropriate dialog box and manage it. After the user has finished interacting with the dialog, it goes away.

Although there are many different types of dialog boxes—for errors, questions, warnings, information, and so on—they are all variations on one of
two Motif widgets. All dialog boxes are implemented as a preconfigured
MessageBox widget or SelectionBox widget. Figure 18.1 shows what a dialog box would look like in a typical Motif application.

Motif MessageBox

¤   The MessageBox is a dialog-type widget that consists of a message Label
widget, a symbol (called a pixmap), a Separator widget, and three Push-
Button widgets. It is used to display a message to the application user.
Convenience functions are provided for the creation of several standard
types of message-style dialogs for things like error messages, warning messages, and asking questions. You can also design and create customized
dialog boxs to suit other needs.

The MessageBox is laid out with the symbol in the top-left corner and the
message to its right. The Separator separates the message at the top from
the PushButtons at the bottom. By default, the Buttons will be labeled
OK, Cancel, and Help and are evenly spaced across the bottom of the MessageBox. The OK button is the "default" button and is activated when the
user presses the return key. Also, by default, when the user activates any
one of the three Button widgets, the MessageBox is automatically
unmanaged.

The contents of the message and the labels for the three PushButtons are
easily modified by changing appropriate resources. The symbol that is used
to the left of the message is also a resource. The resource type for the symbol, however, is type Pixmap, which will be discussed later. Figure 18.2
shows the syntax for the XmCreateMessageBox() function.

The MessageBox widget inherits resources from the Core, Composite,
Constraint, XmManager, and XmBulletinBoard classes. It depends on the
XmBulletinBoard widget class for much of its general dialog behavior. Its
class name is XmMessageBox. Figure 18.3 shows what a MessageBox
would look like.

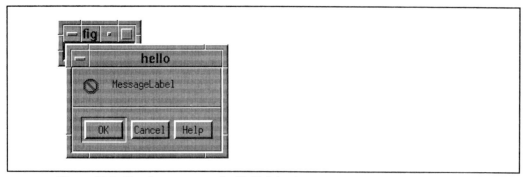

Figure 18.1 Visual appearance of a Motif dialog box.

```
#include <Xm/MessageB.h>

Widget XmCreateMessageBox(parent_id, instance_name, arg_list, arg_count)

Widget      parent_id;
String      instance_name;
ArgList     arg_list;
Cardinal    arg_count;
```

Figure 18.2 XmCreateMessageBox() syntax.

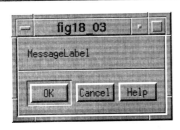

Figure 18.3 Visual appearance of a MessageBox widget.

The XmMessageBox widget class defines a set of resources that are inherited by an instance of a MessageBox widget. Figure 18.4 lists these new resources and their type and access.

When a callback occurs for a MessageBox widget for any one of the callback resources listed in Figure 18.4, a pointer to a structure of type XmAnyCallbackStruct is passed as the call_data parameter to the callback function that is invoked in response. The structure has the following members:

```
Name                          Type (Default Value)                       Access
-----------------------------  ------------------------------------------  ------
XmNcancelCallback             XtCallbackList (NULL)                       C
XmNcancelLabelString          XmString ("Cancel")                        CSG
XmNdefaultButtonType          unsigned char (XmDIALOG_OK_BUTTON)         CSG
XmNdialogType                 unsigned char (XmDIALOG_MESSAGE)           CSG
XmNhelpLabelString            XmString ("Help")                          CSG
XmNmessageAlignment           unsigned char (XmALIGNMENT_BEGINNING)      CSG
XmNmessageString              XmString (NULL)                            CSG
XmNminimizeButtons            Boolean (False)                            CSG
XmNokCallback                 XtCallbackList (NULL)                       C
XmNokLabelString              XmString ("OK")                            CSG
XmNsymbolPixmap               Pixmap (dynamic)                           CSG
```

Figure 18.4 XmMessageBox resources.

```
typedef struct
    {
    int     reason;
    XEvent  *event;
    } XmAnyCallbackStruct;
```

reason   Indicates why the callback was invoked.

event   Pointer to a union of type XEvent which contains information about the actual X event that triggered the callback.

Motif SelectionBox

The SelectionBox is a dialog-type widget that consists of a scrolling List widget for alternatives, an editable Text widget for the selected alternative, Label widgets for the List and Text, a Separator, and three (possibly four) PushButton widgets. Convenience functions are provided for the creation of several standard types of selection-style dialogs for a List of alternatives, a List of filenames, prompting for textual information, and so on. You can also design and create customized dialog boxes to suit other needs.

The SelectionBox is laid out in a vertical orientation. The list Label appears first with the List of alternatives below it. This is followed by the text Label with the Text selection widget below that. The Separator widget is used to separate the List and the Text from the PushButtons at the bottom. By default, the Buttons will be labeled OK, Cancel, and Help and are evenly spaced across the bottom of the SelectionBox. The OK button is the "default" button and is activated when the user presses the return key. Also, by default, when the user activates any one of the three Button widgets, the SelectionBox is automatically unmanaged. The fourth possible Button widget is labeled Apply and is unmanaged by default.

The user can select an item from the list in one of two ways: by scrolling through the List and pointing and clicking on the desired item or by typing the item directly into the Text widget. Clicking on an item in the list causes that item to be displayed in the Text widget. New items can be selected as many times as the user wants. Interaction with the OK Button causes the selected item to be acted on through the callback function attached to that Button.

The contents of the List and Text labels and the labels for the three Push-Buttons are easily modified by changing appropriate resources. The contents of the List widget, as discussed in a previous chapter, are an array of Motif compound strings. This array, a count of the number of List elements, as well as a variety of other List information are also changeable through resources. Figure 18.5 shows the syntax for the XmCreateSelectionBox() function.

The SelectionBox widget inherits resources from the Core, Composite, Constraint, XmManager, and XmBulletinBoard classes. It depends on the XmBulletinBoard widget class for much of its general dialog behavior. Its class name is XmSelectionBox. Figure 18.6 shows what a SelectionBox would look like.

```
#include <Xm/SelectioB.h>

Widget XmCreateSelectionBox(parent_id, instance_name, arg_list, arg_count)

Widget       parent_id;
String       instance_name;
ArgList      arg_list;
Cardinal     arg_count;
```

Figure 18.5 XmCreateSelectionBox() syntax.

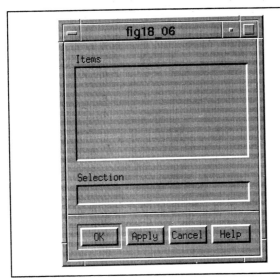

Figure 18.6 Visual appearance of a SelectionBox widget.

The XmSelectionBox widget class defines a set of resources that are inherited by an instance of a SelectionBox widget. Figure 18.7 lists these new resources and their type and access.

When a callback occurs for a SelectionBox widget for any one of the callback resources listed in Figure 18.7, a pointer to a structure of type XmSelectionBoxCallbackStruct is passed as the call_data parameter to the callback function that is invoked in response. The structure has the following members:

```
typedef struct
    {
    int      reason;
    XEvent   *event;
    XmString value;
    int      length;
    } XmSelectionBoxCallbackStruct;
```

```
Name                          Type (Default Value)                    Access
----------------------------  ------------------------------------    ------
XmNapplyCallback              XtCallbackList (NULL)                    C
XmNapplyLabelString           XmString ("Apply")                      CSG
XmNcancelCallback             XtCallbackList (NULL)                    C
XmNcancelLabelString          XmString ("Cancel")                     CSG
XmNdialogType                 unsigned char (dynamic)                 CSG
XmNhelpLabelString            XmString ("Help")                       CSG
XmNlistItemCount              int (0)                                 CSG
XmNlistItems                  XmStringList (NULL)                     CSG
XmNlistLabelString            XmString (NULL)                         CSG
XmNlistVisibleItemCount       int (8)                                 CSG
XmNminimizeButtons            Boolean (False)                         CSG
XmNmustMatch                  Boolean (False)                         CSG
XmNnoMatchCallback            XtCallbackList (NULL)                    C
XmNokCallback                 XtCallbackList (NULL)                    C
XmNokLabelString              XmString ("OK")                         CSG
XmNselectionLabelString       XmString ("Selection")                  CSG
XmNtextAccelerators           XtTranslations (see the documentation)  C
XmNtextColumns                int (20)                                CSG
XmNtextString                 XmString (NULL)                         CSG
```

Figure 18.7 XmSelectionBox resources.

reason   Indicates why the callback was invoked.

event   Pointer to a union of type XEvent which contains information about the actual X event that triggered the callback.

value   Compound string text of item selected or typed in by user.

length   Size in bytes of selected item.

Creating and Managing Dialog Boxes

◻   Dialog boxes have some features in common with menus. Just like a PulldownMenu pane, dialog boxes can be created at any time *but are not managed immediately.* Instead, you wait to manage a dialog box in response to some type of event.

Most Motif programmers will create their dialog boxes right along with all the other widgets in their program. An event handler or callback function is then registered to manage the dialog in response to some user input. For example, when the user chooses the Quit option off the File PulldownMenu, the program may post a dialog box that asks the question "Are you sure you want to quit?"

In this example, a QuestionDialog would be created right along with the MenuBar, the MenuBar CascadeButtons, the PulldownMenus, and the PulldownMenu PushButtons. Just like the PulldownMenu pane, the Question-Dialog widget is not managed at this time. A callback would be registered for one of the Button widgets on one of the PulldownMenu panes such that, when activated, a call is made to a function that will post the dialog box by doing an XtManageChild() on its widget id. Figure 18.8 shows how a dialog box is typically created and managed.

□   Once a dialog box is posted, it stays on the screen until the user interacts with it. By default, when a user interacts with any one of the PushButton widgets, the dialog box will become unmanaged and disappear. This behavior is a result of the XmNautoUnmanage resource that the dialog box inherits from the XmBulletinBoard widget class. The value of this resource is normally True, which indicates that the dialog should automatically unmanage itself when any one of the dialog's Button widgets are activated.

This is the default operation of a dialog. If you want the dialog box to remain on the screen after the user interacts with a Button in the dialog, you should set the XmNautoUnmanage resource for the dialog to False. This would mean that it would be up to your client application code to unmanage the dialog and make it disappear in response to some other user action or event.

□   Dialog boxes have another feature which is important to discuss here. Since a dialog pops up out of nowhere, it can be assumed that it is enclosed in its own Shell widget. All dialog boxes, whether they are MessageBoxes or SelectionBoxes, are created as the children of XmDialogShell widgets. Just as with menus, this allows the dialog box to pop up without being

```
#include <Xm/BulletinB.h>
#include <Xm/MessageB.h>
...
XtEventHandler BPressFunc();
...
    Widget bBoard;
    Widget dialog;
    Arg argList[10];
    ...
    bBoard = XmCreateBulletinBoard(topShell, "bboard", NULL, 0);
    XtSetArg(argList[0], XmNdialogStyle, XmDIALOG_SYSTEM_MODAL);
    dialog = XmCreateWarningDialog(bBoard, "warndialog", argList, 1);
    ...
    XtAddEventHandler(bBoard, ButtonPressMask, False, BPressFunc, dialog);
    XtManageChild(bBoard);
    XtRealizeWidget(topShell);
    ...
XtEventHandler BPressFunc(widget_id, client_data, call_data)
Widget widget_id;
Widget client_data;
XEvent *call_data;
    {
    ...
    XtManageChild(client_data);
    ...
    return;
    }
```

Figure 18.8 Creating and using a dialog box.

squeezed between the other widgets in your application. Unlike menus, these Shell widgets *do not* bypass the window manager and are enclosed in their own separate window decorations. This means that once the dialog pops up, the user can grab the title bar, move it out of the way, and ignore it. This is not always desirable.

The style of interaction that a user has with a dialog box is controlled by another resource that all dialog boxes inherit from the XmBulletinBoard widget class. This resource is the XmNdialogStyle and can be set to one of four possible values:

XmDIALOG_SYSTEM_MODAL	Specifies that the dialog must have a response before X allows you to have any other interaction with any other application on the screen.
XmDIALOG_APPLICATION_MODAL	Specifies that the dialog must have a response before X allows you to have any other interaction with the current application. The user can interact with any other application before responding to the dialog.
XmDIALOG_MODELESS	Specifies that the dialog does not need any type of immediate response. The user can continue with the current application and respond to the dialog at some later time. This is the default.
XmDIALOG_WORK_AREA	Used for nondialog Bulletin-Board widgets where the parent widget is not some type of Shell widget.

◻ One final word about the operation of a dialog—just as with PushButtons on a PulldownMenu pane—there is no automatic action performed in response to a user interacting with a PushButton on a dialog box. If you want your client application to do something when the user clicks on the OK button, you have to set up a callback for it. If you do not register a callback function for the PushButton widgets on a dialog box, the only thing that happens is that it becomes unmanaged.

Each type of dialog box has three callbacks defined in their resource lists. The XmNokCallback and the XmNcancelCallback are defined for both the MessageBox and the SelectionBox widgets. Both these styles of dialog boxes also inherit the XmNhelpCallback from the XmManager widget class. The SelectionBox widget class also defines an XmNapplyCallback. If you want some action to occur when a user activates one of your dialog's PushButtons, you must register a callback function for it. Just as before, call XtAddCallback() using the appropriate XmN...Callback name.

MessageBox Dialogs

◻ There are six preconfigured Motif MessageBox dialogs. You can create your own, but these six styles cover the most common situations in which a message dialog box is needed. The only difference between these six dialog boxes is the symbol that is displayed in the upper-left corner. Figure 18.9 shows the syntax for the convenience functions provided for the creation of these preconfigured MessageBox dialogs. The symbols for each style of dialog are as follows:

ErrorDialog	A circle with a diagonal line through it
InformationDialog	A large, stylized, lowercase i in a serifed font
QuestionDialog	A silhouette of a human head with a question mark in it
WarningDialog	A large, stylized, exclamation point
WorkingDialog	An hourglass
MessageDialog	No symbol

As stated previously, these are the default symbols. When you learn what bitmaps and pixmaps are (a little later), you will be able to create your own custom symbols. As discussed previously, you can install your own symbols in these or other dialogs. Figure 18.10 shows what the different types of MessageBox dialog boxes look like.

◻ You can, of course, create one unique dialog box for every type of user interaction you plan on making from your X/Motif client application. But with some thought and a little work you can decrease the size and increase the speed of your client application through judicious use of dialogs.

Most Motif application programmers will create only one instance of each style of dialog box that they will use. For instance, a programmer may need to inform the user of certain error conditions, ask a couple of questions with a yes/no response, and prompt the user for one or more text responses. In this case the programmer should create one ErrorDialog, one Question-Dialog, and one PromptDialog. In a situation requiring the use of a dialog, an appropriate message is installed in the XmNmessageString resource of

```
#include <Xm/MessageB.h>

Widget XmCreateErrorDialog(parent_id, instance_name, arg_list, arg_count)
Widget XmCreateInformationDialog(parent_id, instance_name, arg_list, arg_count)
Widget XmCreateMessageDialog(parent_id, instance_name, arg_list, arg_count)
Widget XmCreateQuestionDialog(parent_id, instance_name, arg_list, arg_count)
Widget XmCreateWarningDialog(parent_id, instance_name, arg_list, arg_count)
Widget XmCreateWorkingDialog(parent_id, instance_name, arg_list, arg_count)

Widget      parent_id;
String      instance_name;
ArgList     arg_list;
Cardinal    arg_count;
```

Figure 18.9 XmMessageBox dialog convenience functions syntax.

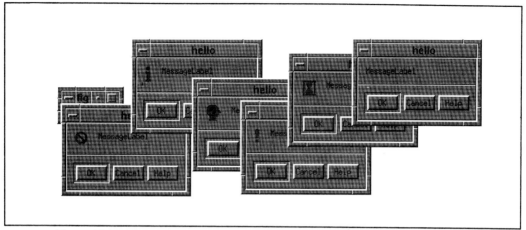

Figure 18.10 Visual appearance of MessageBox dialog boxes.

the dialog box, and it is managed. In another situation requiring the same dialog box, a different string is installed in the XmNmessageString resource before it is managed.

By using this style of programming instead of one dialog per user interaction, you will make your program more efficient. Widgets take time to create, take up space in your application and the server, and require interaction with the server—and dialog boxes are Composite widgets with a Shell, a BulletinBoard, and several Primitive children. To make your client application as efficient as possible, minimize the number of widgets you create and reuse them whenever possible.

SelectionBox Dialogs

¤   There are three preconfigured Motif SelectionBox dialogs. You can create your own, but these three styles cover the most common situations in which a selection dialog box is needed. Figure 18.11 shows the syntax for the convenience functions provided for the creation of these preconfigured Selection-Box dialogs.

```
#include <Xm/SelectioB.h>
#include <Xm/FileSB.h>


Widget XmCreatePromptDialog(parent_id, instance_name, arg_list, arg_count)
Widget XmCreateSelectionDialog(parent_id, instance_name, arg_list, arg_count)
Widget XmCreateFileSelectionDialog(parent_id,instance_name,arg_list,arg_count)


Widget      parent_id;
String      instance_name;
ArgList     arg_list;
Cardinal    arg_count;
```

Figure 18.11 XmSelectionBox dialog convenience functions syntax.

The PromptDialog has a Label widget that you can use to prompt the user for some kind of textual information. The Label is followed by a single-line Text widget for the user's input. A separator appears below the Text widget with the three standard PushButtons below it.

The SelectionDialog follows the same basic form, with one addition. The SelectionDialog adds a List widget with an associated Label above the position of the Text widget and its Label. The Label is for your use to identify the purpose of the List widget. When you click on an item in the List, the text from the selected item gets copied to the Text widget.

The FileSelectionDialog adds one more item. Similar to the SelectionDialog, the FileSelectionDialog adds another single-line Text widget and an associated Label above the List widget. Unlike the other SelectionBox-style dialogs, there is some preprogrammed code associated with this widget. The first Text widget is called the file or directory mask. You enter some type of file or directory name supported by the underlying operating system using any of the filename expansion metacharacters (wildcards) that the file system supports. When the text widget is activated, it searches the file system for all the files that match the pattern and puts them in the list widget. The user then selects an item in the List which gets copied into the last Text widget. When the OK button is activated, the contents of the last Text widget become available to the callback function that was registered for the OK PushButton.

In order to create a FileSelectionDialog in your X/Motif client application, you must include the Programmer's Workbench library (-lPW) on the cc command used to compile your program. In Motif 1.1 the FileSelectionDialog has been expanded to include a directory List widget as well. The user can start with an initial directory in the directory mask text widget, which, when activated, will display all the directories in one list and all the files in the other. To change directories, the user selects an item from the directory list. To act on a file, the user selects an item from the file list. Figure 18.12 shows what the different types of SelectionBox dialog boxes look like.

¤   Remember, widgets take time to create, take up space in your application and the server, and require interaction with the server—and dialog boxes are Composite widgets with a Shell, a BulletinBoard, and several Primitive children. To make your client application as efficient as possible, minimize the number of dialogs you create and reuse them whenever possible.

Create Your Own Dialog

¤   If you run into a situation where one of the preconfigured dialog boxes is not appropriate, you can create your own unique dialog box. Two functions are provided to conveniently create an empty dialog box which you can customize with any children widgets you want. Figure 18.13 shows the syntax for these functions.

Obviously, XmCreateBulletinBoardDialog() creates a dialog box with a BulletinBoard in it, while XmCreateFormDialog() creates a dialog box with a Form in it. Which one you use depends only on how you want to attach the Primitive children widgets to the dialog box. Otherwise, they both provide the same functionality.

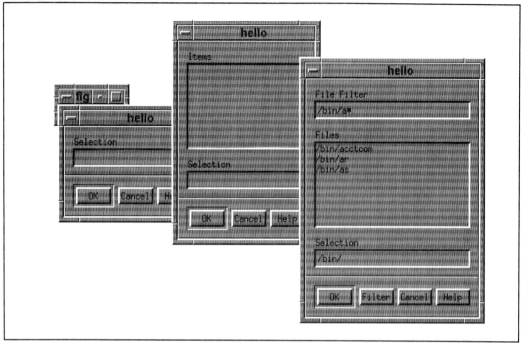

Figure 18.12   Visual appearance of SelectionBox dialog boxes.

```
#include <Xm/BulletinB.h>
#include <Xm/Form.h>

Widget XmCreateBulletinBoardDialog(parent_id,instance_name,arg_list,arg_count)
Widget XmCreateFormDialog(parent_id, instance_name, arg_list, arg count)

Widget      parent_id;
String      instance_name;
ArgList     arg_list;
Cardinal    arg_count;
```

Figure 18.13   Custom dialog convenience functions syntax.

Both functions create an XmDialogShell first and then create their respective Manager widgets as a child. The shell is managed, but the Manager is
not. Just like any other dialog box, when you are ready to display your
custom dialog, you must do an XtManageChild() on it. When you see that
the user is done with your dialog box, you do an XtUnmanageChild() on it
(or use the XmNautoUnmanage resource).

Neither one of these dialogs come with any preconfigured Primitive children. It is up to you to create the dialog first and then create the Primitive
children that you want in the dialog box as children of the Manager widget
that was created for you. In this way, you can create customized dialog
boxes that contain any user interface widgets that you need.

Motif Dialog Box Convenience Functions

◻ What if you wanted to change the XmNsensitive resource on the Help button in a dialog box to render it unavailable for user input? What if you wanted to change the XmNseparatorType resource on the Separator widget to XmSHADOW_ETCHED_OUT? Unfortunately, you don't have direct access to all the resources in all the Primitive widgets that are preconfigured as children of a dialog box.

For this reason three functions are provided to give you access to the widget ids of the Primitive widgets configured into a MessageBox dialog, a SelectionBox dialog, or a FileSelectionBox dialog. Once you have a widget id, you can create an argument list with the appropriate resources and use XtSetValues() to set the resource values in the child widget of the dialog box to change its characteristics.

◻ XmMessageBoxGetChild() is a convenience function which retrieves the widget id of any of the child widgets configured into any one of the MessageBox-style dialogs. You pass it a parameter that indicates which child you are interested in and it will return you its widget id. Figure 18.14 shows the syntax for this function.

The first parameter is the widget id returned from some previous call to an XmCreate...Dialog() function. This is the widget id of the MessageBox-style dialog whose child widget id you are interested in. The second parameter identifies which child widget id you want retrieved and can be one of the following values:

◻ XmDIALOG_CANCEL_BUTTON

◻ XmDIALOG_DEFAULT_BUTTON

◻ XmDIALOG_HELP_BUTTON

◻ XmDIALOG_MESSAGE_LABEL

◻ XmDIALOG_OK_BUTTON

◻ XmDIALOG_SEPARATOR

◻ XmDIALOG_SYMBOL_LABEL

◻ XmSelectionBoxGetChild() is a convenience function which retrieves the widget id of any of the child widgets configured into any one of the SelectionBox-style dialogs. You pass it a parameter that indicates which child you are interested in, and it will return you its widget id. Figure 18.15 shows the syntax for this function.

```
#include <Xm/MessageB.h>

Widget XmMessageBoxGetChild(widget_id, child);

Widget        widget;
unsigned char child;
```

Figure 18.14 XmMessageBoxGetChild() syntax.

```
#include <Xm/SelectioB.h>

Widget XmSelectionBoxGetChild(widget_id, child);

Widget          widget;
unsigned char child;
```

Figure 18.15 XmSelectionBoxGetChild() syntax.

The first parameter is the widget id returned from some previous call to an XmCreate...Dialog() function. This is the widget id of the SelectionBox-style dialog whose child widget id you are interested in. The second parameter identifies which child widget id you want retrieved:

◻ XmDIALOG_APPLY_BUTTON

◻ XmDIALOG_CANCEL_BUTTON

◻ XmDIALOG_DEFAULT_BUTTON

◻ XmDIALOG_HELP_BUTTON

◻ XmDIALOG_LIST

◻ XmDIALOG_LIST_LABEL

◻ XmDIALOG_OK_BUTTON

◻ XmDIALOG_SELECTION_LABEL

◻ XmDIALOG_SEPARATOR

◻ XmDIALOG_TEXT

◻ XmDIALOG_WORK_AREA

◻ XmFileSelectionBoxGetChild() is a convenience function which retrieves the widget id of any of the child widgets configured into a FileSelectionDialog. You pass it a parameter that indicates which child you are interested in, and it will return you its widget id. Figure 18.16 shows the syntax for this function.

The first parameter is the widget id returned from some previous call to an XmCreateFileSelectionDialog() function. This is the widget id of the FileSelectionBox-style dialog whose child widget id you are interested in. The second parameter identifies which child widget id you want retrieved and can be one of the following values:

```
#include <Xm/FileSB.h>

Widget XmFileSelectionBoxGetChild(widget_id, child);

Widget          widget;
unsigned char child;
```

Figure 18.16 XmFileSelectionBoxGetChild() syntax.

◻ XmDIALOG_APPLY_BUTTON

◻ XmDIALOG_CANCEL_BUTTON

◻ XmDIALOG_DEFAULT_BUTTON

◻ XmDIALOG_FILTER_LABEL

◻ XmDIALOG_FILTER_TEXT

◻ XmDIALOG_HELP_BUTTON

◻ XmDIALOG_LIST

◻ XmDIALOG_LIST_LABEL

◻ XmDIALOG_OK_BUTTON

◻ XmDIALOG_SELECTION_LABEL

◻ XmDIALOG_TEXT

Motif Dialog Shells

◻ Each one of the XmCreate...Dialog() functions creates an XmDialogShell widget to support the popup nature of the dialogs. Although you don't usually deal with the Shell widgets that are created for you to parent a dialog box, it is a good idea to know a little more about them to be able to make effective use of them.

The XmDialogShell class is subclassed off the Intrinsics TransientShell widget class. TransientShells are for Shell windows that can be manipulated by the window manager but are not allowed to be iconified separately. They are only iconified if the main application shell is iconified. Transient-Shells were designed with dialog boxes in mind.

The XmDialogShell widget class inherits resources from the Core, Composite, Shell, WMShell, VendorShell, and TransientShell widget classes. Its class name is XmDialogShell, and it does not define any new resources for itself. It does, however, override the XmNdeleteResponse resource that it inherits from the VendorShell widget class.

◻ When referencing the children Button widgets of any of the dialog boxes discussed in this section in a resource file, you have two problems. First, because the widgets within the dialog box are created for you, you don't have an instance name to reference them with. This forces you to use class names. Second, because an XmDialogShell widget is created as the parent of your dialog box for you, there is no way to determine its instance name. This means that you cannot reference a dialog box widget with a completely tight binding. In a resource file you will be forced to use some type of loose binding to reference the children widgets of the dialog box.

A Complete X/Motif Client Application

◻ Using all the concepts and techniques presented in this chapter, we can put together a simple, but complete, X/Motif-based client application. Example 18.1 shows the code for a program that has a BulletinBoard and two dialog boxes in it. An event handler is attached to the BulletinBoard to watch for mouse-down events. When the application receives a mouse-down event it checks to see which button was pressed. If button 1 was pressed a WarningDialog is managed with its XmNdialogStyle set to SYSTEM_-MODAL to keep the user from doing anything except responding to the dialog. For mouse button 2, a PromptDialog is managed with its XmNdialogStyle set to APPLICATION_MODAL to keep the user from doing anything with our application until they respond to the dialog.

Figure 18.17 shows what the program would look like on a typical terminal screen.

Review Questions

¤ Please write down the answers to the following questions:

1. What are dialog boxes used for?

2. How do the two styles of dialog boxes differ?

3. List the two widget classes on which dialog boxes are based.

4. What is a MessageBox used for?

5. List the typical children widgets of a MessageBox.

6. What is a SelectionBox used for?

7. List the typical children widgets of a SelectionBox.

8. When should a dialog box be created?

9. How is a dialog box posted? When should it be posted?

10. How long does a dialog box remain on the screen?

11. What is the XmNautoUnmanage resource used for in a dialog box?

12. What is the XmNdialogStyle resource used for in a dialog box?

13. How do you get your application to execute some code in response to user interaction with a dialog box?

14. List the six different styles of preconfigured MessageBox dialogs and how they differ.

15. Why you should reuse dialog widgets instead of creating one widget for each user interaction?

16. List the three different styles of preconfigured SelectionBox dialogs and how they differ.

17. List the two functions available to create a customized dialog box.

18. How do you access and change the resources associated with the children widgets of the preconfigured dialog boxes?

19. Why is it possible for dialog boxes to pop up out of nowhere and then disappear?

```
#include <stdio.h>
#include <Xm/BulletinB.h>
#include <Xm/MessageB.h>
#include <Xm/SelectioB.h>

XtEventHandler BPressFunc();
Widget topShell;

main(argc, argv)
Cardinal argc;
String argv[];
    {
    Widget bBoard;
    Widget dialogs[2];
    Arg argList[10];

    /* Initialize  the Intrinsics and create a top Shell widget */
    topShell = XtInitialize(argv[0], "Edit", NULL, 0, &argc, argv);

    /* Create the manager widget */
    XtSetArg(argList[0], XmNwidth, 300);
    XtSetArg(argList[1], XmNheight, 200);
    bBoard = XmCreateBulletinBoard(topShell, "bboard", argList, 2);

    /* Create the user interface widgets */
    XtSetArg(argList[0], XmNdialogStyle, XmDIALOG_SYSTEM_MODAL);
    dialogs[0] = XmCreateWarningDialog(bBoard, "warndialog", argList, 1);
    XtSetArg(argList[0], XmNdialogStyle, XmDIALOG_APPLICATION_MODAL);
    dialogs[1] = XmCreatePromptDialog(bBoard, "promptdialog", argList, 1);

    /* Set up event handlers for the widgets */
    XtAddEventHandler(bBoard, ButtonPressMask, False, BPressFunc, dialogs);

    /* Make the program visible on the screen */
    XtManageChild(bBoard);
    XtRealizeWidget(topShell);

    /* Wait for input events */
    XtMainLoop();
    }
```

Example 18.1 X/Motif application program with dialog boxes, part 1.

Exercises

¤   The following exercises are designed to give you the opportunity to practice
     the concepts and facilities presented in this chapter:

```
XtEventHandler BPressFunc(widget_id, client_data, call_data)
Widget widget_id;
Widget client_data[];
XEvent *call_data;
    {

    /* Determine which button invoked this function */
    switch(call_data->xbutton.button)
        {
        case 1:
            XtManageChild(client_data[0]);
            break;
        case 2:
            XtManageChild(client_data[1]);
            break;
        default:
            fprintf(stderr,  "Only mouse buttons 1 and 2 are recognized.\n");
            break;
        }

    /* Return control to the calling function */
    return;
    }
```

Example 18.2 X/Motif application program with dialog boxes, part 2.

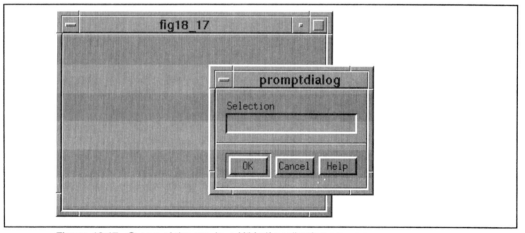

Figure 18.17 Output of the previous X/Motif application program.

1. Modify the program from a previous chapter that had a DrawingArea, three PushButtons, and an OptionMenu. Add an event handler to the DrawingArea that watches for a control-d from the keyboard. In response to the control-d, your application should pop up a QuestionDialog that asks "Are you sure you want to quit?" When the user clicks the OK button, the application will exit. The Cancel button will cause the

application to return and continue. Modify the Help button so that it is not sensitive to user input.

2. Modify the program from a previous chapter that had a MenuBar with three options on it, five Label widgets, and five Text widgets in a MainWindow. Add a PromptDialog that is managed from the Open Button on the File PulldownMenu. The PromptDialog will prompt for the filename of the database to open. When the user activates the OK button, print a message that indicates the name of the file that was received from the user through the Text widget in the PromptDialog. Unmanage the Help button so that it is not visible in the dialog box.

3. Modify the previous program to add a QuestionDialog that is managed from the Quit button on the File PulldownMenu. The QuestionDialog will ask "Are you sure you want to quit?" and exit if the OK button is activated. Unmanage the Help button so that it is not visible in the dialog box.

Color

Introduction

◻ You already know how to work with colors through a resource file in an X/Motif client application. Unfortunately, you cannot use color names directly in the argument lists for the widgets in your client's source code. In this chapter you will learn how to work with colors as pixel values using the RGB (red-green-blue) color model and something called a *colormap*.

Objectives

◻ After completing this chapter, you will be able to:

◻ Describe the basic idea behind the RGB color model.

◻ Explain what a pixel is and what its components are.

◻ List several different RGB intensities for specific colors.

◻ Explain how X establishes color intensities in the RGB model.

◻ Explain why X can't support all possible color values.

◻ Explain what X uses to overcome its color limitations.

◻ Describe how a terminal's display memory is organized and what it is called.

◻ Describe how a pixel value is formed.

❑ Explain what a pixel value is used for.

❑ Explain the term *color width*.

❑ Describe what visual classes are used for.

❑ List three different visual classes in X.

❑ List the macro that retrieves the visual class of a terminal as well as two other macros that get screen characteristics for you.

❑ Explain what the default colormap is.

❑ Explain how a window gets a colormap associated with it.

❑ Explain the term *virtual colormap*.

❑ List the colors that are usually installed in the default colormap automatically.

❑ List the macro that gets the default colormap for you as well as two other colormap related-macros.

❑ Explain where X gets color names from.

❑ Describe how hexadecimal values can be used to describe colors in resource files.

❑ Explain the purpose of the XColor structure.

❑ Explain the difference between shared and private color cells in a colormap.

❑ List the two functions that allocate shared color cells.

❑ Explain what happens if a shared color cell cannot be allocated.

❑ Explain what has to be done first before private color cells can be allocated.

❑ List three functions that store colors in private color cells.

❑ Describe what happens to your colors when your client terminates.

❑ Describe how to free colors previously allocated by your client.

❑ Explain how to create a new colormap.

❑ Describe who is usually responsible for installing colormaps.

❑ Explain how your client can install a colormap.

❑ Explain how to get rid of a colormap.

❑ Describe the ColormapNotify event.

X Color Concepts

❑ The X Window System uses the RGB color model for implementing colors. This color model is also used by most color terminal manufacturers to implement color displays. The RGB color model specifies that any color that you want to display on a screen can be constructed by combining varying intensities of three base colors: red, green, and blue.

This is even how a standard color television set works. The picture is constructed from an array of dots. The screen is some number of dots high and some number of dots wide. These dots — actually called *pixels* (or *picture elements*) — are further subdivided into three smaller dots. One of these subdots, or pixel components, is used to display the color red, one is used for green, and the last is used for blue. The relative brightness of the red component in comparison to the green component and the blue component will determine what color appears to be displayed at that pixel.

For example, if the red component is as bright as it can be, the green component is as bright as it can be, and the blue component is as bright as it can be, then the color that appears to be displayed at that pixel is white. If the red component is as dim as it can be, the green component is as dim as it can be, and the blue component is as dim as it can be, then the color that appears to be displayed at that pixel is black. If the red and green components are at 100 percent intensity (as bright as they can be) while the blue component is at 0 percent intensity (as dim as it can be), then the color displayed at that pixel will be yellow. Figure 19.1 shows some other RGB component relative intensities and their resulting pixel color.

In X, color intensities are established with 16-bit integers for each component with values for the integers ranging from 0 to 65,535. A value of 0 indicates that the color component should be displayed at its lowest intensity (as dim as it can be), while a value of 65,535 indicates that the color component should be displayed at full intensity (as bright as it can be). Since the different colors are defined by the varying intensities of the red, green, and blue values, there are a total of 65,535 to the third power (281,462,092,005,375) possible colors. For a terminal to be able to display all the possible colors at any one point in time, it would have to have enough memory for 3 times 65,535 to the third power 16-bit integers or 1,688,772,552,032,250 bytes!

Most terminals cannot support this much memory so terminal manufacturers and the X Window System have adopted a different approach to dealing with colors. Instead of allowing access to all possible colors, the X Window System lets you access a subset of available colors. You decide which colors you want to use in your client code and install them in a *color lookup*

Color name	Red intensity	Green intensity	Blue intensity
aquamarine	43%	85%	57%
brown	64%	16%	16%
cadet blue	37%	62%	62%
cyan	0%	100%	100%
gold	80%	49%	19%
khaki	62%	62%	37%
magenta	100%	0%	100%
orange	80%	19%	19%
pink	73%	56%	56%
tan	85%	57%	43%
turquoise	67%	91%	91%

Figure 19.1 RGB component intensities for particular colors.

table. When your client is ready to display a particular color at some point on the screen, it tells the terminal to look up that color in the table and use the RGB intensities from that entry for the pixel. The result is that the desired color is displayed at a point on the screen. In X terminology we call a color lookup table a *colormap.*

The memory of a typical color video-display terminal is organized into a series of *bit planes.* A bit plane is an array of bits that is the same number of bits wide as the number of pixels across the width of the screen, the same number of bits high as the number of pixels in the height of the screen, and 1 bit deep. Every terminal will have some finite number of these bit planes in its *frame buffer.* The number of bit planes available is called the *pixel depth* of the terminal. Figure 19.2 illustrates how you would visualize this organization.

One bit in corresponding positions from each plane combine to form a pixel value. Each pixel value is used to store a bit pattern which is equivalent to an integer number. If you have two bit planes, the pixel-value integers can range from 0 to 3, four bit planes can have pixel values from 0 to 15, eight bit planes allow for pixel values up to 255, and so on. This determines the total number of colors that you can have available at any one time.

The pixel value for a particular pixel on the bitmapped color graphic-display terminal does not directly display a color at that point. Instead, the pixel value is used as an index into the color lookup table, or colormap.

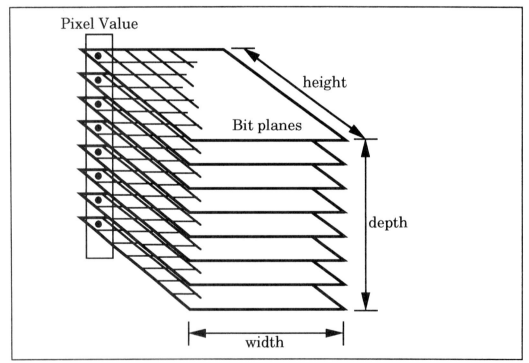

Figure 19.2 Bit plane/pixel organization of a typical color video display terminal.

The color information stored at the colormap entry indexed by the pixel value is the color that is displayed at a particular pixel on the screen.

For example, if the pixel value in row 7, column 3 of the terminal's memory (which is organized into eight bit planes) contains the binary value 00110101 (decimal 53), the terminal would access entry number 53 in the colormap. If colormap entry 53 contained 65,535 for the red component (100 percent), 65,535 for the green component (100 percent), and 0 for the blue component (0 percent), then the actual pixel at row 7, column 3 on the terminal screen would display what appeared to be the color yellow. Figure 19.3 illustrates this mechanism.

When you want to use a particular color from within your X/Motif client application code, there are several things you must do. First, you must access a colormap to store your color in. Then you have to obtain the red,

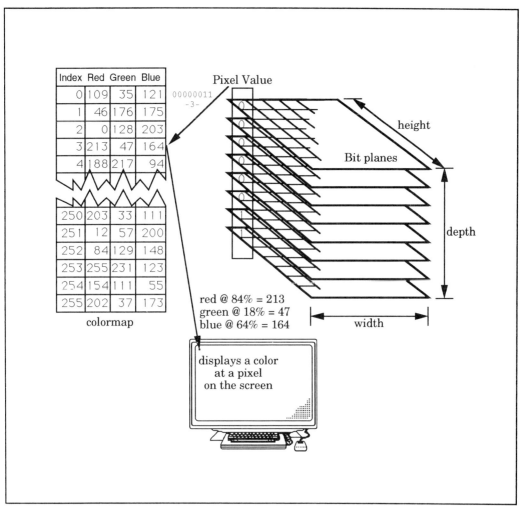

Figure 19.3 Colormap use in pixel value-to-color translation.

green, and blue component intensities for the desired color. Finally, you install the RGB values into the colormap at a particular location to be accessed by a pixel value. The pixel value is what you use in your source code to cause your color to be displayed in some set of pixels on the screen.

☐   Different terminal manufacturers support different color widths. The most common color width seems to be 8 bits for each of the red, green, and blue components. In fact, the color definitions in /usr/lib/X11/rgb.txt use RGB values in the range of 0 to 255 − 8 bits each. Since X uses 16-bit RGB values we usually shift the 8-bit value into the high order byte of the 16-bit color value. On newer terminals the full 16 bits can be used.

X Terminals and Visual Classes

☐   This description of colormapping is necessarily somewhat simplified. There are a wide variety of methods that terminal manufacturers use on different types of terminals. Although the description is typical, monochrome, gray-scale, and low-end color terminals can use a different type of pixel-to-color mapping. Also, newer high-performance color graphic-display terminals are being created that may use the colormap concept in different ways.

For this reason, to get your X/Motif client application to be portable to many different types of terminals, your source code must be written to take differences between terminals into account. The X Window System helps you with this problem by defining something called *Visual Classes*. X defines six different visual classes as shown in Figure 19.4.

☐   Monochrome displays don't really have a colormap. There is only one bit plane with 1 bit per pixel on the screen. This means that there is a direct correspondence between a bit being "on" in the bit plane and a pixel being illuminated at 100 percent on the screen. Standard computer video-display terminals are all monochrome even though some use a white phospher on the screen while others may use green or orange.

Gray-scale displays do have a colormap. Instead of dividing the colormap entries into three parts (for red, green, and blue), there is only one entry that determines the intensity of the one color (usually white) at a particular pixel location on the screen.

| | ------------ Visual Class ----------- | |
Hardware colormap type	Hardware has a Read/Write colormap	Hardware has a Read-only colormap
Monochrome/Gray-scale	GrayScale	StaticGray
Single index for RGB values (as in the previous description)	PseudoColor	StaticColor
Separate indexes for R, G, and B (high-performance color displays)	DirectColor	TrueColor

Figure 19.4 Visual classes for X.

Midrange color displays are the most common. The previous description of the RGB color model applies most directly to this type of display and usually supports either 16 (four bit planes) or 256 (eight bit planes) colors. The popularity of this type of color display system is due to the fact that it provides a flexible color system at a reasonable price.

High-performance color displays use a different colormap technique. Instead of one set of bit planes, newer displays are using three sets of bit planes — one for each of the three primary colors — and three different colormaps. Usually, these types of displays have 24 bits per pixel and, with the colormapping scheme described previously, would have to have a colormap with some 16 million entries. Instead, these displays use 8 of the bits as an index into a 256-entry red colormap, another 8 bits as an index into a 256-entry green colormap, and the last 8 bits as an index into a 256-entry blue colormap (three 256 entry colormaps give 768 color entries). Each screen pixel value is then used to access one entry from each colormap for a total of approximately 16 million possible colors.

¤ Many of the X functions that deal with colors and colormaps will need to know what visual class the terminal that they are displaying on belongs to. For this reason there are several X macros that you will want to become familiar with to obtain necessary information about the type of screen you are working on. Figure 19.5 shows the syntax for these macros.

DefaultVisualOfScreen() returns a pointer to a Visual structure. One of the members of this structure is named class and will contain one of the defined constants GrayScale, StaticGray, PseudoColor, StaticColor, DirectColor, or TrueColor, which indicates the visual class of the screen passed as a parameter.

DefaultDepthOfScreen() returns the integer number of bits per pixel (the number of bit planes) for the screen passed as a parameter. The last four macros return the size of the screen in pixels or millimeters. Don't forget — the screen pointer required as a parameter to these macros can be obtained with a call to the XtScreen() function.

The X Window System and Colormaps

¤ Some newer color video-display terminals can support multiple hardware colormaps. However, most support only one. If the terminal's hardware colormap is read-write (as is most often the case), then an X/Motif client application can create and use several different colormaps.

```
Visual *DefaultVisualOfScreen(screen)
int DefaultDepthOfScreen(screen)
int WidthOfScreen(screen)
int WidthMMOfScreen(screen)
int HeightOfScreen(screen)
int HeightMMOfScreen(screen)

Screen *screen;
```

Figure 19.5 Screen attributes macro syntax.

When an X server starts up and a connection is made to a display, the server creates one colormap called the *default colormap*. This colormap is assigned to the root window and then installed in the display hardware. Every X window that is created as a child of the root window will inherit the colormap of its parent. So, by default, every X window that is created in your client application will inherit the default colormap.

Colormaps, like widgets, are stored in the server. A colormap id is used to identify which colormap is associated with which window in the client application. You can use the default colormap for your application, or you can create custom colormaps for your entire application or subwindows in your application.

The colormap that is associated with a window in your X/Motif client application code is called a *virtual colormap* because it is not necessarily the one currently installed in the display hardware. By default, the Motif window manager (mwm) will install the virtual colormap of the current input focus window into the terminal display hardware for you. Usually, you rely on the window manager to change colormaps, but you can also install a new colormap at any time from your client application code. To see a visual representation of the currently installed colormap, use the standard X client called xshowcmap.

When the X server starts up, it will install at least two colors in the default colormap. These two entries are what the server will use for the colors black and white. Other default colors may also be installed by the server. When the Motif window manager starts up, it will install 12 colors in the default colormap. Motif will create and install colors for the TopShadowColor, BottomShadowColor, Background, and Foreground resources for the widgets in the windows it manages. The current input focus window, all inactive windows, and your program's widgets will each have their own set of four color values.

Again, for your convenience, X supplies several macros that provide easy access to the default colormap. Figure 19.6 shows the syntax for these macros.

The first two macros deal with the default colormap that was created for you and stored in the X server at startup. To get the colormap id of that colormap (needed by other color-processing functions), pass the screen pointer to your screen to DefaultColormapOfScreen(), which returns you something of type Colormap. The CellsOfScreen() macro takes the same

```
Colormap DefaultColormapOfScreen(screen)
int CellsOfScreen(screen)
int MaxCmapsOfScreen(screen)
int MinCmapsOfScreen(screen)
Pixel BlackPixelOfScreen(screen)
Pixel WhitePixelOfScreen(screen)


Screen    *screen;
```

Figure 19.6 Default colormap access macro syntax.

screen pointer as a parameter and returns an integer count of the number of color entries in the default colormap.

The next two macros deal with the capabilities of the terminal hardware. Both macros take a screen pointer as a parameter and return an integer count. MaxCmapsOfScreen() returns the maximum number of installed colormaps that your terminal can support. MinCmapsOfScreen() returns the minimum number of installed colormaps that your terminal can support.

Finally, since the colors that are installed by X as the black and white colors may not actually be black and white, two more macros are provided. BlackPixelOfScreen() returns the pixel value for the color that was installed as black, while WhitePixelOfScreen() returns the pixel value for the color that was installed as white. Both functions take a screen pointer as a parameter and return type Pixel.

Using Colors in Your Application

¤   You have already learned that colors can be specified in a resource file through the use of a valid color name. The color names that X knows about are stored in a database implemented as a flat ASCII text file. This color database contains the names and the RGB values for many different predefined colors. Figure 19.7 shows a sample of some of the entries in the /usr/lib/X11/rgb.txt color database file.

¤   In addition to using color names from the rgb.txt database, you can also specify colors in a more exacting way. In a resource file, if you don't like the exact RGB definition of a color, you can specify your own RGB values in hexadecimal form. Specifying colors in this way gives you more control over what the color will actually look like.

In a resource file you can specify a hexadecimal color value by using a pound sign (#) followed by a 3-, 6-, 9-, or 12-digit hexadecimal number. Which one you use depends on the color width available on your terminal:

```
...
112 219 147        aquamarine
165 42 42          brown
95 159 159         cadet blue
0 255 255          cyan
204 127 50         gold
159 159 95         khaki
255 0 255          magenta
204 50 50          orange
188 143 143        pink
219 147 112        tan
173 234 234        turquoise
...
```

Figure 19.7 Portion of the /usr/lib/X11/rgb.txt color database.

```
#RGB              - 4 bits each of R,  G,  & B
#RRGGBB           - 8 bits each of R,  G,  & B
#RRRGGGBBB        - 12 bits each of R,  G,  & B
#RRRRGGGGBBBB     - 16 bits each of R,  G,  & B
```

Figure 19.8 shows shows several methods for setting the background resource for a label widget to the color aquamarine.

▢   Within your X/Motif client application you can also refer to colors in the rgb.txt database by name or through exact RGB values as you do in a resource file. However, all work with colors in your program's source code is done using the XColor structure definition. Figure 19.9 shows the definition of this new data type.

The XColor structure is used in one of two ways. Just as in a resource file, there are functions that you can call to find a particular color name in the rgb.txt database. When the color is found, it will install it in a colormap of your choice and return you an XColor structure. The structure will have the RGB values for the installed color in it as well as the pixel value needed to reference the color within the colormap.

Another way to use the XColor structure is similar to using the hexadecimal RGB color values in a resource file. You can put the red, green, and blue integer intensity values in the XColor structure yourself and then call another function to install them in a colormap of your choice. The function will return the XColor structure back to you with the pixel value filled in for the colormap entry that was used to install your color. When using the structure in this way, the flags member can contain the bitwise OR of the defined names DoRed, DoGreen, or DoBlue, which indicate which of the color members (red, green, and blue) are to be used in the color definition.

▢   Remember—pixel values are neither colors nor color intensities. *You should only get pixel values as return values from an X function.* Once you have obtained a pixel value, you cannot perform arithmetic or logical

```
*rcmanager.XmLabel.background:          aquamarine
*rcmanager.XmLabel.background:          #70DB93
*rcmanager.XmLabel.background:          #0700DB093
*rcmanager.XmLabel.background:          #007000DB0093
```

Figure 19.8 Different methods for setting color resources.

```
/*
 * Data structure used by color operations
 */
typedef struct {
        unsigned long   pixel;
        unsigned short  red, green, blue;
        char            flags;              /* DoRed, DoGreen, DoBlue */
        char            pad;
} XColor;
```

Figure 19.9 Definition of the XColor structure type.

operations on it, and you should (in fact) consider it to be a "magic number" provided for your use. Pixel values are an index into a colormap, and modifications to that index cannot be guaranteed to produce usable results. Don't mess with a pixel value (unless you are doing rubber-band drawing — more on this later).

Installing Colors in a Colormap

◻ Before you can learn about how to put RGB values into a colormap entry, you have to understand that there are two types of entries (or color cells) in a colormap. If you have a display that is in the visual class of terminals that have a read-write (changeable) colormap, then X supports both shared and private color cells (colormap entries).

A shared color cell is an entry in a colormap that you allocate with a particular color in it for read-only access by yourself or any other client. A colormap with sharable read-only color cells is less likely to run out of free cells. Any client that needs a particular color will scan the colormap for free color cells to install it in, and if none is found, can use a sharable color cell that comes close to the desired color instead.

A private color cell is an entry in a colormap that you allocate with an initial color in it for read-write access by your client alone. No other client application can access the contents of a private color cell. A colormap with many private color cells in it will fill up quickly, leaving fewer cells for use by other applications. However, private read-write color cells allow the owning client application to change the color stored there at any time. If you are using a private color cell to display an object in a particular color on the screen, the color can be changed by simply writing a different RGB color definition into the private color cell.

◻ Allocating sharable color cells is the easiest because you don't have to make sure there are color cells available first. If you want to allocate a shared color cell based on RGB values, then use the XAllocColor() function. If you want to allocate a shared color cell based on a color name from rgb.txt, then use the XAllocNamedColor() function. Figure 19.10 shows the syntax for these two functions.

Notice that the first two parameters to both of these functions are a display pointer and a colormap id. The display pointer identifies which server your application is connected to, and the colormap id identifies the

```
Status XAllocColor(display, colormap, colorcell)
Status XAllocNamedColor(display, colormap, name, colorcell, exact_rgb_values)

Display  *display;
Colormap colormap;
String   name;
XColor   *colorcell;
XColor   *exact_rgb_values;
```

Figure 19.10 XAllocColor() and XAllocNamedColor() syntax.

colormap you want to work with. These two data items will be required for every color function that deals with the contents of a colormap.

With XAllocColor() you have to create an XColor structure containing the desired red, green, and blue values. You also fill in the flags member with the bitwise OR of DoRed, DoGreen, and DoBlue depending on which of the other members contain valid data. When the function is called, with the XColor structure address passed as the last parameter, the color cell will be allocated, the color installed, and the pixel member filled in (returned) with the pixel value necessary to reference the newly installed color.

With XAllocNamedColor() you have to supply a name parameter which is one of the defined color names from rgb.txt. When the function is called, the color cell will be allocated for the name passed as the third parameter. The color will be installed, and two items will be returned in the fourth and fifth parameters, which are both addresses of separate XColor structures. The first of these two structures will contain the pixel value as well as the red, green, and blue values of the color that was actually installed in the colormap—the closest that is capable of being supported by the hardware. The second structure will contain the actual red, green, and blue values as they were specified in the rgb.txt database.

Both of these functions will search the specified colormap for a color that already exists that matches the desired color. If one exists, the pixel value for that color is returned. If one does not exist, they will attempt to allocate a new color cell to store the color in and return a pixel value for the new color cell. If no unallocated color cells exist, both these functions will search the colormap for a color cell that contains a color that is installed that comes closest to the requested color and will return the pixel value for that color.

Don't forget—the display pointer required as the first parameter to these functions can be obtained with a call to the XtDisplay() function. Also, the colormap parameter required as the second parameter to these functions can be obtained with a call to the DefaultColormapOfScreen() macro.

Both these color functions return something of type Status, which will be a 0 if it encounters an error and a 1 if it succeeds. If a color allocation fails, you should probably set the needed pixel value to either BlackPixelOf-Screen() or WhitePixelOfScreen() so that your program can continue and do something instead of simply terminating with an error. Figure 19.11 shows how the XAllocNamedColor() function would be used in a program segment.

In order to allocate private color cells, other functions must be used. Before private colors can be created, color cells must be allocated for them. Once private color cells have been allocated, then, just as with shared color cells, you can allocate colors by name or by RGB values. Figure 19.12 shows the syntax for the XAllocColorCells(), XStoreColor(), XStoreColors(), and XStoreNamedColor() functions.

These four functions use the same first two parameters that the previous color functions used. In the XAllocColorCells() function the next three parameters will be ignored in this book. They are used for drawing techniques where you want to nondestructively overlay one set of graphics over another, with only one of the graphics objects being visible at any one time. These techniques involve some advanced concepts that are beyond the scope of this introductory book. For our purposes they will be set to False, NULL, and 0. The last two parameters are an array of pixel values and the

```
#include <Xm/PushB.h>
...
    Widget myButton[5];
    Display *display;
    Screen *screen;
    Colormap colormap;
    XColor closest;
    XColor exact;
    Arg argList[10];
    Cardinal i;
    static char colors[][7] = {"yellow", "gold", "orange", "red", "maroon"};
    static char labels[][8] = {"button1", "button2", "button3",
                               "button4", "button5", "exit"};
    ...
    display = XtDisplay(topShell);
    screen = XtScreen(topShell);
    colormap = DefaultColormapOfScreen(screen);
    ...
    for(i = 0; i < XtNumber(myButton); ++i)
        {
        XAllocNamedColor(display, colormap, colors[i], &closest, &exact);
        XtSetArg(argList[0], XmNbackground, closest.pixel);
        myButton[i] = XmCreatePushButton(rcManager, labels[i], argList, 1);
        }
    ...
```

Figure 19.11 Using XAllocNamedColor() to allocate shared color cells.

```
Status XAllocColorCells(display, colormap,
                        contiguous, plane_mask, nplanes, pixels, npixels)
Status XStoreColor(display, colormap, colorcell)
Status XStoreColors(display, colormap, colorcells ncolors);
Status XStoreNamedColor(display, colormap, name, pixel flags);


Display        *display;
Colormap        colormap;
Bool            contiguous;
unsigned long   plane_masks[nplanes], pixels[npixels], pixel;
XColor         *colorcell, colorcells[ncolors];
int             nplanes, npixels, ncolors, flags;
String          name;
```

Figure 19.12 XAllocColor(), XStoreColor(), XStoreColors(), and XStoreNamedColor() syntax.

number of elements in the array of pixels. The function will allocate the number of color cells specified in the last parameter. The array will be filled in with the pixel values from the colormap for the color cells that were allocated for you.

Once the color cells have been allocated, you can store RGB color values that you want to use in them. The XStoreColor() function stores a single RGB value in a color cell allocated by XAllocColorCells(). The third parameter is a pointer to an XColor structure which has the red, green, and blue members filled in with the desired RGB values. The flags member has an appropriate combination of DoRed, DoGreen, and DoBlue. The pixel member of the structure must contain the pixel value of the color cell that was returned from XAllocColorCells() where you want to store the color.

The only difference between XStoreColor() and XStoreColors() is that the plural version of the function lets you store more than one color at a time. The description of XStoreColor() applies to XStoreColors() also, except that the last two parameters are an array of XColor structures and a count of the number of elements in the array. You fill in the XColor structures in each element of the array as described above and then pass the number of elements that you filled in as the last parameter.

XStoreNamedColor() lets you store a color in the colormap based on one of the predefined color names in the /usr/lib/X11/rgb.txt color database. In this function the third parameter is the character string name of one of the colors defined in rgb.txt. The fourth parameter is the pixel value for the color cell you want to store the color in returned from XAllocColorCells(). The last parameter is the bitwise OR of the DoRed, DoGreen, and DoBlue flags to indicate which of the RGB values from rgb.txt are to be used in the color cell in the colormap.

☐   Don't forget—the display pointer required as the first parameter to these functions can be obtained with a call to the XtDisplay() function. Also, the colormap parameter required as the second parameter to these functions can be obtained with a call to the DefaultColormapOfScreen() macro.

All these color functions return something of type Status, which will be a 0 if it encounters an error and a 1 if it succeeds. If a color allocation fails, you should probably set the needed pixel value to either BlackPixelOf-Screen() or WhitePixelOfScreen() so that your program can continue and do something instead of simply terminating with an error. Figure 19.13 shows how the XStoreNamedColor() function would be used in a program segment.

```
...
XColor theColor;
Display *display;
Screen *screen;
Colormap colormap;
...
    display = XtDisplay(topShell);
    screen = XtScreen(topShell);
    colormap = DefaultColormapOfScreen(screen);
    ...
    XAllocColorCells(display, colormap, False, NULL, 0, &theColor.pixel, 1);
    XStoreNamedColor(display, colormap, "black", theColor.pixel,
                   DoRed | DoGreen | DoBlue);

    ...
```

Figure 19.13 Using XStoreNamedColor() to fill in a private color cell.

◻   Normally, when an application terminates, any color cells that it has allocated will be freed for use by other programs. However, if you need to free a color cell that you have allocated before your program ends, you can use the XFreeColors() function. This function will work with shared or private color cells. Figure 19.14 shows the syntax for this function.

The first two parameters are the same as any other color function. The third parameter is an array of pixel values. These are the pixel values for the color cells that you want to free. The fourth parameter is the number of pixels that you have specified in the previous array. The last parameter, again, is beyond the scope of this book and should be set to 0.

If the color cells were private, they become available for reuse by you or any other client. If the color cells were shared, they become available only if this is the last client that has allocated the cell. The function will return a status of 1 if is succeeds and 0 if it fails.

◻   Once you have a pixel value−whether a shared or a private pixel value−you can use it wherever a Pixel-type value can be specified. The most obvious use is in the argument lists for the widgets you are creating in your client application. If you go back and look at the resource charts for the various widgets that you have learned about you will see a variety of resources are of type Pixel. The XmNforeground, XmNbackground, XmNtopShadowColor, and XmNbottomShadowColor are all defined to be of type Pixel as are all of the resources that deal with colors.

Using Custom Colormaps

◻   There will be times when allocating color cells in a colormap that the colormap will become full. If this happens with your client code, X supplies functions that allow you to create new colormaps. There are a variety of different functions that let you deal with colormaps in a number of different ways, but we will concentrate on three in this section. These three functions will let you create a colormap, install a colormap into the terminal hardware, and then free a colormap when you are done.

There is an important point to be made about using custom colormaps. Remember that every application that is running installed the colors that it is using into the colormap that is currently installed in the terminal hardware. Typically, for PseudoColor and DirectColor terminals, only one colormap can be used at a time. This means that if you install a new colormap from your application−with different colors defined in the color cells

```
Status XFreeColors(display, colormap, pixels, npixels, planes)

Display        *display
Colormap       colormap;
unsigned long  pixels[npixels];
int            npixels;
unsigned long  planes;
```

Figure 19.14 XFreeColors() syntax.

that other applications are currently using—then you may destroy the visual appearance of all other running applications.

Again, it is usually left up to the window manager to install the colormap of the current input focus window into the terminal hardware for you. Every window inherits a colormap id from its parent, which is usually the id of the colormap created for the root window. Use this colormap whenever possible. If you decide to use a custom colormap, you do so at your own risk. Be aware of the possible consequences and take them into account when writing your client code.

□   To create a custom colormap, use the function XCreateColormap(). This function creates a colormap for your use but does not install it in the terminal hardware. Figure 19.15 shows the syntax for XCreateColormap()

The first parameter identifies the server in which the colormap will be created. The second parameter is a window id used to determine which screen the colormap will be associated with. This value can be obtained with a call to XtWindow() passing it a widget id. The third parameter is a pointer to a visual structure to specify the visual class of the colormap. This parameter can be obtained with a call to DefaultVisualOfScreen() passing it a screen pointer.

The last parameter can be one of two defined names. For PseudoColor, DirectColor, and GrayScale terminals this parameter can be AllocNone or AllocAll. If AllocNone is specified, no color cells are allocated and the client code can use either XAllocColor()-type functions to allocate shared color cells or XAllocColorCells()/XStoreColor()-type functions to allocate private color cells. If AllocAll is specified, all the colormap color cells are automatically allocated as private color cells for your application and you can use XStoreColor()-type functions to store your application-specific RGB values in those cells.

The colormap is actually stored in the server. The return value from XCreateColormap() is a colormap id. When you want to reference your custom colormap as opposed to the default colormap, you use its colormap id to tell the server which colormap you want.

□   Once a colormap is created, to make it active you must install it in the terminal hardware. Again, usually only one colormap is active and available at one time. The window manager automatically installs the colormap of the current input focus window in the hardware for you. But you can install a custom colormap by using the XInstallColormap() function. Figure 19.16 shows the syntax for this function.

The first parameter is the display pointer identifying the display connection for the terminal you want the colormap installed on. The second

```
Colormap XCreateColormap(display, window, visual, allocation)

Display *display;
Window  window;
Visual  *visual;
int     allocation;
```

Figure 19.15 XCreateColormap() syntax.

```
Status XInstallColormap(display, colormap)

Display  *display;
Colormap colormap;
```

Figure 19.16 XInstallColormap() syntax.

parameter is the colormap id for the colormap you want to install. The function returns a Status which should be 1 for success and 0 for failure.

If the hardware supports only one colormap, the virtual colormap specified as the second parameter is loaded into the hardware. All windows that were associated with this colormap will immediately display their chosen colors. Any other windows still on the screen that were associated with the old colormap will display with false colors.

If multiple hardware colormaps are possible and the limit for colormaps has not been reached, then XInstallColormap() installs the specified colormap, keeping any existing ones. In this way, all displayed windows will remain in their true colors. If the maximum number of colormaps are installed, this function will swap out an old colormap for the new one, making it less likely that a number of windows will be displayed with false colors. Again, colormaps are usually installed by the window manager.

Colormaps, just like windows, display connections, and visuals, are called *server resources*. Other server resources include graphics contexts, fonts, cursors, and pixmaps. By *resources*, it is meant that they are data structures that the server uses to keep track of data about objects that it must use to provide its services. Do not confuse *server resources* with *widget resources*. They are two different concepts.

The reason they are stored in the server is because the server uses them directly and frequently. Instead of having to go across the network to your client application to get the data, the server accesses the data directly within its own data space. However, the server does not have unlimited resources. There are only so many colormaps and other resources that the server can create. When your application terminates, any server resources that it had allocated will be freed up. But, if you are done with a particular resource and want to continue doing other things in your client application, you should free up those resources for other applications to use. To free a colormap use the XFreeColormap() function. Figure 19.17 shows its syntax.

The parameters and return values for this function are identical with the XInstallColormap() function. If the specified colormap is installed, it is uninstalled first and then destroyed while the default colormap is installed in its place. If the specified colormap is not installed but still associated with a window, the window attribute for the colormap is changed to the

```
Status XFreeColormap(display, colormap)

Display  *display;
Colormap colormap;
```

Figure 19.17 XFreeColormap() syntax.

defined constant None. The colors displayed with a colormap of None are server-dependent but are usually the colors of the default colormap.

☐   *A Special Note about the XtWindow() Function:* It is important to understand that the XtWindow() function returns a window id. This id is a unique number that is assigned to every X window that the server creates and displays on the screen. If your client application does not have a window displayed on the screen, XtWindow() cannot return a valid window id. Remember — until your client code invokes the XtRealizeWidget() function to realize your top-level Shell widget, there are no windows on the screen. This means that XtWindow cannot return a valid window id until after the XtRealizeWidget() function has been called and your client's windows have been realized! If you must have a window id before you call XtRealizeWidget(), then X supplies a macro called RootWindowOfScreen(), which takes a screen pointer as a parameter and returns the window id of the root window. The root window is realized as soon as the X server starts up and is always available.

ColormapNotify Events

☐   Whenever a change occurs in the colormap associated with a particular window, or the colormap id for a particular window itself changes to a different colormap, a ColormapNotify event is generated for that window. If your application might be affected by changes in the colormap, you will want to watch for these events. You should remember from the discussion of event handlers that this can be accomplished with a call to XtAddEventHandler() and by setting up an event-handling function to process the change in colormaps. The mask value that you would use would be ColormapChangeMask.

When an event-handling function is invoked in response to a ColormapNotify event, the call_data parameter to the function (the third parameter) will still be a pointer to an XEvent. However, the XEvent union member that you will want to access for the colormap information is the xcolormap member which is defined to be of type XColormapEvent. The following code shows you what the XColormapEvent data structure looks like:

```
typedef struct {
    int           type;
    unsigned long serial;    /* # of last request processed by server */
    Bool          send_event;/* true if this came from a SendEvent() */
    Display       *display;  /* Display the event was read from */
    Window        window;
    Colormap      colormap;  /* COLORMAP or None */
    Bool          new;
    int           state;     /* ColormapInstalled,ColormapUninstalled */
} XColormapEvent;
```

The first five members of the structure are, as before, common to all event-handler structures. The window member will be the window id of the window that received a new colormap or whose colormap was changed. The colormap member is the colormap id of the colormap that changed or the defined constant None if the function was invoked in response to an

XFreeColormap() call. The new member of the structure will be True when a new colormap has been assigned to the window or False when the colormap is being installed or uninstalled. The state member indicates whether the colormap is installed or uninstalled.

XAllocColor(), XAllocNamedColor(), XStoreColor(), XStoreColors(), XStoreNamedColor(), XInstallColormap(), and XFreeColormap() all generate this event for those windows that have their associated colormap set to the colormap that was affected. By examining the structure members, you can determine what type of function was called (not the exact function) to generate the event.

A Complete X/Motif Client Application

¤ Using all the concepts and techniques presented in this chapter, we can put together a simple, but complete, X/Motif-based client application. Example 19.1 shows the code for a program that has a RowColumn with several PushButtons in it. Each of the PushButtons has its XmNbackground resource set to a different color. The colors that are used are from the rgb.txt file and are allocated with successive calls to XAllocNamedColor().

Figure 19.18 shows what the program would look like on a typical terminal screen.

Review Questions

¤ Please write down the answers to the following questions:

1. What is the basic idea behind the RGB color model?
2. What is a pixel, and what are its components?
3. List three different RGB intensities for specific colors.
4. How does X establishe color intensities in the RGB model?
5. Why can't X support all possible color values?
6. What does the X Window System use to overcome its color limitations?
7. How is a terminal's display memory organized, and what it is called?
8. How is a pixel value formed?
9. What is a pixel value used for?
10. Explain the term color width.
11. What are visual classes used for?
12. List three different visual classes in X.
13. List the macro that retrieves the visual class of a terminal as well as two other macros that get screen characteristics for you.
14. What is the default colormap?
15. How does a window get a colormap associated with it?

```
#include <stdio.h>
#include <Xm/RowColumn.h>
#include <Xm/PushB.h>

Widget topShell;

XtCallbackProc ExitApplication();
XtCallbackProc PrintMesg();

main(argc, argv)
Cardinal argc;
String argv[];
    {
    Widget rcManager;
    Widget myButton[5];
    Widget exitButton;
    Display *display;
    Screen *screen;
    Colormap colormap;
    XColor closest;
    XColor exact;
    Arg argList[10];
    Cardinal i;
    static char colors[][7] = {"yellow", "gold", "orange", "red", "maroon"};
    static char labels[][8] = {"button1", "button2", "button3",
                               "button4", "button5", "exit"};

    /* Initialize  the Intrinsics and create a top Shell widget */
    topShell = XtInitialize(argv[0], "Edit", NULL, 0, &argc, argv);

    /* Get some server specific information */
    display = XtDisplay(topShell);
    screen = XtScreen(topShell);
    colormap = DefaultColormapOfScreen(screen);

    /* Create the manager widget */
    rcManager = XmCreateRowColumn(topShell, "rcmanager", NULL, 0);

    /* Create the user interface widgets */
    for(i = 0; i < XtNumber(myButton); ++i)
        {
        XAllocNamedColor(display, colormap, colors[i], &closest, &exact);
        XtSetArg(argList[0], XmNbackground, closest.pixel);
        myButton[i] = XmCreatePushButton(rcManager, labels[i], argList, 1);
        XtAddCallback(myButton[i], XmNactivateCallback, PrintMesg, NULL);
        }
    exitButton = XmCreatePushButton(rcManager, labels[5], NULL, 0);
```

Example 19.1 X/Motif application program using colors, part 1.

```
    /* Set up callbacks for the widgets */
    XtAddCallback(exitButton, XmNactivateCallback, ExitApplication, NULL);

    /* Make the program visible on the screen */
    XtManageChildren(myButton, XtNumber(myButton));
    XtManageChild(exitButton);
    XtManageChild(rcManager);
    XtRealizeWidget(topShell);

    /* Wait for input events */
    XtMainLoop();
    }

XtCallbackProc PrintMesg(widget_id, client_data, call_data)
Widget widget_id;
caddr_t client_data;
caddr_t call_data;
    {

    /* Print something on the screen */
    printf("You pressed one of my buttons...\n");

    /* Return control to the calling function */
    return;
    }

XtCallbackProc ExitApplication(widget_id, client_data, call_data)
Widget widget_id;
caddr_t client_data;
caddr_t call_data;
    {

    /* Print something on the screen */
    printf("You just pressed the exit button...\n");
    sleep(3);
    printf("Good Bye!\n");

    /* Return control to the operating system */
    XtCloseDisplay(XtDisplay(topShell));
    exit(0);
    }
```

Example 19.2 X/Motif application program using colors, part 2.

16. Explain the term virtual colormap.

17. List the colors that are automatically installed in the default colormap.

18. List the macro that gets the default colormap for you as well as two

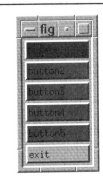

Figure 19.18 Output of the previous X/Motif application program.

other colormap-related macros.

19. Where does X get color names from?

20. How can hexadecimal values be used to describe colors in resource files?

21. What is the purpose of the XColor structure?

22. What is the difference between shared and private color cells in a colormap?

23. List the two functions that allocate shared color cells.

24. What happens if a shared color cell cannot be allocated?

25. What has to be done first before private color cells can be allocated?

26. List three functions that store colors in private color cells.

27. What happens to your colors when your client terminates?

28. How do you free colors previously allocated by your client?

29. How do you create a new colormap?

30. Who is usually responsible for installing colormaps?

31. How can your client install a colormap?

32. How do you get rid of a colormap?

33. Describe the ColormapNotify event.

Exercises

☐ The following exercises are designed to give you the opportunity to practice the concepts and facilities presented in this chapter:

1. Without using a resource file, modify your multibutton program from a previous chapter so that it uses different foreground colors for the labels on the PushButtons being managed by the RowColumn. Leave the fore-

ground color of the exit Button black but make its background color red.

2. Without modifying its resource file, modify the database program that you have been building over the last several sessions (five Text widgets, five Label widgets, and a MenuBar). Make the background color of the Text widgets white.

3. Without modifying its resource file, modify the drawing program that you have been building over the last several sessions (a DrawingArea, two PushButtons, and a color OptionMenu). Make the background color of the DrawingArea widget white. Also, set up a private color cell to contain the value chosen from the color OptionMenu. Set up a callback function that changes the value in the private color cell based on the color PushButton chosen from the OptionMenu.

4. Create a new X/Motif client application that has three Scale widgets, a DrawingArea widget, and a PushButton widget managed by a RowColumn. The Scale widgets should show the titleStrings of Red, Green, and Blue. Have the Scales show their current value in the range of 0 to 255. Set up a callback function such that any time one of the Scale widgets change their value a new RGB value is stored in a private color cell which is used as the background color for the drawing area. The PushButton will be used to exit the program. Feel free to use a resource file if necessary.

20

X Fonts,
Motif Fontlists,
and the X Cursor Font

Introduction

¤ A font is a collection of letters, digits, and other characters that are displayed in one size and style. With the popularity of GUI interfaces, almost everybody recognizes the difference between serifed fonts (with a small terminal line at the end of the main lines constructing a letter), sans-serifed fonts (without the small terminating lines), boldfaced fonts, and italic fonts. X supports a wide variety of fonts for the display of text in different styles and sizes on the screen. In this chapter you will learn how to use fonts in X for different styles of text on the screen (not on a printer). You will also learn how fonts are related to compound strings and how to use the standard X cursors which are also implemented as a font.

Objectives

¤ After completing this chapter, you will be able to:

□ Explain what a font is.

□ Explain how fonts are stored outside X.

□ Describe where fonts are stored.

□ List several different font families.

□ Describe how to determine which fonts are available.

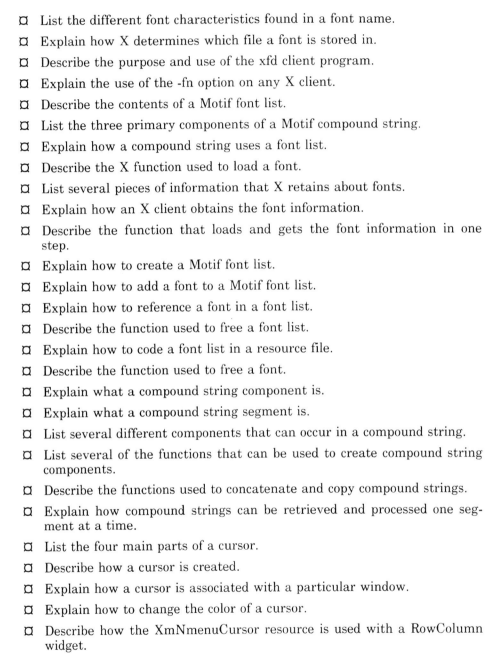

- List the different font characteristics found in a font name.
- Explain how X determines which file a font is stored in.
- Describe the purpose and use of the xfd client program.
- Explain the use of the -fn option on any X client.
- Describe the contents of a Motif font list.
- List the three primary components of a Motif compound string.
- Explain how a compound string uses a font list.
- Describe the X function used to load a font.
- List several pieces of information that X retains about fonts.
- Explain how an X client obtains the font information.
- Describe the function that loads and gets the font information in one step.
- Explain how to create a Motif font list.
- Explain how to add a font to a Motif font list.
- Explain how to reference a font in a font list.
- Describe the function used to free a font list.
- Explain how to code a font list in a resource file.
- Describe the function used to free a font.
- Explain what a compound string component is.
- Explain what a compound string segment is.
- List several different components that can occur in a compound string.
- List several of the functions that can be used to create compound string components.
- Describe the functions used to concatenate and copy compound strings.
- Explain how compound strings can be retrieved and processed one segment at a time.
- List the four main parts of a cursor.
- Describe how a cursor is created.
- Explain how a cursor is associated with a particular window.
- Explain how to change the color of a cursor.
- Describe how the XmNmenuCursor resource is used with a RowColumn widget.

X Font Concepts

- A font is a set of letters, digits, and other characters that has a distinctive appearance on the screen. Each font has characteristics that distinguish it from other fonts on the system. For example, a font may belong to the

Helvetica, Times, or Palatino family; a font may be a roman or an italic font; a font may be 12, 14, or 18 points tall (1 point = 1/72 inch). In general, one font distinguishes itself from the other fonts by the style or characteristics in which it is displayed.

In the X Window System (X11 through Release 4), each font is stored in a separate file. For example, 10-point Helvetica roman would be stored in one file, 10-point Helvetica italic would be stored in another, and 14-point Helvetica bold would be stored in yet another file. Unlike other systems where all the members of the same family are stored in a single file, X stores separate fonts in separate files as bitmaps. (In Release 5 of X, fonts are handled differently.)

Although fonts files can be located anywhere in the file system and accessed through the use of a *font path*, standard fonts are usually stored in the /usr/lib/X11/fonts directory. There are three subdirectories called 100dpi, 75dpi, and misc in this directory where the actual font files are stored. These three subdirectories make up the default font path. The font file names end with the extension .snf (Server Natural Format).

To get a listing of the available fonts, you can use a standard X client called xlsfonts. Simply enter xlsfonts at the operating system prompt from your terminal emulator window to get a listing similar to that shown in Figure 20.1.

Although the font names may appear a bit imposing at first, they are designed to give you a lot of information. The font name consists of 12 fields separated by one or two dashes. Each field tells you something different about the font:

foundry	The company (type foundry) that supplied the font in its digitized form. Adobe and Bitstream are two companies that have donated font families to the X Window System.
family	The style of the font regardless of its size, weight, slant, and so on. Common font families include Helvetica, Palatino, Times, Courier, and New Century Schoolbook.
weight	The thickness of the lines that make up the characters. Medium and bold are two common font line thicknesses.
slant	The angle of the lines that make up the characters. Oblique (o) means italicized, and roman (r) means straight up and down.
set width	The proportionate width of the font. Widths include normal, condensed, narrow, and double width.
pixels	The number of vertical screen pixels required to display a character from the font.
points	The vertical size of a character from the font in tenths of a point.
horizontal resolution	The horizontal resolution in dots (pixels) per inch that the font was designed for.

```
$ xlsfonts
-adobe-courier-bold-o-normal--10-100-75-75-m-60-iso8859-1
-adobe-courier-bold-o-normal--12-120-75-75-m-70-iso8859-1
-adobe-courier-bold-o-normal--14-140-75-75-m-90-iso8859-1
-adobe-courier-bold-o-normal--18-180-75-75-m-110-iso8859-1
-adobe-courier-bold-o-normal--24-240-75-75-m-150-iso8859-1
-adobe-courier-bold-o-normal--8-80-75-75-m-50-iso8859-1
-adobe-courier-bold-r-normal--10-100-75-75-m-60-iso8859-1
-adobe-courier-bold-r-normal--12-120-75-75-m-70-iso8859-1
-adobe-courier-bold-r-normal--14-140-75-75-m-90-iso8859-1
-adobe-courier-bold-r-normal--18-180-75-75-m-110-iso8859-1
-adobe-courier-bold-r-normal--24-240-75-75-m-150-iso8859-1
-adobe-courier-bold-r-normal--8-80-75-75-m-50-iso8859-1
-adobe-courier-medium-o-normal--10-100-75-75-m-60-iso8859-1
-adobe-courier-medium-o-normal--12-120-75-75-m-70-iso8859-1
-adobe-courier-medium-o-normal--14-140-75-75-m-90-iso8859-1
-adobe-courier-medium-o-normal--18-180-75-75-m-110-iso8859-1
-adobe-courier-medium-o-normal--24-240-75-75-m-150-iso8859-1
-adobe-courier-medium-o-normal--8-80-75-75-m-50-iso8859-1
-adobe-courier-medium-r-normal--10-100-75-75-m-60-iso8859-1
-adobe-courier-medium-r-normal--12-120-75-75-m-70-iso8859-1
-adobe-courier-medium-r-normal--14-140-75-75-m-90-iso8859-1
-adobe-courier-medium-r-normal--18-180-75-75-m-110-iso8859-1
-adobe-courier-medium-r-normal--24-240-75-75-m-150-iso8859-1
-adobe-courier-medium-r-normal--8-80-75-75-m-50-iso8859-1
-adobe-helvetica-bold-o-normal--10-100-75-75-p-60-iso8859-1
-adobe-helvetica-bold-o-normal--12-120-75-75-p-69-iso8859-1
...
```

Figure 20.1 Xlsfonts client output.

vertical resolution	The vertical resolution in dots (pixels) per inch that the font was designed for.
spacing	The font is either monospaced (m) or proportional (p).
average width	The mean width of all of the characters in the font measured in tenths of a pixel.
character set	The character set used for the font. The International Standards Organization (ISO) has defined a set of characters that is a superset of the ASCII character set which supports various special characters used in some European languages. The iso8859-1 character set is sometimes referred to as the ISO Latin 1 character set.

One thing that the font name does not do is tell you the name of the file that the font is stored in. X accomplishes the translation between a font name and its filename through the use of a special file located in each font directory. This file is called fonts.dir Figure 20.2 shows what a typical fonts.dir file looks like.

```
$ cat /usr/lib/X11/fonts/75dpi/fonts.dir
126
courBO10.snf        -adobe-courier-bold-o-normal--10-100-75-75-m-60-iso8859-1
courBO12.snf        -adobe-courier-bold-o-normal--12-120-75-75-m-70-iso8859-1
courBO14.snf        -adobe-courier-bold-o-normal--14-140-75-75-m-90-iso8859-1
courBO18.snf        -adobe-courier-bold-o-normal--18-180-75-75-m-110-iso8859-1
courBO24.snf        -adobe-courier-bold-o-normal--24-240-75-75-m-150-iso8859-1
courBO08.snf        -adobe-courier-bold-o-normal--8-80-75-75-m-50-iso8859-1
courB10.snf         -adobe-courier-bold-r-normal--10-100-75-75-m-60-iso8859-1
courB12.snf         -adobe-courier-bold-r-normal--12-120-75-75-m-70-iso8859-1
courB14.snf         -adobe-courier-bold-r-normal--14-140-75-75-m-90-iso8859-1
courB18.snf         -adobe-courier-bold-r-normal--18-180-75-75-m-110-iso8859-1
courB24.snf         -adobe-courier-bold-r-normal--24-240-75-75-m-150-iso8859-1
courB08.snf         -adobe-courier-bold-r-normal--8-80-75-75-m-50-iso8859-1
courO10.snf         -adobe-courier-medium-o-normal--10-100-75-75-m-60-iso8859-1
courO12.snf         -adobe-courier-medium-o-normal--12-120-75-75-m-70-iso8859-1
courO14.snf         -adobe-courier-medium-o-normal--14-140-75-75-m-90-iso8859-1
courO18.snf         -adobe-courier-medium-o-normal--18-180-75-75-m-110-iso8859-1
courO24.snf         -adobe-courier-medium-o-normal--24-240-75-75-m-150-iso8859-1
courO08.snf         -adobe-courier-medium-o-normal--8-80-75-75-m-50-iso8859-1
courR10.snf         -adobe-courier-medium-r-normal--10-100-75-75-m-60-iso8859-1
courR12.snf         -adobe-courier-medium-r-normal--12-120-75-75-m-70-iso8859-1
courR14.snf         -adobe-courier-medium-r-normal--14-140-75-75-m-90-iso8859-1
courR18.snf         -adobe-courier-medium-r-normal--18-180-75-75-m-110-iso8859-1
courR24.snf         -adobe-courier-medium-r-normal--24-240-75-75-m-150-iso8859-1
courR08.snf         -adobe-courier-medium-r-normal--8-80-75-75-m-50-iso8859-1
helvBO10.snf        -adobe-helvetica-bold-o-normal--10-100-75-75-p-60-iso8859-1
helvBO12.snf        -adobe-helvetica-bold-o-normal--12-120-75-75-p-69-iso8859-1
...
```

Figure 20.2 A fonts.dir file.

To get an idea of what the characters in a particular font look like, X supplies another standard client. The xfd (X Font Displayer) client displays a window on the screen and a grid within it. Each cell of the grid is used to display a character from the font. Figure 20.3 shows what the output of the xfd client would look like.

The -fn option is used with xfd to tell it the name of the font you want to see. Follow the -fn with a space and the full name (not the filename) of the font you want displayed.

Once the xfd window has been displayed, the mouse buttons can be used to alter the display. If more characters are available in the font than can fit on the screen, the right mouse button will scroll the font down to view more characters. To scroll up, use the left mouse button. The middle mouse button will display the cell number (in decimal and hexadecimal) that the mouse pointer is currently pointing to.

There are two different ways to terminate the xfd client. With the xfd window as the current input focus window, type either the letter q or a <control>-c.

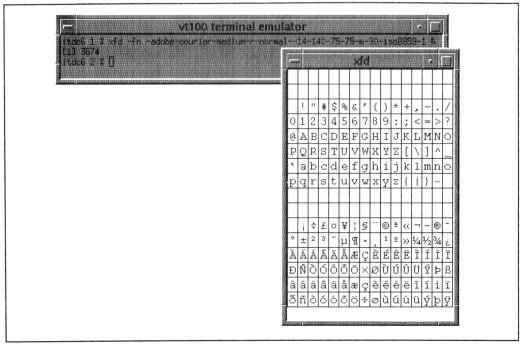

Figure 20.3 Output of the xfd client.

⊡   Many X clients allow you to specify the font that you would like to use to display text with. Several standard options are available and recognized by the command line parsing that XtInitialize() does for you. One of these options, as shown with the xfd client previously, is the -fn option.

Just as with xfd, the -fn option is followed with a font name — not a filename. The font name you specify will be used for the text items that the X client displays on the screen. So, to start another terminal emulator program, you might type something like:

```
xterm -fn "-adobe-courier-medium-o-normal--8-80-75-75-m-50-iso8859-1" &
```

Unfortunately, this is not the way you work with fonts in a Motif application. Because Motif uses compound strings and the font that is used is encoded within the compound string, a different method is needed to work with fonts in Motif.

Motif Font Concepts

⊡   With the exception of the text being entered or displayed within a text widget, all text items in a Motif application are compound strings. The font that is used for the text within a compound string is defined by something called a *character set*. The character set is an identifier, or a name, for a font that exists in a *font list*. A font list is a list of one or more character set name and font name pairs.

You might remember from our discussion of resources in a previous chapter that compound strings are designed to allow text to be displayed without hard-coding language-dependent attributes within a string. The XmString data type is actually a pointer to a data structure that contains three components:

character set   The mapping between the string of characters that make up a text item and the font in which the text will be displayed

direction   The relationship between the keyboard entry order and the display order of the characters in the string

text   The actual characters to be displayed

Compound strings are not the same thing as C language character strings. Characters such as \n and \t that have special meaning in a C character string have no meaning in an XmString. The XmNlabelString of the Label widget which is inherited by the CascadeButton, PushButton, and ToggleButton; XmNitems of the List widget; and the XmNtitleString of the Scale widget are all examples of resources that must be set with compound strings.

When you create a compound string for Motif, one of the parameters for the create function is always the character set to use. The create function will take the character set name and compare it to all the character set names in the font list of the widget it is creating the compound string for. Once it finds a match for a character set, then the associated font name is used for the compound string. Figure 20.4 illustrates this mechanism.

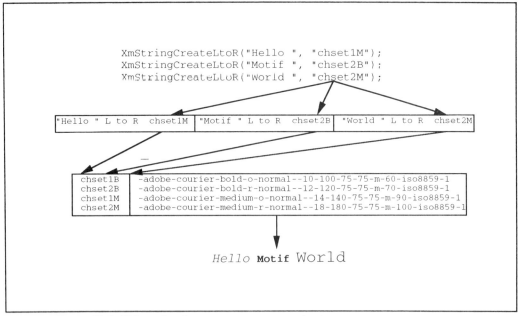

Figure 20.4 Using a font list to create a compound string.

Motif supplies a character set name for use when you don't care what font is used for your compound strings. In the previous discussion of the XmStringCreateLtoR() function you learned about the XmSTRING_-DEFAULT_CHARSET character set to get the first font from the font list.

Many Motif widgets supply a font list resource. Its name is always XmNfontList, and its type is always XmFontList. The default font that Motif uses for its default font list is called *fixed*. One of the main features of the font list concept is a compound string's ability to have multiple text segments and each segment capable of being displayed in a different font.

Loading a Font

¤ As with colormaps, fonts are server resources. The server manages the fonts for your use in an X/Motif client application. In order for the server to manage a font for you, the font must be loaded into the server. This font loading can be accomplished with a call to XLoadFont(). Figure 20.5 shows the syntax for this function.

The first parameter is the display pointer used to access the display connection information needed to determine which server to load the font into. The second parameter is a null-terminated character string which is the name of the font to load. When coding the font name, the case of the letters is not important.

The function returns an identifier which will be used to uniquely identify this font from other loaded fonts in the server. The Font type item returned from XLoadFont() is, in effect, another name for the font. It is this alternate name, which is used in the next step, that is required for using a font in your X/Motif client application.

Getting Font Information

¤ Once the font is loaded, there are a number of characteristics of the font that must be ascertained before X can use the font to display text on the screen. What must be understood here is that X terminals do not handle the details of text display for you the way that a simple 80×24 ASCII display terminal did for you in the past. These details are left up to your client program.

In an older ASCII display terminal, text was usually displayed on a series of 24 lines. These lines were evenly spaced through the height of the screen. The "font" that was used on these lines was designed so that the descenders of the characters on one line did not interfere with the characters displayed on the next line. About the only choice that a few terminal

```
Font XLoadFont(display, name)

Display *display;
String   name;
```

Figure 20.5 XLoadFont() syntax.

manufacturers allowed you was the ability to display 80 or 132 characters per line — normal or condensed text.

Because there are so many variables in an X font, this simple method of handling text is no longer adequate. Fonts can be normal, narrow, condensed, or of double width; fonts can be 8, 10, 12, 14, 18, or any number of points high; fonts can have different sizes of ascenders and descenders; and so on. In fact, a font description is an exacting description that allows very precise display of the characters and lines on an X terminal screen. It is up to you and your client application to make use of this information to display your text in appropriate locations on the screen. Figure 20.6 shows some of the information that X provides with the fonts that you use to display text on the screen.

X gives you access to this information through another data structure. The XFontStruct data type contains all the necessary display information for the font in general and the characters within the font. To query a loaded font for its XFontStruct information, you make a call to the XQueryFont() function. Figure 20.7 shows its syntax.

The first parameter is the display pointer used to access the display connection information needed to determine which server the font was loaded into. The second parameter is the Font type identifier that was returned

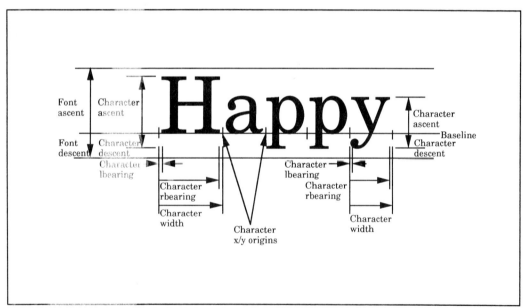

Figure 20.6   Font display information.

```
XFontStruct *XQueryFont(display,  font_id)

Display *display;
Font    font_id;
```

Figure 20.7   XQueryFont() syntax.

from XLoadFont() as a name for the loaded font. This function returns a
pointer to an XFontStruct with all the needed font information in it.

One of the more important members of this data structure is the fid
member. The fid is the actual "font id" that you will use to reference this
font in subsequent functions. Figure 20.8 shows the layout for the
XFontStruct data structure for informational purposes only.

¤   X provides another function that provides the functionality of XLoad-
Font() and XQueryFont() together in one function. The XLoadQueryFont()
function can be called to perform the same operations. Figure 20.9 shows
the syntax for this function.

¤   Once you have the XFontStruct with the fid member, X is ready to use
the font. However, before Motif can use the font for any of its widget's text
resources, there is one more step to be taken. Once you have the

```
/*
 * Font metric information.
 */
typedef struct {
    XExtData        *ext_data;  /* hook for extension to hang data */
    Font            fid;        /* Font id for this font */
    unsigned        direction;  /* hint about direction the font is painted */
    unsigned        min_char_or_byte2; /* first character */
    unsigned        max_char_or_byte2; /* last character */
    unsigned        min_bytel;  /* first row that exists */
    unsigned        max_bytel;  /* last row that exists */
    Bool            all_chars_exist; /* flag if all charas. have non-0 size*/
    unsigned        default_char; /* char to print for undefined character */
    int             n_properties; /* how many properties there are */
    XFontProp       *properties; /* pointer to array of more properties*/
    XCharStruct     min_bounds; /* minimum bounds over all existing char*/
    XCharStruct     max_bounds; /* maximum bounds over all existing char*/
    XCharStruct     *per_char;  /* first_char to last_char information */
    int             ascent;     /* log. extent above baseline for spacing */
    int             descent;    /* log. descent below baseline for spacing */
} XFontStruct;

/*
 * Per character font metric information.
 */
typedef struct {
    short           lbearing;   /* origin to left edge of raster */
    short           rbearing;   /* origin to right edge of raster */
    short           width;      /* advance to next char's origin */
    short           ascent;     /* baseline to top edge of raster */
    short           descent;    /* baseline to bottom edge of raster */
    unsigned short  attributes; /* per char flags (not predefined) */
} XCharStruct;
```

Figure 20.8 Font description data structures.

```
XFontStruct *XLoadQueryFont(display, name)

Display *display;
String  name;
```

Figure 20.9 XLoadQueryFont() syntax.

XFontStruct, you must create a character set name for it and put it into a Motif font list. Figure 20.10 shows a code segment that uses these functions to load some fonts.

Creating a Motif Fontlist

¤   Once again, a font list is nothing more than one or more pairs of character set names (identifiers that you, the programmer, come up with) and font names (as shown with xlsfonts). When a widget uses a compound string for displaying some type of text information, it obtains the character set from the compound string and compares it to all the character sets in the associated font list resource. When it finds a match, it uses the associated font for the text of the compound string.

To create a font list, Motif provides a function called XmFontList-Create(). If you want to add fonts to an already existing font list, you use the function called XmFontListAdd(). Figure 20.11 shows the syntax for both of these functions.

```
...
#define font1 "-adobe-helvetica-bold-r-normal--14-140-75-75-p-82-iso8859-1"
#define font2 "-adobe-helvetica-medium-o-normal--18-180-75-75-p-98-iso8859-1"
#define font3 "-adobe-helvetica-medium-r-normal--24-240-75-75-p-130-iso8859-1"
...
    XFontStruct *font[3];
    ...
    font[0] = XLoadQueryFont(display, font1);
    font[1] = XLoadQueryFont(display, font2);
    font[2] = XLoadQueryFont(display, font3);
    ...
```

Figure 20.10 Using XLoadQueryFont() in a program.

```
XmFontList XmFontListCreate(font, character_set)
XmFontList XmFontListAdd(old_font_list, font, character_set)

XFontStruct    *font;
XmFontList     old_font_list;
XmStringCharSet character_set;
```

Figure 20.11 XmFontListCreate() and XmFontListAdd() syntax.

Both these functions return a *new* font list for use with compound strings. The first function creates a new font list for the font whose XFontStruct you pass as the first parameter. The font will be entered into the font list and associated with character set you specify as the second parameter. This character set can be specified as a simple C character string that you create, or it can be the predefined name XmSTRING_DEFAULT_CHARSET.

The second function creates a new font list and copies the old font list (specified as the first parameter) into it. It then deallocates the old font list before adding the new font. This function then adds the new font for the font whose XFontStruct you pass as the second parameter. The font will be entered into the font list and associated with the character set you specify as the third parameter. This character set can be specified as a simple C character string that you create, or it can be the predefined name XmSTRING_DEFAULT_CHARSET. Do not attempt to reference the old font list after calling this function — it will not exist.

It then becomes easy to reference any of the fonts stored in a font list. Simply, use the character set name that you defined for the font in either one of these two functions as the appropriate parameter to the compound string creation function. Don't forget that both the font list and the compound string are resources specified for a particular widget. It is, of course, possible to use the same font list for multiple widgets either in your client's source code or from within a resource file. Figure 20.12 shows an example of a code segment that creates a font list.

¤   When you are done with a font list, just as with compound strings, you should free the font list. This frees up valuable space that could be used for other things in your client. To free a font list, use the XmFontListFree() function. Figure 20.13 shows its syntax.

¤   Just like any other resource, Motif font lists can be coded within your client application code or within a resource file. The XmNfontList resource can be set for a single widget, a class of widgets, or all widgets within your

```
...
#define font1 "-adobe-helvetica-bold-r-normal--14-140-75-75-p-82-iso8859-1"
#define font2 "-adobe-helvetica-medium-o-normal--18-180-75-75-p-98-iso8859-1"
#define font3 "-adobe-helvetica-medium-r-normal--24-240-75-75-p-130-iso8859-1"
...
    XFontStruct *font[3];
    XmFontList myFontList;
    ...
    font[0] = XLoadQueryFont(display, font1);
    font[1] = XLoadQueryFont(display, font2);
    font[2] = XLoadQueryFont(display, font3);
    myFontList = XmFontListCreate(font[0], "chset1");
    myFontList = XmFontListAdd(myFontList, font[1], "chset2");
    myFontList = XmFontListAdd(myFontList, font[2], "chset3");
    ...
```

Figure 20.12 Creating a font list in a Motif application.

```
void XmFontListFree(font_list)

XmFontList font_list;
```

Figure 20.13 XmFontListFree() syntax.

X/Motif client application. Just as described above, the font list resource can contain entries for one or more font-character set combinations.

Within a resource file, the font list value can be a comma-separated list of one or more sets of font name, equals sign (=), character set name. Remember that the character set name is simply an identifier that you come up with to reference a particular font from within a compound string. Figure 20.14 shows some sample resource entries for font lists in a resource file.

Once the font lists have been created, you can create compound strings using the fonts specified in the list. In the XmStringCreateLtoR() function you specify a character set name from the font list, and the string will be created in the associated font. Figure 20.15 shows some examples based on the font lists created in Figure 20.14.

□   If you are done with a font and you don't need it anymore, you should free it. This only needs to be done if your client will continue executing after the font is freed. Just like most other server resources, when a client terminates, the fonts that were allocated are automatically freed. Figure 20.16 shows the syntax for the XFreeFont() function.

```
...
Edit.rcmanager.button1.fontList:
          -adobe-courier-bold-r-normal--8-80-75-75-m-50-iso8859-1=chset1
*menubar.XmCascadeButton.fontList:   8x13=set1,8x13bold=set2
*fontList:                           5x7=size1,6x10=size2,8x13=size3,9x15=size4
...
```

Figure 20.14 Font lists specified in a resource file.

```
XmString str1, str2, str3;
...
str1 = XmStringCreateLtoR("Exit Program", "chset1");
...
str1 = XmStringCreateLtoR("Edit", "set1");
str2 = XmStringCreateLtoR("File", "set1");
str3 = XmStringCreateLtoR("Help", "set2");
...
str1 = XmStringCreateLtoR("Please enter a filename:", "size4");
str2 = XmStringCreateLtoR("Copyright 1992 ITDC", "size1");
...
```

Figure 20.15 Using font lists to create compound strings.

```
XFreeFont(display, font_structure)

Display      *display;
XFontStruct  *font_structure;
```

Figure 20.16 XFreeFont() syntax.

Compound Strings and Fontlists

¤ To be a little more detailed about the XmString data type, a compound string is created as a collection of one or more components. Each component consists of three parts:

tag   A 1-byte field that identifies the type of the component. This will indicate that the component is a character set, a direction, or a text component.

length   A 2-byte field that indicates how many bytes follow in the third part.

value   A field whose length is specified in the previous part to hold the actual data for the character set, direction, or text information.

Every compound string starts with a special component that contains the total length of all the components that make up the compound string. The subsequent components define the character set, direction, and text for the compound string as was described previously. For the simple compound strings that we have created so far, only three additional components were created.

For more complicated compound strings there can be more than these four components. Each component can define a different character set (font), a different direction, and different text with optional separators. It is possible, for example, to create a compound string with different portions being displayed in different fonts or with different directions and on separate lines.

¤ We have already discussed creating compound strings in their simplest form. The XmStringCreateLtoR() function created a four component compound string. This function created one component each for the total length, a character set (the default fixed character set), a direction (left to right), and a text component that had the actual text information to be displayed. There are several other Motif functions that allow for the creation of compound strings that have more or fewer components. Figure 20.17 shows the syntax for these other compound string creation functions.

The first of these functions creates a simple three-component compound string. XmStringCreate() creates a compound string with a character set component and a text component but no direction component. You can, if you wish, create a direction component with a call to XmStringDirection-Create(). This function creates a two-component compound string that has nothing but a direction component in it. Two directions are currently defined: XmSTRING_DIRECTION_L_TO_R and XmSTRING_-DIRECTION_R_TO_L.

```
XmString XmStringCreate(text, character_set)
XmString XmStringDirectionCreate(direction)
XmString XmStringSegmentCreate(text, character_set, direction, separator)
XmString XmStringSeparatorCreate()


char             *text;
XmStringCharSet   character_set;
XmStringDirection direction;
Boolean           separator;
```

Figure 20.17 Compound string creation function syntax.

The XmStringSegmentCreate() function creates the same type of compound string that XmStringCreateLtoR() did with two exceptions. First, this new function lets you specify the direction for the compound string instead of defaulting to left to right. Second, this function lets you specify a fifth component called a *separator component*. A separator essentially gives you the ability to embed a newline character in a compound string so that when it is displayed it will occupy several different physical lines on the screen.

Notice that in XmStringSegmentCreate() two additional parameters are provided. The next to the last parameter is a direction parameter as specified above. The last parameter is a Boolean value—True if you do want a separator component to appear after the text component; False if you do not want a separator component. The last of these functions, XmStringSeparatorCreate(), lets you create a separator component by itself.

You will notice that each of the preceding functions creates and returns an XmString (compound string) value. Don't forget that a compound string always contains a length component that specifies the length of the entire compound string. Each compound string is a stand-alone entity.

There may be times when you want to combine or copy compound strings and manipulate several XmStrings as a group. Several functions are provided for such manipulations, three of which we present here. Figure 20.18 shows the syntax for the XmStringConcat(), XmStringCopy(), and the XmStringLineCount() functions.

XmStringConcat() appends the second compound string onto the end of the first. Both these compound strings are preserved while the function returns the resulting compound string. If you don't need the component compound strings anymore, it is suggested, as before, that you use the XmStringFree() function to release the memory that was allocated for them.

```
XmString XmStringConcat(string1, string2)
XmString XmStringCopy(string1)
int XmStringLineCount(string1)

XmString string1;
XmString string2;
```

Figure 20.18 XmStringConcat(), XmStringCopy(), and XmStringLineCount() syntax.

Using these functions, you can create portions of compound strings described above and concatenate them together into a single compound string. You might create a character set and text component with XmStringCreate(), a direction component with XmStringDirectionCreate(), a separator component with XmStringSeparatorCreate(), and string them all together with multiple calls to XmStringConcat(). This method provides for the greatest flexibility in creating Motif compound strings.

The XmStringCopy() function copies the compound string you specify as a parameter into a brand-new compound string. The return value is the XmString value for the new compound string. XmStringLineCount takes a compound string as a parameter and returns you an integer count of the number of separator components plus one—the number of lines in the compound string. Figure 20.19 shows a code segment that uses different character sets to construct a multiline and multifont compound string.

In addition to setting compound strings as resources in widgets, you have also learned how to retrieve compound string values from widgets and use them as ASCII strings in your client's data processing. You will remember that you had to do this with the list widget to process the selected item.

```
...
#include <X11/cursorfont.h>

#define font1 "-adobe-helvetica-bold-r-normal--14-140-75-75-p-82-iso8859-1"
#define font2 "-adobe-helvetica-medium-o-normal--18-180-75-75-p-98-iso8859-1"
#define font3 "-adobe-helvetica-medium-r-normal--24-240-75-75-p-130-iso8859-1"
...
    XFontStruct *font[3];
    XmFontList myFontList;
    XmString label;
    XmString segment;
    ...
    font[0] = XLoadQueryFont(display, font1);
    font[1] = XLoadQueryFont(display, font2);
    font[2] = XLoadQueryFont(display, font3);
    myFontList = XmFontListCreate(font[0], "chset1");
    myFontList = XmFontListAdd(myFontList, font[1], "chset2");
    myFontList = XmFontListAdd(myFontList, font[2], "chset3");
    label = XmStringSegmentCreate("Press here to",
            "chset1", XmSTRING_DIRECTION_L_TO_R, True);
    segment = XmStringSegmentCreate("EXIT",
            "chset2", XmSTRING_DIRECTION_R_TO_L, True);
    label = XmStringConcat(label, segment);
    segment = XmStringSegmentCreate("the application",
            "chset3", XmSTRING_DIRECTION_L_TO_R, False);
    label = XmStringConcat(label, segment);
    ...
```

Figure 20.19 Creating a multiline and multifont compound string.

The function you learned about to retrieve a compound string was called XmStringGetLtoR().

You now know that a compound string is composed of different components. A text component, a direction component, a character set component, and a separator component combine to form a compound string segment. You may want to access a compound string one segment at a time. There are three functions that allow you to do this. XmStringInitContext() creates an XmStringContext, which is analogous to a pointer to a segment within a compound string. XmStringGetNextSegment() retrieves the next segment pointed to by the XmStringContext pointer so that you can use it in your client code. And finally, when done, XmStringFreeContext() frees the XmStringContext and deallocates the memory associated with it. Figure 20.20 shows the syntax for these three functions.

XmStringInitContext() takes the address of an XmStringContext as its first parameter and an XmString as its second. This function sets up a pointer in the second parameter compound string for subsequent "Gets" with XmStringGetNextSegment(). The "pointer" is returned in the variable whose address was passed as the first parameter. XmStringInitContext() returns True if it was successful in allocating the context and False if it failed.

Once the context, or pointer, has been allocated, you can call XmStringGetNextSegment() to get the XmString segment that the XmStringContext is currently pointing to. Successive calls to this function return successive segment information from the compound string. Note that the first parameter is a pointer to the context that was allocated with XmStringInitContext() and is incremented with each successive call to XmStringGetNextSegment(). The remaining parameters are addresses of variables that will be filled in with compound string information. This function returns True if it was successful in its operation and False otherwise.

□   When you are finished obtaining the parts of a compound string, you should free the XmStringContext that you used. XmStringFreeContext() is used for this purpose. It takes the pointer to the XmStringContext that is no longer needed and returns nothing. Figure 20.21 shows its syntax.

```
Boolean XmStringInitContext(context, string)
Boolean XmStringGetNextSegment(context,
                        text, character_set, direction, separator);
void XmStringFreeContext(context);

XmStringContext     *context;
XmString            string;
char                **text;
XmStringCharSet     *character_set;
XmStringDirection   *direction;
Boolean             *separator;
```

Figure 20.20 XmString...InitContext(), ...GetNextSegment(), and ...FreeContext() syntax.

```
void XmStringFreeContext(context)

XmStringContext *context;
```

Figure 20.21 XmStringFreeContext() syntax.

X Cursor Font

One other standard font that X supplies is a font that consists of several different cursor shapes. Cursors are provided in a variety of shapes and sizes. Standard cursor shapes include several different styles of arrows, several different styles of hands with a pointing finger, a coffee mug, the starship Enterprise, a watch, a heart, and even Gumby. Figure 20.22 shows the standard cursor shapes.

All cursors (just like all fonts) are bitmaps that are displayed on the screen. The cursor bitmap moves around the screen in response to the movement of the mouse. In X, a cursor actually consists of four parts:

❑ A cursor bitmap that determines the shape of the cursor

❑ A mask bitmap that determines which pixels on the screen will be affected by the cursor in its current position

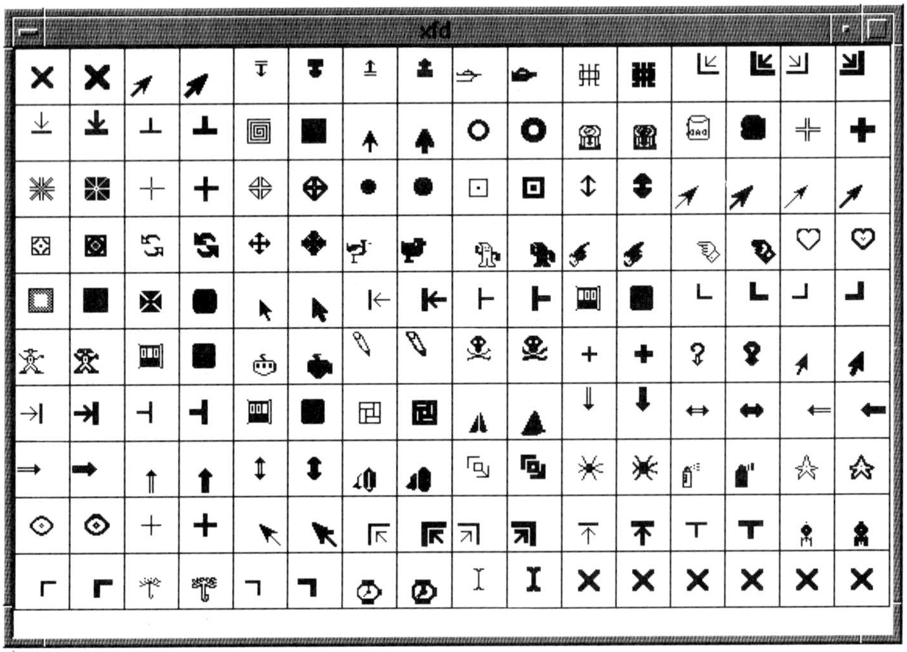

Figure 20.22 Standard cursor shapes.

    □ Two pixel values—one for the foreground color and one for the background

    □ A hot spot—the X/Y location on the screen that is reported when a pointer event occurs; the actual on-screen location of the mouse

The cursor bitmap defines the exact shape of the cursor and will be displayed in the foreground color of the cursor. The mask bitmap is almost identical to the cursor bitmap except that it is one pixel wider in all directions. The mask allows a one-pixel background color to be displayed around the perimeter of the cursor. The mask also defines which portion of the rectangular area that surrounds the cursor will be transparent so that the underlying window will be visible around the cursor shape.

□   Unlike using regular fonts, you do not have to load the cursor font before you can use it—X does this for you. However, you must tell the server which cursor shape you want to use and create an actual cursor from it. This is accomplished with a call to XCreateFontCursor(). Figure 20.23 shows its syntax.

The first parameter to this function is the display pointer that identifies which server you are connected to while the second parameter is a defined name that identifies which of the standard shapes you want for a cursor. The function returns type Cursor, which can then be associated with some window in your client application code.

The defined names that are used to identify which cursor shape you want to use are defined in the required header file <X11/cursorfont.h>. There is one name for each of the standard cursors. Figure 20.24 shows what some of these defined names look like.

□   Once the cursor has been created, it must be associated with a particular window on the screen. This is done so that when the pointer location moves into that window, the cursor will change to the desired shape. This association between a cursor shape and a window is accomplished with a call to the XDefineCursor() function. Figure 20.25 shows its syntax.

The first parameter to this function is the display pointer that identifies which server you are connected to, while the second parameter is the window id of the window you want the cursor associated with. Don't forget that the window id for a particular widget can be obtained with a call to the XtWindow() function. The last parameter is the Cursor data type that was returned from the call to XCreateFontCursor. If XDefineCursor() is not called for a particular window on the screen, the window will inherit its parent's cursor.

```
#include <X11/cursorfont.h>

Cursor XCreateFontCursor(display, cursor_shape)

Display      *display;
unsigned int cursor_shape;
```

Figure 20.23 XCreateFontCursor() syntax.

```
$ cat /usr/include/X11/cursorfont.h
/* $XConsortium: cursorfont.h,v 1.2 88/09/06 16:44:27 jim Exp $ */
#define XC_num_glyphs 154
#define XC_X_cursor 0
#define XC_arrow 2
#define XC_based_arrow_down 4
#define XC_based_arrow_up 6
#define XC_boat 8
#define XC_bogosity 10
#define XC_bottom_left_corner 12
#define XC_bottom_right_corner 14
#define XC_bottom_side 16
#define XC_bottom_tee 18
#define XC_box_spiral 20
#define XC_center_ptr 22
#define XC_circle 24
#define XC_clock 26
#define XC_coffee_mug 28
#define XC_cross 30
#define XC_cross_reverse 32
#define XC_crosshair 34
#define XC_diamond_cross 36
#define XC_dot 38
#define XC_dotbox 40
#define XC_double_arrow 42
#define XC_draft_large 44
#define XC_draft_small 46
#define XC_draped_box 48
#define XC_exchange 50
#define XC_fleur 52
#define XC_gobbler 54
#define XC_gumby 56
...
```

Figure 20.24 Cursor names for the XCreateFontCursor() function.

```
XDefineCursor(display,  window,  cursor)

Display *display;
Window  window;
Cursor  cursor;
```

Figure 20.25 XdefineCursor() syntax.

☐   If a cursor's default foreground and background colors conflict with the colors of the underlying window, you may want to change them. XRecolorCursor() provides a mechanism for giving different foreground and background colors to a cursor you have defined. Figure 20.26 shows the syntax for this function.

```
XRecolorCursor(display, cursor, foreground_color, background_color)

Display *display;
Cursor  cursor;
XColor  *foreground_color;
XColor  *background_color;
```

Figure 20.26 XRecolorCursor() syntax.

The first parameter to this function is the display pointer that identifies which server you are connected to, while the second parameter is the Cursor data type that was returned from the call to XCreateFontCursor. The last two parameters are used to specify the Red, Green, and Blue values for the background and foreground colors of the cursor. Figure 20.27 shows a code segment that defines a new cursor.

```
...
#include <Xm/PushB.h>
#include <X11/cursorfont.h>
...
Display *display;
Screen *screen;
Window window;
Colormap colormap;
...
    Widget myButton;
    Cursor myCursor;
    XColor closest[2];
    XColor exact[2];
    Arg argList[10];
    Cardinal i;
    ...
    i = 0;
    XtSetArg(argList[i], XmNwidth, 180); ++i;
    XtSetArg(argList[i], XmNheight, 110); ++i;
    myButton = XmCreatePushButton(topShell, "hello", argList, i);
    ...
    display = XtDisplay(myButton);
    screen = XtScreen(myButton);
    window = XtWindow(myButton);
    colormap = DefaultColormapOfScreen(screen);
    ...
    myCursor = XCreateFontCursor(display, XC_trek);
    XAllocNamedColor(display, colormap, "red", &closest[0], &exact[0]);
    XAllocNamedColor(display, colormap, "coral", &closest[1], &exact[1]);
    XRecolorCursor(display, myCursor, &closest[0], &closest[1]);
    XDefineCursor(display, window, myCursor);
    ...
```

Figure 20.27 Defining a new cursor for an application.

□   If you are done with a cursor and you don't need it anymore, you should free it. This needs to be done only if your client will continue executing after the cursor is freed. Just like most other server resources, when a client terminates, the cursors that were allocated are automatically freed. Figure 20.28 shows the syntax for the XFreeCursor() function.

□   Motif supplies one other method of setting a cursor with respect to menus. The RowColumn widget is the basis for the Motif menu system and supplies an additional resource for the cursor shape in a menu. The XmNmenuCursor resource can be set in a resource file or within your client application code by using the XmSetMenuCursor() function to define a different cursor shape for menus.

    It is important to note that the cursor for each client can only be set once – at menu creation time – and cannot be changed thereafter. Also note that only one menu cursor shape is allowed for each client application. You cannot have different cursor shapes for different menus.

□   *A Special Note about the XtWindow() Function:* It is important to understand that the XtWindow() function returns a window id. This id is a unique number that is assigned to every X window that the server creates and displays on the screen. If your client application does not have a window displayed on the screen, XtWindow() cannot return a valid window id. Remember – until your client code invokes the XtRealizeWidget() function to realize your top-level Shell widget, there are no windows on the screen. This means that XtWindow cannot return a valid window id until after the XtRealizeWidget() function has been called and your client's windows have been realized! If you must have a window id before you call XtRealizeWidget(), X supplies a macro called RootWindowOfScreen() which takes a screen pointer as a parameter and returns the window id of the root window. The root window is realized as soon as the X server starts up and is always available.

A Complete X/Motif Client Application

□   Using all the concepts and techniques presented in this chapter, we can put together a simple, but complete, X/Motif-based client application. Example 20.1 shows the code for a program that has a single PushButton in it. The PushButton window has a new cursor defined for it with different colors. A font list is defined with three fonts in it for use in the compound string for the label on the PushButton.

    Figure 20.29 shows what the program would look like on a typical terminal screen.

```
XFreeCursor(display, cursor)

Display *display;
Cursor  cursor;
```

Figure 20.28 XFreeCursor() syntax.

```
#include <stdio.h>
#include <Xm/PushB.h>
#include <X11/cursorfont.h>

#define font1 "-adobe-helvetica-bold-r-normal--14-140-75-75-p-82-iso8859-1"
#define font2 "-adobe-helvetica-medium-o-normal--18-180-75-75-p-98-iso8859-1"
#define font3 "-adobe-helvetica-medium-r-normal--24-240-75-75-p-130-iso8859-1"

Display *display;
Screen *screen;
Window window;
Colormap colormap;
Widget topShell;
XtCallbackProc ButtonPushed();

main(argc, argv)
Cardinal argc;
String argv[];
    {
    Widget myButton;
    XFontStruct *font[3];
    XmFontList myFontList;
    XmString label;
    XmString segment;
    Cursor myCursor;
    XColor closest[2];
    XColor exact[2];
    Arg argList[10];
    Cardinal i;

    /* Initialize  the Intrinsics and create a top Shell widget */
    topShell = XtInitialize(argv[0], "Edit", NULL, 0, &argc, argv);

    /* Create the user interface widgets */
    i = 0;
    XtSetArg(argList[i], XmNwidth, 180); ++i;
    XtSetArg(argList[i], XmNheight, 110); ++i;
    myButton = XmCreatePushButton(topShell, "hello", argList, i);

    /* Set up callbacks for the widgets */
    XtAddCallback(myButton, XmNactivateCallback, ButtonPushed, NULL);

    /* Make the program visible on the screen */
    XtManageChild(myButton);
    XtRealizeWidget(topShell);
```

Example 20.1 X/Motif application program using fonts and cursors, part 1.

```
/* Get some server specific information */
display = XtDisplay(myButton);
screen = XtScreen(myButton);
window = XtWindow(myButton);
colormap = DefaultColormapOfScreen(screen);

/* Get the font information */
font[0] = XLoadQueryFont(display, font1);
font[1] = XLoadQueryFont(display, font2);
font[2] = XLoadQueryFont(display, font3);
myFontList = XmFontListCreate(font[0], "chset1");
myFontList = XmFontListAdd(myFontList, font[1], "chset2");
myFontList = XmFontListAdd(myFontList, font[2], "chset3");
label = XmStringSegmentCreate("Press here to",
            "chset1", XmSTRING_DIRECTION_L_TO_R, True);
segment = XmStringSegmentCreate("EXIT",
            "chset2", XmSTRING_DIRECTION_R_TO_L, True);
label = XmStringConcat(label, segment);
segment = XmStringSegmentCreate("the application",
            "chset3", XmSTRING_DIRECTION_L_TO_R, False);
label = XmStringConcat(label, segment);

/* Set the new label in the PushButton */
i = 0;
XtSetArg(argList[i], XmNfontList, myFontList); ++i;
XtSetArg(argList[i], XmNlabelString, label); ++i;
XtSetValues(myButton, argList, i);

/* Get a new cursor for the window */
myCursor = XCreateFontCursor(display, XC_trek);
XAllocNamedColor(display, colormap, "red", &closest[0], &exact[0]);
XAllocNamedColor(display, colormap, "coral", &closest[1], &exact[1]);
XRecolorCursor(display, myCursor, &closest[0], &closest[1]);
XDefineCursor(display, window, myCursor);

/* Wait for input events */
XtMainLoop();
}
```

Example 20.2 X/Motif application program using fonts and cursors, part 2.

Review Questions

◻ Please write down the answers to the following questions:

   1. What is a font?

```
XtCallbackProc ButtonPushed(widget_id, client_data, call_data)
Widget widget_id;
caddr_t client_data;
caddr_t call_data;
    {

    /* Print something on the screen */
    printf("Good Bye!\n");

    /* Return control to the operating system */
    XtCloseDisplay(XtDisplay(topShell));
    exit(0);
    }
```

Example 20.3 X/Motif application program using fonts and cursors, part 3.

Figure 20.29 Output of the previous X/Motif application program.

2. How are fonts stored outside X?

3. Where are fonts stored?

4. List three different font families.

5. How do you determine which fonts are available?

6. List four different font characteristics found in a font name.

7. How does X determine which file a font is stored in?

8. What is the purpose of the xfd client program?

9. How do you use the xfd client program?

10. Why do you use the -fn option on any X client?

11. What is contained in a Motif font list?

12. List the three primary components of a Motif compound string.

13. How does a compound string use a font list?

14. Which X function is used to load a font?

15. List three pieces of information that X retains about fonts.

16. How does an X client obtain the font information?

17. Which function loads and gets the font information in one step?

18. How do you create a Motif font list?

19. How do you add a font to a Motif font list?

20. How do you reference a font in a font list?

21. Which function is used to free a font list?

22. How do you code a font list in a resource file?

23. Which function is used to free a font?

24. What is a compound string component?

25. What is a compound string segment?

26. List four different components that can occur in a compound string.

27. List two of the functions that can be used to create compound string segments.

28. Which functions are used to concatenate and copy compound strings?

29. How can compound strings be retrieved one segment at a time?

30. List the four main parts of a cursor.

31. How is a cursor created?

32. How is a cursor associated with a particular window?

33. How do you change the color of a cursor?

34. How is the XmNmenuCursor resource used with a RowColumn widget?

Exercises

¤ The following exercises are designed to give you the opportunity to practice the concepts and facilities presented in this chapter:

1. Modify the multibutton program from the previous chapter so that the label of each PushButton is displayed in a different font. Use the xlsfonts and xfd clients to help you decide which fonts you want to use. Make sure that the font for the exit button is a large, bold font.

2. Modify the drawing program that you have been building over the last several sessions. Set the cursor for the drawing area to a cross hair. Also, change the font for the labels on all widgets to a large, bold Helvetica font.

3. Modify the database program that you have been building over the last several sessions. Set the cursor for all the menus to a left-pointing hand. Also, change the font for all the widgets to an italic New Century Schoolbook font.

21

A Motif
Case Study
Example Program

Introduction

Up to this point, the code examples shown in this book have presented only a user interface. That is to say that there have been no complete working applications that you can use to see how a real Motif application would be structured. In this chapter we present the source code to a complete, albeit simple, Motif application program.

For our case study, we have taken the code for the database program that you have been working on over the last several sessions, modified it, and filled it out into a complete working Motif client application. The main modification to the user interface is that the message-command Text widget in the MainWindow has been removed. The code has also been reorganized for better readability and understanding.

In looking through the code you will notice that there is no error checking done in the X/Motif code and very little error checking in the operating system and file interface code. This was done on purpose. The hope is that with all the extraneous code removed, you will be able to read and understand it better. It will also be easier to see some of the real problems and issues that confront a typical graphic-user interface programmer.

This implementation is a *very simple,* but fully functioning program. The algorithms used to do the actual data processing are not very fancy – using brute force and KISS (keep it simple and stupid) principles – and would not be used in production code. Again, the major purpose of this case study is to show some of the design and implementation details that you will be facing as you start to create your own graphic-user interface client applications using Motif and the X Window System.

So, here is the code:

```
/**********************************************************************
*                 G L O B A L   D E F I N I T I O N S                 *
**********************************************************************/

/*
 * Intermodule interfaces for the operating system input/output library,
 * the C library string handling functions,  and the Motif widgets.
 */
#include <stdio.h>
#include <string.h>
#include <Xm/BulletinB.h>
#include <Xm/MainW.h>
#include <Xm/RowColumn.h>
#include <Xm/Label.h>
#include <Xm/Text.h>
#include <Xm/CascadeB.h>
#include <Xm/PushB.h>
#include <Xm/SelectioB.h>
#include <Xm/MessageB.h>

/*
 * Interface definitions for the Unix operating system system-call-level
 * error codes and error messages.
 */
extern int errno;
extern int sys_nerr;
extern char *sys_errlist[];

/*
 * Function return type declarations for callback functions.
 */
XtCallbackProc AskFile();
XtCallbackProc OpenFile();
XtCallbackProc AskExit();
XtCallbackProc CloseFunc();
XtCallbackProc ExitFunc();
XtCallbackProc CancelExit();
XtCallbackProc AllowAdd();
XtCallbackProc AddRec();
XtCallbackProc AskWhichRecV();
XtCallbackProc ViewRec();
XtCallbackProc AskWhichRecR();
XtCallbackProc RemoveRec();
XtCallbackProc HelpUser();

/*
 * Function return type declarations for application specific functions.
 */
void CreateManagers();
```

```
void CreateWorkArea();
void CreateMenu();
void CreateDialogs();

/*
 * Structure declarations for client_data being
 * passed to callback functions.
 */
struct getFile
    {
    Widget fPromptDialog;
    Widget fErrorDialog;
    String fileName;
    FILE *inFile;
    Widget editButton;
    };
struct widgetList
    {
    Widget *wList;
    Cardinal wCount;
    String *fileName;
    FILE **inFile;
    Widget ePromptDialog;
    Widget eErrorDialog;
    };
struct helpItems
    {
    Widget hInfoDialog;
    Cardinal msgNo;
    };

/**********************************************************************
 *                   M A I N   R O U T I N E                         *
 **********************************************************************/

int main(argc, argv)
Cardinal argc;
String argv[];
    {

    /*
     * Application-wide widget definitions.
     * Passed and returned as needed to and from other functions.
     */
    Widget topShell;
    Widget mwMgr;
    Widget bbMgr;
    Widget labRcMgr;
    Widget txtRcMgr;
    Widget theLabel[5];
    Widget theText[5];
```

```
Widget mBar;
Widget theCascade[3];
Widget fileBtns[3];
Widget editBtns[3];
Widget helpBtns[3];
Widget helpFileBtns[3];
Widget helpEditBtns[3];
Widget promptDialog;
Widget questDialog;
Widget errorDialog;
Widget infoDialog;

/*
 * Callback structure definitions.
 */
struct getFile dataBase;
struct widgetList theItems;
struct helpItems helpData;

/*
 * Initialize the intrinsics and create a shell widget.
 */
topShell = XtInitialize(argv[0], "Edit", NULL, 0, &argc, argv);

/*
 * Create the user interface widgets.
 */
CreateDialogs(topShell,
    &promptDialog, &questDialog, &errorDialog, &infoDialog);
CreateManagers(topShell, &mwMgr, &bbMgr, &txtRcMgr, &labRcMgr);
CreateWorkArea(topShell, txtRcMgr, theText,
    XtNumber(theText), labRcMgr, theLabel, XtNumber(theLabel));
CreateMenu(mwMgr, &mBar, theCascade, XtNumber(theCascade),
    fileBtns, XtNumber(fileBtns), editBtns, XtNumber(editBtns),
    helpBtns, XtNumber(helpBtns), helpFileBtns,
    XtNumber(helpFileBtns), helpEditBtns, XtNumber(helpEditBtns));

/*
 * Set up the callbacks for the menu options from the file
 * pulldown menu.  [0] == Open,  [1] == Close,  [2] == Quit.
 */
dataBase.fPromptDialog = promptDialog;
dataBase.fErrorDialog = errorDialog;
dataBase.inFile = NULL;
dataBase.editButton = theCascade[1];
XtAddCallback(fileBtns[0], XmNactivateCallback,
    AskFile, &dataBase);
XtAddCallback(fileBtns[1], XmNactivateCallback,
    CloseFunc, &dataBase);
XtAddCallback(fileBtns[2], XmNactivateCallback,
    AskExit, questDialog);
```

```
/*
 * Set up the callbacks for the menu options from the edit
 * pulldown menu.   [0] == Add,  [1] == View,  [2] == Remove.
 */
theItems.wList = theText;
theItems.wCount = XtNumber(theText);
theItems.fileName = &dataBase.fileName;
theItems.inFile = &dataBase.inFile;
theItems.ePromptDialog = promptDialog;
theItems.eErrorDialog = errorDialog;
XtAddCallback(editBtns[0], XmNactivateCallback,
    AllowAdd, &theItems);
XtAddCallback(editBtns[1], XmNactivateCallback,
    AskWhichRecV, &theItems);
XtAddCallback(editBtns[2], XmNactivateCallback,
    AskWhichRecR, &theItems);

/*
 * Set up the callbacks for the text widgets.
 * [0] == Last name,  [1] == First name,  [2] == Age,
 * [3] == Salary,  [4] == Title.
 */
XtAddCallback(theText[0], XmNactivateCallback, AddRec, &theItems);
XtAddCallback(theText[1], XmNactivateCallback, AddRec, &theItems);
XtAddCallback(theText[2], XmNactivateCallback, AddRec, &theItems);
XtAddCallback(theText[3], XmNactivateCallback, AddRec, &theItems);
XtAddCallback(theText[4], XmNactivateCallback, AddRec, &theItems);

/*
 * Set up the callbacks for the menu options
 * from the help pulldown menu.
 */
XtAddCallback(helpBtns[2], XmNactivateCallback,
    HelpUser, &infoDialog);
XtAddCallback(helpFileBtns[0], XmNactivateCallback,
    HelpUser, &infoDialog);
XtAddCallback(helpFileBtns[1], XmNactivateCallback,
    HelpUser, &infoDialog);
XtAddCallback(helpFileBtns[2], XmNactivateCallback,
    HelpUser, &infoDialog);
XtAddCallback(helpEditBtns[0], XmNactivateCallback,
    HelpUser, &infoDialog);
XtAddCallback(helpEditBtns[1], XmNactivateCallback,
    HelpUser, &infoDialog);
XtAddCallback(helpEditBtns[2], XmNactivateCallback,
    HelpUser, &infoDialog);

/*
 * Associate the main application widget components with their
 * specific main window widget area.
```

```
        */
        XmMainWindowSetAreas(mwMgr, mBar, NULL, NULL, NULL, bbMgr);


        /*
         * Manage all of the user interface widgets except the pulldown
         * menus and the dialog boxes.
         */
        XtManageChildren(theLabel, XtNumber(theLabel));
        XtManageChildren(theText, XtNumber(theText));
        XtManageChild(labRcMgr);
        XtManageChild(txtRcMgr);
        XtManageChild(bbMgr);
        XtManageChild(mBar);
        XtManageChildren(theCascade, XtNumber(theCascade));
        XtManageChildren(fileBtns, XtNumber(fileBtns));
        XtManageChildren(editBtns, XtNumber(editBtns));
        XtManageChildren(helpBtns, XtNumber(helpBtns));
        XtManageChildren(helpFileBtns, XtNumber(helpFileBtns));
        XtManageChildren(helpEditBtns, XtNumber(helpEditBtns));
        XtManageChild(mwMgr);


        /*
         * Make the application visible on the screen and wait for events.
         */
        XtRealizeWidget(topShell);
        XtMainLoop();
        }

/*************************************************************************
 *   C A L L B A C K   S U B R O U T I N E S  -- Listed Alphabetically  *
 *************************************************************************/

/*
 * Callback function to add a record to the data base.
 */
XtCallbackProc AddRec(widget_id, client_data, call_data)
Widget widget_id;
struct widgetList *client_data;
caddr_t call_data;
    {

    /*
     * Local data definitions.
     */
    Widget message;
    XmString errorText;
    Arg argList[10];
    Cardinal i;
    Cardinal j;
    char *recData[5];
```

```
    /*
     * Get the text data from the strings in the text widgets.
     */
    for(i = 0; i < client_data->wCount; ++i)
        recData[i] = XmTextGetString(client_data->wList[i]);


    /*
     * Determine if any of the text widgets are empty and display an
     * error if found.  Record must be complete before adding.
     */
    if(*recData[0] == '\0' || *recData[1] == '\0' ||
        *recData[2] == '\0' || *recData[3] == '\0' ||
        *recData[4] == '\0')
        {
        message = XmMessageBoxGetChild(
            client_data->eErrorDialog, XmDIALOG_MESSAGE_LABEL);
        errorText = XmStringCreateLtoR(
            "The record is not complete!", XmSTRING_DEFAULT_CHARSET);
        j = 0;
        XtSetArg(argList[j], XmNlabelString, errorText); ++j;
        XtSetValues(message, argList, j);
        XmStringFree(errorText);
        XtManageChild(client_data->eErrorDialog);
        }

    /*
     * Otherwise,  go ahead and add the record to the data base.
     */
    else
        {
        fseek(*client_data->inFile, 0L, 2);
        fprintf(*client_data->inFile, "%s:%s:%s:%s:%s\n",
            recData[0], recData[1], recData[2], recData[3], recData[4]);
        j = 0;
        XtSetArg(argList[j], XmNeditable, False); ++j;
        XtSetArg(argList[j], XmNcursorPositionVisible, False); ++j;
        for(i = 0; i < client_data->wCount; ++i)
            {
            XtSetValues(client_data->wList[i], argList, j);
            XmTextSetString(client_data->wList[i], "");
            }
        }

    /*
     * Return to the calling function.
     */
    return;
    }

/*
 * Callback function to allow data to be entered into the text widgets.
```

```
*/
XtCallbackProc AllowAdd(widget_id, client_data, call_data)
Widget widget_id;
struct widgetList *client_data;
caddr_t call_data;
    {

    /*
     * Local data definitions.
     */
    Arg argList[10];
    Cardinal i;
    Cardinal j;

    /*
     * Make the cursor visible and allow data entry in each text widget.
     */
    j = 0;
    XtSetArg(argList[j], XmNeditable, True); ++j;
    XtSetArg(argList[j], XmNcursorPositionVisible, True); ++j;
    for(i = 0; i < client_data->wCount; ++i)
        XtSetValues(client_data->wList[i], argList, j);

    /*
     * Return to the calling function.
     */
    return;
    }

/*
 * Callback function to verify a quit operation.
 */
XtCallbackProc AskExit(widget_id, client_data, call_data)
Widget widget_id;
Widget *client_data;
caddr_t call_data;
    {

    /*
     * Local data definitions.
     */
    Widget message;
    XmString pString;
    Arg argList[10];
    Cardinal j;

    /*
     * Put together the dialog box and manage it.
     */
    message =
        XmMessageBoxGetChild(*client_data, XmDIALOG_MESSAGE_LABEL);
```

```
        pString = XmStringCreateLtoR(
            "Are you sure you want to quit?", XmSTRING_DEFAULT_CHARSET );
        j = 0;
        XtSetArg(argList[j], XmNlabelString, pString); ++j;
        XtSetValues(message, argList, j);
        XmStringFree(pString);
        XtManageChild(*client_data);

        /*
         * Set up the callbacks for the buttons on the dialog.
         */
        XtAddCallback(*client_data, XmNokCallback,
            ExitFunc, client_data);
        XtAddCallback(*client_data, XmNcancelCallback,
            CancelExit, client_data);

        /*
         * Return to the calling function.
         */
        return;
        }

/*
 * Callback function to prompt for a data base name to open.
 */
XtCallbackProc AskFile(widget_id, client_data, call_data)
Widget widget_id;
struct getFile *client_data;
caddr_t call_data;
    {

    /*
     * Local data definitions.
     */
    Widget message;
    XmString pString;
    XmString errorText;
    Arg argList[10];
    Cardinal j;

    /*
     * Check to see if a data base file is open.
     * If not,  put together a dialog box to prompt
     * for a name and manage it.
     */
    if(client_data->inFile == NULL)
        {
        pString = XmStringCreateLtoR(
            "Please enter the database name:",
            XmSTRING_DEFAULT_CHARSET );
        j = 0;
```

```
        XtSetArg(argList[j], XmNselectionLabelString, pString); ++j;
        XtSetValues(client_data->fPromptDialog, argList, j);
        XmStringFree(pString);
        XtAddCallback(client_data->fPromptDialog, XmNokCallback,
            OpenFile, client_data);
        XtManageChild(client_data->fPromptDialog);
        }

    /*
     * Otherwise,  put together a dialog for the error indicating
     * a data base is already open and manage it.
     */
    else
        {
        message = XmMessageBoxGetChild(
            client_data->fErrorDialog, XmDIALOG_MESSAGE_LABEL);
        errorText = XmStringCreateLtoR(
            "A data base is already open!", XmSTRING_DEFAULT_CHARSET);
        j = 0;
        XtSetArg(argList[j], XmNlabelString, errorText); ++j;
        XtSetValues(message, argList, j);
        XmStringFree(errorText);
        XtManageChild(client_data->fErrorDialog);
        }

    /*
     * Return to the calling function.
     */
    return;
    }

/*
 * Callback function to prompt for last name of record to remove.
 */
XtCallbackProc AskWhichRecR(widget_id, client_data, call_data)
Widget widget_id;
struct widgetList *client_data;
caddr_t call_data;
    {

    /*
     * Local data definitions.
     */
    Widget text;
    Widget message;
    XmString pString;
    XmString errorText;
    Arg argList[10];
    Cardinal i;
    Cardinal j;
```

```
    /*
     * Set up the dialog box to prompt for the last name.
     */
    text = XmSelectionBoxGetChild(
        client_data->ePromptDialog, XmDIALOG_TEXT);
    XmTextSetString(text, "");
    pString = XmStringCreateLtoR(
        "Enter Last Name for record to remove:",
        XmSTRING_DEFAULT_CHARSET);
    j = 0;
    XtSetArg(argList[j], XmNselectionLabelString, pString); ++j;
    XtSetValues(client_data->ePromptDialog, argList, j);
    XmStringFree(pString);

    /*
     * Add a callback for the ok button to remove the record.
     * Clear out all of the text widgets and manage the dialog.
     */
    XtAddCallback(client_data->ePromptDialog, XmNokCallback,
        RemoveRec, client_data);
    for(i = 0; i < client_data->wCount; ++i)
        XmTextSetString(client_data->wList[i], "");
    XtManageChild(client_data->ePromptDialog);

    /*
     * Return to the calling function.
     */
    return;
    }

/*
 * Callback function to prompt for last name of record to view.
 */
XtCallbackProc AskWhichRecV(widget_id, client_data, call_data)
Widget widget_id;
struct widgetList *client_data;
caddr_t call_data;
    {

    /*
     * Local data definitions.
     */
    Widget text;
    Widget message;
    XmString pString;
    XmString errorText;
    Arg argList[10];
    Cardinal i;
    Cardinal j;

    /*
```

```
 * Set up the dialog box to prompt for the last name.
 */
text = XmSelectionBoxGetChild(
    client_data->ePromptDialog, XmDIALOG_TEXT);
XmTextSetString(text, "");
pString = XmStringCreateLtoR(
    "Enter Last Name for record to view:",
    XmSTRING_DEFAULT_CHARSET);
j = 0;
XtSetArg(argList[j], XmNselectionLabelString, pString); ++j;
XtSetValues(client_data->ePromptDialog, argList, j);
XmStringFree(pString);

/*
 * Add a callback for the ok button to view the record.
 * Clear out all of the text widgets and manage the dialog.
 */
XtAddCallback(client_data->ePromptDialog, XmNokCallback,
    ViewRec, client_data);
for(i = 0; i < client_data->wCount; ++i)
    XmTextSetString(client_data->wList[i], "");
XtManageChild(client_data->ePromptDialog);

/*
 * Return to the calling function.
 */
return;
}

/*
 * Callback function to cancel a quit operation.
 */
XtCallbackProc CancelExit(widget_id, client_data, call_data)
Widget widget_id;
Widget *client_data;
caddr_t call_data;
    {

    /*
     * Remove the callbacks that were set up
     * on the quit question dialog.
     */
    XtRemoveCallback(*client_data, XmNokCallback,
        ExitFunc, client_data);
    XtRemoveCallback(*client_data, XmNcancelCallback,
        CancelExit, client_data);

    /*
     * Return to the calling function.
     */
    return;
```

```
            }

     /*
      * Callback function to close a data base file.
      */
     XtCallbackProc CloseFunc(widget_id, client_data, call_data)
     Widget widget_id;
     struct getFile *client_data;
     caddr_t call_data;
         {

         /*
          * Local data definitions.
          */
         Widget message;
         Widget text;
         XmString line1;
         XmString line2;
         XmString line3;
         XmString line4;
         XmString errorText;
         Arg argList[10];
         Cardinal j;
         int rc;

         /*
          * Close the data base.  If successful,  clear the data base
          * name from the open prompt dialog,  and don't allow edits
          * from the edit menu.
          */
         rc = fclose(client_data->inFile);
         if(rc == 0)
             {
             text = XmSelectionBoxGetChild(
                 client_data->fPromptDialog, XmDIALOG_TEXT);
             XmTextSetString(text, "");
             *client_data->fileName = '\0';
             client_data->inFile = NULL;
             XtSetSensitive(client_data->editButton, False);
             }

         /*
          * Otherwise,  put together an error dialog describing the
          * error and manage it.
          */
         else
             {
             message = XmMessageBoxGetChild(
                 client_data->fErrorDialog, XmDIALOG_MESSAGE_LABEL);
             line1 = XmStringSegmentCreate(
                 "Could not close data base:", XmSTRING_DEFAULT_CHARSET,
```

```
                         XmSTRING_DIRECTION_L_TO_R, True);
               line2 = XmStringSegmentCreate(
                   client_data->fileName, XmSTRING_DEFAULT_CHARSET,
                   XmSTRING_DIRECTION_L_TO_R, True);
               line3 = XmStringSegmentCreate(
                   "Operating system reason:", XmSTRING_DEFAULT_CHARSET,
                   XmSTRING_DIRECTION_L_TO_R, True);
               line4 = XmStringSegmentCreate(
                   sys_errlist[errno], XmSTRING_DEFAULT_CHARSET,
                   XmSTRING_DIRECTION_L_TO_R, False);
               errorText = XmStringConcat(line1, line2);
               errorText = XmStringConcat(errorText, line3);
               errorText = XmStringConcat(errorText, line4);
               j = 0;
               XtSetArg(argList[j], XmNlabelString, errorText); ++j;
               XtSetArg(argList[j], XmNalignment, XmALIGNMENT_CENTER); ++j;
               XtSetValues(message, argList, j);
               XmStringFree(line1);
               XmStringFree(line2);
               XmStringFree(line3);
               XmStringFree(line4);
               XmStringFree(errorText);
               XtManageChild(client_data->fErrorDialog);
               }

       /*
        * Return to the calling function.
        */
       return;
       }

   /*
    * Callback function to exit the application.
    */
   XtCallbackProc ExitFunc(widget_id, client_data, call_data)
   Widget widget_id;
   caddr_t client_data;
   caddr_t call_data;
       {

       /*
        * Return to the operating system.
        */
       exit();
       }

   /*
    * Callback function to display the help dialog boxes.
    */
   XtCallbackProc HelpUser(widget_id, client_data, call_data)
   Widget widget_id;
```

```
Widget *client_data;
caddr_t call_data;
    {

    /*
     * Local data definitions.
     */
    Widget message;
    XmString pString;
    XmString lString;
    Arg argList[10];
    Cardinal i;
    Cardinal j;
    char *labelString;
    static char *helpLbl[] =
        {"Help", "Open", "Close", "Quit", "Add", "View", "Remove"};
    static char *helpMsg[] =
        {"Use this menu option to get help on the other menu options.",
         "Use this menu option to open a data base file.",
         "Use this menu option to close a data base file.",
         "Use this menu option to quit the data base application.",
         "Use this menu option to add a record.  Arrow between fields.",
         "Use this menu option to view a record from the data base.",
         "Use this menu option to remove a record from the data base."};

    /*
     * Get the label off of the activated widget to determine
     * which help button was actually chosen.
     */
    j = 0;
    XtSetArg(argList[j], XmNlabelString, &lString); ++j;
    XtGetValues(widget_id, argList, j);
    XmStringGetLtoR(lString, XmSTRING_DEFAULT_CHARSET, &labelString);

    /*
     * Prepare to change the message on the help information dialog.
     */
    message =
        XmMessageBoxGetChild(*client_data, XmDIALOG_MESSAGE_LABEL);
    for(i = 0; i < XtNumber(helpLbl); ++i)

        /*
         * After determining which button,  change the message.
         */
        if(strcmp(labelString, helpLbl[i]) == 0)
            {
            pString =
                XmStringCreateLtoR(
                helpMsg[i], XmSTRING_DEFAULT_CHARSET);
            j = 0;
            XtSetArg(argList[j], XmNlabelString, pString); ++j;
```

```
                XtSetValues(message, argList, j);
                XmStringFree(pString);
                break;
                }

    /*
     * Manage the help dialog with the appropriate message.
     */
    XtManageChild(*client_data);

    /*
     * Return to the calling function.
     */
    return;
    }

/*
 * Callback function to actually open a database file.
 */
XtCallbackProc OpenFile(widget_id, client_data, call_data)
Widget widget_id;
struct getFile *client_data;
caddr_t call_data;
    {

    /*
     * Local data definitions.
     */
    Widget text;
    Widget message;
    XmString line1;
    XmString line2;
    XmString line3;
    XmString line4;
    XmString errorText;
    Arg argList[10];
    Cardinal j;

    /*
     * Remove the callback that just invoked us and get the
     * data base file name from the prompt dialog.
     */
    XtRemoveCallback(client_data->fPromptDialog, XmNokCallback,
        OpenFile, client_data);
    text = XmSelectionBoxGetChild(
        client_data->fPromptDialog, XmDIALOG_TEXT);
    client_data->fileName = XmTextGetString(text);

    /*
     * Open the data base file and if unsuccessful put together an error
     * dialog and manage it to describe the error.
```

```
        */
        client_data->inFile = fopen(client_data->fileName, "r+");
        if(client_data->inFile == (FILE *) 0)
            {
            message = XmMessageBoxGetChild(
                client_data->fErrorDialog, XmDIALOG_MESSAGE_LABEL);
            line1 = XmStringSegmentCreate(
                "Could not open data base:", XmSTRING_DEFAULT_CHARSET,
                XmSTRING_DIRECTION_L_TO_R, True);
            line2 = XmStringSegmentCreate(
                client_data->fileName, XmSTRING_DEFAULT_CHARSET,
                XmSTRING_DIRECTION_L_TO_R, True);
            line3 = XmStringSegmentCreate(
                "Operating system reason:", XmSTRING_DEFAULT_CHARSET,
                XmSTRING_DIRECTION_L_TO_R, True);
            line4 = XmStringSegmentCreate(
                sys_errlist[errno], XmSTRING_DEFAULT_CHARSET,
                XmSTRING_DIRECTION_L_TO_R, False);
            errorText = XmStringConcat(line1, line2);
            errorText = XmStringConcat(errorText, line3);
            errorText = XmStringConcat(errorText, line4);
            j = 0;
            XtSetArg(argList[j], XmNlabelString, errorText); ++j;
            XtSetArg(argList[j], XmNalignment, XmALIGNMENT_CENTER); ++j;
            XtSetValues(message, argList, j);
            XmStringFree(line1);
            XmStringFree(line2);
            XmStringFree(line3);
            XmStringFree(line4);
            XmStringFree(errorText);
            XtManageChild(client_data->fErrorDialog);
            }

    /*
     * Otherwise,  if successful,  allow the edit menu to operate.
     */
    else
        XtSetSensitive(client_data->editButton, True);

    /*
     * Return to the calling function.
     */
    return;
    }

/*
 * Callback function to actually remove a record.
 */
XtCallbackProc RemoveRec(widget_id, client_data, call_data)
Widget widget_id;
struct widgetList *client_data;
```

```
caddr_t call_data;
    {

    /*
     * Local data definitions.
     */
    Widget text;
    Cardinal i;
    char *lastName;
    char *bufPos;
    char cmdBuf[BUFSIZ];
    char nameData[50];
    int length;

    /*
     * Remove the callback that just invoked us and get the data base
     * file name from the prompt dialog.
     */
    XtRemoveCallback(client_data->ePromptDialog, XmNokCallback,
        RemoveRec, client_data);
    text = XmSelectionBoxGetChild(
        client_data->ePromptDialog, XmDIALOG_TEXT);
    lastName = XmTextGetString(text);

    /*
     * Construct a Unix command to remove the
     * requested record and execute it.
     */
    strcpy(nameData, lastName);
    strcat(nameData, ":");
    sprintf(cmdBuf, "grep -v '^%s' %s > /tmp/$$; mv /tmp/$$ %s\n",
        nameData, *client_data->fileName, *client_data->fileName);
    fclose(*client_data->inFile);
    system("sync; sync");
    system(cmdBuf);
    *client_data->inFile = fopen(*client_data->fileName, "r");

    /*
     * Return to the calling function.
     */
    return;
    }

/*
 * Callback function to display a record in the text widgets.
 */
XtCallbackProc ViewRec(widget_id, client_data, call_data)
Widget widget_id;
struct widgetList *client_data;
caddr_t call_data;
    {
```

```
/*
 * Local data definitions.
 */
Widget text;
Widget message;
Cardinal i;
Cardinal j;
Boolean found = False;
Arg argList[10];
XmString errorText;
char *lastName;
char *bufPos;
char fileBuf[BUFSIZ];
char nameData[50];
int length;

/*
 * Remove the callback that just invoked us and get the
 * last name that was entered in the prompt dialog.
 */
XtRemoveCallback(client_data->ePromptDialog, XmNokCallback,
    ViewRec, client_data);
text = XmSelectionBoxGetChild(
    client_data->ePromptDialog, XmDIALOG_TEXT);
lastName = XmTextGetString(text);

/*
 * Make a local copy of the last name,  tack a ":" on the end
 * and get the length of the resulting string.
 */
strcpy(nameData, lastName);
strcat(nameData, ":");
length = strlen(nameData);
fseek(*client_data->inFile, 0L, 0);

/*
 * Look for a record with a matching last name.
 */
while(fgets(fileBuf, BUFSIZ, *client_data->inFile) != NULL)
    if(strncmp(nameData, fileBuf, length) == 0)
        {

        /*
         * When found,  parse the record up into fields (tokens).
         */
        found = True;
        bufPos = strtok(fileBuf, ":");
        for(i = 0; bufPos != NULL; ++i)
            {
            XmTextSetString(client_data->wList[i], bufPos);
```

```
                        bufPos = strtok(NULL, ":");
                        }
                    break;
                    }

        /*
         * If not found,  put together an error dialog
         * to describe the error.
         */
        if(! found)
            {
            message = XmMessageBoxGetChild(
                client_data->eErrorDialog, XmDIALOG_MESSAGE_LABEL);
            errorText = XmStringCreateLtoR(
                "Record not found!", XmSTRING_DEFAULT_CHARSET);
            j = 0;
            XtSetArg(argList[j], XmNlabelString, errorText); ++j;
            XtSetValues(message, argList, j);
            XmStringFree(errorText);
            XtManageChild(client_data->eErrorDialog);
            }

        /*
         * Return to the calling function.
         */
        return;
        }

/*************************************************************************
 *    C L I E N T    S U B R O U T I N E S  -- Listed Alphabetically    *
 *************************************************************************/

/*
 * Application-defined function to create all needed dialog boxes.
 */
void CreateDialogs(shell, pDialog, qDialog, eDialog, iDialog)
Widget shell;
Widget *pDialog;
Widget *qDialog;
Widget *eDialog;
Widget *iDialog;
    {

    /*
     * Local data definitions.
     */
    Widget dialogHelpButton;
    Widget dialogCancelButton;

    /*
     * Create a prompt dialog and unmanage its help button.
```

```
     */
    *pDialog = XmCreatePromptDialog(shell, "pdialog", NULL, 0);
    dialogHelpButton =
        XmSelectionBoxGetChild(*pDialog, XmDIALOG_HELP_BUTTON);
    XtUnmanageChild(dialogHelpButton);

    /*
     * Create a question dialog and unmanage its help button.
     */
    *qDialog = XmCreateQuestionDialog(shell, "qdialog", NULL, 0);
    dialogHelpButton =
        XmMessageBoxGetChild(*qDialog, XmDIALOG_HELP_BUTTON);
    XtUnmanageChild(dialogHelpButton);

    /*
     * Create an error dialog and unmanage its help and cancel buttons.
     */
    *eDialog = XmCreateErrorDialog(shell, "edialog", NULL, 0);
    dialogHelpButton =
        XmMessageBoxGetChild(*eDialog, XmDIALOG_HELP_BUTTON);
    XtUnmanageChild(dialogHelpButton);
    dialogCancelButton =
        XmMessageBoxGetChild(*eDialog, XmDIALOG_CANCEL_BUTTON);
    XtUnmanageChild(dialogCancelButton);

    /*
     * Create an information dialog and unmanage
     * its help and cancel buttons.
     */
    *iDialog = XmCreateInformationDialog(shell, "idialog", NULL, 0);
    dialogHelpButton =
        XmMessageBoxGetChild(*iDialog, XmDIALOG_HELP_BUTTON);
    XtUnmanageChild(dialogHelpButton);
    dialogCancelButton =
        XmMessageBoxGetChild(*iDialog, XmDIALOG_CANCEL_BUTTON);
    XtUnmanageChild(dialogCancelButton);

    /*
     * Return to the calling function.
     */
    return;
    }

/*
 * Application-defined function to create all needed manager widgets.
 */
void CreateManagers(shell, mgr1, mgr2, mgr3, mgr4)
Widget shell;
Widget *mgr1;
Widget *mgr2;
Widget *mgr3;
```

```
Widget *mgr4;
    {

    /*
     * Create the manager widgets.
     */
    *mgr1 = XmCreateMainWindow(shell, "mwmanager", NULL, 0);
    *mgr2 = XmCreateBulletinBoard(*mgr1, "bbmanager", NULL, 0);
    *mgr3 = XmCreateRowColumn(*mgr2, "rcmanager2", NULL, 0);
    *mgr4 = XmCreateRowColumn(*mgr2, "rcmanager1", NULL, 0);

    /*
     * Allow for the arrow keys to move between the text widgets
     */
    XmAddTabGroup(*mgr3);

    /*
     * Return to the calling function.
     */
    return;
    }

/*
 * Application-defined function to create the menu bar
 * and associated pulldowns.
 */
void CreateMenu(mgr, menu, cBtns, cBtnCnt, fBtns, fBtnCnt, eBtns,
    eBtnCnt, hBtns, hBtnCnt, hfBtns, hfBtnCnt, heBtns, heBtnCnt)
Widget mgr;
Widget *menu;
Widget cBtns[];
Cardinal cBtnCnt;
Widget fBtns[];
Cardinal fBtnCnt;
Widget eBtns[];
Cardinal eBtnCnt;
Widget hBtns[];
Cardinal hBtnCnt;
Widget hfBtns[];
Cardinal hfBtnCnt;
Widget heBtns[];
Cardinal heBtnCnt;
    {

    /*
     * Local data definitions.
     */
    Widget pullMenu[3];
    Widget helpPullMenu[2];
    Arg argList[10];
    Cardinal i;
```

```
    Cardinal j;
    char instNameConvBuff[10];
    static char menuInstName[][5] = {"file", "edit", "help"};

    /*
     * Create the menu bar.
     */
    *menu = XmCreateMenuBar(mgr, "menubar", NULL, 0);
    for(i = 0; i < XtNumber(pullMenu); ++i)
        {

        /*
         * Create the pulldown menus.
         */
        sprintf(instNameConvBuff, "%spm", menuInstName[i]);
        pullMenu[i] =
            XmCreatePulldownMenu(*menu, instNameConvBuff, NULL, 0);

        /*
         * Create the cascade buttons for the menu bar and
         * associate them with a pulldown menu.
         */
        sprintf(instNameConvBuff, "%scb", menuInstName[i]);
        j = 0;
        XtSetArg(argList[j], XmNsubMenuId, pullMenu[i]); ++j;
        cBtns[i] =
            XmCreateCascadeButton(*menu, instNameConvBuff, argList, j);
        }

    /*
     * Make the edit button insensitive until a data base
     * has been opened.   And,  specify which button is the
     * help button for the menu bar.
     */
    XtSetSensitive(cBtns[1], False);
    j = 0;
    XtSetArg(argList[j], XmNmenuHelpWidget, cBtns[2]); ++j;
    XtSetValues(*menu, argList, j);

    /*
     * Create the push buttons for the file menu.
     */
    for(i = 0; i < fBtnCnt; ++i)
        {
        sprintf(instNameConvBuff, "%sbtn%d", menuInstName[0], i + 1);
        fBtns[i] =
            XmCreatePushButton(pullMenu[0], instNameConvBuff, NULL, 0);
        }

    /*
     * Create the push buttons for the edit menu.
```

```
    */
    for(i = 0; i < eBtnCnt; ++i)
        {
        sprintf(instNameConvBuff, "%sbtn%d", menuInstName[1], i + 1);
        eBtns[i] =
            XmCreatePushButton(pullMenu[1], instNameConvBuff, NULL, 0);
        }

    /*
     * Create the push buttons for the help menu.
     */
    for(i = 0; i < hBtnCnt; ++i)
        {
        if(i == 2)
            {
            sprintf(instNameConvBuff, "%sbtn%d", menuInstName[i], i+1);
            hBtns[i] =
                XmCreatePushButton(
                pullMenu[2], instNameConvBuff, NULL, 0);
            }
        else
            {
            sprintf(instNameConvBuff, "%shpm", menuInstName[i]);
            helpPullMenu[i] =
                XmCreatePulldownMenu(
                pullMenu[2], instNameConvBuff, NULL,0);
            sprintf(instNameConvBuff, "%sbtn%d", menuInstName[2], i+1);
            j = 0;
            XtSetArg(argList[j], XmNsubMenuId, helpPullMenu[i]); ++j;
            hBtns[i] =
                XmCreateCascadeButton(
                pullMenu[2], instNameConvBuff, argList,j);
            }
        }

    /*
     * Create the push buttons for the file option off of the help menu.
     */
    for(i = 0; i < hfBtnCnt; ++i)
        {
        sprintf(instNameConvBuff, "hfbtn%d", i + 1);
        hfBtns[i] =
            XmCreatePushButton(
            helpPullMenu[0], instNameConvBuff, NULL, 0);
        }

    /*
     * Create the push buttons for the edit option off of the help menu.
     */
    for(i = 0; i < heBtnCnt; ++i)
        {
```

```
            sprintf(instNameConvBuff, "hebtn%d", i + 1);
            heBtns[i] =
                XmCreatePushButton(
                helpPullMenu[1], instNameConvBuff, NULL, 0);
            }

    /*
     * Return to the calling function.
     */
    return;
    }

/*
 * Application-defined function to create the widgets in the work area.
 */
void CreateWorkArea(shell, txtMgr, text, txtCount,
    lblMgr, label, lblCount)
Widget shell;
Widget txtMgr;
Widget text[];
Cardinal txtCount;
Widget lblMgr;
Widget label[];
Cardinal lblCount;
    {

    /*
     * Local data definitions.
     */
    Display *theDisplay;
    Screen *theScreen;
    Colormap theColormap;
    XColor installedColor;
    XColor colorDefinition;
    Arg argList[10];
    Cardinal i;
    Cardinal j;
    static char labelInstName[][8] =
        {"label1", "label2", "label3", "label4", "label5"};
    static char textInstName[][8] =
        {"text1", "text2", "text3", "text4", "text5"};

    /*
     * Get the color for the background of the text widgets.
     */
    theDisplay = XtDisplay(shell);
    theScreen = XtScreen(shell);
    theColormap = DefaultColormapOfScreen(theScreen);
    XAllocNamedColor(theDisplay,
        theColormap, "white", &installedColor, &colorDefinition);
```

```
/*
 * Create the text and label widgets.
 */
j = 0;
XtSetArg(argList[j], XmNbackground, installedColor.pixel); ++j;
XtSetArg(argList[j], XmNeditable, False); ++j;
XtSetArg(argList[j], XmNcursorPositionVisible, False); ++j;
XtSetArg(argList[j], XmNtraversalOn, True); ++j;
for(i = 0; i < txtCount; ++i)
    text[i] = XmCreateText(txtMgr, textInstName[i], argList, j);
for(i = 0; i < lblCount; ++i)
    label[i] = XmCreateLabel(lblMgr, labelInstName[i], NULL, 0);


/*
 * Return to the calling function.
 */
return;
}
```

The code in the preceding example uses a Motif concept called a *tab group* to allow the arrow keys to move input focus back and forth among the text widgets. In OSF/Motif 1.0 you must explicitly enable tab groups as was done in this case study program. In OSF/Motif 1.1 tab groups are enabled automatically. This concept will be discussed in a later chapter. In the following code, we have included the resource file that was used with the preceding application:

```
!*******************************************************************************
!*                       R E S O U R C E S                                    *
!*******************************************************************************
!
!Resources for the main window manager.
!
session_23.mwmanager.showSeparator:                      True
!
!Resources for the label row column manager.
!
session_23.mwmanager.bbmanager.rcmanager1.x:             10
session_23.mwmanager.bbmanager.rcmanager1.y:             10
session_23.mwmanager.bbmanager.rcmanager1.isAligned:     true
session_23*bbmanager.rcmanager1.entryAlignment:          alignment_end
!
!Resources for the text row column manager.
!
session_23.mwmanager.bbmanager.rcmanager2.x:             100
session_23.mwmanager.bbmanager.rcmanager2.y:             10
!
!Resources for the label widgets.
!
session_23*bbmanager.rcmanager1.label1.labelString:      Last Name
session_23*bbmanager.rcmanager1.label1.marginHeight:     5
```

```
session_23*bbmanager.rcmanager1.label2.labelString:      First Name
session_23*bbmanager.rcmanager1.label2.marginHeight:     5
session_23*bbmanager.rcmanager1.label3.labelString:      Age
session_23*bbmanager.rcmanager1.label3.marginHeight:     5
session_23*bbmanager.rcmanager1.label4.labelString:      Salary
session_23*bbmanager.rcmanager1.label4.marginHeight:     5
session_23*bbmanager.rcmanager1.label5.labelString:      Title
session_23*bbmanager.rcmanager1.label5.marginHeight:     5
!
!Resources for the text widgets.
!
session_23*bbmanager.rcmanager2.XmText.maxLength:        20
!
!Resources for all menus
!
session_23*menuCursor:                                  hand2
!
!Resources for the cascade buttons on the menu bar.
!
session_23.mwmanager.menubar.filecb.labelString:        File
session_23.mwmanager.menubar.editcb.labelString:        Edit
session_23.mwmanager.menubar.helpcb.labelString:        Help
!
! Wildcard references are used here because you don't know the
! instance name of the XmMenuShell widget that was created for
! you by the XmCreate...Menu() call
!
!Resources for the file pulldown menu buttons.
!
session_23*filepm.filebtn1.labelString:                 Open
session_23*filepm.filebtn2.labelString:                 Close
session_23*filepm.filebtn3.labelString:                 Quit
!
!Resources for the edit pulldown menu buttons.
!
session_23*editpm.editbtn1.labelString:                 Add
session_23*editpm.editbtn2.labelString:                 View
session_23*editpm.editbtn3.labelString:                 Remove
!
!Resources for the help pulldown menu buttons.
!
session_23*helppm.helpbtn1.labelString:                 File
session_23*helppm.helpbtn2.labelString:                 Edit
session_23*helppm.helpbtn3.labelString:                 Help
session_23*filehpm.hfbtn1.labelString:                  Open
session_23*filehpm.hfbtn2.labelString:                  Close
session_23*filehpm.hfbtn3.labelString:                  Quit
session_23*edithpm.hebtn1.labelString:                  Add
session_23*edithpm.hebtn2.labelString:                  View
session_23*edithpm.hebtn3.labelString:                  Remove
!
```

```
!Resources for all dialog boxes.
!
session_23*XmMessageBox.dialogStyle:          dialog_application_modal
session_23*XmSelectionBox.dialogStyle:        dialog_application_modal
!
!Resources for all compound strings.
!
session_23*fontList:  -adobe-new*century*schoolbook-medium-i-normal--14*
```

Figure 21.1 shows what the program would look like on a typical terminal screen.

☐ Hopefully, after reading through the code and the resources, you will have a good idea of the work involved in writing a graphic-user interface program. One of the overriding concepts is that the user is always in control – not you. You have to retrieve the inputs from the user and manage them in a way that is user-friendly and makes sense.

☐ The program shown in this chapter, although complete, leaves a lot to be desired in terms of style, maintainability, and other factors. The Xlib library provides a low-level data and procedural abstraction over the X Protocol. The Xt Intrinsics provides yet another level of abstraction with the widget concept. You, in your program code, should provide another level of abstraction – application-level abstraction – to make the purpose of the application more readable, maintainable, and understandable.

Although X and Motif are not object-oriented programming systems, an object-oriented approach should be taken when designing Motif-based client applications. With the advent of programming languages such as C + +, almost every programmer now recognizes the advantages of data and procedural abstractions that object-oriented languages provide. With application-supplied object-oriented mechanisms and techniques the programmer can hide low-level details for a greater understanding of the program's design and purpose, isolate dependencies between modules so that a change in one module will have little or (ideally) no effect on code in

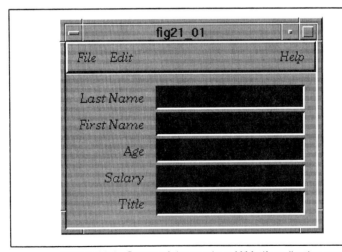

Figure 21.1 Output of the previous X/Motif application program.

other modules, and allow for the establishment of communication mechanisms among a program's components.

◻ It is strongly suggested that you do not spread the widget creation functions throughout your source code. Collect them together in one or more creation functions that are located physically close to one another. Also, do not spread the callback functions throughout your source code. They should be collected together to enhance the readability of your program's code.

To implement features of an application-level abstraction it is recommended that you do not implement the client application's functionality in the callback function definitions. This is better accomplished by having the callback functions call other functions to do the needed client data-processing. This was not done for the example client in this chapter to make the code a little more readable and understandable from an instructional point of view.

◻ All of the callback functions should be collected together in one place so that anybody reading your code can study the user-interface and the nonuser-interface components separately. This keeps the reader from being distracted by the functions that implement your client's functionality. And, since non-trivial Motif client applications are usually quite large, always break your source code into several modules keeping related functions together in the same module.

Finally, as suggested previously, you should use higher levels of abstraction for both the user-interface components and the non-user-interface components of your client programs. For example, you might use a simple procedural abstraction to implement a menu-creation function. File-level abstraction could be used to create a reusable help system that could be instantiated once in a client application. And, higher levels of abstraction could be used to create multiply instantiable objects such as a text-edit object with menus.

◻ Writing a graphic-user interface program using Motif and the X Window System is not a trivial task. It requires lots of thought, lots of planning, and a lot of code. Writing a GUI program that is easy to use and widely accepted by your users requires a great deal of work on your part. But when done well, gives you a great feeling of accomplishment.

Graphics
Context

Introduction

◻ The X Window system uses a bitmapped graphic display terminal for its operation. Bitmapped graphics allow you to place a foreground color in a set of pixels and a background color in another set of pixels to form graphics objects. These graphics objects allow for the formation of windows and other items on the screen. In this chapter you will learn some of the basic concepts of X graphics and the use of an important graphics data structure called a *graphics context*.

Objectives

◻ After completing this chapter, you will be able to:

◻ List the two places where X drawing functions can draw graphics objects.

◻ Explain some of the work X goes through to get a graphics object drawn.

◻ Explain the purpose of a graphics context.

◻ Describe where a graphics context is stored.

◻ Explain the impact of expose events on graphics operations.

◻ Describe the function needed to create a graphics context.

◻ List several members of the graphics context.

- ❏ Explain how to change the default values in a newly created graphics context.

- ❏ Describe the purpose of several of the graphics context structure members.

- ❏ Explain what is meant by *rubber-band* drawing.

- ❏ Describe the function used to change the contents of an existing graphics context.

- ❏ List several convenience functions that can change one or more members of a graphics context.

- ❏ Explain which function is used to free a graphics context.

- ❏ Explain how to draw a line with an X drawing function.

- ❏ Explain how to draw text with an X drawing function.

- ❏ Describe the operation of backing store.

- ❏ List two other methods of handling redrawing in response to an expose event.

Graphics Concepts

❏ The X Window System provides a wide variety of functions to perform graphics operations. These *graphics primitives*, as they are called, allow you to draw points, lines, rectangles, arcs, and so on. The graphics operations are performed using bitmapped graphics techniques where a bitmap is used to determine which pixels are turned on with the foreground color and which pixels are turned off with the background color.

In X, graphics operations can be performed in only two places. You can call the graphics primitives (functions) to draw in an on-screen window (which you are already familiar with) or in an off-screen pixmap. A pixmap, like a window, is an array in memory organized into a series of bit planes. Also, just like a window, corresponding bits in the bit planes combine to form pixels. The only difference between a window and a pixmap is that one is on the screen where graphics can be displayed immediately and the other is not. Windows and pixmaps are collectively referred to as drawables.

When working with graphics in X, you are not drawing lines on a blank "sheet of paper." Instead, a graphics object is first drawn in a temporary off-screen pixmap. The drawing is accomplished by using mathematical formulas to decide which pixels in the temporary pixmap are to be affected. Then, a variety of other operations may be performed on the graphic. The foreground color is applied to some pixels, the background color is applied to others; the thickness and style of the lines may be modified; patterns may be applied to the pixmap in the form of stipples or tiles; and finally, the resulting pixmap is displayed at a specific location on the screen. But it is not necessarily copied from the temporary pixmap to the screen window. Instead, you can direct the bits of the off-screen pixmap to be combined with the bits of the on-screen window in a bitwise operation.

☐   Because so much information is required to draw a graphic on the screen, there would have to be a ridiculous number of arguments to each graphics function—even to draw a simple point. Most of these graphics parameters don't change much from function to function, so X11 has bundled the parameters together into a data structure. This data structure is called a *graphics context*. A graphics context is used to gather together all the parameters required for a particular type or style of graphics operation.

All graphics operations—whether drawing text, points, lines, or anything—require the use of a graphics context. The graphics context, or GC as it is called, contains all the data necessary to determine the style of how a particular graphics object will be drawn. Usually, there is one GC for a graphics object. However, since a variety of styles of drawing may be used in a client program, you may have a variety of GCs. There may be one GC for all graphics objects, one GC for each graphics object, or many GCs for a single graphics object.

GCs are server resources. You will recall that this means that the data space allocated for the structure is stored in the server. Since all graphics operations are actually performed by the server, it is more convenient for the server to access a local data structure instead of requesting that the GC be sent across the network from the client. Usually, one of the main reasons that a particular data item (resource) is stored in the server is to reduce network traffic and to make the associated operations as fast as possible.

☐   It is important to understand that once a graphic has been drawn on the screen, X has no memory of the operation. X does not remember that you drew a square at one position on the screen, a circle at another location, and a line that may connect the two. The only memory that X has of your graphics operations is in the form of the pixels displayed on the screen.

When a portion of your graphic is hidden by an overlapping window, if that window moves or goes away and your graphics window receives an expose event, *X does not know how to redraw the graphic.* When a widget receives an expose event for its windows, the widget redraws itself. This is part of the code that the widget writer wrote into the widget. If you want a graphic objects to redraw itself when its window receives an expose event, you have to write the code necessary to remember what was drawn and redraw it.

Some servers have a feature that can do the redrawing of graphics objects for you. This feature is called *backing store.* If backing store is available and it is enabled, you can specify that it be used on a window-by-window basis. With backing store turned on for a graphics window, any drawing you do in that window will also be performed into an off-screen backing store pixmap. When your graphics window receives an expose event for that window then it will copy the affected portions from the backing store pixmap back to the screen window.

Backing store is a very "expensive" resource for the server. It requires the server to allocate a lot of memory that it may or may not have to use. When it is used, the copying of pixels from one place to another is very slow and time-consuming. It is much more efficient for the client to remember what was drawn and to simply redraw it when necessary.

◻   One other limitation of graphics in X through Release 4 is that it does not support three-dimensional graphics. You can use the two-dimensional graphics that are provided to imitate three-dimensional drawings, but 3-D is not directly supported. With Release 5, some graphics extensions will be added to support three-dimensional graphics objects.

Creating a Graphics Context

◻   Since all graphics operations require a GC, the first thing you need to do is create one. The XCreateGC() function creates a graphics context in the server, fills it in with some default values, and then returns you a graphics context id to reference it with. Figure 22.1 shows the syntax for this function.

The first parameter is the display pointer that, as we have seen, is required as the first parameter to almost every Xlib function. The second parameter, called a *drawable,* can be either a window id (X data type Window) or a pixmap id (X data type Pixmap). Since you haven't learned a lot about Pixmaps yet this parameter will be the window id of the screen window you are going to draw in.

The GC structure has a number of members in it that determine the style of the graphics object you are drawing. These members are allocated with some default values. If you don't like the default values, the last two parameters let you place a different initial value into the GC members. The last parameter is the address of an XGCValues structure and contains a copy of all the user-accessible components of a graphics context. The following code shows you what the XGCValues structure looks like:

```
typedef struct {
    int             function;   /* logical operation */
    unsigned long plane_mask; /* plane mask */
    unsigned long foreground; /* foreground pixel */
    unsigned long background; /* background pixel */
    int             line_width; /* line width */
    int             line_style; /* LineSolid, LineOnOffDash, LineDoubleDash */
    int             cap_style;  /* CapNotLast,CapButt,CapRound,CapProjecting */
    int             join_style; /* JoinMiter, JoinRound, JoinBevel */
    int             fill_style; /* FillSolid, FillTiled, */
                                /* FillStippled, FillOpaeueStippled */
    int             fill_rule;  /* EvenOddRule, WindingRule */
```

```
GC XCreateGC(display, drawable, value_mask, values)

Display       *display;
Drawable       drawable;
unsigned long value_mask;
XGCValues     *values;
```

Figure 22.1 XCreateGC() syntax.

```
    int           arc_mode;     /* ArcChord, ArcPieSlice */
    Pixmap        tile;         /* tile pixmap for tiling operations */
    Pixmap        stipple;      /* stipple 1 plane pixmap for stippling */
    int           ts_x_origin;/* offset for tile or stipple operations */
    int           ts_y_origin;
    Font          font;         /* default text font for text operations */
    int           subwindow_mode; /* ClipByChildren, IncludeInferiors */
    Bool          graphics_exposures; /* Should exposures be generated */
    int           clip_x_origin; /* origin for clipping */
    int           clip_y_origin;
    Pixmap        clip_mask;    /* bitmap clipping; other calls for rects */
    int           dash_offset;/* patterned/dashed line information */
    char dashes;
} XGCValues;
```

When you use an XGCValues structure to tell XCreateGC() about the GC
values that you want to change, you will probably not change all the
members. Instead, it is more typical to change only a few of the members
from their default values. The third parameter to XCreateGC() is used to
identify which members of the XGCValues structure you have filled in with
new data. The value_mask parameter is a mask value which is the bitwise
OR of one or more defined names that correspond to members of the
XGCValues structure. Figure 22.2 lists the default values and these
defined names for you.

Figure 22.3 shows a short code segment that creates a graphics context.

Meaning of Various GC Members

The function member is used to determine how the bits in the pixel of the
thing you are drawing (the source) are combined with the bits in the pixel of
the thing you are drawing on (the destination). A variety of bitwise operations are provided. Figure 22.4 summarizes the defined names for the function operations and their definitions.

The two most common functions are GXcopy and GXxor. The copy function does just what the name says. It copies the source graphic that you are
drawing directly to the destination, replacing the pixels of the destination
with the pixels of the source. If you know the coordinates and size of the of
the graphics item that you are going to draw, then GXcopy will be the
function you use.

The GXxor function allows for rubber-band drawing. Rubber-band drawing is used when you don't know the coordinates and size of the graphics
item you are going to draw. Instead, you track the mouse pointer movement and mouse button clicks to determine the origin and size of the
graphic. With the GXxor function, the source and destination bits are combined in such a way that if the drawing operation is repeated, the screen
returns to its original condition. So for each pixel of ButtonMotion you draw
the graphics object twice with the GXxor function — once to draw the line
and once to erase the line. When the mouse button is released, you draw
the final object with the GXcopy function.

```
                                                      value_mask names used
       XGCValues structure members        Default value   to override   defaults
------------------------------------  ------------------  -----------------------
typedef struct {
    int            function;          GXcopy              GCFunction
    unsigned long  plane_mask;        all 1's             GCPlaneMask
    unsigned long  foreground;        0                   GCForeground
    unsigned long  background;        1                   GCBackground
    int            line_width;        0                   GCLineWidth
    int            line_style;        LineSolid           GCLineStyle
    int            cap_style;         CapButt             GCCapStyle
    int            join_style;        JoinMiter           GCJoinStyle
    int            fill_style;        FillSolid           GCFillStyle
    int            fill_rule;         EvenOddRule         GCFillRule
    int            arc_mode;          ArcPieSlice         GCArcMode
    Pixmap         tile;              Pixmap filled with  GCTile
                                         foreground pixel
    Pixmap         stipple;           Pixmap filled with  GCStipple
                                         all 1's
    int            ts_x_origin;       0                   GCTileStipXOrigin
    int            ts_y_origin;       0                   GCTileStipYOrigin
    Font           font;              Implementation      GCFont
                                         dependent
    int            subwindow_mode;    ClipByChildren      GCSubwindowMode
    Bool           graphics_exposures; True               GCGraphicsExposures
    int            clip_x_origin;     0                   GCClipXOrigin
    int            clip_y_origin;     0                   GCClipYOrigin
    Pixmap         clip_mask;         None                GCClipMask
    int            dash_offset;       0                   GCDashOffset
    char           dashes;            4                   GCDashList
} XGCValues;
```

Figure 22.2 Value_mask names and default values for a GC using an XGCValues structure.

A Special Note about Color Pixel Values and Rubber-Band Drawing: Although this book does not attempt to show or teach practical graphics techniques, there is something you should know about rubber-band drawing. With this particular graphics technique, the program will typically set the foreground color to the exclusive OR of the current foreground and background colors. Even though you were previously told not to "mess" with pixel values, this technique allows for typical rubber-banding. When the combination foreground color is GXxor'ed with the background pixel value already on the screen, the result will be the true foreground color. And when the combination foreground color is GXxor'ed with the foreground color pixel value already on the screen, the result will be the true background color. This technique allows for a reverse video effect when the line you are currently rubber-banding (drawing) crosses over an already existing (foreground color) pixel on the screen.

```
...
Display *display;
Screen *screen;
Window root;
GC myGC;
...
    XGCValues myValues;
    ...
    display = XtDisplay(topShell);
    screen = XtScreen(topShell);
    root = RootWindowOfScreen(screen);
    ...
    myValues.line_width = 4;
    myValues.cap_style = CapRound;
    myGC = XCreateGC(display, root, GCLineWidth | GCCapStyle, &myValues);
    ...
```

Figure 22.3 Creating a graphics context.

```
Defined function value name          Function definition
------------------------------       ------------------------------

GXclear                              0
GXand                                    source AND     destination
GXandReverse                             source AND NOT destination
GXcopy                                   source
GXandInverted                        NOT source AND     destination
GXnoop                                                  destination
GXxor                                    source XOR     destination
GXor                                     source OR      destination
GXnor                                NOT source AND NOT destination
GXequiv                              NOT source XOR     destination
GXinvert                             NOT               destination
GXorReverse                              source OR NOT  destination
GXcopyInverted                       NOT source
GXorInverted                         NOT source OR      destination
GXnand                               NOT source OR NOT  destination
GXset                                1
```

Figure 22.4 Function names for a graphics context.

□ The plane_mask is used to determine which of the bit planes in a pixel are affected during a graphics operation. One bit in the plane_mask represents one bit plane in the array of pixel values. If the plane_mask bit is a 1, that bit plane will be affected. If the plane_mask bit is 0, that plane will not be affected. The plane_mask is used for advanced drawing techniques that are beyond the scope of this introductory book.

□ The foreground and background pixel values are used to determine the color of the object you are drawing (foreground) and its background color. Usually, the foreground and background colors are chosen to be distinctively different from one another so that the graphic being drawn is easily visible on the screen. If an item needs to be erased from the screen, it is a simple matter to change the foreground color to the background color and redraw the object.

All the line characteristics members deal with the style of the lines that X draws for you. There are six of them. The line_width member specifies the width of the graphics lines. A nonzero number is the number of pixels wide that a line should be drawn. A linewidth of zero specifies that a single pixel line be drawn as fast as possible. Zero-width lines are drawn with a different algorithm and may not visually mix well with non-zero-width lines.

The line_style determines whether the line is drawn as a solid or dashed line. There are three possible values. LineSolid specifies that a solid line be drawn. LineOnOffDash specifies that a dashed line be drawn with only the foreground color and that spaces between the dashes not be drawn. LineDoubleDash specifies specifies that a solid line be drawn but that dashes be implemented by alternating the foreground and background colors.

The cap_style determines the style in which a line ends. There are four possible values. CapNotLast specifies that for a linewidth of 0 or 1 that the endpoint not be drawn. CapButt specifies that the line "butt" up against the endpoint. CapRound specifies that the end of the line be rounded past the endpoint with a diameter equal to the linewidth. CapProjecting speci-fies that the line project past the endpoint one half of the linewidth.

The join_style determines how corners are drawn for wide lines. There are three possible values. JoinMiter specifies that the outer edges of the two lines should be extended to meet at an angle. JoinRound specifies that the two lines should be joined with an arc with a diameter equal to the line-width. JoinBevel specifies that the endpoints of the outer edges be joined with a straight line.

The last two line style characteristics are dashes and dash_offset. Both of these are related to customizing a dashed line. Dashes specifies the length of the dashes for a customized dashed line. Dash_offset specifies the starting point for customized dashed lines. Figure 22.5 gives you a visual indication of how the various line characteristics will look on the screen.

The fill_style determines how an area enclosed by a graphics object should be filled. There are four possible values. FillSolid specifies that the area should be filled with the foreground pixel value. FillTiled specifies that the area should be filled in a repetitive tiled fashion using the rectangular pixmap member called *tile*. FillStippled specifies that the area be filled with the foreground color masked off by the member called *stipple*. FillOpa-queStippled is the same as FillStippled except that the masked off pixels are filled in with the background color.

The fill_rule determines which parts of an overlapping enclosed graphics object are filled and which are not filled. There are two possibilities. EvenOddRule specifies that if an area overlaps on itself an odd number of times, it is not filled — even numbers of overlaps are filled. WindingRule specifies that overlapping areas are always filled.

The arc_mode determines how an arc is enclosed for filling. There are two possibilities. ArcChord specifies that a straight line be drawn to con-nect the two endpoints of the arc. ArcPieSlice specifies that a straight line be drawn from each endpoint of the arc to its center.

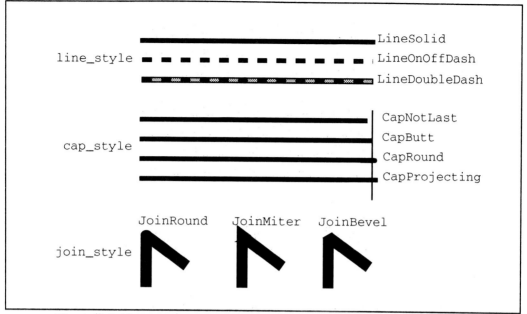

Figure 22.5 The visual effects of the various line characteristics.

The ts__x__origin and ts__y__origin determine where a tile or stipple pattern should start. The X/Y-coordinates are specified with respect to the origin of the area being tiled or stippled. Figure 22.6 gives you a visual indication of how the various fill characteristics will look on the screen.

◻ The font determines which font is used when you use X functions to draw text on the screen. This member specifies a font id (fid) returned in the XFontStruct structure from XQueryFont(). The font member has absolutely no effect on the font used for labels, titles, or text in any of the Motif widgets.

◻ The subwindow__mode determines whether graphics can be seen through a child window when it obscures its parent where the graphics are being drawn. There are two possible values. ClipByChildren specifies that when a graphics object is drawn in an area that is obscured by a child window, it will not be visible. IncludeInferiors specifies that graphics will appear through visible children even if they have opaque backgrounds. Window managers use this second value when displaying rubber-band lines for a window that is being moved or resized.

◻ The graphics__exposures determines whether expose events should be generated under certain special circumstances. In copying (not drawing) of one graphics area to another, there may be conditions where part of the destination area is obscured or unavailable. In these cases the obscured or missing part of the graphic must be drawn in some other way. A True value specifies that an expose event will be generated for the destination window if the copy operation cannot copy the entire graphic as described above. A False value indicates that no event should be generated.

◻ The clip__mask determines which pixels of the destination drawable will be affected by a graphics operation. The clip__mask is a bitmap that

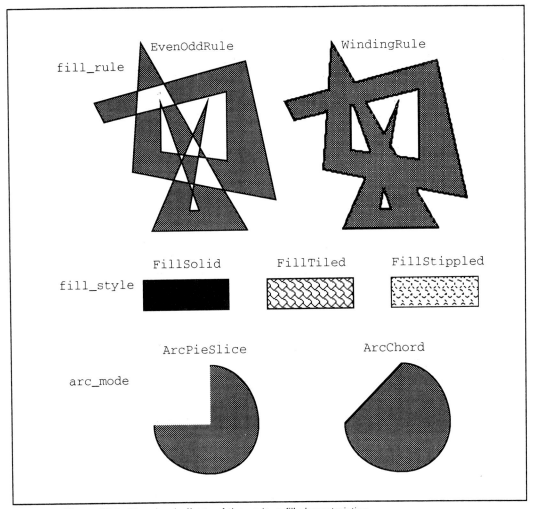

Figure 22.6 The visual effects of the various fill characteristics.

specifies where drawn pixels will appear (with a 1 bit) and where drawn pixels will not appear (with a 0 bit). The origin of this bitmap is specified with respect to the destination drawable using clip__x__origin and clip__y__-origin.

Changing the Graphics Context Programmatically

If you have a graphics context that you want to use for a new graphics operation but it still has the data for the old graphics operations in it, you can change its contents. The XChangeGC() function allows you to change the contents of a GC. Figure 22.7 shows the syntax for this function.

The first parameter is the display pointer required by most XLib functions. The second parameter specifies the id of the GC that you want to change. The last two parameters serve the same purpose in XChangeGC as

```
XChangeGC(display, gc, value_mask, values)

Display         *display;
GC              gc;
unsigned long   value_mask;
XGCValues       *values;
```

Figure 22.7 XChangeGC() syntax.

they did on XCreateGC(). The third parameter is the bitwise OR of the defined names of the members of the XGCValues structure that you have filled in and whose address you are passing through the fourth parameter. Figure 22.8 shows a short code segment that uses XChangeGC().

X also provides a number of convenience functions that allow you to change one or more members of a GC without the overhead of an XGCValues data structure. Although these functions are more convenient to use, there is no real advantage to using them as opposed to XChangeGC(). Figure 22.9 lists these convenience functions.

Figure 22.10 shows a short code segment that uses some of these convenience functions.

□   Just like any other server resource, when you are done with a GC, you should free it. Freeing a GC frees up space in the server's memory and gives the server fewer things to keep track of. XFreeGC() is the function you use to do this. Figure 22.11 shows its syntax.

Drawing a Line

□   One of the many graphics objects you can draw in X is a simple straight line. The XDrawLine() function allows you to draw a straight line between two defined points. Figure 22.12 shows the syntax for this function.

```
...
Display *display;
Screen *screen;
Window root;
GC myGC;
...
    XGCValues myValues;
    ...
    display = XtDisplay(topShell);
    screen = XtScreen(topShell);
    root = RootWindowOfScreen(screen);
    ...
    myValues.line_style = LineOnOffDash;
    myValues.join_style = JoinBevel;
    myGC = XChangeGC(display, myGC, GCLineStyle | GCJoinStyle, &myValues);
    ...
```

Figure 22.8 Changing a graphics context.

```
XSetArcMode(display, gc, arc_mode)
XSetBackground(display, gc, background)
XSetClipMask(display, gc, clip_mask)
XSetClipOrigin(display, gc, clip_x_origin, clip_y_origin)
XSetDashes(display, gc, dash_offset, dash_list, n)
XSetFillRule(display, gc, fill_rule)
XSetFillStyle(display, gc, fill_style)
XSetFont(display, gc, font)
XSetForeground(display, gc, foreground)
XSetFunction(display, gc, function)
XSetGraphicsExposures(display, gc, graphics_exposures)
XSetLineAttributes(display, gc, line_width, line_style, cap_style, join_style)
XSetPlaneMask(display, gc, plane_mask)
XSetState(display, gc, foreground, background, function, plane_mask)
XSetStipple(display, gc, stipple)
XSetSubwindowMode(display, gc, subwindow_mode)
XSetTile(display, gc, tile)
XSetTSOrigin(display, gc, ts_x_origin, ts_y_origin)
```

Figure 22.9 Functions to change members of a graphics context.

```
...
Widget topShell;
Display *display;
XColor white;
XColor red;
XFontStruct *myFont;
GC myGC;
...
    display = XtDisplay(topShell);
    myGC = XCreateGC(display, root, NULL, NULL);
    ...
    XSetFont(display, myGC, myFont->fid);
    XSetForeground(display, myGC, white.pixel);
    ...
    XSetBackground(display, myGC, red.pixel);
    XSetLineAttributes(display, myGC, 4, LineSolid, CapRound, JoinRound);
    ...
```

Figure 22.10 Changing a graphics context with other functions.

```
XFreeGC(display, gc)

Display *display;
GC      gc;
```

Figure 22.11 XFreeGC() syntax.

```
XDrawLine(display, drawable, gc, x1, y1, x2, y2)

Display  *display;
Drawable drawable;
GC       gc;
int      x1, y1;
int      x2, y2;
```

Figure 22.12 XDrawLine() syntax.

The first parameter is the display pointer required by almost every Xlib function. The second parameter is the window id of the window you will be drawing the line in. The third parameter is the graphics context to use for this drawing operation. The line will be drawn between the endpoints specified by the fourth and fifth parameters and the sixth and seventh parameters. Figure 22.13 shows a short code segment that draws a line.

The X/Y-coordinates for both endpoints are specified with respect to the origin of the window (drawable) that you are drawing in. The coordinates are usually obtained from the XEvent union received from a ButtonDown, ButtonUp, or a ButtonMotion event. You can use the ButtonMotion event to track the mouse movement and draw a rubber-band line using the GXxor function (with the foreground and background colors exclusive-ORed together as the foreground color). When the mouse button is released, you can use the GXcopy function to draw the permanent line. To erase a drawn

```
...
#include <Xm/DrawingA.h>
...
Display *display;
Screen *screen;
Window root;
Window window;
GC myGC;
    ...
    display = XtDisplay(topShell);
    screen = XtScreen(topShell);
    root = RootWindowOfScreen(screen);
    myGC = XCreateGC(display, root, NULL, NULL);
    i = 0;
    XtSetArg(argList[i], XmNheight, 200); i++;
    XtSetArg(argList[i], XmNwidth, 200); i++;
    draw = XmCreateDrawingArea(topShell, "draw", argList, i);
    window = XtWindow(draw);
    ...
    XSetForeground(display, myGC, red.pixel);
    XSetLineAttributes(display, myGC, 4, LineSolid, CapRound, JoinRound);
    XDrawLine(display, window, myGC, 10, 103, 180, 103);
    ...
```

Figure 22.13 Drawing a line in X.

```
    /* Return control to the calling function */
    XtAddEventHandler(draw, ExposureMask, False, drawIt, NULL);

    /* Make the program visible on the screen */
    XtManageChild(draw);
    XtRealizeWidget(topShell);

    /* Wait for input events */
    XtMainLoop();
    }

XtEventHandler drawIt(widget_id,  client_data, call_data)
Widget widget_id;
caddr_t client_data;
caddr_t call_data;
    {
    static XTextItem myText = {"Hello World", 11, 0, None};
    Window window = XtWindow(widget_id);

    /* Draw something on the screen */
    XSetFont(display, myGC, myFont->fid);
    XSetForeground(display, myGC, white.pixel);
    XDrawText(display, window, myGC, 20, 100, &myText, 1);
    XSetForeground(display, myGC, red.pixel);
    XSetLineAttributes(display, myGC, 4, LineSolid, CapRound, JoinRound);
    XDrawLine(display, window, myGC, 10, 103, 180, 103);

    /* Return control to the calling function */
    return;
    }
```

Example 22.2 X/Motif application program with a graphics context, part 2.

Figure 22.16 Output of the previous X/Motif application program.

text?

9. What is the purpose of three of the graphics context structure members?

10. What is meant by rubber-band drawing?

11. Which function is used to change the contents of an existing graphics context?

12. List several convenience functions that can change one or more members of a graphics context.

13. Which function is used to free a graphics context?

14. How do you draw a line with an X drawing function?

15. How do you draw text with an X drawing function?

16. How does backing store operate?

17. List two other methods of handling redrawing in response to an expose event.

Exercises

☐ The following exercises are designed to give you the opportunity to practice the concepts and facilities presented in this chapter:

1. Modify the drawing program that you have been working on over the last several chapters. Cause the Line PushButton to allow you to draw a line. The easy way to accomplish this would be to watch for two ButtonDown events and to cause the line to be drawn between the two X/Y-coordinate pairs. A more difficult exercise would be to do rubber-band drawing of the line by watching for the initial ButtonDown event, tracking the ButtonMotion events, and drawing the final line on the next ButtonUp event.

2. Modify the previous program to cause the color OptionMenu to allow for different color lines.

3. Modify the previous program to cause the linewidth PopupMenu to allow for different linewidths.

Drawing
Graphics Objects
(Optional)

Introduction

◻ In addition to being able to draw lines and text, the X Window System supplies a number of other graphics primitives to draw other graphics objects. In this chapter you will learn about more functions to draw other graphics objects as well as how to clear and copy window areas.

Objectives

◻ After completing this chapter, you will be able to:

◻ Explain why a graphics object isn't drawn directly on the screen.

◻ Describe the two places graphics operations can be performed.

◻ Explain an X client's responsibility with respect to graphics and expose events.

◻ List the three things all graphics functions have in common.

◻ List the two functions that can draw points on the screen.

◻ Describe the X data type that can hold a point description.

◻ List the two functions that can draw lines — connected and unconnected.

◻ Describe the X data type that can hold a line segment description.

◻ List the two functions that can draw rectangles on the screen.

◻ Describe the X data type that can hold a rectangle description.

◻ List the two functions that can draw arcs on the screen.

◻ Describe the X data type that can hold an arc description.

◻ Explain which function is used to draw polygons on the screen.

◻ Explain which function is used to clear the contents of a window.

◻ Explain which function is used to copy an area from one drawable to another.

Graphics Review

◻ Several points should be reviewed before you learn about the rest of the functions that allow you to draw different graphics objects. Remember, drawing in X is not the same as drawing on a "blank sheet of paper." Drawing is first performed off-screen and then processed and possibly modified according to the contents of the graphics context. Only after this has been done is your graphics object copied to a window on the screen.

And, although you haven't learned a lot about them yet, drawing can also be accomplished in something called a *pixmap*. All graphics operations are performed in a *drawable*. X defines a drawable as either an on-screen window id or an off screen pixmap id. Wherever you see a drawable specified, remember that you can use either a window or a pixmap.

Another important point to remember is that you and your client application are responsible for redrawing graphics objects in response to an expose event. Although backing store may be available, it is an expensive resource to use. Your program should come up with some other technique of remembering and redrawing graphics objects when a hidden portion of a graphics window gets exposed.

Although we haven't really talked about it yet, there is a common misconception about graphics objects that has to do with resizing a graphics window. Some people think that when the graphics window gets resized, the graphic inside the window ought to resize proportionately. This is not the case. In X, if you want a graphic object to resize in response to the resizing of its window—whether its lines or text—you have to write the code to do the resizing. Your program can watch for resize events and erase and then redraw the graphics in a new, proportionately different size.

One final word in review. All graphics functions have a point of commonality. All the X functions that draw a graphics object have the same first three parameters. The first parameter is always the display pointer that identifies the display connection to the server that you want to do your drawing on. The second parameter is always the drawable—the window id or pixmap id—where you are going to do your drawing. Finally, the third parameter is always the GC, or graphics context, to be used in specifying the style and characteristics of your drawing.

The rest of this chapter introduces you to the many other drawing functions available in the X Window System.

Drawing Points

◻ Two more of the X functions available to draw objects allow you to draw a point or a collection of points. These two functions are XDrawPoint() and XDrawPoints(). Figure 23.1 shows their syntax.

XDrawPoint() draws a single point on the screen. The point's location is determined by the parameters X and Y. These coordinates are specified relative to the origin of the drawable.

XDrawPoints() draws multiple points on the screen. The definition of the points occurs in an array of type XPoint. Each array element contains an integer X value and an integer Y value. The number of points (the number of elements in the array) is specified in the following parameter.

The mode parameter determines how the X/Y-coordinates of a point are interpreted. There are two possible values. CoordModeOrigin specifies that the X/Y-coordinates of the point are calculated with respect to the origin of the drawable. CoordModePrevious specifies that the X/Y-coordinates of the point are calculated with respect to the X/Y-coordinates of the previous point in the array. Figure 23.2 shows a short code segment that draws some points.

Drawing Lines and Segments

◻ In addition to XDrawLine() discussed in the previous chapter, there are two other functions available to draw lines. XDrawLines() draws multiple connected line segments. XDrawSegments() draws multiple unconnected line segments. Figure 23.3 shows their syntax,

XDrawLines() draws multiple lines on the screen. Each line is drawn connecting one point in the array to the next. A total of number_of_points minus 1 lines are drawn. The definition of the points occurs in an array of type XPoint. Each array element contains an integer X value and an integer Y value. The number of points (the number of elements in the array) is specified in the following parameter.

```
XDrawPoint(display, drawable, gc, x, y)
XDrawPoints(display, drawable, gc, points, number_of_points, mode)

Display  *display;
Drawable drawable;
GC       gc;
int      x, y;
XPoint   *points;
int      number_of_points;
int      mode;

typedef struct {
    short x, y;
} XPoint;
```

Figure 23.1 XDrawPoint() and XDrawPoints() syntax.

```
...
#include <Xm/DrawingA.h>
...
Display *display;
Screen *screen;
Window root;
Window window;
GC myGC;
...
    static XPoint myPoints[] = { 3,   3,   3,   6,   3,   9,   3, 12,
                                 6,   3,   6,   6,   6,   9,   6, 12,
                                 9,   3,   9,   6,   9,   9,   9, 12,
                                12,   3,  12,  6,  12,   9,  12, 12};
    ...
    display = XtDisplay(topShell);
    screen = XtScreen(topShell);
    root = RootWindowOfScreen(screen);
    myGC = XCreateGC(display, root, NULL, NULL);
    ...
    i = 0;
    XtSetArg(argList[i], XmNheight, 200); i++;
    XtSetArg(argList[i], XmNwidth, 200); i++;
    draw = XmCreateDrawingArea(topShell, "draw", argList, i);
    window = XtWindow(draw);
    ...
    XSetForeground(display, myGC, white.pixel);
    XDrawPoints(display, window, myGC, myPoints, 16, CoordModeOrigin);
    ...
```

Figure 23.2 Drawing points with X.

The mode parameter determines how the X/Y-coordinates of a point are interpreted. There are two possible values. CoordModeOrigin specifies that the X/Y-coordinates of the point are calculated with respect to the origin of the drawable. CoordModePrevious specifies that the X/Y-coordinates of the point are calculated with respect to the X/Y-coordinates of the previous point in the array.

XDrawSegments() draws multiple lines on the screen. The definition of the lines occurs in an array of type XSegment. Each array element contains four integer numbers representing two X/Y-coordinates as the endpoints of a line. The number of segments (the number of elements in the array) is specified in the following parameter.

Drawing Rectangles

◻ Two more of the X functions available to draw objects allows you to draw a rectangle or a collection of rectangles. These two functions are XDrawRectangle() and XDrawRectangles(). Figure 23.4 shows their syntax,

```
XDrawLines(display, drawable, gc, points, number_of_points, mode)
XDrawSegments(display, drawable, gc, segments, number_of_segments)

Display  *display;
Drawable drawable;
GC       gc;
int      x, y;
XPoint   *points;
int      number_of_points;
int      mode;
XSegment *segments
int      number_of_segments;

typedef struct {
    short x, y;
} XPoint;

typedef struct {
    short x1, y1, x2, y2;
} XSegment;
```

Figure 23.3 XDrawLines() and XDrawSegments() syntax,

```
XDrawRectangle(display, drawable, gc, x, y, width, height)
XDrawRectangles(display, drawable, gc, rectangles, number_of_rectangles)

Display      *display;
Drawable     drawable;
GC           gc;
int          x, y;
unsigned int width, height;
XRectangle   *rectangles;
int          number_of_rectangles;

typedef struct {
    short x, y;
    unsigned short width, height;
} XRectangle;
```

Figure 23.4 XDrawRectangle() and XDrawRectangles() syntax.

XDrawRectangle() draws a single rectangle on the screen. The rectangle's location is determined by the parameters X and Y. Its width and height are also specified as parameters. The X/Y-coordinates are specified relative to the origin of the drawable.

XDrawRectangles() draws multiple rectangles on the screen. The definition of the rectangles occurs in an array of type XRectangle. Each array element contains an X/Y-coordinate origin as well as width and height. The number of rectangles (the number of elements in the array) is specified in the following parameter. Figure 23.5 shows a short code segment that draws a rectangle.

Drawing Arcs

Two more of the X functions available to draw objects allows you to draw an arc or a collection of arcs. These two functions are XDrawArc() and XDrawArcs(). Figure 23.6 shows their syntax,

XDrawArc() draws a single arc on the screen. The arc's location is determined by the parameters X and Y. The size and shape of the arc are determined by the height, width, angle1, and angle2 parameters as shown in Figure 23.7. The coordinates are specified relative to the origin of the drawable and the angles are measured in 64ths of a degree.

XDrawArcs() draws multiple arcs on the screen. The definition of the arcs occurs in an array of type XArc. Each array element contains the X/Y origin, the height and width, and the two angles required for an arc as in XDrawArc(). The number of arcs (the number of elements in the array) is specified in the following parameter. Figure 23.8 shows a short code segment that draws an arc.

```
...
#include <Xm/DrawingA.h>
...
Display *display;
Screen *screen;
Window root;
Window window;
GC myGC;
...
    display = XtDisplay(topShell);
    screen = XtScreen(topShell);
    root = RootWindowOfScreen(screen);
    myGC = XCreateGC(display, root, NULL, NULL);
    ...
    i = 0;
    XtSetArg(argList[i], XmNheight, 200); i++;
    XtSetArg(argList[i], XmNwidth, 200); i++;
    draw = XmCreateDrawingArea(topShell, "draw", argList, i);
    window = XtWindow(draw);
    ...
    XSetForeground(display, myGC, green.pixel);
    XSetLineAttributes(display, myGC, 4, LineOnOffDash, CapRound, JoinRound);
    XDrawRectangle(display, window, myGC, 5, 50, 190, 100);
    ...
```

Figure 23.5 Drawing rectangles with X.

```
XDrawArc(display, drawable, gc, x, y, width, height, angle1, angle2)
XDrawArcs(display, drawable, gc, arcs, number_of_arcs)

Display       *display;
Drawable       drawable;
GC             gc;
int            x, y;
unsigned int width, height;
int            angle1, angle2;
XArc          *arcs;
int            angle1, angle2;

typedef struct {
    short x, y;
    unsigned short width, height;
    short angle1, angle2;
} XArc;
```

Figure 23.6 XDrawArc() and XDrawArcs() syntax.

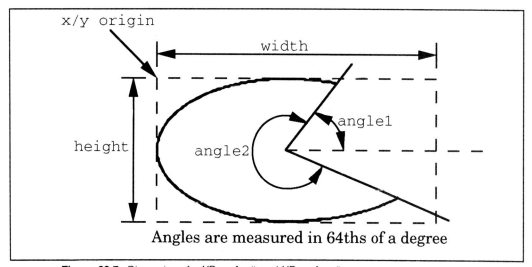

Figure 23.7 Dimensions for XDrawArc() and XDrawArcs().

Drawing Filled Rectangles and Arcs

◻ There are two more functions that are similar in operation to the XDrawRectangle() functions and two more functions that are similar in operation the the XDrawArc() functions. The main difference between these new functions and their relatives is that the graphics object that is drawn is also filled with the foreground color or a tile.

```
...
#include <Xm/DrawingA.h>
...
Display *display;
Screen *screen;
Window root;
Window window;
GC myGC;
...
    display = XtDisplay(topShell);
    screen = XtScreen(topShell);
    root = RootWindowOfScreen(screen);
    myGC = XCreateGC(display, root, NULL, NULL);
    ...
    i = 0;
    XtSetArg(argList[i], XmNheight, 200); i++;
    XtSetArg(argList[i], XmNwidth, 200); i++;
    draw = XmCreateDrawingArea(topShell, "draw", argList, i);
    window = XtWindow(draw);
    ...
    XSetForeground(display, myGC, yellow.pixel);
    XSetBackground(display, myGC, red.pixel);
    XSetLineAttributes(display, myGC, 6, LineDoubleDash, CapRound, JoinRound);
    XDrawArc(display, window, myGC, 0, 0, 200, 200, 360 * 64, 360 * 64);
    ...
```

Figure 23.8 Drawing arcs with X.

XFillRectangle() and XFillRectangles() draw a rectangle or rectangles just like XDrawRectangle() and XDrawRectangles(). They take the same parameters and draw filled rectangles instead of empty rectangles. However, the dimensions of the Fill versions of the functions do not produce a rectangle that is of exactly the same size as the non-Fill functions.

XFillArc() and XFillArcs() draw an arc or arcs just like XDrawArc() and XDrawArcs(). They take the same parameters and draw filled arcs instead of empty arcs. However, the dimensions of the Fill versions of the functions do not produce an arc that is exactly the same size as the non-Fill functions.

It is interesting to note that the Fill functions do not produce the exact same graphics object as do the non-Fill functions. For example, XFillRectangle() produces a rectangle that is one pixel shorter in both the height and width than the corresponding XDrawRectangle with the exact same parameters. Fixing this problem for a rectangle is relatively easy by adjusting the parameters.

There is also a difference between the way that XDrawArc() and XFillArc() draw an arc on the screen. However, fixing this problem in a portable manner is a more difficult proposition.

Drawing Filled Polygons

¤ There is one Fill function that does not have a corresponding Draw function. XFillPolygon() will draw a multiside object on the screen, ensure that it is closed, and then fill the closed area. Figure 23.9 shows the syntax for this function.

XFillPolygon() draws multiple lines on the screen. Each line is drawn connecting one point in the array to the next. A total of number_of_points lines are drawn. If the last point does not coincide with the first point, a line is drawn connecting them. The enclosed area is then filled with the foreground color or tiled with the tile pixmap according to the contents of the graphics context.

The definition of the points occurs in an array of type XPoint. Each array element contains an integer X value and an integer Y value. The number of points (the number of elements in the array) is specified in the following parameter.

The shape parameter allows the server to optimize its performance in filling the enclosed area on the basis of its shape. There are three possible values. *Complex* specifies that the path of the lines forming the object may self-intersect and that the GC fill rule should be consulted to determine how filling should take place. *Nonconvex* specifies that the lines of the object do not intersect but that the object is not wholly convex. *Convex* specifies that all the lines form a wholly convex object. If Nonconvex or Convex are specified and the drawn polygon does not fit the description, the results of the fill operation are undefined.

The mode parameter determines how the X/Y-coordinates of a point are interpreted. There are two possible values. CoordModeOrigin specifies that the X/Y-coordinates of the point are calculated with respect to the origin of the drawable. CoordModePrevious specifies that the X/Y-coordinates of the point are calculated with respect to the X/Y-coordinates of the previous point in the array. Figure 23.10 shows a short code segment that draws a filled polygon.

```
XFillPolygon(display, drawable, gc, points, number_of_points, shape, mode)

Display   *display;
Drawable  drawable;
GC        gc;
int       x, y;
XPoint    *points;
int       number_of_points;
int       shape;

typedef struct {
    short x, y;
} XPoint;
```

Figure 23.9 XFillPolygon() syntax.

```
...
#include <Xm/DrawingA.h>
...
Display *display;
Screen *screen;
Window root;
Window window;
GC myGC;
...
    static XPoint poPoints[] = { 75, 150,  70, 125, 125,  120, 100, 175};
    ...
    display = XtDisplay(topShell);
    screen = XtScreen(topShell);
    root = RootWindowOfScreen(screen);
    myGC = XCreateGC(display, root, NULL, NULL);
    ...
    i = 0;
    XtSetArg(argList[i], XmNheight, 200); i++;
    XtSetArg(argList[i], XmNwidth, 200); i++;
    draw = XmCreateDrawingArea(topShell, "draw", argList, i);
    window = XtWindow(draw);
    ...
    XSetLineAttributes(display, myGC, 8, LineSolid, CapButt, JoinBevel);
    XSetForeground(display, myGC, BlackPixelOfScreen(screen));
    XFillPolygon(display, window, myGC, poPoints, 4, Convex, CoordModeOrigin);
    ...
```

Figure 23.10 Drawing filled polygons with X.

Clearing and Copying Areas

There are two more operations that are useful when doing graphics. Many times you need the ability to clear an area on the screen of all of its foreground pixels. You also, from time to time, need to copy one area of a window to another area or into another window or pixmap. The XClearArea() function performs a clearing operation for you. Figure 23.11 shows the syntax for this function.

```
XClearArea(display, window, x, y, width, height, exposures)

Display        *display;
Window         window;
int            x, y;
unsigned int   width, height;
Bool           exposures;
```

Figure 23.11 XClearArea() syntax.

Notice that the XClearArea() function works only on a window and cannot be used on a pixmap. The area that is cleared is determined by the X/Y-coordinates of the origin as well as a width and height. If height is zero, the window is cleared from the Y point to the bottom of the window. If the width is zero, the window is cleared from the X point to the right edge of the window.

The clearing is accomplished by filling the area to be cleared with the background color. If the window has a background tile defined for it, the area is tiled instead. The exposures parameter specifies whether one or more expose events should be generated for the clear operation. Its value can be True or False.

¤   The XCopyArea() function is used to copy a rectangular area from one drawable to another. This function doesn't care if the drawables are windows, pixmaps, or some combination. Figure 23.12 shows the syntax for XCopyArea().

An area from the source drawable is copied to the destination drawable. The area that is copied is defined by the origin specified with source__x and source__y as well as a width and a height. The area will be copied to an area in the destination that is the same size starting at the coordinate specified by destination__x and destination__y.

A Complete X/Motif Client Application

¤   Using all the concepts and techniques presented in this chapter, we can put together a simple, but complete, X/Motif-based client application. Example 23.1 shows the code for a program that has DrawingArea in it. The program uses several of the drawing functions presented in this chapter to draw some objects in the DrawingArea. Points, lines, rectangles, circles, text, and polygons are represented.

Figure 23.13 shows what the program would look like on a typical terminal screen.

```
XCopyArea(display, source, destination, gc,
          source_x, source_y, width, height, destination_x, destination_y)

Display       *display;
Drawable      source;
Drawable      destination;
GC            gc;
int           source_x, source_y;
unsigned int  width, height;
int           destination_x, destination_y;
```

Figure 23.12 XCopyArea() syntax.

```
#include <stdio.h>
#include <Xm/DrawingA.h>
#define FONT1 \
    "-adobe-new century schoolbook-bold-r-normal--24-240-75-75-p-149-iso8859-1"

XtEventHandler drawIt();

Widget topShell;
Display *display;
Screen *screen;
Window root;
Colormap colormap;
XFontStruct *myFont;
XColor white;
XColor red;
XColor green;
XColor yellow;
XColor exact;
GC myGC;

main(argc, argv)
Cardinal argc;
String argv[];
    {
    Widget draw;
    Arg argList[10];
    Cardinal i;

    /* Initialize  the Intrinsics and create a top Shell widget */
    topShell = XtInitialize(argv[0], "Edit", NULL, 0, &argc, argv);

    /* Get some server specific information */
    display = XtDisplay(topShell);
    screen = XtScreen(topShell);
    root = RootWindowOfScreen(screen);
    colormap = DefaultColormapOfScreen(screen);
    myFont = XLoadQueryFont(display, FONT1);
    XAllocNamedColor(display, colormap, "white", &white, &exact);
    XAllocNamedColor(display, colormap, "red", &red, &exact);
    XAllocNamedColor(display, colormap, "green", &green, &exact);
    XAllocNamedColor(display, colormap, "yellow", &yellow, &exact);
    myGC = XCreateGC(display, root, NULL, NULL);

    /* Create the user interface widgets */
    i = 0;
    XtSetArg(argList[i], XmNheight, 200); i++;
    XtSetArg(argList[i], XmNwidth, 200); i++;
    draw = XmCreateDrawingArea(topShell, "draw", argList, i);
```

Example 23.1 X/Motif application program drawing some graphics objects, part 1.

```
     /* Set up event handlers for the widgets */
     XtAddEventHandler(draw, ExposureMask, False, drawIt, NULL);

     /* Make the program visible on the screen */
     XtManageChild(draw);
     XtRealizeWidget(topShell);

     /* Wait for input events */
     XtMainLoop();
     }

XtEventHandler drawIt(widget_id,  client_data, call_data)
Widget widget_id;
caddr_t client_data;
caddr_t call_data;
     {
     Window window = XtWindow(widget_id);
     static XTextItem myText = {"Hello World", 11, 0, None};
     static XPoint myPoints[] = { 3,   3,   3,   6,   3,   9,   3, 12,
                                   6,   3,   6,   6,   6,   9,   6, 12,
                                   9,   3,   9,   6,   9,   9,   9, 12,
                                  12,   3,  12, 6,  12,   9,  12, 12};
     static XPoint poPoints[] = { 75, 150,  70, 125, 125,  120, 100, 175};

     /* Draw something on the screen */
     XSetFont(display, myGC, myFont->fid);
     XSetForeground(display, myGC, white.pixel);
     XDrawText(display, window, myGC, 20, 100, &myText, 1);
     XSetForeground(display, myGC, red.pixel);
     XSetLineAttributes(display, myGC, 2, LineSolid, CapRound, JoinRound);
     XDrawLine(display, window, myGC, 10, 103, 180, 103);
     XSetForeground(display, myGC, white.pixel);
     XDrawPoints(display, window, myGC, myPoints, 16, CoordModeOrigin);
     XSetForeground(display, myGC, green.pixel);
     XSetLineAttributes(display, myGC, 4, LineOnOffDash, CapRound, JoinRound);
     XDrawRectangle(display, window, myGC, 5, 50, 190, 100);
     XSetForeground(display, myGC, yellow.pixel);
     XSetBackground(display, myGC, red.pixel);
     XSetLineAttributes(display, myGC, 6, LineDoubleDash, CapRound, JoinRound);
     XDrawArc(display, window, myGC, 0, 0, 200, 200, 360 * 64, 360 * 64);
     XSetLineAttributes(display, myGC, 8, LineSolid, CapButt, JoinBevel);
     XSetForeground(display, myGC, BlackPixelOfScreen(screen));
     XFillPolygon(display, window, myGC, poPoints, 4, Convex, CoordModeOrigin);

     /* Return control to the calling function */
     return;
     }
```

Example 23.2 X/Motif application program drawing some graphics objects, part 2.

Figure 23.13 Output of the previous X/Motif application program.

Review Questions

¤   Please write down the answers to the following questions:

1. Why isn't a graphics object drawn directly on the screen?
2. Where are the two places where graphics operations can be performed?
3. What is an X client's responsibility with respect to graphics and expose events?
4. List the three things all graphics functions have in common.
5. List the two functions that can draw points on the screen.
6. What is the X data type that can hold a point description?
7. List the two functions that can draw lines – connected and unconnected.
8. What is the X data type that can hold a line segment description?
9. List the two functions that can draw rectangles on the screen.
10. What is the X data type that can hold a rectangle description?
11. List the two functions that can draw arcs on the screen.
12. What is the X data type that can hold an arc description?
13. Which function is used to draw polygons on the screen?
14. Which function is used to clear the contents of a window?
15. Which function is used to copy an area from one drawable to another?

Exercises

¤ The following exercises are designed to give you the opportunity to practice the concepts and facilities presented in this chapter:

1. Modify the drawing program that you have been working on over the last several chapters. Cause the Circle PushButton to allow you to draw a circle. The easy way to accomplish this would be to watch for two ButtonDown events and to cause the circle to be drawn in a rectangle bounded by the two X/Y-coordinate pairs. A more difficult exercise would be to do rubber-band drawing of the circle by watching for the initial ButtonDown event, tracking the ButtonMotion events, and drawing the final circle on the next ButtonUp event. Make sure that the color OptionMenu and the linewidth PopupMenu apply to the lines used to draw the circle as well as the straight lines.

2. Modify the previous program to add a button that allows you to draw rectangles. Apply the same capabilities that are already available with the lines and circles, with respect to colors and linewidths, to a rectangle.

Pixmaps
and Bitmaps
(Optional)

Introduction

◻ Pixmaps have been mentioned for the last several chapters as alternative graphics objects. In this chapter we will finally present the pixmap concept in more detail. You will learn how to create pixmaps and work with pixmaps in your X/Motif client programs. You will also learn about a special type of pixmap called a *bitmap*.

Objectives

◻ After completing this chapter, you will be able to:

◻ Explain what a pixmap is.

◻ Describe the memory organization of a pixmap.

◻ List several different uses for pixmaps.

◻ Explain which function is used to create a pixmap.

◻ Describe where pixmaps are stored.

◻ Explain which function is used to get rid of a pixmap.

◻ Describe how to clear a pixmap.

◻ Explain which function is used to copy a pixmap.

◻ Explain the difference between a pixmap and a bitmap.

- Describe the purpose of the bitmap program.
- Describe the output of the bitmap program.
- Explain which function is used to convert a bitmap into a pixmap.
- Describe the location of the standard X bitmaps.
- Explain the purpose of the xsetroot program.
- Describe how to construct a cursor and the function you use to do it.

Pixmap Concepts

Quite simply, a pixmap is an off-screen array in memory that can be used as an alternate graphics or drawing area. The memory is organized into a series of bit planes. A bit plane is an array of bits that is some number of bits wide, some number of bits high (organized as a rectangular area), and 1 bit deep. All pixmaps will have a finite number of these bit planes. The number of bit planes available determines the *depth* of the pixmap. Figure 24.1 illustrates how you would visualize this organization.

One bit from each plane combines with bits in corresponding positions from other planes (1 bit from each plane) to form a pixel value. Each pixel value is used to store a bit pattern which is equivalent to an integer number. If you have two bit planes, the pixel value integers can range from 0 to 3, four bit planes can have pixel values from 0 to 15, eight bit planes allow for pixel values of up to 255, and so on. Just like pixel values for the screen, this determines the total number of colors that you can have

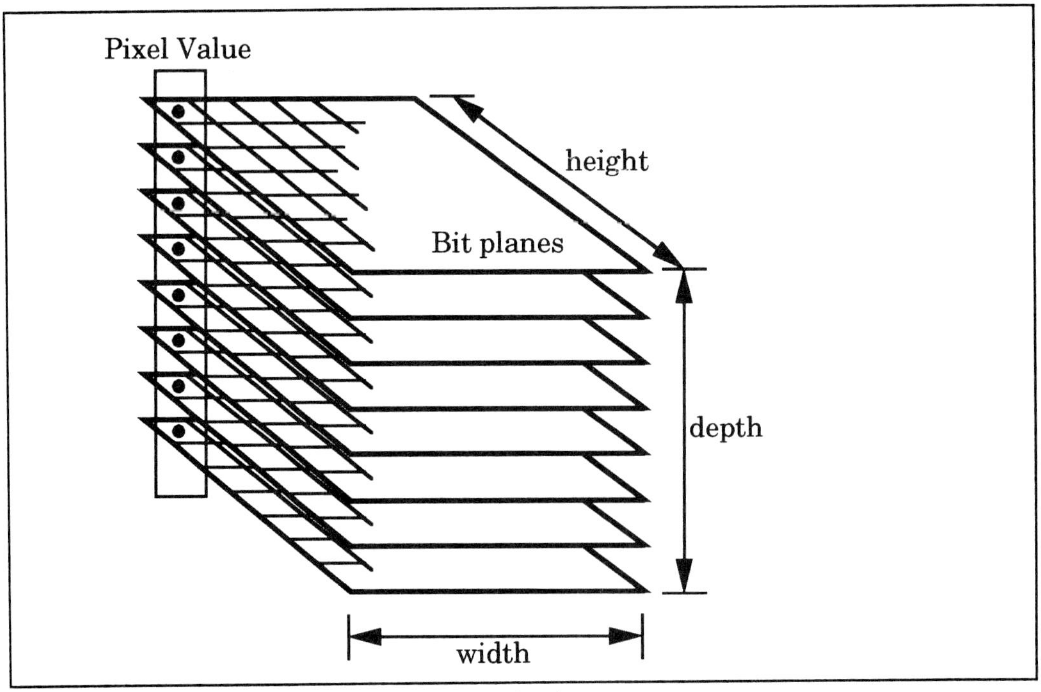

Figure 24.1 Bit plane/pixel organization of a pixmap.

available at any one time. Usually, you create a pixmap that is of the same depth as that of your screen.

The pixel value is used as an index into the color lookup table, or colormap. The color information stored at the colormap entry indexed by the pixel value is the color that will be displayed at a particular pixel when the pixmap is copied to the screen. Remember—anything that you can draw in a window on the screen can also be drawn in a pixmap—they are both called *drawables*.

Pixmaps have a variety of different uses in X:

◻ Pixmaps can be used to simulate the backing store concept so that you can redraw graphics when an expose event is received.

◻ Motif uses pixmaps for the symbols in the standard dialog boxes.

◻ The iconified windows that the Motif window manager creates in response to interaction with the minimize button contains a pixmap.

◻ Most cursors are implemented as a pair of pixmaps—one for the cursor shape and one for the mask that is usually one pixel bigger than the cursor in all directions.

Creating a Pixmap

◻ Pixmaps are another server resource. They are created in the server, and the server keeps track of them for you. To create a pixmap you use the XCreatePixmap() function. Figure 24.2 shows its syntax.

The first parameter is the display pointer that identifies the display connection for the server on which you want to create the pixmap. The server uses the second parameter to determine which screen the pixmap will be stored on (the pixmap can only be used on this screen). The last three parameters specify the size of the pixmap. The width and height specify the dimensions of the pixmap rectangle, and the depth must be the same as that of the screen on which it will eventually be displayed.

◻ Please remember that the server keeps track of many different kinds of things. In addition to managing the keyboard input and screen display, there are several other data items that the server has to manage for you. Windows, GCs, fonts, cursors, colormaps, and now pixmaps are all created in and managed by the server. The server's memory space is not unlimited, and with the possibility of several clients running with the same

```
Pixmap XCreatePixmap(display, drawable, width, height, depth)

Display        *display;
Drawable       drawable;
unsigned int width;
unsigned int height;
unsigned int depth;
```

Figure 24.2 XCreatePixmap() syntax.

server and all of them requesting their own server resources, you must try to keep your use of the server resources to a minimum.

When you are done with a pixmap and you do not need it anymore, you should get rid of it to free up server memory space. To free a pixmap, call the XFreePixmap() function. Figure 24.3 shows its syntax.

Clearing and Copying Pixmaps

¤   There are two operations that are useful when doing graphics with pixmaps. Frequently you need the ability to clear an area in a pixmap of all its foreground pixels. You also, from time to time, need to copy one area of a pixmap to another area or into another pixmap or window. The XClearArea() function does not work on pixmaps. Instead, you must use the XFillRectangle() function to simulate clearing an area of a pixmap. Figure 24.4 shows the syntax for this function.

The area that is cleared is determined by the X, Y, width, and height parameters. Remember that the Fill versions of the Draw functions do not draw the exact same figure. In particular, XFillRectangle() actually draws a rectangle that is one pixel smaller than the specified height and width.

The clearing is accomplished by filling the area to be cleared with the background color specified in the GC parameter. If the GC has a background tile defined for it, the area is tiled instead.

¤   The XCopyArea() function is used to copy a rectangular area from one drawable to another. This function doesn't care if the drawables are windows, pixmaps, or some combination. Figure 24.5 shows the syntax for XCopyArea().

An area from the source drawable is copied to the destination drawable. The area that is copied is defined by the origin specified with source__x and source__y as well as a width and a height. The area will be copied to an area in the destination that is the same size starting at the coordinate specified by destination__x and destination__y.

```
XFreePixmap(display, pixmap)

Display *display;
Pixmap  pixmap;
```

Figure 24.3 XFreePixmap() syntax.

```
XFillRectangle(display, drawable, gc, x, y, width, height)

Display       *display;
Drawable      window;
GC            gc;
int           x, y;
unsigned int width, height;
```

Figure 24.4 XFillRectangle() syntax.

```
XCopyArea(display, source, destination, gc,
          source_x, source_y, width, height, destination_x, destination_y)

Display        *display;
Drawable       source;
Drawable       destination;
GC             gc;
int            source_x, source_y;
unsigned int   width, height;
int            destination_x, destination_y;
```

Figure 24.5 XCopyArea() syntax.

Bitmap Concepts

¤   A bitmap is a very simple concept. Bitmaps are simply pixmaps with a pixel depth of one. It should be obvious, then, that bitmaps don't have a color associated with them. A pixel value in a bitmap can have only one of two values: 1 (on) for black and 0 (off) for white.

Bitmaps are often used to store graphic items in operating system files. It is fairly simple to put together a binary or hexadecimal pattern of 1s and 0s to represent which bits should be on and which bits should be off in a bitmap. This type of graphic representation can be easily stored in and read from a file by an X client program. Storing and reading pixmaps with their associated colormaps in a portable way would be a little more involved.

¤   In fact, X supplies a standard client program that allows you to create an X-format bitmap file with an easy-to-use point-click interface. The client, called bitmap, puts a grid and a series of buttons on the screen that allows you to create a bitmap in a manner similar to that used in many popular paint programs.

The bitmap program lets you draw points, lines, and circles. There are capabilities to clear all the bits or set all the bits in an area. Buttons are provided to invert, copy, and move areas. The bitmap program can even be used to create cursors with a facility that lets you decide where the hot spot will be. You can see what your bitmap will look like in two pixmaps that are displayed at the bottom of the bitmap window. One of the pixmaps shows your bitmap in normal mode while the other displays it in reverse video mode.

To start the bitmap client, simply enter "bitmap filename" at the operating system prompt. The filename is the name of the file in which you want the bitmap data stored. The filename can optionally be followed by two numbers separated by a lowercase x. These two numbers represent the width and the height of the bitmap being created. The default size is 16×16. Figure 24.6 shows what the bitmap program would look like on the screen.

Once the bitmap program is started, you can use the mouse to point and click in the grid to set bits in the bitmap. Mouse button 1 turns on a bit, while mouse button 2 turns it off. Each one of the buttons along the right-hand side provides some additional functionality with respect to the graphic

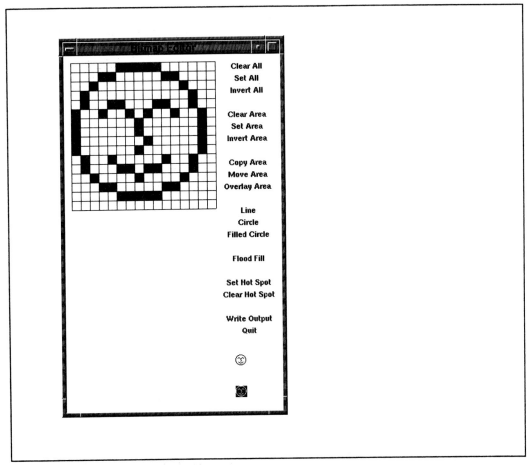

Figure 24.6 Output of the bitmap program.

that you are trying to create. When you are done, there is a button near the bottom of the window that allows you to write the bitmap data out to the file you originally named on the command line. Then, finally, there is another button to quit the application.

The output of the bitmap program is standard C source code in ASCII text format. Defines are set up for the size and, if this was for a cursor, the hot spot location. This is followed by an array definition that is initialized with hexadecimal integer data that corresponds to the bitmap. This bitmap data format is created by an X function called XWriteBitmapFile() and can be read and processed in a number of ways. Figure 24.7 shows what an X11 standard bitmap format file looks like.

Creating a Pixmap from a Bitmap

Although there are some uses for bitmaps by themselves in some advanced drawing applications, in order to make use of the bitmap as a graphic on the screen, it must be converted to a pixmap. Since the file is actually C

```
$ cat /usr/include/X11/bitmaps/wingdogs
#define wingdogs_width 32
#define wingdogs_height 32
static char wingdogs_bits[] = {
   0x60, 0x00, 0x00, 0x00, 0xc0, 0x00, 0x00, 0x00, 0x80, 0x03, 0x00, 0x00,
   0x20, 0x0f, 0x00, 0x00, 0x40, 0x3e, 0x00, 0x00, 0xc0, 0x7f, 0x00, 0x80,
   0x84, 0xff, 0x00, 0xc0, 0x86, 0xff, 0x00, 0xc0, 0x07, 0xff, 0x21, 0xe0,
   0x0f, 0xfe, 0x23, 0xf0, 0x0f, 0xfe, 0x23, 0xfc, 0x1d, 0xfe, 0x13, 0xfe,
   0x39, 0xfc, 0x13, 0xff, 0x3f, 0xfc, 0x83, 0xff, 0x9f, 0xfc, 0xc1, 0xff,
   0x0f, 0xfe, 0xe0, 0xff, 0xf3, 0xff, 0xff, 0xff, 0xf9, 0xff, 0xff, 0xff,
   0xfc, 0xff, 0xff, 0x7f, 0xf6, 0xff, 0xff, 0x1f, 0xfb, 0xff, 0xff, 0x07,
   0xf8, 0xfd, 0xff, 0x03, 0xbc, 0xf9, 0xff, 0x01, 0x3c, 0xf9, 0xff, 0x01,
   0x3e, 0xf0, 0xf7, 0x00, 0x1f, 0xe0, 0x77, 0x00, 0x1f, 0x80, 0x77, 0x00,
   0x8f, 0x00, 0x6f, 0x00, 0xc7, 0x00, 0x6e, 0x80, 0x07, 0x00, 0x7c, 0x80,
   0x0d, 0x00, 0xf8, 0x80, 0x1f, 0x00, 0xf0, 0x01};
```

Figure 24.7 Bitmap file format.

source code, it can be included and then processed by XCreatePixmapFrom-BitmapData(). Figure 24.8 shows the syntax for this function.

With the XCreatePixmapFromBitmapData() function, you must first #include the file that contains the bitmap data. You must specify the drawable to identify the screen that you want the pixmap associated with as the second parameter. The next three parameters make up the bitmap data and are obtained from the #include'ed file. *Data* is the name of the array that contains the bitmap data. *Width* and *height* are the defined names for the width and height of the bitmap.

When the pixmap is created, it is created with a depth specified in the last parameter. Pixels will be filled in with the foreground color wherever there is a 1 bit in the bitmap and the background color where there are 0 bits. The id of the newly created pixmap is returned by the function.

¤   There are a number of predefined bitmaps that come standard with the X Window System. The files for these bitmaps are stored in the /usr/include/X11/bitmaps directory. Although most of these files are used by X for a variety of purposes, you can read and display them with the bitmap client application just like any other bitmap file.

```
Pixmap XCreatePixmapFromBitmapData(display, drawable, data,
                                   width, height, foreground, background, depth)

Display        *display;
Drawable       drawable
char           *data;
unsigned int   width;
unsigned int   height;
unsigned long  foreground;
unsigned long  background;
unsigned int   depth;
```

Figure 24.8 XCreatePixmapFromBitmapData() syntax.

The xsetroot client application can be used to take a bitmap file and use it as a tile for the root window of the screen. Three options to the xsetroot client will be of interest. The -bitmap option is followed by the name of the file that contains the bitmap data. The -fg and -bg options are used to specify color names from rgb.txt for the foreground and background colors, respectively.

Cursor Pixmaps

If you don't like the cursors that are defined in the standard cursor font, X allows you to create your own cursor shapes using two pixmaps. The XCreatePixmapCursor() function is called to create a cursor using these pixmaps. Figure 24.9 shows the syntax for this function.

Both the source and mask pixmaps have a depth of 1 – they are both bitmaps. The source bitmap specifies the shape of the desired cursor. The 1 bits indicate the foreground color, and the 0 bits indicate the background color.

The mask pixmap is usually the same as the source but one pixel bigger in all directions. This pixmap specifies the bits of the cursor that are to be displayed. The 1 bits indicate those pixels that will be displayed, and the 0 bits indicate where the underlying screen will show through. If no mask value is present, all of the pixels in the cursor will be displayed.

The foreground and background XColor structures are used to specify the red, green, and blue values to be created for the cursor's foreground and background color. The last two parameters specify the coordinates of the cursor's hot spot.

A Complete X/Motif Client Application

Using all the concepts and techniques presented in this chapter, we can put together a simple, but complete, X/Motif-based client application. Example 24.1 shows the code for a program that has DrawingArea and uses one of the predefined bitmaps for a background. The program converts the bitmap into a pixmap and installs it as the background for the DrawingArea.

```
Cursor XCreatePixmapCursor(display, source, mask,
                           foreground, background, x_hot_spot, y_hot_spot)

Display       *display;
Pixmap        source;
Pixmap        mask;
XColor        foreground;
XColor        background;
unsigned int  x_hot_spot;
unsigned int  y_hot_spot;
```

Figure 24.9 XCreatePixmapCursor() syntax.

```
#include <stdio.h>
#include <Xm/DrawingA.h>
#include <Xll/bitmaps/wingdogs>

#define FONT1 \
    "-adobe-new century schoolbook-bold-r-normal--24-240-75-75-p-149-iso8859-1"

XtEventHandler drawIt();

Widget topShell;
Display *display;
Screen *screen;
Window root;
Colormap colormap;
Cardinal depth;
XFontStruct *myFont;
XColor white;
XColor red;
XColor green;
XColor orange;
XColor exact;
GC myGC;

main(argc, argv)
Cardinal argc;
String argv[];
    {
    Widget draw;
    Pixmap myPixmap;
    Arg argList[10];
    Cardinal i;

    /* Initialize  the Intrinsics and create a top Shell widget */
    topShell = XtInitialize(argv[0], "Edit", NULL, 0, &argc, argv);
```

Example 24.1 X/Motif application program using a pixmap, part 1.

Figure 24.10 shows what the program would look like on a typical terminal screen.

Review Questions

¤ Please write down the answers to the following questions:

1. What is a pixmap?

```
/* Get some server specific information */
display = XtDisplay(topShell);
screen = XtScreen(topShell);
root = RootWindowOfScreen(screen);
colormap = DefaultColormapOfScreen(screen);
depth = DefaultDepthOfScreen(screen);
myFont = XLoadQueryFont(display, FONT1);
XAllocNamedColor(display, colormap, "white", &white, &exact);
XAllocNamedColor(display, colormap, "red", &red, &exact);
XAllocNamedColor(display, colormap, "green", &green, &exact);
XAllocNamedColor(display, colormap, "orange", &orange, &exact);
myPixmap = XCreatePixmapFromBitmapData(display, root, wingdogs_bits,
    wingdogs_width, wingdogs_height, green.pixel, orange.pixel, depth);
    myGC = XCreateGC(display, root, NULL, NULL);

/* Create the user interface widgets */
i = 0;
XtSetArg(argList[i], XmNheight, 200); i++;
XtSetArg(argList[i], XmNwidth, 200); i++;
XtSetArg(argList[i], XmNbackgroundPixmap, myPixmap); i++;
draw = XmCreateDrawingArea(topShell, "draw", argList, i);

/* Set up event handlers for the widgets */
XtAddEventHandler(draw, ExposureMask, False, drawIt, NULL);

/* Make the program visible on the screen */
XtManageChild(draw);
XtRealizeWidget(topShell);

/* Wait for input events */
XtMainLoop();
}
```

Example 24.2 X/Motif application program using a pixmap, part 2.

2. How is memory organized for a pixmap?

3. List several different uses for pixmaps.

4. Which function is used to create a pixmap?

5. Where are pixmaps stored?

6. Which function is used to get rid of a pixmap?

7. How do you clear a pixmap?

8. Which function is used to copy a pixmap?

```
XtEventHandler drawIt(widget_id,  client_data, call_data)
Widget widget_id;
caddr_t client_data;
caddr_t call_data;
    {
    Window window = XtWindow(widget_id);
    static XTextItem myText = {"Hello World", 11, 0, None};
    static XPoint poPoints[] = { 75, 150,  70, 125, 125,  120, 100, 175};
    Pixel black = BlackPixelOfScreen(screen);
    Pixmap myPixmap;

    /* Draw something on the screen */
    XSetFont(display, myGC, myFont->fid);
        XSetForeground(display, myGC, white.pixel);
    XDrawText(display, window, myGC, 20, 100, &myText, 1);
        XSetForeground(display, myGC, red.pixel);
    XSetLineAttributes(display, myGC, 2, LineSolid, CapRound, JoinRound);
    XDrawLine(display, window, myGC, 10, 103, 180, 103);

    /* Return control to the calling function */
    return;
    }
```

Example 24.3 X/Motif application program using a pixmap, part 3.

Figure 24.10 Output of the previous X/Motif application program.

9. What is the difference between a pixmap and a bitmap?

10. What is the purpose of the bitmap program?

11. What is the output of the bitmap program?

12. Which function is used to convert a bitmap into a pixmap?

13. Where are the standard X bitmaps located?

14. What is the purpose of the xsetroot program?

15. How do you construct a cursor, and which function do you use to do it?

Exercises

The following exercises are designed to give you the opportunity to practice the concepts and facilities presented in this chapter:

1. Pick one or two of the standard bitmaps out of the /usr/include/X11/-bitmaps directory, and use the bitmap client to look at them.

2. Pick a bitmap from the /usr/include/X11/bitmaps directory as well as two colors from the /usr/lib/X11/rgb.txt file, and use the xsetroot client to change the root window background.

3. Use the bitmap client to create a new bitmap. Give the bitmap graphic a database look-and-feel. Modify the database program that you were building a few chapters ago. Each one of the MessageBox style dialog boxes that you created inherits a pixmap resource called XmNsymbolPixmap. Convert your bitmap into a pixmap, and change this resource to use your bitmap for the dialog box symbol instead of the default.

Motif
Window Manager
(Optional)

Introduction

¤ Sometimes, when writing a X/Motif client application, just writing the C code is not enough. There will be times when you will want more control over the window management functions controlling the windows of your application. For this reason, it is important to understand how you can control and configure mwm – the Motif window manager. In this chapter you will learn about the resources and other features that can be used to configure mwm.

Objectives

¤ After completing this chapter, you will be able to:

  ¤ Describe the purpose of a window manager.

  ¤ List three different window manager programs.

  ¤ List some of the user controls typically provided by a window manager.

  ¤ Explain how to start a window manager.

  ¤ Explain which files are used by xinit and xdm at startup.

  ¤ Describe the contents of the startup files for xinit and xdm.

  ¤ List four of the standard command-line options and what they do.

◻ Explain Motif's input selection model.

◻ List the two types of keyboard focus policy and explain how they differ.

◻ Explain the purpose of a widget's highlight area.

◻ List the resources that need to be set to see a widget's highlight.

◻ Describe the concept of keyboard traversal.

◻ List the two things that must be done to use keyboard traversal.

◻ Explain how you traverse the children of a manager that have been added as a tab group.

◻ List the two functions used to work with tab groups.

◻ Describe the restrictions that some widgets have with respect to tab groups.

◻ Use resources to configure mwm and its ability to manage other client windows.

◻ Explain the purpose of the .mwmrc and system.mwmrc files.

◻ Describe the syntax used to specify button bindings to mwm.

◻ Describe the syntax used to specify key bindings to mwm.

◻ Describe the syntax used to specify menu descriptions to mwm.

Purpose of a Window Manager

◻ By way of a review, you will remember that the purpose of a window manager is to manage the X Terminal's root window space. The X Window System installs the root window on the bitmapped graphic display terminal screen, and when a window manager is running, it further controls the mapping, placing, moving, and resizing of any other windows to be displayed by any other client. The window manager is just another X client that has special privileges when it comes to manipulating windows on the terminal screen.

You should also remember that up through X11R3 window managers are not required in the X Window System. But in Release 4 and later releases, they will be required. Although a particular widget set may be delivered with a window manager, a widget set does not depend on a particular window manager. Mwm is the standard Motif window manager but any Motif application can be run just as well with awm (the Athena window manager), uwm (the universal window manager), twm (Tom's window manager), or any other window manager.

From a previous chapter you will recall that mwm provides a distinctive three-dimensional appearance that enhances the visual appearance of the Motif widgets. Controls are provided to move, resize, and restack windows. The Motif window manager has many other features, functions, and facilities that let you control the operation of the window manager in a variety of different ways. The purpose of this chapter, then, is to introduce you to some of these capabilities.

¤ If a window manager was not started for you (your terminal emulator window does not have its client decorations), you can start it yourself. Simply type mwm as a command in the terminal emulator window and *make sure you run it in the background.* You can also arrange to have mwm executed automatically for you when you start X with either xdm or xinit.

When the xinit command is executed, it looks for a startup batch file in your home directory called .xinitrc (just as the Bourne shell in UNIX looks for a .profile file or MS/DOS looks for an autoexec.bat file). This batch file contains all the commands that you want executed whenever you run xinit. The xdm command looks for a file called .xsession. (Other commands that start X will probably use different files.)

It is in these startup batch files that your terminal emulator client is started. Any other client that you want to run when you start X is also entered as a command in these files — including a window manager. An important point to remember about these files is that any client that puts up a window and waits for input (even if it is just input to close the window as in an xclock or xlogo) *must be run in the background.* If you don't run them in the background, then, just like any other command in a batch file, it will wait until it completes before going on to the next command in the file.

Every X client in these batch files except the last command is run in the background. When the last command in these files finishes executing, X terminates, the server shuts down, and control of the terminal screen is returned to the operating system. Example 25.1 shows what a typical .xinitrc file might look like for the xinit command. The corresponding .xsession file for xdm would be virtually identical.

The -fg and -bg options on the xsetroot command as well as the -title and -geometry options on the xterm commands are standard X client command-line options. These options can be specified on any X client and are parsed

```
$ cat .xinitrc
resources=$HOME/.Xdefaults
bitdir=/usr/include/X11/bitmaps
stty erase '^h'
TERM=vt100
export TERM

if [ -f $resources ]
then
        xrdb -load $resources
fi
xsetroot -bitmap $bitdir/itdc6 -fg MediumAquamarine -bg firebrick
xlogo &
xclock &
mwm &
xterm -title "vt100 terminal emulator" -geometry 80x24+40+40 -ls &
exec xterm -title "vt100 terminal emulator" -geometry 80x24+10+10 +ls
```

Example 25.1 A typical .xinitrc file for xinit.

and analyzed through the argc and argv parameters passed to XtInitialize().
Figure 25.1 shows a complete list of all standard options that are recognized.

All the color options are followed by a color name selected from the
/usr/lib/X11/rgb.txt file or a hexadecimal color specification as described in
the chapter on color. The font option is followed by a standard font name as
described in the chapter on fonts. The -xrm option is followed by a quoted
resource specification as described in the chapter on resources.

The -display option describes the combination of server and screen, and
on which host in the network that the client should display its output on.
The format of the string that follows -display is [host]:server#[.screen#]
(with the brackets ([ ]) indicating an optional item). The default value is
typically unix:0.0, which indicates the local system (unix means the local
system), server number 0 (:0), and screen number 0 (.0). This information
can also be specified in the DISPLAY environment variable.

The -title and -name options are both followed by character strings. The
string that follows the -title option will be placed into the title bar by mwm.
The string that follows the -name option modifies how the application will
interpret resource files.

The -geometry option is followed by a geometry string of the form
width×height±xoffset±yoffset [with the parenthesis (( )) indicating that a
choice must be made between items separated by a vertical bar (|)] and
controls the initial size and position of the client window. All values are
usually specified in pixels with the width being separated from the height

```
Option            X resource name    Description
-----------       ---------------     ------------------------------------------------

-background       background          Background color of window
-bg                                   An abbreviation for -background
-bordercolor      borderColor         Color of window border
-bd                                   An abbreviation for -bordercolor
-borderwidth      borderWidth         Border width of a window in pixels
-bw                                   An abbreviation for -borderwidth
-display          display             Display for client to run on
-font             font                Font for text display
-fn                                   An abbreviation for -font
-foreground       foreground          Foreground color for drawing or text in window
-fg                                   An abbreviation for -foreground
-geometry         geometry            Initial window placement and size
-iconic                               Start the application in iconified form
-name             name                Name of application
-reverse          reverseVideo        Reverse foreground and background colors
-rv                                   An abbreviation for -reverse
+rv               reverseVideo        Don't reverse foreground and background colors
-synchronous      synchronous         Synchronous mode--useful for debugging
-title            title               Window title--used by mwm in the title bar
-xrm              next argument       For resource specification
```

Figure 25.1 Standard command-line options.

by a lowercase X, the height from the origin's X offset by a plus or minus sign, and the origin's X offset from its Y offset by another plus or minus sign. Positive offsets are calculated from the upper-left corner of the root window, while negative offsets are calculated from lower-right corner of the root window. Some clients interpret these numbers differently – the xterm looks at the width and height as the numbers of columns and rows of text.

¤ Another purpose of the window manager is to manage input focus.

Motif's Input Selection Model

¤ The Motif input selection model specifies that a window must be selected (have input focus) before an action is performed on it (with keyboard or mouse button input). With the window manager this is a fairly straightforward concept.

With any number of clients executing in an X session, only one of them can have input focus at a time. With your experience to this point you should have noticed that the window that has input focus under mwm has client decorations of a color different from that of the inactive windows. This one window is the only client application that can receive input from the keyboard or the mouse.

Specifying which window gets input focus can be done in one of two ways. If mwm's keyboardFocusPolicy resource is set to explicit, the user must click mouse button 1 in a window to move input focus to that window. If the keyboardFocusPolicy is set to pointer, whichever window the mouse pointer is currently in will be the window that gets input focus. Figure 25.2 shows how this resource would be set in a resource file. Explicit policy is the default.

¤ Determining which widget in an application has focus is a little more difficult proposition. From our discussion of resources you may remember that each widget in your X/Motif client application has the ability to display a highlight area. The highlight area is an area around each widget instance that becomes visible when the widget receives input focus. So, you can tell which widget has input focus by looking for the one displaying its highlight.

However, the highlight will become visible around the widget that has input only if one of two conditions is in effect. With the XmNhighlightOnEnter resource set to True, either the VendorShell's XmNkeyboardFocusPolicy is set to pointer or the widget's XmNtraversalOn is set to True. (*traversal* is defined as the movement of input focus from widget to widget using keyboard keystrokes instead of pointer motion or mouse clicks.) Figure 25.3 shows the two sets of resource entries that could be used to make use of the highlight area to identify which widget has input focus.

¤ In order to use keyboard traversal, there are two things you must do. First, you must set the traversalOn resource to true. However, just setting the traversalOn resource to True is not enough – the name is

```
Mwm*keyboardFocusPolicy: pointer
```

Figure 25.2 Setting mwm's keyboardFocusPolicy.

```
Mwm*keyboardFocusPolicy:                    explicit
*traversalOn:                               true
*highlightOnEnter:                          true
*highlightColor:                            red
*highlightThickness:                        5


   -- OR --


Mwm*keyboardFocusPolicy:                    pointer
*highlightOnEnter:                          true
*highlightColor:                            red
*highlightThickness:                        5
```

Figure 25.3 Resources for highlighting the input focus widget.

misleading – the second thing required for keyboard traversal is to add tab groups. It is important to note that the traversalOn resource has no effect at all unless the XmNkeyboardFocusPolicy is set to explicit.

A tab group is either a primitive or a manager widget that can have input focus passed to it from some other widget when the user presses the <tab> key on the keyboard. Pressing <shift><tab> on the keyboard will move input focus to the previous tab group. The order in which tab groups are added determines the order of keyboard traversal using the tab key. If a manager widget is added as a tab group, input focus can move between its children by using the arrow keys. The order in which the children are added to the manager determines the order of keyboard traversal using the arrow keys on the keyboard.

A widget can be added as a tab group for keyboard traversal using the function XmAddTabGroup(). A widget configured as a tab group can be removed from keyboard traversal using the function XmRemoveTabGroup(). Figure 25.4 shows the syntax for these two functions.

There are certain widgets that must be added as their own separate tab group and cannot be placed in a manager that is added as a tab group. The List widget, multiline Text widgets, OptionMenu widgets, and ScrollBar widgets cannot be the child of a manager widget that has been identified as a tab group because each of these widgets uses the arrow keys for its specific operation. If all these widgets were placed in a tab group manager, there would be confusion as to how the arrow keys should be interpreted.

```
#include <Xm/Xm.h>

void XmAddTabGroup(tab_group)
void XmRemoveTabGroup(tab_group)

Widget tab_group;
```

Figure 25.4 XmAddTabGroup() and XmRemoveTabGroup() syntax.

□   In Motif 1.1 the XmNtraversalOn resource is true by default. Also, every widget is automatically added as a tab group. Since the default XmNkeyboardFocusPolicy is explicit, this means that keyboard traversal is enabled automatically in 1.1. To disable keyboard traversal, simply set the XmNtraversalOn resource for all your widgets to False.

Motif Window Manager Resources

□   Since mwm is just another client application program, there are a number of mwm resources that can be applied to the window manager and to the client windows it controls. These mwm resources can be grouped into three classifications:

component appearance	These resources control the visual appearance of the client decorations and other user interface components under the control of mwm.
specific appearance and behavior	These resources control the look-and-feel of mwm in general and are not set for separate user interface components.
client-specific	These resources can be set for a particular client or class of clients and specify client-specific icon and client decoration look-and-feel.

All these resources can be specified in any of the resource files mentioned in the chapter on resource files. The syntax for these resource specifications is identical to all other resource specifications you have used in the previous chapters with some additions that are specific to the mwm client.

□   The component appearance resources are used to change the visual appearance of all the user interface components of mwm. The syntax for these resources can be specified as

```
Mwm*resource_name: value
```

where resource__name is the name of the resource whose value you want changed and value is the value that you want to change the resource to. This type of resource specification will affect all user interface components controlled by mwm. If you want only specific classes of user interface components affected, the syntax is

```
Mwm*(menu|icon|client|feedback)*resource_name: value
```

where the parentheses (( )) indicate that a choice must be made between the items separated by vertical bars (|). The keyword menu specifies that only mwm menus will be affected, icon will cause only icons to be affected, client specifies that only client decorations will be affected, and feedback causes mwm feedback mechanisms (such as the outline of a window being moved) to be affected.

To affect only the title area of the client decorations, the syntax can be specified as

```
Mwm*client*title*resource_name: value
```

where the keyword title specifies that the mwm button, the title area, the minimize button, and the maximize button should be affected. You can also modify a specific menu that you have created in your .mwmrc file (more on this later) by using the syntax

```
Mwm*menu*menu_name*resource_name: value
```

where the menu__name is the name of a menu that you have created. Figure 25.5 shows the names and types of the component appearance resources.

```
                          All Window Manager Parts

Name                             Value Type (Default Value)
------------------------------   ---------------------------------------
background                       color (varies [1])
backgroundPixmap                 string [2] (varies [1])
bottomShadowColor                color (varies [1])
bottomShadowPixmap               string [2] (varies [1])
fontList                         string [3] ("fixed")
foreground                       color (varies [1])
saveUnder                        True/False (False)
topShadowColor                   color (varies [1])
topShadowPixmap                  string [2] (varies [1])


                       Frame and Icon Components Only

Name                             Value Type (Default Value)
------------------------------   ---------------------------------------
activeBackground                 color (varies [1])
activeBackgroundPixmap           string [2] (varies [1])
activeBottomShadowColor          color (varies [1])
activeBottomShadowPixmap         string [2] (varies [1])
activeForeground                 color (varies [1])
activeTopShadowColor             color (varies [1])
activeTopShadowPixmap            string [2] (varies [1])

[1] The default is chosen based on the visual class of the screen
[2] Specified as a pixmap image name or bitmap file name
[3] An X11R3 font name
```

Figure 25.5 Mwm component appearance resources.

□   The specific appearance and behavior resources apply to the look-and-feel of mwm as a whole and do not apply to specific user interface components. The syntax for specifying these resources is

```
Mwm*resource_name: value
```

Figure 25.6 shows the names and types of the specific appearance and behavior resources.

□   The client-specific resources apply to the look-and-feel of specific clients or classes of clients that mwm controls. The syntax for specifying these resources is

```
Mwm*client_name_or_class*resource_name: value
```

where client_name_or_class is the instance name or class name of an application. These resources can be specified for all clients regardless of name or class with

```
Mwm*resource_name: value
```

Figure 25.7 shows the names and types of the client-specific resources.

□   As before, the Motif documentation describes each of these resources in detail and gives lists of the possible values for each one. To include all that information in this book would make it much larger and difficult to use as a study guide for learning Motif (which is the intent). Once again, have a good set of reference documentation handy before you start to write applications or configure the window manager in Motif.

□   When the Motif window manager (mwm) starts up, it looks for its own "startup batch file" in your home directory. This file is a special type of resource file and is named .mwmrc. The .mwmrc file can contain three types of things:

button bindings   Descriptions of what actions to take in response to specific mouse buttons being pressed

key bindings   Descriptions of what actions to take in response to specific keyboard keys being pressed

menu descriptions   Descriptions of menus that are posted by mwm and the actions to take in response to chosen items

If Motif cannot find .mwmrc in your home directory, it will go to the /usr/lib/X11 directory and look for a file called system.mwmrc. In either case one of these files is read, and its contents are used to further configure the window manager's operation. Figure 25.8 shows what a typical .mwmrc file would look like.

```
Name                              Value Type (Default Value)
--------------------------------  -------------------------------------
autoKeyFocus                      True/False (True)
autoRaiseDelay                    milliseconds (500)
bitmapDirectory                   directory (/usr/include/X11/bitmaps)
buttonBindings                    string (NULL)
cleanText                         True/False (True)
clientAutoPlace                   True/False (True)
colormapFocusPolicy               string (keyboard)
configFile                        file (.mwmrc)
deiconifyKeyFocus                 True/False (True)
doubleClickTime                   milliseconds (500)
enforceKeyFocus                   True/False (True)
fadeNormalIcon                    True/False (False)
frameBorderWidth                  pixels (5)
iconAutoPlace                     True/False (True)
iconBoxGeometry                   string (6x1+0-0)
iconBoxName                       string (iconbox)
iconBoxTitle                      string (Icons)
iconClick                         True/False (True)
iconDecoration                    string (varies)
iconImageMaximum                  widthxheight in pixels (50x50)
iconImageMinimum                  widthxheight in pixels (32x32)
iconPlacement                     string (left bottom)
iconPlacementMargin               pixels (varies)
interactivePlacement              True/False (False)
keyBindings                       string (system)
keyboardFocusPolicy               string (explicit)
limitResize                       True/False (True)
lowerOnIconify                    True/False (True)
maximumMaximumSize                widthxheight in pixels (2*screen width/height)
moveThreshold                     pixels (4)
passButtons                       True/False (False)
passSelectButton                  True/False (True)
positionIsFrame                   True/False (True)
positionOnScreen                  True/False (True)
quitTimeout                       milliseconds (1000)
resizeBorderWidth                 pixels (10)
resizeCursors                     True/False (True)
showFeedback                      string (all)
startupKeyFocus                   True/False (True)
transientDecoration               string (system title)
transientFunctions                string (-minimize -maximize)
useIconBox                        True/False (False)
wMenuButtonClick                  True/False (True)
wMenuButtonClick2                 True/False (True)
```

Figure 25.6 Mwm specific appearance and behavior resources.

```
Name                            Value Type (Default Value)
------------------------------  --------------------------------------
clientDecorations               string (all)
clientFunctions                 string (all)
focusAutoRaise                  True/False (True)
iconImage                       pathname ((image))
iconImageBackground             color (icon background)
iconImageBottomShadowColor      color (icon bottom shadow)
iconImageBottomShadowPixmap     color (icon bottom shadow pixmap)
iconImageForeground             color (icon foreground)
iconImageTopShadowColor         color (icon top shadow)
iconImageTopShadowPixmap        color (icon top shadow pixmap)
matteBackground                 color (background)
matteBottomShadowColor          color (bottom shadow color)
matteBottomShadowPixmap         color (bottom shadow pixmap)
matteForeground                 color (foreground)
matteTopShadowColor             color (top shadow color)
matteTopShadowPixmap            color (top shadow pixmap)
matteWidth                      pixels (0)
maximumClientSize               widthxheight (fill the screen)
useClientIcon                   True/False (False)
windowMenu                      string (string)
```

Figure 25.7 Mwm client-specific resources.

The syntax used to specify the key bindings, mouse bindings, and menu descriptions is given in the following sections.

Motif Keyboard Bindings

α   The window manager can look for and act on key press events (key release events are ignored) within several different contexts during an X session. Within your .mwmrc file, a key binding set is created and given a name. A particular key binding set is made active by setting the XmNkeyBindings resource for your client to the desired key binding set name. The specified key bindings will replace the default key bindings for that client. The syntax for a key binding set is as follows:

```
Keys binding_set_name
{
    key    context    function
    ...
    key    context    function
}
```

where the binding__set__name is the name you have created for the binding set to be installed in the XmNkeyBindings resource. The key is a specification of which key sequence you want to watch for and has a syntax of

```
Menu RootMenu
{
    "Root Menu"          f.title
    no-label             f.separator
    "New Window"         f.exec "xterm &"
    "Shuffle Up"         f.circle_up
    "Shuffle Down"       f.circle_down
    "Refresh"            f.refresh
    no-label             f.separator
    "Restart..."         f.restart
}


Menu DefaultWindowMenu MwmWindowMenu
{
    "Restore"    _R      Alt<Key>F5      f.normalize
    "Move"       _M      Alt<Key>F7      f.move
    "Size"       _S      Alt<Key>F8      f.resize
    "Minimize"   _n      Alt<Key>F9      f.minimize
    "Maximize"   _x      Alt<Key>F10     f.maximize
    "Lower"      _L      Alt<Key>F3      f.lower
    no-label                             f.separator
    "Close"      _C      Alt<Key>F4      f.kill
}



Keys DefaultKeyBindings
{
    Shift<Key>Escape           icon|window          f.post_wmenu
    Meta<Key>space             icon|window          f.post_wmenu
    Meta<Key>Tab               root|icon|window     f.next_key
    Meta Shift<Key>Tab         root|icon|window     f.prev_key
    Meta<Key>Escape            root|icon|window     f.next_key
    Meta Shift<Key>Escape      root|icon|window     f.prev_key
    Meta Ctrl Shift<Key>exclam root|icon|window     f.set_behavior
    Meta<Key>F6                window               f.next_key transient
}

Buttons DefaultButtonBindings
{
    <Btn1Down>          frame|icon      f.raise
    <Btn2Down>          frame|icon      f.post_wmenu
    <Btn1Down>          root            f.menu  RootMenu
    Meta<Btn1Down>      icon|window     f.lower
    Meta<Btn2Down>      window|icon     f.resize
    Meta<Btn3Down>      window          f.move
}
```

Figure 25.8 Typical .mwmrc file.

```
[modifier_list]<Key>key_name
```

where the optional modifier__list is a blank-separated list of one or more of the keywords Ctrl, Shift, Alt or Meta, Lock, Mod1, Mod2, Mod3, Mod4, or Mod5. The string <Key> is literal and the key_name identifies the key on the keyboard that the binding is being defined for. Key names are specified as keysym names, as was discussed in the chapter on X events, with the XK__ prefix removed.

The context is a specification of which item (X window) on the screen must have input focus for the key press to take effect and is a vertical bar (|)-separated list of one or more of the keywords root, icon, window, title, frame, border, or app. And, the function is an mwm internal function to execute when the specified key press event occurs in the specified context. A list of available functions is given in Figure 25.9.

Motif Mouse Button Bindings

The window manager can look for and act on button press events (button release events are ignored) within several different contexts during an X session. Within your .mwmrc file a button binding set is created and given a name. A particular button binding set is made active by setting the XmNbuttonBindings resource for your client to the desired button binding set name. The specified button bindings will be merged with the default button bindings for that client. The syntax for a button binding set is as follows:

```
Buttons binding_set_name
{
    button    context    function
    ...
    button    context    function
}
```

where the binding__set__name is the name you have created for the binding set to be installed in the XmNbuttonBindings resource. The button is a specification of which button press you want to watch for and has a syntax of

```
[modifier_list]<button_event_name>
```

where the modifier__list is the same as was described for key bindings. The angle brackets (< >) are literal, and the button_event_name is chosen from the following:

```
Function                              Description
------------------------------------  ----------------------------------------
f.beep                                Ring terminal bell.
f.circle_down [icon|window]           Put window currently on top of window
                                         stack on bottom.
f.circle_up [icon|window]             Put bottom window on top of stack.
f.exec command                        Execute specified operating system
                                         command.
f.focus_color                         Set colormap focus to a client window.
f.focus_key                           Set keyboard focus to a client window.
f.kill                                Terminate a client application
f.lower [-client_name]                Lower a client window to bottom of stack.
f.maximize                            Display a client window with maximum
                                         size.
f.menu menu_name                      Cause a menu or cascade menu to display.
f.minimize                            Display a client window as an icon.
f.move                                Allow a client window to be moved
                                         interactively.
f.next_cmap                           Install next colormap in colormap list.
f.next_key [icon|window|transient]    Set keyboard input focus to next icon,
                                         window,  or transient window.
f.nop                                 Do nothing.
f.normalize                           Display a client window with normal
                                         size.
f.pack_icons                          Relayout icons based on layout policy.
f.pass_keys                           Enable/disable (toggle) key binding set.
f.post_wmenu                          Post the window manager menu.
f.prev_cmap                           Install previous colormap in colormap
                                         list.
f.prev_key [icon|window|transient]    Set keyboard input focus to previous icon,
                                         window,  or transient window.
f.quit_mwm                            Terminates mwm but not X.
f.raise [-client_name]                Raise a client window to top of stack.
f.raise_lower                         Raise a client window if partially obscured
                                         otherwise lower a client window.
f.refresh                             Redraw all windows.
f.refresh_win                         Redraw a client window.
f.resize                              Allow a client window to be resized
                                         interactively.
f.restart                             Terminate and restart mwm.
f.send_msg message_number             Send a client message of a type specified
                                         by message_number.
f.separator                           Display a separator in a menu.
f.set_behavior                        Restart mwm with a different behavior.
f.title                               Display a title in a menu.
```

Figure 25.9 Functions available for key bindings, button bindings, and menus.

```
Btn1Down    -Button 1 Press            Btn3Click  -Button 3 Press/Release
Btn1Up      -Button 1 Release          Btn3Click2 -Button 3 Double Click
Btn1Click   -Button 1 Press/Release    Btn4Down   -Button 4 Press
Btn1Click2  -Button 1 Double Click     Btn4Up     -Button 4 Release
Btn2Down    -Button 1 Press            Btn4Click  -Button 4 Press/Release
Btn2Up      -Button 2 Release          Btn4Click2 -Button 4 Double Click
Btn2Click   -Button 2 Press/Release    Btn5Down   -Button 5 Press
Btn2Click2  -Button 2 Double Click     Btn5Up     -Button 5 Release
Btn3Down    -Button 3 Press            Btn5Click  -Button 5 Press/Release
Btn3Up      -Button 3 Release          Btn5Click2 -Button 5 Double Click
```

The context and the function are the same as those described for key bindings.

Motif Window Manager Menus

◻ The two mwm menus that you are familiar with, the window manager menu and the root menu, are both handled with menu descriptions in your .mwmrc or the system.mwmrc file. Other menus can be created with this mechanism, too. A key binding or a button binding can be used to post a menu using the f.menu function followed by a menu_name. (One menu cascading from another menu is also possible.) The menu_name identifies a menu description with the following syntax:

```
Menu menu_name
{
    label   [mnemonic]   [accelerator]   function
    ...
    label   [mnemonic]   [accelerator]   function
}
```

where the label is the quoted string that will appear as the Label on the PushButton used to implement a menu choice. The optional mnemonic is a literal underscore (_) followed by one of the characters in the Label. This character will be underlined in the Label to indicate that the menu choice can be activated from the keyboard by typing the letter. The optional accelerator is a key event specification (with the same syntax used for key bindings) that identifies how to activate a menu choice from the keyboard without posting the menu.

Review Questions

◻ Please write down the answers to the following questions:

1. What is the purpose of a window manager?

2. List three different window manager programs.

3. List some of the user controls typically provided by a window manager.

4. How do you start a window manager?

5. Which files are used by xinit and xdm at startup?

6. What do you put in the startup files for xinit and xdm?

7. List four of the standard command-line options and what they do.

8. What is Motif's input selection model?

9. List the two types of keyboard focus policy and explain how they differ.

10. What is the purpose of a widget's highlight area?

11. List the resources that need to be set to see a widget's highlight.

12. What is keyboard traversal?

13. List the two things that must be done to use keyboard traversal.

14. How do you traverse the children of manager that has been added as a tab group?

15. List the two functions used to work with tab groups.

16. What restrictions do some widgets have with respect to tab groups?

17. List five resources used to configure mwm, and describe their purpose.

18. What is the purpose of the .mwmrc and system.mwmrc files?

19. What syntax is used to specify button bindings to mwm?

20. What syntax is used to specify key bindings to mwm?

21. What syntax is used to specify menu descriptions to mwm?

Exercises

The following exercises are designed to give you the opportunity to practice the concepts and facilities presented in this chapter:

1. Determine whether there are any other window managers available on your system (awm, uwm, twm, etc). Window managers, along with most other X binaries, are usually located in /usr/bin/X11. If another window manager is available, use the command appropriate to your operating system to terminate mwm and start another window manager in its place.

2. Restart mwm.

3. Modify the startup batch file appropriate to the command you use to start X so that the xlogo, xclock, and another xterm are started automatically the next time you start X.

4. Exit X and restart to see the previous changes take effect.

5. Execute another xclock with a background color of wheat, a foreground color of forest green, and a title of "time."

6. Within your .Xdefaults file or the resource manager property of the root window, change your keyboard focus policy to the opposite of what it is now. Terminate and restart X (you may need to restart only mwm) to

see how the new policy operates.

7. Modify any one of your previous multiwidget programs and enable keyboard traversal in it. Set up the tab groups so that you can move input focus between widgets with the keyboard.

8. Within your .Xdefaults file or the resource manager property of the root window, set up the mwm resources necessary to display the icon box. Let the icon box show one row of four icons, and give the box a title of "My Icons."

9. If you don't have a .mwmrc file already, copy the system.mwmrc file to your home directory. Modify the root window menu to add options to execute your database programs and drawing programs from the previous chapters. Terminate and restart X (you may need to restart only mwm) to see the new menu options.

X11R4, X11R5, Motif 1.1, and Motif 1.2 (Optional)

Introduction

¤ Although the X Window System Version 11 Release 3 is still in common usage, Release 4 is starting to become more prevalent in the industry, and Release 5 has been announced and will become available soon. Also, the original version of OSF/Motif was 1.0, but Version 1.1 became available with Release 4 of X. With X11R5, OSF has also announced a newer version of Motif—OSF/Motif 1.2. This chapter outlines some of the differences between the different versions of both X and Motif.

Objectives

¤ After completing this chapter, you will be able to:

¤ List several new functions or features of the X Window System Version 11 Release 4.

¤ List several new functions or features of the X Window System Version 11 Release 5.

¤ List several new functions or features of OSF/Motif Version 1.1.

¤ List several new features of OSF/Motif Version 1.2.

X11 Release 4

◻ For the most part, programs written for Release 3 should be source code compatible with Release 4. With respect to the topics that have been presented in this book about the Xlib library, Release 4 has added some new functions of interest:

XGetGCValues()   This function uses a mask value to fill in a XGCValues structure with the values returned by the server from some specific graphics context.

XKeysymToString()   This function converts the Keysym returned in XLookupString() into an actual C character string.

XListDepths()   This function returns an array of integers that indicates the screen depths (bits per pixel) that the screen supports. Some newer terminals can support multiple screen depths.

XScreenNumberOfScreen()   This function returns the integer screen number of a specified screen pointer. Remember – X allows any one terminal to have up to three screens.

XStringToKeysym()   This function is the opposite of the one listed above and converts a C character string into a Keysym just like the one returned from XLookupString().

There are many other new and changed Xlib functions related to topics that were not presented in this book.

◻ Within the Intrinsics, new functions have been added for better support of application contexts. Remember, application contexts allow for multiple, logically separate applications to reside within the same physical address space. Additionally, application contexts allow X applications to run without change on hardware that does not support separate address spaces for each process. The functions that we have discussed in this book that have changed include:

XtAppAddTimeOut()   This function adds a timeout function to an application context to be invoked after a specified time limit has expired.

XtAppAddWorkProc()   This function adds a work procedure function to an application context to be invoked when there are no input events to process.

XtAppInitialize()   This function initializes the Intrinsics for an application context, opens a display connection, and creates a top-level shell widget.

XtAppMainLoop()   This function watches for input events for an application context and causes the appropriate callback and event-handler functions to be invoked in response.

It is important to note that if you decide to use the XtApp...() functions, you must use all of them consistently. You cannot intermix the "App" and the "non-App" functions in the same program. There are many other new Xt functions that use application contexts related to topics that were not presented in this book.

□   Another new feature in the Intrinsics is the concept of variable argument list functions. Many of the Xt functions deal with widgets, and these widgets often need what the Intrinsics call an "argument list" to supply initial resource settings. You used argument lists as the last two parameters to all of the XmCreate...() functions.

The Xt library has been extended with a number of functions which allow you to specify the resource names and values directly as parameters to a creation function. This keeps you from having to perform what appeared to be two steps to create a single widget with calls to both XtSetArg() and XmCreate...() functions. However, the arguments to these functions can be quite numerous and can require several lines of coding. The functions that we have discussed in this book that have changed include:

XtVaAppInitialize()	This function initializes the Intrinsics for an application context, opens a display connection, and creates a top-level shell widget.
XtVaCreateManagedWidget()	This function is similar to the XmCreate...() function calls that we have discussed. It creates an instance of a widget belonging to a specific widget class and manages it at the same time.
XtVaCreateWidget()	This function is the Intrinsics equivalent to the XmCreate...() function calls that we have discussed. It creates an instance of a widget belonging to a specific widget class.
XtVaGetValues()	This function retrieves resource values from an already existing widget.
XtVaSetValues()	This function sets resource values in an already existing widget.

There are many other new Xt functions that use variable argument lists related to topics that were not presented in this book.

□   A new data type has been added to the Xt Intrinsics. The type XtPointer is used in place of caddr__t to be more portable across a wider range of hardware platforms. Caddr_t is defined in <sys/types.h>, which was included for you in the <X11/Intrinsic.h> header file in Release 3. Because of this, and other new data types, some vendors' versions of Release 4 do not include <sys/types.h> for you anymore.

On those systems that do not support ANSI-compiant C compilers, the X Window System's definition of XtPointer will be defined over a char *. In ANSI-compliant compilers it will be defined over void *. The purpose of XtPointer (as is void * in ANSI C) is to be a generic pointer type. As a generic pointer type, it should always be cast to a valid pointer type before it is used.

◻   An interesting addition to Release 4 of the X11 X Window System is the support for nonrectangular windows. This feature is not part of Xlib or Xt but, instead, was added as an optional extension. This extension, called the SHAPE extension, allows you to change the shape of a window to be the same shape as a bitmap.

In order to use the SHAPE extension, you must include the extensions library when compiling your program. Add -lXext on the cc command line to have the linker use and search the libXext.a library. This library is usually included before the -lXlib if the library ordering is important for your compiler and linker.

For more information about the SHAPE extension, look for *X11 Nonrectangular Window Shape Extension* by Keith Packard of the MIT X Consortium. It is part of the standard X11R4 release documentation from MIT.

X11 Release 5

◻   Release 5 of the X11 X Window System became available in September 1991. It usually takes a full year or more before new releases of X start becoming available on a wide range of hardware from the different computer vendors. So, you shouldn't expect to see R5 in wide use until late 1992 or early 1993. However, there are several new features that you should be aware of:

◻   PEX: Three-dimensional graphics capabilities for X

◻   Scalable fonts and a font server

◻   Internationalization services for application programs

◻   Color management services for device independent color

◻   There currently exists a library of three-dimensional graphics functions called the Programmer's Hierarchical Interactive Graphics System (PHIGS). The PHIGS library has been implemented as an International Standards Organization (ISO) standard and is available for a wide variety of systems. However, with X11, up through Release 4, only two-dimensional graphics have been available.

With X11R5 the MIT X Consortium has included PEX – the PHIGS Extensions to X. Finally, three-dimensional graphics are available with the X Window System. This will allow X to be applied to entirely new types of applications.

The release tape for Release 5 contains a sample PEX implementation consisting of three parts. It includes the server extensions for PHIGS, the application programmer interface (functions) for ISO standard PHIGS, and the application programmer interface for PHIGS PLUS, which has not been defined as a standard yet. Also included are the manual pages and other documentation for both PEX server developers and application programmers.

The MIT X Consortium also delivers a variety of PEX demo programs on the release tape. These programs can be used as coding examples for anyone interested in working with the PHIGS three-dimensional graphics capabilities available with PEX.

◻   As described in this book, with X11 up through Release 4, an X application program that uses different fonts must use a font of some predefined
size. With Release 5, X introduces the concept of scalable fonts. Adobe's
PostScript font description language is an example of scalable fonts where
the characters of the font are described with mathematical formulas instead
of using bitmaps.

Previously, each different-sized font was stored in a separate file. For
example, in a standard X11R3 implementation, there were 24 separate
files used to store the bitmaps for the Helvetica font: one each for 8, 10,
12, 14, 18, and 24 point sizes; each point size was available in a bold
weight and a medium weight; and each size and weight combination, in a
regular and an oblique slant.

In Release 5 Helvetica is described in one file. If a different size, weight,
or slant is needed, the mathematical formulas used to describe the font are
altered to fit. Two scalable font (sometimes called *outline font*) formats are
used: Adobe's Type 1 PostScript format and Bitstream's Speedo format.

When an application requests an arbitrary-sized font, X will supply a
visually appealing bitmapped version of the font if the appropriate outline
font description is available in either of the two formats. If the outline font
is missing, X will scale an old-style bitmap font for the application. Scaled
bitmapped fonts are not very good-looking but are ensured to be the
requested size.

Release 5 also supplies and makes allowances for a font server. A font
server runs independently of the X servers and can satisfy font requests for
a number of different servers at the same time. The font server is designed
to provide font services for both scaled and bitmapped fonts.

An advantage of the font server concept comes into play in a network of
computers running the X Window System. Previously, font files had to be
maintained in the file system of each user's display server. This is no longer
true with a font server. The server can run on any one machine in the network and satisfy font requests to any server on any other machine in the
network. Obviously, this will simplify X administration in network
environments.

One other change is in the format of the font files themselves. X11R5
still supports the nonportable Server Normal Format (SNF) format but has
defined a new format called PCF. PCF is the Portable Compiled Format for
fonts and is more portable across a wider variety of machines.

◻   X11R5 provides a number of ways that an application can adapt itself to
the language of its users. Release 5 calls this its "internationalization services." This involves some modifications to Xlib to support the ANSI C-
defined "locale" mechanism and support for compound strings. Related to
the internationalization efforts the MIT X Consortium has provided new
fonts for Hebrew and Kanji in the new PCF format.

◻   X11R5 also supplies something called Xcms − the X color management
system. With Xcms X applications can specify colors in a calibrated,
device-independent manner. Before Xcms X users were forced to live with
the fact that color terminals from different manufacturers displayed the
same color slightly differently. Xcms allows applications to specify a cali-
bration for colors that display perceptually identical colors on different terminals.

❑   Finally, X11R5 includes many bug fixes, useful enhancements, and some other new features. Notably, all X header files now contain ANSI C function prototypes and a new client called editres, which allows for interactive exploration and resource manipulation in a running Xt client application, and the X resource manager has been rewritten to run faster and take up less memory, which improves startup performance for client applications.

OSF/Motif 1.1

❑   With the release of X11R4, the Open Software Foundation came out with a new release of the Motif Toolkit: Version 1.1. OSF/Motif 1.1 includes the normal bug fixes, enhancements, and so on, which can be classified into several groups:

   ❑ Using the R4 Intrinsics

   ❑ Memory utilization improvements

   ❑ Resource specifications in a resource file

   ❑ Performance enhancements

   ❑ Type changes for the Position and Dimension types

❑   Motif 1.1 was changed to ensure compatibility with the R4 Intrinsics. Specifically, OSF made sure that Motif supports the R4 concept of an application context correctly. Remember that if you use any of the XtApp...() functions, you must use them all consistently – no "non-App" functions are allowed.
      Motif has also defined its own VendorShell class in 1.1 that overrides and replaces the Xt VendorShell class. This should have no effect on application programmers.

❑   Many of the enhancements that have been made revolve around improved memory usage. Changes are in the areas of sharing certain types of information, improving the implementation of the callback mechanism, combining memory allocations when possible, and fixing memory leaks.
      Memory leaks are those instances where a function allocates a chunk of memory that it needs for its processing and then "forgets" to free the memory. This "forgetfulness" causes some programs to start to grow. It is theoretically possible that these memory leaks could cause a Motif-based process to exceed its process size limits and then terminate abnormally. This was a very big problem in Motif 1.0 but has been fixed in 1.1.

❑   Motif 1.0 lets you specify defined resource values in a resource file by removing the leading Xm from the defined name. For example, the XmN-topAttachment resource for the Form widget could be defined as XmATTACH_FORM in the source code but had to be specified ATTACH_FORM or attach_form in a resource file. Motif 1.1 allows you to use either the full name or the abbreviated name in a resource file.

❑   Many of the widgets have had their internal processing algorithms rewritten to improve memory utilization and increase their speed of execution. Simply recompile your 1.0 applications with the 1.1 libraries to see a noticeable speed improvement.

◻ For compatibility with the X11R4 Intrinsics, Motif 1.1 has redefined the data types Position and Dimension to be short int instead of int. You must make sure that if you are using these two data types in your program, you use them consistently throughout. Do not use a variable of type int to pass or receive data defined as Position or Dimension—your program could break if you are not careful.

◻ If all you are doing is moving a Motif 1.0 program to 1.1, there are only a few things you need to be careful of:

 ◻ If you are using any of the R4 XtApp...() functions in your program (or any function that takes an application context as a parameter) and you are passing NULL as the application context, you have to change the function call to pass an actual application context. Passing NULL in Motif 1.1 will not produce a compile error but will cause the executable program to terminate with a bus error.

 ◻ If you are using a Text widget with a corresponding XmNtopPosition resource, you must change the name of the resource at every occurrence both in your source code and in any resource files. The XmNtopPosition resource for the Text widget has been renamed XmNtopCharacter. This change was made to resolve a conflict with the Form widget that also has an XmNtopPosition resource.

 ◻ If you are using a PanedWindow widget with a corresponding XmNmaximum or XmNminimum resource, you must change the names of those resources at every occurrence both in your source code and in any resource files. The XmNmaximum resource for the PanedWindow widget has been renamed XmNpaneMaximum, and the XmNminimum resource has been renamed to XmNpaneMinimum. This change was made to resolve a conflict with the Scale and ScrollBar widgets that also have an XmNmaximum and XmNminimum resource.

◻ Most of the changes in 1.1 that affect those Motif features that we have discussed in this book are listed below. This is not a complete list of all the changes between 1.0 and 1.1.

Motif 1.1 Changes to Metaclass Widgets

◻ The XmManager widget class has been changed:

 ⇒ The XmNnavigationType resource has been added for adding tab groups automatically. Tab groups let you move input focus from one widget to another by pressing the <tab> key on the keyboard.

 ⇒ The XmNstringDirection resource has been added so that children widgets that support this resource can inherit it from XmManager if it is not specified explicitly for the child widget itself.

◻ The XmGadget class has been changed:

 ⇒ The XmNnavigationType resource has been added.

⟹ Gadgets that have common data values will share them. This is called *instance cacheing* and results in a substantial reduction in memory requirements for gadgets.

◻ The XmPrimitive class has been changed:

⟹ The XmNnavigationType resource has been added.

◻ The VendorShell class has been changed:

⟹ The XmNdefaultFontList resource has been added so that children widgets that support this resource can inherit it from VendorShell if it is not specified explicitly for the child widget itself.

⟹ The VendorShell widget class has been moved to the Motif library.

Motif 1.1 Changes to Primitive Widgets and Gadgets

◻ Changes that are common to all widgets and gadgets:

⟹ If a widget has an XmNfontList resource that is not set at the time the widget is created, a search is made up the widget instance tree for a BulletinBoard widget. The child widget will inherit the BulletinBoard's XmNfontList resource. If there is no BulletinBoard or other manager subclassed off BulletinBoard, the child widget will inherit the XmNdefaultFontList from the VendorShell widget class.

⟹ The XmNmultiClick resource has been added to determine whether multiple mouse button clicks (double clicks, triple clicks, etc.) should be kept or discarded. There are two possible values: XmMULTI-CLICK_DISCARD and XmMULTICLICK_KEEP. The time interval between clicks that determines a multiclick operation is 200 ms (milliseconds) by default but can be set with a call to XtSetMultiClick-Time().

◻ The XmLabel and XmLabelGadget classes have been changed:

⟹ The XmNmnemonic resource has been changed from type char in 1.0 to type KeySym in 1.1. The KeySym value is converted to an XmString using the XmNmnemonicCharSet resource. This change is backward-compatible, and no changes to your source code are required.

⟹ The XmNmnemonicCharSet resource has been added to identify the character set that the XmNmnemonic character is associated with.

◻ The XmList class has been changed:

⟹ The XmListItemPos() function has been added to return the position of an item from a List.

⟹ The XmListGetMatchPos() function has been added to return True or False based on whether a specified item appears in a List.

⇒ The XmListGetSelectedPos() function has been added to return an array containing the positions of all the items that are currently selected in a List.

⇒ The XmListAddItems() function has been added to add any number of items to a List.

⇒ The XmListDeleteItems() function has been added to delete any number of items from a List based on the items.

⇒ The XmListDeleteItemsPos() function has been added to delete any number of items from a List based on item positions.

⇒ The XmListDeleteAllItems() function has been added to delete all items from a List.

⇒ The XmListReplaceItems() function has been added to allow for the replacement of items in a List without deleting and inserting.

⇒ The XmListReplaceItemsPos() function has been added to allow for the replacement of items in a List at a specific position.

⇒ The XmListSetAddMode() function has been added to allow for programmatic control of the add mode in a List in the extended selection model.

⇒ The XmListCallbackStruct has been modified by adding a member called selected_item_positions. This is a pointer to an integer array containing the positions of the items currently selected in a List.

⇒ A new selection mode is defined called the Add mode. This mode was added to enhance the compatibility of the List widget with the IBM Common User Access definition.

⇒ The XmNdoubleClickInterval resource has had its default value changed to dynamic. If the resource is not explicitly set for a List by the application, it inherits the default value defined by the new R4 Intrinsics multiclick model.

◻ The XmPushButton and XmPushButtonGadget classes have been changed:

⇒ The XmNshowAsDefault resource has been changed to Boolean. When True, then the PushButton will have an extra shadow drawn around it. In 1.0, this resource was used to specify the width of the shadow around the button as well as whether it was the default button.

⇒ The XmNdefaultButtonShadowThickness resource has been added to specify the width of the shadow around the default button.

⇒ There is now a two-pixel space between the default button's default shadow and the highlight area. There was no space in 1.0.

◻ The XmScrollBar class has been changed:

⟹ The user interaction with a ScrollBar has been modified to conform with the new version of the Style Guide.

⟹ The colors used for the ScrollBar have changed. The slider trough now defaults to the select color, the color of the slider now defaults to the background color, and the color of the arrows also defaults to the background color.

⟹ The XmNprocessingDirection resource default value has been changed to depend on the value of the XmNorientation resource. If the XmNorientation is set to XmVERTICAL, XmNprocessingDirection is set to XmMAX_ON_BOTTOM. For XmHORIZONTAL, it is set to XmMAX_ON_RIGHT. These values can be overridden.

◻ The XmText class has been changed:

⟹ Three different cursors are now available for the Text widget. Which one appears depends on what state the Text widget is in. The caret (destination cursor) is used to copy or move a primary selection to a new location. The I-beam (insertion cursor) is the standard cursor used in normal Text operations. The stippled I-beam is used for a newly defined Add mode.

⟹ The Add mode allows the insertion cursor to be moved away from the primary selection to allow text to be added to a Text widget without affecting the selected text. XmTextGetAddMode() and XmTextSet-AddMode() functions have been added for the support of Add mode.

⟹ XmTextCopy(), XmTextCut(), XmTextPaste(), and XmTextRemove() functions have been added to support clipboard cut-and-paste operations.

⟹ New keyboard bindings have been added to make the Text widget comply with the Style Guide. Keyboard bindings are those actions that take place when the user interacts with the Text widget through the keyboard.

⟹ The XmTextInsert() function has been added to simplify the use of the XmTextReplace() function.

⟹ The XmTextGetBaseline() function has been added to get the X-coordinate of the first character of the first line relative to the 0 position of a Text widget.

⟹ The XmTextGetSource() function has been added for the support of sources. Text widgets can share sources so that editing in one source can be reflected in another source.

⟹ The XmTextSetSource() function has been added for support of sources.

⟹ The XmTextGetTopCharacter() function has been added to retrieve the position of the first character that is displayed in a Text widget.

⟹ The XmTextSetTopCharacter() function has been added to set the position of the first character that is displayed in a Text widget.

⟹ The XmTextGetCursorPosition() function has been added to retrieve the position of the insertion cursor.

⟹ The XmTextSetCursorPosition() function has been added to set the position of the insertion cursor.

⟹ The XmTextGetLastPosition() function has been added to retrieve the position of the last character in the text buffer.

⟹ The XmTextGetSelectionPosition() function has been added to retrieve the left and right positions of the primary selection.

⟹ The XmTextSetHighlight() function has been added to highlight text within a Text widget. This function does not make the highlighted text a primary selection.

⟹ The XmTextShowPosition() function has been added to force the text at a given position to be displayed.

⟹ The XmTextScroll() function has been added to scroll the text in a Text widget.

⟹ The XmTextPosToXY() function has been added to retrieve the relative X/Y-coordinates for a given text position.

⟹ The XmTextXYToPos() function has been added to retrieve the character position nearest to a given X/Y-location.

⟹ The new resources XmNsource, XmNselectionArrayCount, and XmNverifyBell have been added to the Text widget. The XmNtopPosition resource has been renamed to XmNtopCharacter because of a conflict with the constraint resource by the same name.

⟹ Two new callbacks have been defined. XmNgainPrimaryCallback and XmNlosePrimaryCallback are used in conjunction with an application that has a MenuBar with an edit PulldownMenu. These callbacks are used to set the XmNsensitive resource on the cut, copy, and paste PushButtons on the edit PulldownMenu to make the options available or unavailable at the appropriate times.

⟹ A new type of Text widget is defined called an XmTextField. The TextField widget gives the same functionality as a single-line Text widget with a significant increase in performance and a significant decrease in memory usage. The operation of the TextField is for the most part identical with the operation of a single-line Text widget.

¤   The XmToggleButton and XmToggleButtonGadget classes have been changed:

⟹ The label on the ToggleButton can be removed by setting the XmNlabelString or the resource name to a null string (""). The toggle indicator will be centered in the ToggleButton with a size that must be specified with the new resource called XmNindicatorSize.

⟹ When the XmNindicatorType of the ToggleButton is set to XmONE__OF__MANY, the toggle indicator acquires a diamond shape instead of the normal square (XmN__OF__MANY). The shadow width of the diamond indicator has been increased to three pixels for a better visual appearance.

⟹ The XmToggleButtonGetState() and the XmToggleButtonSetState() functions work with gadgets as well as widgets in 1.1.

Motif 1.1 Changes to Manager Widgets

▫ The XmBulletinBoard class has changed:

⟹ If a BulletinBoard is the child of a WMShell, the shell's XmNtitleEncoding resource is set according to the BulletinBoard's XmNdialogTitle resource. This supports the guidelines specified in the X Inter-Client Communications Conventions Manual.

▫ The XmDrawingArea class has changed:

⟹ The XmNinputCallback has been changed so that all input events can be passed to the callback at the application's discretion. The callback is now implemented using translations and actions as opposed to an event handler.

▫ The XmForm class has changed:

⟹ The Form widget now calculates its initial size according to the sizes and constraints of its children.

⟹ The Form widget now draws a shadow around itself if the inherited XmNshadowThickness is set to nonzero.

▫ The XmMainWindow class has changed:

⟹ The XmNcommandWindowLocation resource has been added to allow the MainWindow's command Text widget location to comply with the Style Guide or to retain compatibility with Motif 1.0.

⟹ The XmNmessageWindow resource has been added to allow for a second Text widget to be placed at the bottom of the MainWindow for messages to the user from the application.

⟹ The XmMainWindowSep3() function has been added to give access to a Separator gadget to be placed in the MainWindow between the message Text widget and the widget above it. This function complements the two existing functions XmMainWindowSep1() and XmMainWindowSep2().

▫ The XmPanedWindow class has changed:

⟹ The PanedWindow now allows the user to interact with the sashes on the window-pane separators with keyboard keystrokes to resize the panes.

$\Longrightarrow$ The constraint resources XmNminimum and XmNmaximum have had their names changed to XmNpaneMinimum and XmNpaneMaximum to resolve a conflict with resources for the ScrollBar and Scale that had the same name.

◻ The XmScale class has changed:

$\Longrightarrow$ The XmNscaleMultiple resource has been added to allow the user to slide the slider in the trough in large increments using keyboard interaction.

$\Longrightarrow$ The XmNprocessingDirection resource default value has been changed to depend on the value of the XmNorientation resource. If the XmNorientation is set to XmVERTICAL, XmNprocessingDirection is set to XmMAX__ON__BOTTOM. For XmHORIZONTAL, it is set to XmMAX__ON__RIGHT. These values can be overridden.

◻ The XmScrolledWindow class has changed:

$\Longrightarrow$ New keyboard interactions that were defined in the Style Guide have been added.

$\Longrightarrow$ Resources that are defined for the XmScrolledWindow, XmList, and XmText classes can now be passed directly to the XmCreateScrolledText() and XmCreateScrolledList() functions through their argument lists.

Motif 1.1 Changes to Dialog Widgets

◻ In Motif 1.0, with a Dialog posted, the return key would always activate the XmNdefaultButtonType (usually the OK button) instead of the button currently having input focus. Motif 1.1 allows the current input focus button to receive the activate event.

The XmBulletinBoard class, the basis for all Dialogs, has three FontList resources: XmNbuttonFontList, XmNlabelFontList, and XmNtextFontList. These resources are used by children widgets (of the appropriate type) attached to the BulletinBoard. If none of these resources are set, the BulletinBoard will search up through the widget instance tree looking for another manager widget that is subclassed off of a BulletinBoard or a Shell. If found, the FontList resource will be set from that parent. If not found, the FontList resources will be set from the XmNdefaultFontList from the VendorShell class.

◻ The XmDialogShell class has changed:

$\Longrightarrow$ A new XmNdialogStyle value has been added. The value of XmDIALOG__FULL__APPLICATION__MODAL now allows for full modality in applications that use multiple Shell widgets. With the old-style value XmDIALOG__APPLICATION__MODAL, children of other Shell widgets remain active even though modal operation may be in effect. XmDIALOG__APPLICATION__MODAL has been renamed to XmDIALOG__PRIMARY__APPLICATION__MODAL. Modal resources only apply to children of the XmDialogShell widget.

◻   The XmFileSelectionBox class has changed:

⟹   The Motif 1.1 FileSelectionBox has been expanded to add another List
     widget to the left of the existing List widget. The original top Text
     widget (or the XmNdirSpec resource) is used to enter a directory
     mask, and the directory that is selected by the mask will have its sub-
     directories listed in the left List widget and its files listed in the right
     List widget. Double-clicking on one of the directories will cd (change
     directory) into that directory and display its subdirectories and files in
     the two List widgets.

⟹   Nine new resources have been added to the FileSelectionBox:

     1. XmNdirListLabelString is the text of the Label above the direc-
         tory list.

     2. XmNdirListItems is the array of compound string items in the
         directory list.

     3. XmNdirListItemCount is a count of the number of items in the
         directory list.

     4. XmNfileTypeMask controls the type of files that are shown in the
         file list.

     5. XmNdirectory specifies the directory whose contents are shown in
         the Lists.

     6. XmNpattern specifies the regular expression controlling the files
         displayed in the file list.

     7. XmNnoMatchString specifies the compound string message to be
         displayed when no files in the XmNdirectory are found to match
         the XmNpattern.

     8. XmNqualifySearchDataProc identifies a function to use for prepar-
         ing data for a call to the XmNdirSearchProc or XmNfileSearch-
         Proc functions.

     9. XmNdirectoryValid is used to signify that a specified directory is a
         valid directory name with appropriate permissions.

⟹   The List widgets have always become ScrolledList widgets if the file
     or directory names were too long to fit in the List. In 1.1, this is also
     true, but the Lists will automatically scroll to ensure that the
     filename part of the path is displayed instead of the leading directory
     names.

Motif 1.1 Changes to Menu Widgets

◻   Popup- and PulldownMenu panes can now be posted from any widget, not
     just its parent, through the use of a "post from" list added to the menu
     widgets. The XmAddToPostFromList() function adds another widget from
     which the menu can be posted to its "post from" list. The XmGetPos-
     tedFromWidget() function retrieves the widget id from which a menu was

posted for context determination in a callback. And, XmRemoveFromPost-FromList() removes a widget from a menu's "post from" list.

□   Four new menu creation convenience functions have been added: XmCreateSimpleMenuBar(), which creates a MenuBar widget; XmCreateSimplePopupMenu(), which creates a PopupMenu widget; XmCreateSimplePulldownMenu(), which creates a PulldownMenu widget; and XmCreateSimpleOptionMenu(), which creates an OptionMenu widget using the following new resources:

1.   XmNbuttonType specifies an array of Label, Separator, or Button types to use in the simple menu.

2.   XmNbuttons specifies a list of compound strings to use on the Labels of the Labels or Buttons in the simple menu.

3.   XmNbuttonCount specifies the number of items (Labels, Separators, Buttons) to create in the simple menu.

4.   XmNbuttonAccelerators specifies a list of ASCII strings used as accelerators on the Buttons in the simple menu.

5.   XmNbuttonAcceleratorText specifies a list of compound strings to display for the accelerators on the Buttons in the simple menu.

6.   XmNbuttonMnemonics specifies a list on mnemonics for the Buttons in the simple menu.

7.   XmNbuttonMnemonicCharSets specifies a list of character sets to use for the mnemonics on the Buttons in the simple menu.

8.   XmNoptionLabel specifies the Label to be used in a simple Option-Menu.

9.   XmNpostFromButton specifies the position of the button in a simple MenuBar used to post a specific simple PulldownMenu pane.

10. XmNsimpleCallback specifies the function to call for the activate callback from any Button in a simple menu.

Motif 1.1 Changes to Support ANSI C

□   One other change in Motif 1.1 is compliance with ANSI C. The 1.1 header files support both old-style function return-type declarations and the new ANSI C prototype function definitions. The ANSI C is the default. If you want to use the older-style C function definitions, you must include a preprocessor define for the name __NO__PROTO either in your source code or with a -D cc command-line option.

OSF/Motif 1.2

□   With the release of X11R5, the Open Software Foundation came out with yet another new release of the Motif Toolkit—Version 1.2. OSF/Motif 1.2 includes the normal bug fixes, enhancements, and so on, which can be classified into several groups:

- ❑ Using the R5 Intrinsics
- ❑ Internationalization
- ❑ Drag and drop
- ❑ Tear-off menus
- ❑ Performance

❑ OSF/Motif 1.2 will support state-of-the-art i18n. (Internationalization – starts with the letter i, meanders along for 18 letters, and ends with an n: from Oliver Jones.) This includes support for the ANSII C locale model, X11R5 input method support, X11R5 FontSet support, and multibyte and wide character support.

The X11R5 input method is a method of translating multiple keystrokes into a single character for foreign languages. This involves a separate process that reads keystrokes from the keyboard and performs any needed translations before the character is passed to the server and on to your client. For example, the key sequence "alt e ^" might be used to represent the French letter e with a circumflex on top. Motif 1.2 supports the operation of the new input method process.

The X11R5 FontSet concept is an integral component of the R5 support for compound strings. Just like the old-style Motif FontList, the R5 FontSet allows for multiple fonts to be displayed in a single text string variable. Motif 1.2 compound strings support these new X compound string and FontSet concepts.

OSF/Motif 1.2 also provides support for many of the new ANSII C i18n efforts. Included in this is support for the locale mechanism as well as multibyte characters and wide characters.

❑ The long-awaited drag and drop functionality is now available in OSF/Motif 1.2. Drag and drop lets you implement a Unix cp (copy), mv (move), or ln (link) operation within the confines of a graphic-user interface. With a click-hold-drag operation using the mouse, you can arrange to copy, move, or link one file to another file or into a directory.

This feature would allow for the implementation of features that are found in other common graphic-user interfaces. Things like removing a file by dragging the file icon and dropping it on a trash can icon or printing a file by dragging a file icon to a printer icon are made possible with the drag and drop functionality.

The drag and drop operation is dependent on two definitions: a draggable icon and a drop site. The draggable icon is simply a pixmap for an icon that can be dragged while the drop site is an area where an object can be dropped. Drop sites are associated with a widget and have resources that can be viewed as constraint resources on the manager. The drag and drop functionality is implemented through the standard Motif callback mechanism.

❑ Tear-off menus allow the user to display a menu pane through standard menu posting mechanisms and then "tear it off", leave it posted, and continue to use both items from the menu pane and items from the main application area at the same time. The metaphor for tear-off menus is a cut-off coupon.

SOLUTIONS

To inquire about solutions to the
exercises in this book, return this card
or call 1-800-752-5448.

**If you would like information regarding
any of the courses listed below, please check
the appropriate box:**

❑ UNIX Fundamentals
❑ The C Programming Language
❑ Programming with C Libraries
❑ Advanced C Language
❑ System Administration
❑ Advanced System Administration
❑ Informix SQL Applications Development
❑ Informix 4GL Applications Development
❑ Informix ESQL/C Interface
❑ UNIX Internals
❑ UNIX
❑ C++
❑ Other _____

❑ ON-SITES-Tell me more about ITDC's on-
site educational courses.

ITDC
4000 Executive Park Drive/Suite 310
Cincinnati, Ohio 45241
1-800-752-5448

NAME: _____

TITLE: _____

COMPANY: _____

ADDRESS: _____

CITY: _____

STATE: _____ ZIP: _____

PHONE: _____

❑ I am not currently in the market for ITDC's
services, but would like to be on a mailing list.

BUSINESS REPLY MAIL
FIRST CLASS MAIL PERMIT NO. 17396 CINCINNATI, OH

POSTAGE WILL BE PAID BY ADDRESSEE

ITDC

4000 Executive Park Drive/Suite 310
Cincinnati, OH 45241

When a tear-off menu is posted, the first menu item is a dashed Separator line. If any other item from the menu is selected, the menu operates as a standard OSF/Motif menu pane. However, if the dashed Separator is selected, the menu pane will get its own client decorations and the user can manipulate the menu pane as if it were any other top-level shell or dialog box window.

◻ Most of the Motif 1.2 performance improvements are due to improvements made to X11R5. Many OSF member organizations made contributions to the Xt Toolkit, which improved the operation of the Intrinsics. The translation manager was completely recoded for better performance.

OSF/Motif 1.2 was completely reorganized for less thrashing and guarantees that nothing will be slower than the 1.1 implementation. The ScrolledText widget now scrolls much faster due to new internal data structures but breaks compatibility for Text widget subclasses. Also, 1.2 has reduced the amount of dynamic memory used.

Review Questions

◻ Please write down the answers to the following questions:

1. List several new functions or features of the X Window System Version 11 Release 4.

2. List several new functions or features of the X Window System Version 11 Release 5.

3. List several new functions or features of OSF/Motif Version 1.1.

4. List several new features of OSF/Motif Version 1.2.

Index

ABOUT THE AUTHOR

William Parrette is the manager of Education Services at
I.T.D.C., Inc., where he is responsible for providing
consultation and software development services to the
UNIX marketplace. In the course of his work at I.T.D.C.,
he has trained thousands of students in the use of UNIX.
Mr. Parrette has also held positions as an independent
software development specialist, a systems software
programmer, and a software engineer.